An Introduction to Japanese Society
Fourth Edition

Now in its fourth edition, *An Introduction to Japanese Society* remains essential reading for students of Japanese society.

Internationally renowned scholar Yoshio Sugimoto uses both English and Japanese sources to update and expand upon his original narrative in this sophisticated yet highly readable text. This book explores the breadth and diversity of Japanese society, with chapters covering class, geographical and generational variation, work, education, gender, minorities, popular culture, and the establishment. Updates include an exploration of the 'Cool Japan' phenomenon and the explosion of Japanese culture overseas. This edition also features the latest research into Japanese society, updated statistical data, and coverage of recent events, including the 2011 earthquake and tsunami, and the change in government.

Written in a clear and engaging style, *An Introduction to Japanese Society* provides an insight into all aspects of a diverse and ever-evolving contemporary Japan.

Yoshio Sugimoto is Professor Emeritus in the School of Social Sciences and Communications at La Trobe University in Melbourne, Australia.

An Introduction to Japanese Society

Fourth Edition

Yoshio Sugimoto

CAMBRIDGE
UNIVERSITY PRESS

CAMBRIDGE
UNIVERSITY PRESS

477 Williamstown Road, Port Melbourne, VIC 3207, Australia

Cambridge University Press is part of the University of Cambridge.

It furthers the University's mission by disseminating knowledge in the pursuit of education, learning and research at the highest international levels of excellence.

www.cambridge.org
Information on this title: www.cambridge.org/9781107626676

First published 1997
Second edition 2003
Third edition 2010
Reprinted 2011 (twice), 2012, 2013
Fourth edition 2014

Cover designed by Liz Nicholson, designBITE

A catalogue record for this publication is available from the British Library

A Cataloguing-in-Publication entry is available from the catalogue of the National Library of Australia at www.nla.gov.au

ISBN 978-1-107-62667-6 Paperback

Contents

List of figures

List of tables

Preface to the fourth edition

Writing a revised and expanded edition of a book is akin to renovating a house. Extensions must be added to the existing structure to give space to fresh realities, while other sections require updating or redesigning. Although the main structure of this book has stood the test of time since its initial publication in 1997, keeping up with the changing features of Japanese society in the 2010s requires me to amend many of its parts, a task which has been both exhausting and intellectually rewarding.

The readers of the past three editions will find some new furnishings and appliances in the renovated house, including sections on the spread of Japan's pop culture abroad and the 'Cool Japan' debate; the Fukushima nuclear explosion and its aftermath; the 'history war' between some Japanese and some in neighboring countries; and the expansion of English-language education and its implications. In all chapters, I have made considerable changes to reflect the rise of new developments and the fall of old patterns, while updating demographic data as much as possible.

For the renovation to be completed, I owe a great deal to academics and students, from all across the globe, with whom I have had lively discussions for the past few years at lectures, seminars, and conferences. In addition, numerous emails and letters I exchanged with readers of the previous editions around the world helped me reconsider, reconstruct, and refine many points. I am grateful for their warm encouragements and constructive criticisms.

By coincidence, I have finished writing the fourth edition in Kyoto, Japan, my hometown where I grew up. I wrote in the preface to the first edition that completing a book is always a liberating experience for me and it still is. I hope that readers will share some of my delight in treading the paths outlined in this text.

Yoshio Sugimoto
Kyoto
April 2014

Map of Japan

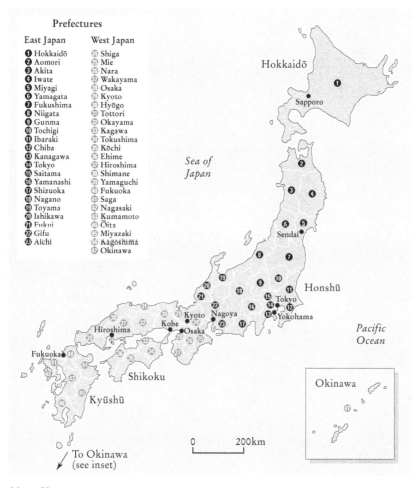

Prefectures

East Japan	West Japan
❶ Hokkaidō	㉔ Shiga
❷ Aomori	㉕ Mie
❸ Akita	㉖ Nara
❹ Iwate	㉗ Wakayama
❺ Miyagi	㉘ Osaka
❻ Yamagata	㉙ Kyoto
❼ Fukushima	㉚ Hyōgo
❽ Niigata	㉛ Tottori
❾ Gunma	㉜ Okayama
❿ Tochigi	㉝ Kagawa
⓫ Ibaraki	㉞ Tokushima
⓬ Chiba	㉟ Kōchi
⓭ Kanagawa	㊱ Ehime
⓮ Tokyo	㊲ Hiroshima
⓯ Saitama	㊳ Shimane
⓰ Yamanashi	㊴ Yamaguchi
⓱ Shizuoka	㊵ Fukuoka
⓲ Nagano	㊶ Saga
⓳ Toyama	㊷ Nagasaki
⓴ Ishikawa	㊸ Kumamoto
㉑ Fukui	㊹ Ōita
㉒ Gifu	㊺ Miyazaki
㉓ Aichi	㊻ Kagoshima
	㊼ Okinawa

Hokkaidō
Sapporo

Sea of
Japan

Sendai

Honshū

Tokyo
Yokohama

Pacific
Ocean

Nagoya
Kyoto
Kobe
Osaka
Hiroshima

Fukuoka

Shikoku

Kyūshū

Okinawa

0   200km

To Okinawa
(see inset)

Map of Japan

1 The Japan Phenomenon and the Social Sciences

I Multicultural Japan

1 Sampling Problem and the Question of Visibility

Hypothetical questions sometimes inspire the sociological imagination. Suppose that a being from a different planet arrived in Japan and wanted to meet a typical Japanese, one who best typified the Japanese adult population. Whom should the social scientists choose? To answer this question, several factors would have to be considered: gender, occupation, educational background, and so on.

To begin with, the person chosen should be a female, because women outnumber men in Japan; sixty-five million women and sixty-two million men live in the Japanese archipelago. With regard to occupation, she would definitely not be employed in a large corporation but would work in a small enterprise, since only one in eight workers is employed in a company with three hundred or more employees. Nor would she be guaranteed lifetime employment, since those who work under this arrangement are concentrated in large companies. She would not belong to a labor union, because less than one in five Japanese workers is unionized. She would not be university educated. Less than one in five Japanese have a university degree, even though today nearly half of the younger generation gains admission to a university for a four-year degree. Table 1.1 summarizes these demographic realities.

The identification of the average Japanese would certainly involve much more complicated quantitative analysis. But the alien would come closer to the 'center' of the Japanese population by choosing a female, non-unionized, and non-permanent employee in a small business without university education than by choosing a male, unionized, permanent employee with a university degree working for a large company.

When outsiders visualize the Japanese, however, they tend to think of men rather than women, career employees in large companies rather than non-permanent workers in small firms, and university graduates rather than high school leavers, for these are the images presented on

Table 1.1   Japan's population distribution in millions

Variable	Majority	Minority
Gender[a]	Female: 65.40 (51%)	Male: 61.93 (49%)
Employees by firm size[b]	Small firms[e]: 47.99 (85%)	Large firms[f]: 8.3 (15%)
Education[c]	Without university education: 70.8 (80%)	University graduates: 17.7 (20%)
Union membership[d]	No: 45.3 (82%)	Yes: 9.9 (18%)

Sources:

[a] Population estimates (final) as of 1 March 2013, Ministry of Internal Affairs and Communications 2013.

[b] Ministry of Internal Affairs and Communications in 2012. The data cover all private-sector establishments except individual proprietorship establishments in agriculture, forestry, and fishery.

[c] Population census conducted in 2010. University graduates do not include those who have completed junior college and technical college. Figures do not include pupils and students currently enrolled in schools and pre-school children.

[d] Ministry of Health, Labour and Welfare in 2012.

[e] Less than 300 employees.

[f] More than 300 employees.

television and in newspaper and magazine articles. Some academic studies have also attempted to generalize about Japanese society on the basis of observations of its male elite sector and have thereby helped to reinforce this sampling bias.[1] Moreover, because a particular cluster of individuals who occupy high positions in a large company have greater access to mass media and publicity, the lifestyles and value orientations of those in that cluster have acquired a disproportionately high level of visibility in the analysis of Japanese society at the expense of the wider cross-section of its population.

Since the 1990s, a fresh trend – possibly a new stereotype – has spread, with images of Japanese obsessed with *manga* and *anime* and their associated merchandise, and with the portrayal of Japan as the land of fanatic consumers of pop culture. *Manga* stands out within Japan's diverse pop culture through the diffusion of *manga*-based images around the world. Although no reliable information about the exact numbers of *manga* readers in Japan is available, Table 1.2 shows findings related to the question. Given that some figures include readers of non-*manga* magazines and books, it is far from the case that *manga* readers can be classified as a representative majority of the Japanese at large, let alone as typical. In spite of worldwide awareness, they are most likely a minority of the population. Furthermore, as Figure 1.1 exhibits, the consumption of *manga* magazines and *manga* books in Japan has declined over time, even while their visibility has increased abroad.

[1] See Mouer and Sugimoto 1986, p. 150.

Table 1.2 *Manga* readership in Japan

Category of reader	% of population
Those who read books (including *manga*) as hobbies (2011)[a]	39.7
Those who read magazines, *manga or* books for more than fifteen minutes per day on weekdays (2010 and 2005)[b]	17.9 and 18.3
Those who read one or more *manga* books per month (2011)[c]	31.5

Sources:
[a] Ministry of Internal Affairs and Communications 2012, Questionnaire A.
[b] NHK Hōsō Bunka Kenkyūsho (NHK Broadcasting Culture Research Institute) 2011, p. 190, and 2006, p. 214.
[c] Nihon Shoseki Shuppan Kyōkai (Japan Book Publishers Association) 2011, p. 125.
Note: The third survey above is based on online non-random samples.

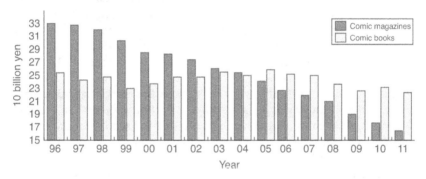

Figure 1.1 Estimated sales of comic books and comic magazines in Japan (1996–2011)
Source: Research Institute for Publications 2010, p. 230.

2   Homogeneity Assumptions and the Group Model

Although a few competing frameworks for understanding Japanese society are discernible, a discourse that is often labeled as *Nihonjinron* (theories of Japaneseness) has persisted as the long-lasting paradigm that regards Japan as a uniquely homogeneous society. The so-called group model of Japanese society represents the most explicit and coherent formulation of this line of argument, although it has drawn serious criticism from empirical, methodological, and ideological angles.[2] Put most succinctly, the model is based upon three lines of argument.

First, at the individual, psychological level, the Japanese are portrayed as having a personality which lacks a fully developed ego or independent self. The best known example of this claim is Doi's notion of *amae*,

---

[2] Befu 1980; Sugimoto and Mouer 1980; Dale 1986; Sugimoto and Mouer 1989; Yoshino 1992. See also Neustupný 1980.

which refers to the allegedly unique psychological inclination among the Japanese to seek emotional satisfaction by prevailing upon and depending on their superiors.[3] They feel no need for any explicit demonstration of individuality. Loyalty to the group is a primary value. Giving oneself to the promotion and realization of the group's goals imbues the Japanese with a special psychological satisfaction.

Second, at the interpersonal, intra-group level, human interaction is depicted in terms of Japanese group orientation. According to Nakane, for example, the Japanese attach great importance to the maintenance of harmony *within* the group. To that end, relationships between superiors and inferiors are carefully cultivated and maintained. One's status within the group depends on the length of one's membership in the group. Furthermore, the Japanese maintain particularly strong interpersonal ties with those in the same hierarchical chain of command within their own organization. In other words, vertical loyalties are dominant. The vertically organized Japanese contrast sharply with Westerners, who tend to form horizontal groups which define their membership in terms of such criteria as class and stratification that cut across hierarchical organization lines.[4]

Finally, at the inter-group level, the literature has emphasized that integration and harmony are achieved effectively *between* Japanese groups, making Japan a 'consensus society'. This is said to account for the exceptionally high level of stability and cohesion in Japanese society, which has aided political and other leaders in their efforts to organize or mobilize the population efficiently. Moreover, the ease with which the energy of the Japanese can be focused on a task has contributed in no small measure to Japan's remarkably rapid economic growth during the post–World War II period. From a slightly different angle, Ishida argues that inter-group competition in loyalty makes groups conform to national goals and facilitates the formation of national consensus.[5]

For decades, Japanese writers have debated the essence of 'Japaneseness'. Numerous books have been written under such titles as *What Are the Japanese?* and *What Is Japan?*[6] Many volumes on *Nihon-rashisa* (Japanese-like qualities) have appeared.[7] Social science discourse in Japan abounds with examinations of *Nihon-teki* (Japanese-style) tendencies in business, politics, social relations, psychology, and so on. Some researchers are preoccupied with inquiries into the 'hidden shape',[8] 'basic layer', and 'archetype'[9] of Japanese culture. These works portray Japanese society as highly homogeneous, with only limited internal variation, and

---

[3] Doi 1973.   [4] Nakane 1967, 1970, and 1978.   [5] Ishida 1983, pp. 23–47.
[6] For example, Umesao 1986; Yamamoto 1989; Sakaiya 1991 and 1993; Umehara 1990.
[7] For example, Hamaguchi 1988; Watanabe 1989; Kusayanagi 1990.
[8] Maruyama, Katō, and Kinoshita 1991.   [9] For example, Takatori 1975.

give it an all-embracing label. Hamaguchi, for example, who presents what he calls a contextual model of the Japanese, maintains that the concept of the individual is irrelevant in the study of the Japanese, who tend to see the interpersonal relationship itself (*kanjin*) – not the individuals involved in it – as the basic unit of action.[10] Amanuma argues that the Japanese core personality is based on the drive for *ganbari* (endurance and persistence), which accounts for every aspect of Japanese behavior.[11] Publishing in Japanese, a Korean writer, Lee, contends that the Japanese have a unique *chijimi shikō*, a miniaturizing orientation which has enabled them to skillfully miniaturize their environment and products, ranging from *bonsai* plants, small cars, and portable electronic appliances to computer chips.[12] The list of publications that aim to define Japanese society with a single key word is seemingly endless, and, although the specific appellation invariably differs, the reductive impulse is unchanged.

At least four underlying assumptions remain constant in these studies. First, it is presumed that *all* Japanese share the attribute in question – be it *amae* or miniaturizing orientation – regardless of their class, gender, occupation, and other stratification variables. Second, it is also assumed that there is virtually no variation among the Japanese in the degree to which they possess the characteristic in question. Little attention is given to the possibility that some Japanese may have it in far greater degree than others. Third, the trait in question, be it group-orientation or *kanjin*, is supposed to exist only marginally in other societies, particularly in Western societies. That is, the feature is thought to be uniquely Japanese. Finally, the fourth presupposition is an ahistorical assumption that the trait has prevailed in Japan for an unspecified period of time, independently of historical circumstances. Writings based on some or all of these propositions have been published in Japan ad nauseam and have generated the genre referred to as *Nihonjinron*. Although some analysts have challenged the validity of *Nihonjinron* assertions on methodological, empirical, and ideological grounds, the discourse has retained its popular appeal, attracting many readers and maintaining a commercially viable publication industry.

The notion of Japan being homogeneous goes in tandem with the claim that it is an exceptionally egalitarian society with little class differentiation. This assertion is based on scattered observations of company life. Thus, with regard to resource distribution, some contrast the relatively modest salary gaps between Japanese executive managers and their employees with the marked discrepancy between the salaries of American business executives and their workers. Focusing on the alleged

---

[10] Hamaguchi 1985 and 1988. For a debate on this model, see Mouer and Sugimoto 1987, pp. 12–63.

[11] Amanuma 1987.   [12] Lee 1984.

weakness of class consciousness, others point out that Japanese managers are prepared to get their hands dirty, wear the same blue overalls as assembly workers in factories, and share elevators, toilets, and company restaurants with low-ranking employees.[13] Still others suggest that Japanese managers and rank-and-file employees work in large offices without status-based partitions, thereby occupying the workplace in an egalitarian way. Furthermore, public opinion polls taken by the Prime Minister's Office have indicated that eight to nine out of ten Japanese classify themselves as middle class. While there is debate as to what this figure means, it has nevertheless strengthened the *images* of egalitarian Japan. A few observers have gone so far as to call Japan a 'land of equality'[14] and a 'one-class society'.[15] Firmly entrenched in all these descriptions is the portrayal of the Japanese as identifying themselves primarily as members of a company, alma mater, faction, clique, or other functional group, rather than as members of a class or social stratum.

3   Diversity and Stratification

The portrayal of Japan as a homogeneous and egalitarian society is, however, contradicted by many observations that reveal it is a more diversified and heterogeneous society than this stereotype suggests. Two frameworks, one emphasizing ethnic diversity and the other stressing class differentiation, appear to have taken root around the turn of the twentieth century that challenge *Nihonjinron* images of Japanese society.

(a)   Minority Issues and the Multi-ethnic Model

The notion of Japan as a racially homogeneous society has come under question as a consequence of the growing visibility of foreign migrants in the country. The shortage of labor in particular sectors of Japan's economy has necessitated the influx of workers from abroad for the past quarter of a century or so, making the presence of various ethnic groups highly conspicuous. Throughout manufacturing cities and towns across the nation, Japanese Brazilians, descendants of Japanese migrants to Brazil, work in large numbers. At many train stations and along major city roads, multilingual signs and posters, including those in English, Korean, Chinese, and Portuguese, depending upon the area, are prominently displayed.

In rural Japan, a significant number of farmers marry women from other Asian countries in order to help with farm and domestic work

---

[13] White and Trevor 1984.   [14] Tominaga 1982.   [15] De Roy 1979.

because of a shortage of Japanese women willing to share a rural lifestyle. Women from neighboring Asian countries also form indispensable support staff in medical institutions, nursing care centers, and welfare facilities. International marriages peaked in 2006, with some 6 percent of all marriages in Japan being between Japanese and non-Japanese nationals.[16] The ratio is nearly 10 percent in Tokyo.

In the national sport of professional sumo wrestling, overseas wrestlers, particularly those from Mongolia, Eastern Europe, and Hawaii, occupy the summit levels of the top sumo ranks of Grand Champion, Champion, and others. In the popular sport of professional baseball, American, Korean, Taiwanese, and other international players have become familiar public faces. On national television, many Korean soap operas attract exceptionally high ratings.

These casual observations have drawn attention to the reality that Japan has an extensive range of minority issues, ethnic and quasi-ethnic, which proponents of the homogeneous Japan thesis tend to ignore. One can identify several minority groups in Japan even if one does so narrowly, referring only to groups subjected to discrimination and prejudice because of culturally generated ethnic myths, illusions, and fallacies, as Chapter 7 will detail.

In Hokkaidō, the northernmost island of the nation, more than twenty thousand Ainu live as an indigenous minority. Their situation arose with the first attempts of Japan's central regime to unify the nation under its leadership around the sixth and seventh centuries and to conquer the Ainu territories in northern Japan. In addition, some two to three million *burakumin* are subjected to prejudice and many of them are forced to live in separate communities, partly because of an unfounded myth that they are ethnically different.[17] Their ancestors' plight began in the feudal period under the Tokugawa shogunate, which ruled the nation for two and a half centuries from the seventeenth century and institutionalized an outcast class at the bottom of a caste system. Though the class was legally abolished after the Meiji Restoration, in 1868, discrimination and prejudice have persisted. Some four hundred thousand permanent Korean residents without Japanese citizenship, called *Zainichi*, form the largest long-term foreign minority group in Japan. Their problem originated with Japan's colonization of Korea at the beginning of the twentieth century, and the Japanese importation of Koreans as cheap labor for industries. More than two million foreign workers, both documented and undocumented, live in the country as a result of their influx into the

---

[16] Ministry of Health, Labour and Welfare 2013f.

[17] This is why some observers called them 'Japan's invisible race' (De Vos and Wagatsuma 1966).

Table 1.3 Estimated proportions of ethnic and pseudo-ethnic minorities in selected countries

Band	% of total population in minority groups	Countries
1	1–4	Bangladesh 2011, Egypt JL, Hungary 2011, North Korea JL, South Korea JL
2	5–8	Czech Republic 2011, Greece 2011, Japan 2013, Iceland 2013, Mongolia 2010, Portugal 2001
3	9–12	Austria 2001, China 2012, Denmark 2012, Finland 2010, Netherlands 2013

Sources: National census data or government estimates produced in the years specified in subscripts.
JL: Lehmeyer 2006.

Japanese labor market since the 1980s, mainly from Asia and the Middle East, in their attempt to earn quick cash in the appreciated Japanese yen. Finally, more than 1.4 million Okinawans, who live in the Ryūkyū Islands at the southern end of Japan, face occasional bigotry based on the belief that they are ethnically different and incur suspicion because of the islands' longstanding cultural autonomy.

As a conservative estimate, the total membership of these groups is about six to seven million, which represents some 5 percent of the population of Japan.[18] If one includes those who marry into these minority groups and suffer the same kinds of prejudice, the number is greater. In the Kansai region, where *burakumin* and Korean residents are concentrated, the proportion of the minority population exceeds 10 percent. These ratios may not be as high as those in migrant societies, such as the United States, Canada, and Australia,[19] but they seem inconsistent with the claim that Japan is a society uniquely lacking minority issues. These issues tend to be obfuscated, blurred, and even made invisible in Japan, partly because the principal minority groups do not differ in skin color and other biological characteristics from the majority of Japanese.

In international comparison, Japan does not rank uniquely high in its composition of minority groups which exist because of their ethnicity or the ethnic frictions that surround them. Table 1.3 lists some of the nations whose ethnic minority groups constitute less than 12 percent of the population. Given that the Japanese figure is 5 percent, Japan's position would be somewhere in the second band. Admittedly, different groups

[18] De Vos and Wetherall 1983, p. 3, provide a similar estimate. Nakano and Imazu 1993 also provide an analogous perspective.
[19] These societies are perhaps 'unique' in their high levels of ethnic and racial diversity.

and societies define minority groups on the basis of different criteria, but that is exactly the point. The boundaries of ethnic and racial groups are imagined, negotiated, constructed, and altered over time and space. In defining them, administrative agencies, private institutions, voluntary organizations, individual citizens, and marginalized groups themselves have different and competing interests and perspectives. Furthermore, international numerical comparisons of ethnic minority groups are complicated and compounded by the fact that the government of each country has different criteria for defining and identifying ethnic minorities. The case here is not that each figure in the table is definitive but that Japan seems to be unique, not in its absence of minority issues, but in the decisiveness with which the government and other organizations attempt to ignore their existence.

For the past couple of decades, studies that undermine the supposed ethnic homogeneity of Japanese society have amassed. Befu, who challenges what he calls the hegemony of homogeneity,[20] shows how deeply seated 'primordial sentiments' spelled out in *Nihonjinron* are and reveals how they play key roles in hiding the experiences and even the existence of various minority groups. In tracing the origin of the 'myth of the ethnically homogeneous nation', Oguma demonstrates that this notion started to take root only after Japan's defeat in World War II; in prewar years Japan was conceptualized as a diverse nation incorporating a mixture of Asian peoples with which the Japanese were thought to share blood relations. The transition from the prewar mixed nation theory to the postwar homogeneous nation theory is a rather recent conversion.[21] Weiner argues that the alleged racial purity of the Japanese is an illusion and discusses the realities of minority groups subjected to prejudice and discrimination.[22] Lie, in his aptly titled book *Multiethnic Japan*,[23] argues that Japan is a society as diverse as any other and discusses the ways in which the 'specter of multiethnicity' haunts the hegemonic assumption of monoethnicity. Building on his studies on *Zainichi* Koreans, Fukuoka suggests that there are several types of 'non-Japanese' on the basis of lineage, culture, and nationality, the three analytical criteria that sensitize us to multiple dimensions of what it is to be Japanese.[24] Covering a significant time span, from the archaeological past to the contemporary period, historians and sociologists put together a volume titled *Multicultural Japan*,[25] which focuses on the fluctuations in 'Japanese' identities and shows that Japan has had multiple ethnic presences in one form or another over centuries. The accumulation of these scholarly studies has led to a discourse that can be labeled as the multi-ethnic model of

---

[20] Befu 2001.   [21] Oguma 2002.   [22] Weiner 2009.   [23] Lie 2001.
[24] Fukuoka 2000, p. xxx.   [25] Denoon et al.1996.

Japanese society. It is still a moot point as to whether this new framework has wide acceptance at Japan's grassroots level.

Though regions themselves do not constitute ethnic groups in the conventional sense, regional identities are only one step away from that of the nation.[26] Japan is divided into two subcultural regions, eastern Japan with Tokyo and Yokohama as its center, and western Japan with Osaka, Kyoto, and Kobe as its hub. The two regions differ in language, social relations, food, housing, and many other respects. The subcultural differences between the areas facing the Pacific and those facing the Sea of Japan are also well known. Japan has a wide variety of dialects. A Japanese from Aomori Prefecture, the northernmost area of Honshū Island, and one from Kagoshima, the southernmost district in Kyūshū Island, can scarcely comprehend each other's dialects. Different districts have different festivals, folk songs, and local dances. Customs governing birth, marriage, and death differ so much regionally that books explaining the differences are quite popular.[27] The exact degree of domestic regional variation is difficult to assess in quantitative terms and by internationally comparative standards, but there is no evidence to suggest that it is lower in Japan than elsewhere.

(b)   Social Stratification and the Class Model

The image of Japan as an egalitarian society experienced a dramatic shift at the beginning of the twenty-first century with the emerging claim that Japan is *kakusa shakai*, literally a 'disparity society', a socially divided society with sharp class differences and glaring inequality, a point which Chapter 2 will examine in some detail. This view appears to have gained ground among the populace during Japan's prolonged recession in the 1990s, the so-called lost decade, and in the 2000s when the then second-largest economy in the world experienced a further downturn as a consequence of the global financial crisis. Although job stability used to be the hallmark of Japan's labor market, two in five employees are now 'non-regular workers' whose employment status is precarious. Even 'regular' employees who were guaranteed job security throughout their occupational careers have been thrown out of employment because of their companies' poor business outcomes and the unsatisfactory performance of their own work. In mass media, at one end of the spectrum, the new rich who have almost instantly amassed vast wealth in such areas as information technology, new media, and financial manipulation are celebrated and lionized as fresh billionaires. At the other end of the spectrum are the unemployed, the homeless, day laborers, and other

[26] Anderson 1983.   [27] For example, Shufu to Seikatsusha 1992.

Table 1.4 Gini index of some OECD countries in the late 2000s

Country (above average)	Gini index	Country (below average)	Gini index
USA	0.378	Germany	0.295
UK	0.345	Ireland	0.293
Italy	0.337	France	0.259
Australia	0.336	Finland	0.259
Japan	0.329	Sweden	0.259
Canada	0.324	Norway	0.250
Korea	0.315	Denmark	0.248

Source: Adapted from Organization for Economic Cooperation and
    Development 2011a, p. 45.

Notes:

1. The values are based on the distribution of household disposable incomes, corrected for household size and deflated by the
   consumer price index.
2. The mean average of the Gini indices of all OECD countries
   was 0.31.

marginalized members of society who are said to form *karyū shakai* (the
underclass), revealing a discrepancy which gives considerable plausibil-
ity to the imagery of *kakusa shakai*. In regional economic comparisons,
affluent metropolitan lifestyles often appear in sharp contrast with the
deteriorated and declining conditions of rural areas.

Comparative studies of income distribution suggest that Japan cannot be regarded as uniquely egalitarian. On the contrary, it ranks high
among major advanced capitalist countries with a significant level of
unequal income distribution. Table 1.4 confirms this pattern, with the
international comparative analysis of the Gini index, which measures the
degree to which a given distribution deviates from perfect equality (with
larger figures indicating higher levels of inequality).

Japan's relative poverty rate, an indicator of the percentage of low-
income earners, was one of the highest among the thirty member
nations of the Organization for Economic Cooperation and Development (OECD) (see Table 1.5).[28] The relative poverty rate represents the
percentage of income earners whose wage is below half of the median
income. One in six workers lives under the poverty line in Japan, a reality
that hardly makes the country a homogeneous middle-class society.

Even to casual observers, the stratification of Japanese society is discernible in a variety of areas. Those who own or expect to inherit land
and other assets have a considerable advantage over those who do not,

---

[28] The Japanese figure, 15.7 percent, which the OECD used, was recorded for 2006. It
rose to 16.7 in 2009. See Ministry of Health, Labour and Welfare 2010.

Table 1.5 Relative poverty rates in some OECD countries 2011 (%)

Country (high rate)	Relative poverty rate	Country (low rate)	Relative poverty rate
USA	17.3	Ireland	9.8
Japan	15.7	Germany	8.9
Korea	15.0	Sweden	8.4
Australia	14.6	Finland	7.9
Italy	11.4	Norway	7.8
Canada	11.4	France	7.2
UK	11.3	Denmark	6.1

Source: Adapted from Organization for Economic Cooperation and Development 2011a.
Note: The mean average of all OECD countries was 11.3.

and asset differentials are so wide that it could be argued that Japan is a class society based upon land ownership.[29] In the area of consumer behavior, those who possess or expect to inherit properties such as houses and land spend lavishly on high-class, fashionable, and expensive goods, while those without such property assets are restricted to more mundane purchases designed to make ends meet, a pattern that has continued for more than two decades.[30] The Social Stratification and Mobility (SSM) project, conducted by a team of Japanese sociologists over the past fifty years, identifies in its 2005 survey five distinct clusters in the Japanese male adult population on the basis of such major stratification variables as education, occupation, and income.[31] With regard to opportunities for education, students from families of high educational and occupational backgrounds have a much better chance of gaining admission to high-prestige universities,[32] and this pattern has persisted over time. A majority of the students of the University of Tokyo, the most prestigious university in Japan, are the sons and daughters of company managers, bureaucrats, academics, teachers, and other professionals.[33] Moreover, although approximately half of high-school leavers advance to universities for four-year degrees,[34] entry into many universities is non-competitive, with a considerable number accepting applicants without formal entrance examinations and, overall, nine out of ten university applicants gaining admission. Thus, most Japanese students have little to do with the widely publicized 'examination hell'.

Subcultural groups are reproduced inter-generationally through the inheritance of social and cultural resources. Mindful of the

---

[29] Shimono 1991.   [30] Ozawa 1989 predicted this polarization.   [31] Hayashi 2008.
[32] SSM 95a, IV, p. 167.   [33] Tokyo Daigaku Kōhō Iinkai 2012.
[34] Ministry of Education and Science 2013a.

inter-generational reproduction of social advantages and cultural prestige, the mass media have sarcastically used the term *nanahikari-zoku* in reference to those who have attained prominence thanks to the 'seven colorful rays of influence emanating from their parents'. Unlike company employees, professionals, and managers, small independent proprietors frequently hand over their family businesses to one of their children.[35] In the world of entertainment, numerous sons and daughters of established entertainers and television personalities have achieved their status with the aid of their parents' national celebrity. The SSM study also suggests that the class characteristics of parents significantly condition their children's choice of spouse.[36] Ostensibly spontaneous selections of partners are patterned in such a way that the class attributes of parents creep into the decision-making process, whether consciously or not.

Gender differences in value orientation are arguably more pronounced than ever with the gradual rise of feminist consciousness at various levels. Opinion surveys have consistently shown that more women than men disagree with the notion of home being the woman's place. The proportion of women who feel that marriage is not necessary if they can support themselves invariably outnumbers that of men.[37] Women show much more commitment than men to community and school activities, neighborhood associations, hobby and sport groups, cooperatives, and other locally based interests.[38]

These observations of social diversification and segmentation, and of the polarization of lifestyles, imply that Japanese society is not as classless and egalitarian as the conventional theory suggests; it is not only diversified horizontally but also stratified vertically like other advanced capitalist societies.

(c) Multicultural Model

Although the two frameworks – the multi-ethnic model and the social stratification model – stress different aspects of diversity and variation in Japanese society, one can combine them into a more comprehensive perspective that locates both ethnic diversity and social stratification as key elements of Japanese society. Table 1.6 illustrates the location of this perspective, which can be labeled the multicultural model of Japanese society, the model that forms the basis of this book.

Subcultures proliferate in Japan, in spheres including ethnicity, region, gender, age, occupation, education, and so forth. To the extent that

---

[35] Ishida 2010, pp. 44–5.   [36] See Chapter 2, Section III.
[37] Kokuritsu Josei Kyōiku Kaikan 2012, p. 178.
[38] See, for example, Iwama 2011, pp. 331–3.

Table 1.6   Four models of Japanese society

	Class variation	
Ethnic diversity	No	Yes
No	Group model	Multi-class model
Yes	Multi-ethnic model	Multicultural model

subculture is defined as a set of value expectations and lifestyles shared by a section of a given population, Japanese society reveals an abundance of subcultural groupings along these lines. As a conglomerate of subcultures, Japan may be viewed as a multicultural society, or a multi-subcultural society. Furthermore, most subcultural units are rank-ordered in terms of access to various resources, including economic privilege, political power, social prestige, information, and knowledge. In this sense, Japan as a multicultural society is multi-stratified as well as multi-ethnic.

Let us pose another hypothetical question. Suppose that our curious being from another planet has capped all adult Japanese with hats of different colors (visible only through special glasses) depending upon their educational background: blue hats for university graduates, yellow hats for those who have completed high school, and red hats for those who have completed middle school or less. The alien might also place invisible color marks on the foreheads of all working Japanese: white on employees in large corporations, gray on those in medium-sized firms, and black on those in small enterprises. If we wore glasses that made these colors visible, would we see different color combinations depending on the location of our observations? Would the color mixtures differ between an exclusive golf club on the outskirts of Tokyo, a meeting at a *buraku* community in Kyoto, a museum in Nara, a *karaoke* bar in a fishing village in Hokkaidō, a *pachinko* pinball parlor in Hiroshima, a parent–teacher meeting at a prestigious private high school in Yokohama, and so on?

The alien could use many more invisible colors, denoting the value of an individual's assets (such as properties and stocks), the individual's occupational position, region of residence or origin, and minority/majority status. If we were to see these colors, how would they be distributed and in what patterns would they cluster? These are questions that a multicultural model of Japanese society can attempt to address by rejecting the thesis of a homogeneous and egalitarian Japan.

4   Control of Ideological Capital

Japanese culture, like the cultures of other complex societies, comprises a multitude of subcultures. Some are dominant, powerful, and controlling, and form core subcultures in given dimensions. Examples are the subculture of management in the occupational dimension, the subculture of the large corporation in the firm size dimension, male subculture in the gender dimension, and Tokyo subculture in the regional dimension. Other subcultures are more marginal and may be called the peripheral subcultures. Some examples are part-time worker subculture, small business subculture, female subculture, and rural subculture.

Core subcultures have ideological capital to define the normative framework of society. Even though the lifetime employment and the company-first dogma associated with the subculture of the large corporation apply to less than a quarter of the workforce, that part of the population has provided a model which all workers are expected to emulate, putting their companies ahead of their individual interests. The language of residents in uptown Tokyo is regarded as standard Japanese not because of its linguistic superiority but because of those residents' social proximity to the national power center.

Dominating in the upper echelons of society, core subcultural groups are able to control the educational curriculum, influence the mass media, and prevail in the areas of publishing and publicity. They outshine their peripheral counterparts in establishing their modes of life and patterns of expectations in the national domain and presenting their subcultures as the national culture. The samurai spirit, the kamikaze vigor, and the soul of the Yamato race,[39] which some male groups uphold as part of the dominant male subculture, are promoted as representing Japan's national culture. And although the liberalization of the domestic agricultural market affects many consumers positively, producer groups that have vested interests in maintaining the status quo and are connected with the country's leadership have often succeeded in presenting their interests as those of the entire nation.

More generally, the slanted views of Japan's totality tend to proliferate because writers, readers, and editors of publications on the general characteristics of Japanese society belong to the core subcultural sphere. Sharing their subcultural base, they conceptualize and hypothesize in a similar way, confirm their portrayal of Japan among themselves, and rarely seek outside confirmation. In many *Nihonjinron* writings, most examples and illustrations are drawn from the elite sector, including male employees in managerial tracks of large corporations and high-ranking officials of the national bureaucracy.[40]

Core subcultural groups overshadow those on the periphery in intercultural transactions too. Foreign visitors to Japan, who shape the images

[39] The Japanese phrase for this is *Yamato damashii*. Most Japanese are popularly presumed to belong to the Yamato race.

[40] Kawamura 1980; Sugimoto and Mouer 1995, pp. 187–8.

of Japan in their own countries, interact more intensely with core subcultural groups than with peripheral ones. In cultural exchange programs, Japanese who have houses, good salaries, and university education predominate among the host families, language trainers, and introducers of Japanese culture. Numerically small but ideologically dominant, core subcultural groups are the most noticeable to foreigners and are capable of presenting themselves to the outside world as representative of Japanese culture.

To recapitulate the major points: Japanese society embraces a significant degree of internal variation in both ethnic and stratificational senses. It comprises a variety of subcultures based on occupation, education, asset holdings, gender, ethnicity, age, and so forth. In this sense, Japan is multicultural and far from being a homogeneous, monocultural entity. One can grasp the complexity and intricacy of Japanese society perhaps only when one begins to see it as a mosaic of rival groups, competing strata, and various subcultures.

II   Multicultural Paradigm

1   Temporal Fluctuations in Understanding Japan

At popular levels, the Japanese self-images have been fairly consistent over time, as a time-series study spanning half a century demonstrates. The Institute of Statistical Mathematics survey results shown in Table 1.7 suggest that the Japanese regard themselves, and have done so more or less unchangingly over the past five decades, as industrious, well mannered, generous, and patient, while being uncreative and cheerless. Regardless of whether these self-portrayals reflect social realities or not, such images have taken hold and have fixed in the minds of many Japanese, forming the bedrock of *Nihonjinron* culture. These self-perceptions are not derived from systematic comparative analysis, though the characterization of any society would have to be based upon its comparison with other societies. To that extent, the Japanese self-images represented here are popular stereotypes.

At a more conceptual and theoretical level, Japanese society has inspired social scientists over several decades to address a complex set of issues. For the past few decades, the pendulum of Japan's images overseas has swung back and forth between positive and negative poles, and between universalist and particularist approaches. As Table 1.8 displays, seven distinctive phases are discernible during the postwar years.[41]

---

[41] See Kawamura 1980, pp. 56–7; Mouer and Sugimoto 1986, pp. 57–8.

Table 1.7   The Japanese self-image: Responses to the question, Which words represent the characteristics of the Japanese? (1958–2008)

Characteristic	1958	1963	1968	1973	1983	1988	1998	2003	2008
	% of respondents choosing characteristic, by year								
Diligent	55	60	61	66	69	72	71	66	67
Courteous	47	43	47	37	47	50	50	48	60
Kind	50	42	45	31	42	38	42	41	52
Persevering	48	55	58	52	60	50	51	46	49
Idealistic	32	23	23	21	30	27	23	20	20
Rational	11	8	10	13	22	22	18	17	17
Liberal	15	10	12	9	17	14	13	14	15
Easy-going	19	15	13	14	12	13	14	14	11
Cheerful	23	14	13	9	12	9	8	8	10
Creative	8	7	8	7	11	10	7	9	9

Source: Adapted from Institute of Statistical Mathematics 2009, Table 9.1.
Notes:
1. The question was not asked in the surveys conducted in 1978 and 1993.
2. The figures are the percentages of people who chose the items in the left column in the survey year. Because the respondents were allowed to make multiple choices, the total of each year exceeds 100 percent. The surveys were based on random samples.

The first phase, immediately following the end of World War II and continuing through the 1950s, saw a flow of writings which characterized the defeated Japan as a backward, hierarchical, and rather exotic society which Western societies should educate. In particular, Benedict's *The Chrysanthemum and the Sword*[42] had a most significant impact on the postwar development of Japanese studies. Methodologically, Benedict took a 'patterns of culture' approach which assumed that Japanese society could best be understood as a social or cultural whole composed of a rather homogeneous set of individuals. Benedict used anthropological techniques for describing small societies with relatively undifferentiated populations in her study of the complex society of Japan. Substantively, Benedict highlighted what she regarded as the most common denominators in Japanese social organization which contrasted markedly with their counterparts in the West. The influence of the anthropological framework can be seen in *Village Japan*,[43] *Japanese Factory*,[44] and *Tokugawa Religion*.[45] This vein of literature set the stage for the persistent style of analysis in which Japanese society was portrayed as both monolithic and unique.

In the second phase, which dominated the 1960s, modernization theory provided a framework within which Japan was assessed in a more

[42] Benedict 1946.   [43] Beardsley, Hall, and Ward 1959.
[44] Abegglen 1958.   [45] Bellah 1957.

Table 1.8 Fluctuations in the frameworks and analytical tools of Japanese studies in English-language publications (1945–2000)

Phase	US–Japan relationship	Evaluation of Japan	Possibility of convergence	Conceptual tools	Key words	Focus on internal variation
1945–60	Japan's total dependence on the US	Negative and positive	No	Particularistic	On, giri, oyabun, kobun	No
1955–70	Japan as the showcase of the US model	Positive	Yes/no (modernization)	Universalistic	Evolutionary change	No
1965–80	Japan's high economic growth and emerging competition with the US	Positive	No (unique Japan)	Particularistic	Amae, tate shakai, groupism	No
1970–90	Japan out-performing the US in some areas of the economy and technology	Positive	Yes (reverse convergence)	Universalistic/ particularistic	Japan as number one	No
1980–90	Intense trade war between Japan and the US	Negative	No (different capitalism)	Universalistic	Enigma, threat	No
1990–	Japan's recession and the US boom	Negative	Yes (global standard)	Universalistic	Borderlessness, structural reform	Yes/no
2000–	Japan as soft power, the US recession and the rise of China	Negative and positive	Yes (cultural capitalism)	Particularistic/ universalistic	Manga, animation, sushi	Yes/no

positive light. The mainstream of American scholarship began to regard Japan as a successful case of evolutionary transformation without revolutionary disruption. In the context of the intense Cold War, the United States establishment also began to see Japan as the showpiece of the non-communist model of development in Asia. The five-volume series on the modernization of Japan published by Princeton University Press represented the culmination of the collective efforts to examine Japan on the basis of a set of universalistic criteria. Using the yardstick of pattern variables developed by Parsons,[46] a leading sociological theorist of modernization, one of the most influential volumes, entitled *Social Change in Modern Japan*,[47] attempted to measure the degree to which Japan exemplified the expected changes from traditional to modern patterns. While using the universalistic model as its overall framework, however, the empirical findings of the series were equivocal, pointing out a number of distinctive features of Japan's modernization.

The third phase saw the revival of a more particularistic approach, lasting for about a decade from the late 1960s. Partly as a reaction to the universalistic modernization framework, there was emphasis on the supposed uniqueness of Japanese psychology, interpersonal relations, and social organization. The notion of *amae*, which Doi[48] spotlighted as the key to unlock the psychological traits of the Japanese, attracted much attention. Reischauer[49] contended that the Japanese were essentially group-oriented and differed fundamentally from individualistic Westerners. According to Nakane,[50] Japanese social organizations were vertically structured and apt to cut across class and occupational lines, unlike their Western counterparts, which were horizontally connected and inclined to transcend company kinship lines. These writings were published when the Japanese economy began to make some inroads into the United States market. To a considerable extent, they reflected increasing confidence in the Japanese way on the part of both Japanese and Western writers.

The fourth phase, which commenced in the early 1970s and persisted for two decades, witnessed waves of 'learn-from-Japan' campaigns. Japan's management practices, industrial relations, and education programs were praised as the most advanced on earth and endorsed as what other societies should emulate. Against the background of a gradual decline of American hegemony in the international economy and a visible ascendancy of Japanese economic performance, Vogel's *Japan as Number One*[51] was one of a number of works which championed what was regarded as the Japanese model. Many who wrote along these lines suggested the possibility of injecting some Japanese elements into

---

[46] Parsons 1951.   [47] Dore 1967.   [48] Doi 1973.
[49] Reischauer 1977.   [50] Nakane 1967, 1970, and 1978.   [51] Vogel 1979.

the Western system to revitalize it. In the main, this argument emphasized transferable, transplantable, and therefore transcultural attributes
of Japanese society.

The fifth phase, which started in around 1980 and continued in the
1990s, witnessed the rise of the revisionists, who saw the Japanese social
system in a much more critical light than previously. Johnson, the author
of *MITI and the Japanese Miracle*,[52] argues that Japanese capitalism is a
different kind of capitalism, based on the developmental state in which
the national bureaucracy plays a pivotal role in shaping national policy
for Japan's national interests only. He cautions that this structure poses
an increasingly grave threat to the wellbeing of the international community. In a similar vein, Wolferen addresses *The Enigma of Japanese
Power*[53] and maintains that the Japanese system, in which leaders lack
accountability, makes each citizen unhappy. Against the background of
Japan's economic superpower status, the intensification of trade friction
between Japan and the West, and the rise of Japan-bashing, the revisionist writings point to the strategies with which Western societies may be
able to contain the influence of Japan and make its social system more
compatible with theirs. The revisionist analysis attaches importance to
the institutional peculiarities of Japanese society and their consequences
both domestically and overseas.

The sixth phase started after the collapse of the so-called bubble
economy, with the commencement of the unprecedentedly prolonged
recession that persisted throughout the 1990s and continued into the
beginning of the twenty-first century. During this period, Japanese
advocates of *Nihonjinron* lost confidence in promoting Japan's cultural
uniqueness, let alone attributing to it the characteristics of the Japanese
economy. Overseas observers also gradually lost interest in the once hotly
debated 'Japanese model'. Many opinion-makers from business consul-
tants to media columnists started calling for the globalization of Japanese
society and for structural reform at various social and economic levels. Such titles as *The End of the Nation State* and *The Borderless World*
hit the bestseller lists.[54] The cultural elite of the Japanese establishment
appears to have abandoned justifying the economic and political behavior
of the Japanese in terms of cultural uniqueness and to have advocated
the necessity of integrating Japan into the international community.

Furthermore, the critical analysis of *Nihonjinron* initiated by a hand-
ful of social scientists in the late 1970s and the 1980s[55] gradually took

---

[52] Johnson 1982.   [53] Wolferen 1990.   [54] See Ohmae 1990 and 1995.
[55] For example, Sugimoto and Mouer 1980; Befu 1990a; Mouer and Sugimoto 1986; and
Dale 1986.

root in Japan's intellectual community,[56] making it difficult for cultural essentialists to naively write about Japan's 'cultural essence' without qualifications. Imported from the West, cultural studies became popular among Japanese social scientists and established itself as a new genre, called *karuchuraru sutadiizu*, which challenges epistemological assumptions about the primacy of the nation state as the fundamental unit of social analysis.

Although the tide of overt *Nihonjinron* has somewhat waned, it continues to exert persistent influence over Japan's intellectual life. For instance, in psychology, Kitayama and his associates assert that Japanese culture and the Japanese mind interact with one another, that Japanese conceptions of individuality emphasize the 'relatedness of individuals with each other'. Hence, while American culture values an independent view of the self, Japanese culture assumes an interdependent view of the self.[57] In economics, Arai maintains that the Japanese system of mutual trust in corporations must be upheld as the basis for the revival of the Japanese economy.[58] The key concepts that prevail in *Nihonjinron*-style stereotyping – group orientation, mutual cooperation, in-group harmony, and a sense of unity with nature, egalitarianism, and racial uniformity – continue to frame many contemporary attempts to analyze and understand Japanese society in the 1990s and the 2000s.

During this time, the polemic surrounding so-called Asian values has echoed and, in effect, reinforced many controversial aspects of *Nihonjinron*. Proclaimed by Singapore's ex–Prime Minister Lee Kwan Yu, Malaysian ex–Prime Minister Mahathir Bin Mohamad,[59] and other political leaders and intellectuals in Southeast Asia, Asian values are defined in contradistinction to Western ones and assert that Asians value groups ahead of individuals. This, then, is almost a pan-Asian version of *Nihonjinron*, which explains why Mahathir and the Japanese nationalist Shintarō Ishihara were able to join forces to write a bestselling book on how to say 'No' to the United States and other Western countries.[60] It is noteworthy that the advocacy of Asian values arose only once countries in the region had attained a measurable level of development and could compete with the West economically. Cultural nationalism, like *Nihonjinron* and the notion of Asian values, appears to flourish when a society reaches a significant level of economic maturity and can defend its national sense of self against other ideologies.

---

[56] See, for example, Yoshino 1992 and 1997; Oguma 2002; Amino 1990, 1992, 1994, and 2000; Takano and Ōsaka 1999; Befu 2001; and Takano 2008.

[57] Markus and Kitayama 1991; Kitayama 1998; Kitayama, Markus, Matsumoto, and Norsakkunkit 1997.

[58] Arai 2000.   [59] Mahathir 1999.   [60] Mahathir and Ishihara 1996.

In the seventh and latest phase, dating from the end of the last century as shown in Table 1.8, Japan's images around the world have been resurrected with the global spread of Japanese cultural goods, ranging from *manga* and *anime* through computer games to sushi and sashimi. Dubbed 'Cool Japan', these commodities have received enthusiastic acceptance in some quarters of Japanese society and overseas, with Japan showing a playful, fun-loving, and 'postmodern' face in stark contrast with its serious, diligent, and monotonous appearance during earlier decades. The products are packaged as being technologically sophisticated, suave, and refined with a touch of humor and light-heartedness. These representations reflect the expansion of the sphere of what one might call cultural capitalism, which thrives on outputting knowledge and information products – as distinct from industrial capitalism, which is based on the production of material and physical goods – a point that Chapter 4 examines in detail. While Japan's industrial capitalism displayed the faces of hardworking, scrupulous, rigid, and bureaucratic businessmen in gray suits, Japanese cultural capitalism attempts to display funny, fashionable, unassuming, maverick, and at times bizarre individuals in various modes.[61] McGray's oft-cited notion, Japan's Gross National Cool,[62] epitomizes these attributes and points to how Japanese cultural capitalism might develop and appropriate new areas of production and consumption, even if the nation's industrial capitalism stagnates. However, one should not lose sight of the fact that the global enhancement of Japan's cultural merchandise owes much to the success of the nation's industrial commodities; the notion that Japan's industrial goods, such as cars and electronic appliances, are of high quality has aided the expansion of the idea that Japanese cultural products are of a similarly high standard.

To attain soft domination in worldwide competition, Japan's cultural export industry requires calculations of the positives and negatives of two rival representations. At one end of the spectrum, exoticism is considered to be good business. The supposed peculiarities of Japanese culture in housing, architecture, gardening, food, clothing, and so on attract tourism on the appeal of mystery, divergence, and 'otherness'. At the other end, the trans-spatial and trans-cultural appearance of products – such as high-tech robots, super-modern city life, and suave gadgets – are market-friendly to the extent that their narratives can be entertaining and captivating in any cultural milieu, thus appealing to a wide range of global consumers, cutting across national and ethnic lines.

---

[61] To put it differently, the emphasis has shifted from the top items to the bottom ones in Table 1.7.

[62] McGray 2002.

The success of cultural export products depends much on the ways in which these two orientations interact and coalesce. On the whole, the Japanese cultural industry finds it profitable to present its products in a globally palatable and hybrid fashion, while it also does not forget to inject some elements of 'Japaneseness' to underscore their national background. Although many Japanese *manga* and *anime* characters have 'un-Japanese' big and round eyes and manipulate pan-cultural techno-logical devices, the landscape, customs, and symbols that are associated with 'Japan' form indispensable components of these cultural export products. Doraemon, the main character in a globally popular anima-tion for children, uses a highly sophisticated *dokodemo* door (a door to wherever you like) while he lives in a Japanese house with *tatami* mats and interacts with very Japanese-looking friends. The imagery is neither completely exotic, foreign, and inscrutable nor fully cosmopolitan, trans-national, and trans-boundary, but it is a balanced mixture of both, to the extent that it proves of much benefit and interest to the expansion of Japan's cultural capitalism.

This process has unfolded alongside the main features of *Nihonjinron*. The assumption of Japanese homogeneity has hardly been questioned, and the traditional continuity and supremacy of Japanese culture have been underscored. It is argued, for example, that Japan's *manga* and ani-mation products have a long domestic history and were exposed to diverse markets long before their popularity exploded abroad in recent decades. The oldest Japanese *manga* is believed to be *chōjū giga*, illustrated in the twelfth century on horizontal picture scrolls by a high priest in Kyoto and featuring personified and playing frogs, rabbits, monkeys, birds, and other animals in a caricature fashion. Some famous artists drew com-ical pictures in *ukiyo-e* (colored woodblock prints of the demimonde) during the feudal period. These partial historical episodes are used to advance the notion of the continuous superiority of Japan's national culture despite their tenuous linkage with the current propagation of Japanese *manga*.[63] As the final section of Chapter 9 explores, it remains to be seen if the new Cool Japan discourse represents postmodern coun-terculture or postmodern *Nihonjinron*.

At the beginning of the twenty-first century the Japanese national ethos continues to be glorified in a variety of cultural arenas. Saitō, for instance, produced many bestselling works that admire the beauty of the Japanese language.[64] In praise of the 'dignity of the Japanese nation', Fujiwara maintained that the Japanese must revive the samurai spirit rather than pursuing democracy and must restore Japan's traditional warm emotions and feelings rather than adhere to Western-style logic.[65] In the sphere

---

[63] Iwabuchi 2007, p. 83.   [64] For example, Saitō 2001.   [65] Fujiwara 2005.

of food culture, in 2006, Japan's Ministry of Agriculture, Forestry, and Fisheries tried to draw a plan to provide certificates of 'authenticity' to a limited number of overseas Japanese–food restaurants, an attempt that eventually went nowhere. The *Nihonjinron* belief that there is something genuinely Japanese remains deeply ingrained in Japan's cultural establishment.

It is important to remember that the rise of Japan's cultural industry received international recognition only after its soft power status was debated in the United States, though Japanese cultural goods have been most extensively exported and linked to the cultural markets of Asia. To be accepted in the United States, Japan's animation entrepreneurs have been willing to cut or change some scenes and even story lines. The success of Japanimation owes much to considerable 'de-Japanization' and partial 'Americanization'.

Since the middle of the twentieth century, Japan's economic performance on the international stage in general and the changing political and economic relationships between Japan and the United States in particular have shaped the framework of analysis of Japan. Observed from outside, the analytical tools used to assess Japanese society have alternated between particularistic and universalistic types, while foreign evaluation of Japanese society has swung between positive and negative appraisals.

2   The Convergence Debate

At the highest level of abstraction, the so-called convergence debate has made Japan the focal point of analysis for decades. The debate itself is as old as social sciences and has had many twists and turns. At one end of the continuum, convergence theorists have maintained that all industrial societies become akin in their structural arrangements and value orientations because the logic of industrialism entails a common batch of functional imperatives. At the other end, anti-convergence theorists have argued that the cultural background and historical tradition of each society are so firmly entrenched that the advent of industrialism cannot simply mold them into a uniform pattern; no convergence eventuates, because each culture develops its own style of industrial development on the basis of its own momentum and dynamics. Japan provides a logical testing ground for this debate since it is the only nation outside the Western cultural tradition that has achieved a high level of industrialization. On balance, a majority of Japan specialists, be they culturologists or institutionalists, have tended to underscore the unique features of Japanese society, thereby siding either explicitly or implicitly with the anti-convergence stance. Yet this position has presupposed that the West continues to lead the direction of industrialism, though the Japanese pattern deviates from it.

Many convergence theorists see the so-called unique features of Japanese society mostly as the expression of the nation's late development, lagging behind the early-developer countries. Tominaga, for example, regards four patterns of transformation in progress for decades in Japan as pointers that suggest it is becoming increasingly like advanced Western societies.[66]

First, Japan's demographic composition is changing from one in which a young labor force comprises an overwhelming majority of the population to one in which the aged comprise the larger portion. The proportion of those who are sixty-five years of age or older exceeded the 10 percent mark in France in the 1930s, in Sweden and the United Kingdom in the 1940s, in Germany and Switzerland in the 1950s, and in the United States and Italy in the 1970s, while Japan arrived at this stage in the middle of the 1980s. This means that the comparative demographic advantage that Japan enjoyed in the past has begun to disappear. If the present trend continues, Japan will become the nation with the highest ratio of aged in its population in the early part of the twenty-first century, thus completing the catch-up cycle.

Second, Japan's family and kinship groups have dwindled and even disintegrated in a similar way to those of Europe and the United States. Nuclear families are now the norm, and the percentage of singles has increased. While the anti-convergence theorists use the Japanese family system and kinship networks as a cornerstone of their argument for the distinctive character of Japanese society, Tominaga underscores their decline and suggests that the Japanese are undergoing a Western-type experience somewhat belatedly.

Third, so-called Japanese management is changing. There are many signs that the twin institutions of permanent employment and seniority-based wage structure cannot sustain themselves. Company loyalty is weakening among young employees. The aging profile of the corporate demographic structure makes it difficult for starting workers to expect smooth and automatic promotions at the later stages of their careers. Head-hunting is becoming rampant, and inter-company mobility is rising. In the long run, the convergence theory predicts, the Japanese employment structure and its concomitant management styles will more resemble Western patterns.

Fourth, the emphasis of the Japanese value system is gradually shifting from collectivism to individualism. The rising number of students enrolled in universities and other institutions of higher education leads

[66] The description below follows Tominaga 1988, pp. 2–50.

to the mass production of citizens exposed and oriented to individualistic and rational thinking. The disintegration of the family and kinship
systems, plus the gradual dissolution of the local community, tends to
liberate individuals from intense social constraints imposed by these traditional structures. As Japanese workers become accustomed to material
affluence, their legendary work ethic tends to dissipate and their lifestyles
become more hedonistic. In this process, the Japanese are inclined to lose
a sense of devotion to the groups and organizations to which they belong
and to experience the state of *anomie* (**normlessness**), much as do citizens
of advanced industrialized societies in the West.

Convergence theorists concede that these four transformations have
not yet run their course but maintain that they head undeniably in the
direction of convergence with advanced industrialized societies, contrary
to the view of unique-Japan theorists, who frequently ignore the significance of different levels of development and make erroneous static comparisons between Japan and Western societies. It would be fair for social
scientists to compare Japan's present features with their counterparts in
Western countries a few decades ago.

The convergence debate gained another twist with Dore's formulation of the reverse convergence hypothesis.[67] According to his argument,
industrialized societies are converging on a set of patterns observed not
in Euro-American societies but in Japan. This proposition finds considerable support with the proliferation of so-called Japanese-style management around the world: an increasing number of industrial and indus-
trializing societies appear to have adopted the systems of multi-skilling,
just-in-time, and enterprise-based labor negotiations. In terms of the
role of the state in industrial policy implementation, many Western analysts have made a positive assessment of the coordination and orchestra-
tion functions of national public bureaucracy à la Japanese Ministry of
International Trade and Industry.[68] In the sphere of education, too, the
Japanese-style structured and regimented mode of teaching has attracted
international attention and made inroads into some education systems
abroad. In the area of law enforcement, the Japanese *kōban* police-box
system is being instituted in many parts of the world.

The reverse convergence perspective signaled a new phase in the debate
in which the West was no longer regarded as the trailblazer in industrial
development. Advancing this line of thinking further, another position
which could be labeled the multiple convergence thesis has gained ground
in recent years. It postulates that two or more types of development are
observable, depending on when industrialization began or the type of
cultural background that predominated. The proposition suggests that

[67] Dore 1973.   [68] Johnson 1982 and 1990.

Table 1.9 Four positions in the convergence debate

The West is the dominant pattern?	One point of convergence?	
	Yes	No
Yes	Convergence thesis	Anti-convergence thesis
No	Reverse convergence thesis	Multiple convergence thesis

these types generate plural patterns of convergence in structures and values. Table 1.9 maps the relative locations of the four perspectives under discussion.

The multiple convergence perspective has many versions. One of them is the so-called late-developer hypothesis that Anglo-American capitalism was a unique type of development of early industrializers, while late-developer societies such as Japan had to evolve different social configurations to cope with different domestic and international constraints. Murakami,[69] for example, contends that, unlike Anglo-American societies, Japan, Germany, Italy, and other late-developing countries could not achieve political integration suitable to industrialization at its initial phase. To cope, these countries had to devise a strategy of catch-up industrialization by preserving some elements of traditional heritage while establishing a powerful bureaucracy that steered the process of development.

Reflecting the swift rise of Asian economies since the 1980s, another version points to the possibility of 'Confucian capitalism',[70] in which the ethic of obedience to authorities and emphasis on selfless devotion to work lead to a path of development different from the Western type but conducive to rapid economic growth. Similar arguments have surfaced under the rubrics of the 'East Asian model',[71] 'Oriental capitalism',[72] the 'Pacific Century',[73] and so on. Japan's economic structure is regarded as the most refined and polished of this type.

In a broader perspective, some theorists explore the ways in which different types of civilizations take different routes of development. Civilization in this context includes not only culture but social organizations, structures, and institutions. This approach attempts to place different civilizations in some evolutionary hierarchy in which Japan occupies a position near the top.[74] As early as the 1950s, Umesao[75] proposed an ecological model of the history of civilizations in which he attempted to

---

[69] Murakami 1984a.   [70] Dore 1987.   [71] Berger and Hsiao 1988.
[72] Twu 1990.   [73] Burenstam Linder 1986; Borthwick 1992.
[74] For example, Itō 1985.   [75] See Umesao 2002.

demonstrate that Japan belonged to the same civilization zone as Western Europe in having an internally stimulated process of 'autogenic succession' and attaining higher levels of development than continental Asia and Eastern Europe. In more recent years, Murakami, Kumon, and Satō[76] have argued that Japanese society is built upon what they call *ie* civilization, which emphasizes quasi-kinship lineage and functional hierarchy. They maintain that the *ie* principle permeates Japanese history as a 'genotype', playing a central role in the formation of Japanese-style capitalism. They refute the assumption of unilinear development and argue for a model of multilinear development in which the Japanese pattern represents a distinctive type. Huntington[77] sees the fundamental division of the world in the clash of several civilizations, singling out Japan as the only non-Western civilization that has succeeded in the quest to become modern without becoming Western. Civilizational scholars, including Eisenstadt and Arnason,[78] have recently published some important books on Japanese civilization in which it is argued that Japan's case is unique and represents a civilization sui generis, unparalleled in other parts of the world.

All these generalizations use civilizations as the units of analysis and explain multiple patterns of development in terms of macro-cultural variables. The multiple convergence thesis perhaps represents a return to emphasis on cultural variables in the convergence debate and reflects the fluctuations in the tone of another debate – that concerning cultural relativism.

3   The Cultural Relativism Debate

Given the multicultural features of Japanese society, can sociological analysis do justice to them by adopting a multicultural perspective? Can the analysis of societies be free from ethnocentric assumptions? These questions emerge against the backdrop of increasingly multicultural realities and rising tides of ethnic confidence around the world.

The Japan phenomenon poses a wide range of questions about the ethnocentric nature of Western sociology. The issue is looming large rather belatedly, partly because the founding fathers of sociology, and their followers, until very recently used Western Europe, the United States, and a very limited number of non-Western societies as the empirical settings for the construction of theories of modernity and modernization. In the writings of Marx, Weber, and Durkheim, for instance, China, India, and Pacific islands are studied primarily as traditional societies for comparative purposes, but none of these scholars made any meaningful reference

---

[76] Murakami, Kumon, and Satō 1979; Murakami 1984b.   [77] Huntington 1993.
[78] Eisenstadt 1996; Arnason 2002.

to Japan. Even today, Habermas, who talks much about the need to redefine the concept of modernity, makes little mention of Japan.

In anthropology, it is almost trite to distinguish two types of concepts. One type consists of emic concepts, which are specific and peculiar to a particular culture and meaningful only to its members. The other type consists of etic concepts, which are applicable to all cultures, transcending national and ethnic boundaries.[79] Most sociological concepts are assumed to be etic, but it can be argued that they were initially emic concepts of Euro-American societies which became etic notions because of the cultural hegemony of Western nations. Here one should not lose sight of the extent to which sociology contains elements of cultural imperialism, although this does not mean that proper research cannot often determine their applicability in diverse cultural settings.[80] Cultural relativists would argue that the time is ripe for a wide range of Japanese emic concepts to be examined and used in comparative analysis of advanced capitalism.

At the conceptual level, the *Nihonjinron* literature provides a wide repertoire of emic notions that can be tested and scrutinized for cross-cultural studies. This may be an important contribution of this genre, because, with some refinement and elaboration of conceptual boundaries and substance, Japan-based notions can be developed as viable tools for sociological analysis. White[81] and others maintain, for example, that indigenous definitions of women's lives differ between Japan and the West. They also argue that feminism has different meanings depending on the cultural context, thereby making it impossible for a universally valid model of women's lives to be developed. Doi's notion of *amae*, which he regards as peculiar to the Japanese personality, may be used as a conceptual tool of comparative analysis. When these concepts are used as variables for cross-cultural studies, it may be that Japanese society does not always exhibit these characteristics in the highest possible degree. A quantitative comparative study of Australia, Hawaii, Japan, Korea, and the mainland United States, for example, shows that the level of *kanjin* (interperson) orientation, which Hamaguchi contends is emic to the Japanese, is lower in Japan than in any other country and lowest among Japanese men.[82]

---

[79] See Befu 1989 for a discussion of these two types of concepts in the context of Japanese studies.

[80] Clammer 2001 takes a comparative, non-Western perspective seriously and attempts to bring the study of Japanese society into dialogue with some recent developments in cultural studies.

[81] White 1987b.

[82] Kashima, Yamaguchi, Kim, Choi, Gelfand, and Yuki 1996. The same study also demonstrates that the level of *kanjin* orientation is consistently higher among women than among men in all the societies under analysis. See also Hofstede 1984.

At the theoretical level, some scholars, notably Befu and Deutsch-mann,[83] maintain that theories of bureaucracy, as developed in the Western sociological tradition, are 'culture-bound'. Large bureaucratic corporations in Japan tend to give priority to such paternalistic arrangements as company housing, company leisure facilities, and company excursions. At the level of interpersonal interaction, an elaborate system of particularistic arrangements enables superiors to maneuver their subordinates with great ease. In corporations, every supervisor spends an enormous amount of time paying personal attention to employees under his charge, beyond the call of his job specifications. He entertains his subordinates in pubs, bars, restaurants, and clubs after working hours, serves as a formal go-between in their wedding ceremonies, listens to personal problems of their families, and even attends the funerals of their grandparents. None of these activities is formally required, yet no manager in a Japanese firm could retain his position without them; the expectation is that his subordinates, in return, are willing to devote their time to work and to commit themselves to it beyond the call of their job specifications. This inordinate exchange of expressive resources between superiors and subordinates characterizes Japan's bureaucratic organizations.

Befu and Deutschmann contend that the particularistic qualities of Japanese bureaucratic organization contradict the key thesis of Western theories of bureaucracy – that bureaucracy's most efficient mode is a legal-rational one. From Weber to Merton, sociologists of modern bureaucratic organization have argued that its operation must be governed by universalistic law, formal criteria, and 'functional specificity' and must transcend particularistic interactions, affective considerations, and 'functional diffuseness'. This is one of the reasons why nepotism is regarded as dysfunctional in formal organizations in the Western model of bureaucracy. Those researchers who find Japanese bureaucracy essentially non-Weberian suggest the possibility that the legal–rational approach may not be the only way of achieving bureaucratic efficiency; the opposite, which the Japanese pattern represents, is another possible path.[84]

On a different front, Kuwayama pinpoints the power relationship inherent in what he calls the academic world system, in which the global intellectual community is divided into core (center) and periphery

---

[83] Befu 1990b; Deutschmann 1987. The discussion below follows Befu's argument.

[84] The Befu-Deutschmann argument is possibly subject to debate on two grounds: many analysts of Western bureaucratic organization have pointed out a number of informal and non-rational elements in it, and the Japanese bureaucracy is basically a highly formalistic system and expressive ties may be a matter of nuance. The exact opposite of legal–rational bureaucracy would be pure nepotism or patrimonialism.

(margin).[85] Focusing on anthropology, he maintains that the core is made up of the United States, Great Britain and, to a lesser extent, France, while areas outside these countries, including Japan, constitute the academic periphery. More broadly, in core countries it is not only anthropologists but social scientists in general who maintain an academic hegemony throughout the world. Their writings are in international circulation and form required reading for researchers in the periphery, who study and even imitate their theories, methods, findings, and styles of writing to keep abreast with scholarship in the metropolitan West. The converse is untrue to the extent that academics in the core can afford to ignore the scholarship in the periphery or to dismiss it as unsophisticated, immature, or underdeveloped.

As a peripheral country, Japan is, by and large, at the receiving end of such one-way traffic from core areas. A new academic trend in the United States and Western Europe, be it cultural studies, postmodernism, or postcolonialism, is translated into Japanese and studied intensely, often with a few Japanese scholars serving as its interlocutors and interpreters to the Japanese academic community. In comparison, very few Japanese scholarly books are translated into English and other Western languages, and most remain unknown in the core countries, despite the accumulation of significant studies in Japanese academia. This asymmetry often enables social scientists in core areas to criticize Japan's 'native' research as vague, inarticulate, or vaporous without realizing that their yardsticks may be ethnocentric.

4   Subcultural Relativism

Studies of development and social change certainly require comparative analyses of national averages. When carefully made, nation-level summaries and generalizations help one take a snapshot and global view of each society. One should not underestimate the importance of this approach, while avoiding the pitfall of stereotyping. A multicultural approach to Japanese society sensitizes one to such a danger and provides some guideposts to avoid it.

In addition to examining Japanese emic concepts at societal level, studies can probe the patterns of distribution of various emic notions of subcultural groups within Japan – for example, women's versus men's emics, emics of inhabitants in the Kantō area versus those in the Kansai area, and elite emics versus mass emics. This approach implies that researchers can invoke the concept of cultural relativism not only cross-culturally between

---

[85] Kuwayama 2004. On the same issue, see Kosaka and Ogino 2008.

Table 1.10   A four-person case comparing subcultural dimensions

Subcultural dimensions	Nation	
	Japan	Germany
Business executive, large corporation, male, large city	Mr Toyota	Mr Müller
Worker, small firm, female, small town	Ms Honda	Ms Schmitz

Japanese culture and other national cultures, but intra-culturally, between subcultural groupings within Japan itself.

The multicultural framework will allow systematic comparative analysis of Japanese subcultures and their counterparts in other societies. One can compare, for example, the quality of life of small-shop owners in Japan and Britain, the lifestyles of school dropouts in Japan and Germany, the life satisfaction of part-time female workers in Japan and France, and so on. One can also compare distributions of social resources and value orientations across different groups in Japan with those in other countries. Such analyses would spotlight some hitherto unanalyzed social groups and their subcultures and rectify national stereotypical biases.

To highlight the point, we may think of another hypothetical situation, where four individuals – two from Japan and two from Germany – get together, as shown in Table 1.10. Those from Japan are Mr Toyota, a business executive of a large corporation in Tokyo, and Ms Honda, a shop assistant in a small shop in a small town in Shikoku. Those from Germany are Mr Müller, an executive director of a large firm in Frankfurt, and Ms Schmitz, a clerk in a small firm in a small town in northern Germany. We assume that they can communicate in a common language. Which pair would be most similar in their thought and behavior patterns? According to the conventional national culture argument, Mr Toyota and Ms Honda would form one cluster and Mr Müller and Ms Schmitz the other, because the pairs would be based on shared national culture. The subcultural model suggests the possibility that the close pairs may be Mr Toyota and Mr Müller on the one hand and Ms Honda and Ms Schmitz on the other, membership of each pair being determined by similarities of gender, occupation, firm size, and place of residence.

5   The Desirability Debate

In the current climate of ambivalence of Western nations towards Japan, analysts are often tempted to join either a 'Japan-admiring camp' or a 'Japan-bashing camp' and to portray Japanese society in simplistic black-and-white terms. Yet as Japan is a multifaceted, complex society, one would perhaps have to start with a kind of 'trade-off' model that focuses on the ways in which both desirable and undesirable elements are interlinked. To the extent that Japanese society is an integrated system, its observers would be required to examine the processes in which its various parts depend on many others, and upon which the overall functioning of Japanese society depends. Pattern A may be an outcome of Pattern B, which may in turn be a consequence of Pattern C. From this perspective, every institutional sphere contains Janus-faced arrangements.

In work, for example, the permanent-employment system is regarded as a scheme that provides job stability, company loyalty, and job commitment. In exchange, however, most workers in this category find it difficult to disobey company orders, which at times require great sacrifices. When married male employees are asked to transfer to a firm or a branch office distant from their place of residence, one in four reluctantly choose to live away from their families as so-called 'company bachelors'. In community life, low crime rates in cities are closely related to the costs of criminal activities: harsh prison conditions, merciless methods used to force suspects to confess, and the penetration of police into private lives of citizens. In terms of the seller–purchaser relationship, Japan is an extremely efficient, high-speed consumer-oriented society where commodities are available at all hours and delivered on time without fail at the request of the customer. Such flexible dynamism is supported behind the scenes by the cheap labor of casual workers who work in convenience stores and for delivery companies.

With these trade-offs criss-crossing the Japanese social system, any simplistic argument for importing a particular element of that system into another country requires careful analysis; as long as that element depends on the operation of further elements, its transplantation would be ineffective unless the whole package were imported. The 'learn-from-Japan' campaigners must be aware that in this process good things would be accompanied by bad.

6   Legitimation of Double Codes

In this context, one must be mindful that dominant subcultural groups rely heavily on an ideology which discourages transparent and forthright interactions between individuals. While indirectness, vagueness, and ambiguity are facets of human behavior in any society, the Japanese norm explicitly encourages such orientations in a wide range of situations. Double codes are legitimized in many spheres of Japanese life, thereby creating a world beneath the surface. The Japanese language has several concept pairs which distinguish between sanitized official appearance and hidden reality. The distinction is frequently invoked between the facade, which is normatively proper and correct, and the actuality, which may be publicly unacceptable but adopted privately or among insiders. In analyzing Japanese society, one should caution against confusing these two aspects and pay special attention to at least three such pairs.[86]

One set is *tatemae* and *honne*. *Tatemae* refers to a formally established principle which is not necessarily accepted or practiced by the parties involved. *Honne* designates true feelings and desires which cannot be openly expressed because of the strength of *tatemae*. If *tatemae* corresponds to 'political correctness', *honne* points to hidden, camouflaged, and authentic sentiment. Thus, an employee who expresses dedication to his company boss in accordance with the corporate *tatemae* of loyalty and harmony may do so because of his *honne* ambition for promotion and other personal gains. Or an advocate of the *tatemae* principle of the unique place of Japanese rice in Japanese culture may be a farmer whose *honne* lies in the promotion of his agricultural interests.

Another pair is likened to two sides of a coin or any other flat object with *omote* (the face) and *ura* (the back). The implication is that *omote* represents the correct surface or front, which is openly permissible, whereas *ura* connotes the wrong, dark, concealed side, which is publicly unacceptable or even illegal. Thus, in the business world, *ura* money flows with *ura* negotiations and *ura* transactions. Wheeler-dealers use various *ura* skills to promote their interests. At some educational institutions, students whose parents have paid *ura* fees to school authorities buy their way into the school through the '*ura* gate' (back door). In community life, *ura* stories (inside accounts) are more important than *omote* explanations.

The third pair consists of *soto* (outside or exterior) and *uchi* (inside or interior). When referring to individuals' group affiliation, the dichotomy is used to distinguish between outsiders and insiders, or between members of an out-group and those of an in-group. When talking to outsiders, company employees often refer to their firm as *uchi*, drawing a line between 'them' and 'us'. One cannot candidly discuss sensitive matters in *soto* but can straightforwardly break confidentiality in *uchi* situations. In the context of human interaction, while *soto* aspects of individuals or groups represent their superficial outward appearances, their *uchi* facets account for their fundamental essence and real dispositions. For instance, a female worker may make a pretense of being obedient to her male supervisor in *soto* terms but may in fact be quite angry about his arrogant behavior in her *uchi*.

[86] See, for example, Shibata 1983; Nitoda 1987.

These dichotomies also exist in other cultures and languages. In Japanese society, however, these particular forms of duality are invoked in public discourse time and again to defend the publicly unacceptable sides of life as realities to be accepted. According to the dominant social code, the *honne* of the *uchi* members should be winked at, and the *ura* of their activities must be purposely overlooked. The legitimation of duality underlying the Japanese vocabulary provides a pretext for corrupt activities.

In the *ura* side of business transactions, for example, Japanese companies use the category of *shito hitoku kin* (expenses unaccounted for) to conceal the identity of the recipient of the expenditure. They can do this as long as they declare those expenses to be subject to taxation. The corporate world uses this method extensively to hide secret pay-offs, kickbacks, and political donations. About half the expenditures unaccounted for in the construction industry are thought to be undisclosed political donations of this nature.[87] The *honne* of the participants in these deals is to promote the mutual interests of *uchi* networks of business and politics.

The notion that the dual codes must be seen as facts of life is sometimes used to justify murky collusion known as *dangō*, the illegal practice most predominant in construction tendering for public works projects. Companies which take part in *dangō* engage in artful pre-tender arrangements where they agree in advance among themselves on their bids and on which company will be the successful tenderer. In return, it is agreed that the unsuccessful companies are entitled to a certain share of the successful company's profits. The practice of *dangō* rests upon the prevailing 'closed' tender system in which a government body designates several companies as entitled to tender. As the number of companies designated is normally limited to ten or so, they can easily engage in pre-tender negotiations and come to mutually agreed clandestine deals. To win designation, companies vie with each other for the arbitrary favor of bureaucrats and the influence of politicians, and this also tends to create an environment for corruption. The practice rests upon the *ura* operations of *uchi* insiders attempting to materialize their *honne* of profit maximization among themselves.

To accomplish the *ura* part of their business exchanges, Japanese companies spend enormous amounts on entertainment expenses. The *tatemae* and *omote* justifications of these expenses include the importance of informal contacts and communications. Many important political policy decisions are made by politicians who wine and dine in high-class Japanese-style restaurants (called *ryōtei*) where *ura*-type trading is done behind closed doors. Similarly, local government officials used to

[87] MM, 29 June 1993, p. 26.

entertain their national counterparts in these and other restaurants in order to secure high allocations of national government subsidies, a now illegal *ura* practice which citizens' groups have criticized as illegitimate use of taxpayers' money. In the sphere of environmental politics, while the Japanese government presents Japan's whaling as 'scientific' in *omote* terms, Japanese environmental groups claim that its *ura* reality is 'commercial'.

Studies of Japanese society are incomplete if researchers examine only its *tatemae*, *omote*, and *soto* aspects. Only when they scrutinise the *honne*, *ura*, and *uchi* sides of Japanese society can they grasp its full picture. To be Japan-literate, researchers should not confuse outward appearances with inside realities when examining a society in which double codes play significant roles.

III   Towards a Multicultural Analysis

To reiterate the main points of the discussion: this book takes issue with two types of monoculturalism that have long pervaded studies of Japanese society. First, it explicitly challenges descriptions of Japan as a culturally homogeneous society with little internal variation and contests the view that Japan is 'uniquely unique' among advanced industrial societies in being uniform, classless, egalitarian, and harmonious, with little domestic variety and diversity. Second, it wishes to be sensitive to Japanese emic concepts as well as established etic notions of the social sciences and to avoid the pitfall of two types of conceptual monoculturalism. On one hand, it seeks to avoid the assumptions of those who claim that Japan can be understood fully only with the application of Japan-specific conceptual yardsticks, as seen in the influential so-called *Nihonjinron* writings, the discourse which tries to highlight the presumably unique aspects of Japan and the Japanese. On the other hand, it does not follow those social scientists who have sought to investigate the Japanese situation exclusively in terms of the concepts and rhetoric of Western social sciences. It intends to be pluralistic regarding the use of emic and etic concepts and to count on many fine published studies which have been based upon such pluralism.

Seeking to avoid these two sorts of monoculturalism, the book suggests that two types of multicultural approaches would allow the sociological pulse of contemporary Japan to be taken in a realistic way. One is a multicultural research focus that spotlights the domestic stratification and subcultural differentiation of Japanese society; the other is an international, multicultural conceptual paradigm for the understanding of Japan.

This book consists of four major themes. The first (Chapters 2 and 3) presents an overview of class and stratification in Japan, and of Japan's demographic variation, preparatory to depicting Japanese society. The second (Chapters 4 and 5) addresses stratification based upon achievement criteria, such as occupation and education, and investigates the degree of class reproduction in these spheres. The third theme (Chapters 6 and 7) is the way in which Japanese society is stratified on the basis of gender and ethnicity, two ascriptive criteria that are determined at birth and are generally unalterable thereafter. The fourth (Chapters 8, 9, and 10) explores the patterns of trade-off and tug-of-war between forces of control and dissent in the Japanese social system.

Students of Japanese society must be mindful of the complex patterns of diversity in Japanese society and sensitive to the types of devices used to monitor its functioning. By attending closely to Japan's intra-societal multicultural reality and adopting a perspective of inter-societal conceptual multiculturalism in cross-cultural analysis, we may perhaps be able to see a new horizon in our endeavor to understand Japanese society from an international perspective.

In doing this, one must be careful to identify the merits and demerits of two types of cultural relativism: one emphasizing cultural relativity *within* a society, the other stressing the cultural relativity *between* societies. On one hand, inter-cultural relativism tends to prioritize the internal uniformity of each culture and thereby falls into the trap of *Nihonjinron* and other forms of 'cultural essentialism'. On the other hand, intra-cultural relativism invariably underplays the importance or denies the existence of inter-societal cultural relativity, often rendering its proponents insensitive to Eurocentric or other forms of international or trans-ethnic cultural imperialism. This means that a *negative correlation* exists between intra- and inter-societal cultural relativism. The more we emphasize inter-societal cultural differences, the more cultural homogeneity we presume, thereby affirming an assumption of internal cultural imperialism. However, the more we stress the significance of intra-societal cultural relativism, the more we tend to play down the threat of external cultural domination and ethnocentrism. This dilemma, which the Japanese case so clearly illustrates, has placed the theory of the 'relativity of relativities' on the contemporary intellectual agenda.

2 Class and Stratification: An Overview

The public discourse on class and stratification in Japan experienced a dramatic paradigm shift towards the end of the twentieth century. Although widely portrayed as an egalitarian and predominantly middle class society during the period of high economic growth until the early 1990s, Japan has suddenly been deemed a society divided along class lines under the prolonged stagnation that has characterized the Japanese economy for a couple of decades.

In the heyday of the 'Japanese miracle', the spectacular comeback of Japan's economy after the devastation of World War II, a considerable amount of literature suggested that the basic rifts in Japan were not those between social classes but were these between corporate groups.[1] It was argued that in Japan 'it is not really a matter of workers struggling against capitalists or managers but of Company A ranged against Company B'.[2] Some went so far as to claim that the Western notions of class and stratification did not find expression in the daily realities of the Japanese. Others contended that class-consciousness was weaker in Japan than in Western countries.[3] Often-publicized government statistics which showed that some 90 percent of Japanese regarded themselves as belonging to the 'middle class' appeared to bear out this line of thinking.

However, with the economic recession in the 1990s and the 2000s, the public perception has shifted to emphasize the advent of 'disparity society' with marked divisions between classes with rival interests. Satō maintains that the sharp decline of social mobility of the privileged upper middle white-collar sector has resulted in what he calls the breakdown of middle class society. Tachibanaki, who led a debate over deepening inequality, argues that the level of social inequality in Japanese society has increased so much that it ranks among the most highly disparate societies in the world.[4] The new discourse has gained further ground since the worldwide financial crisis from 2008 onwards. Suddenly, it is widely argued that middle class society has collapsed and *kakusa shakai*

---

[1] The most influential books which take this line are Nakane 1967, 1970, and 1978.
[2] Nakane 1970, p. 87.   [3] Reischauer 1977, pp. 161–2.   [4] Tachibanaki 2005.

Table 2.1 Class identification and middle-class consciousness (%) (1965–2012)

Class Period	Upper	Upper middle (A)	Middle middle (B)	Lower middle (C)	Lower	Middle total (A)+(B)+(C)
1965–69	0.6	7.1	51.6	28.8	7.7	87.5
1970–74	0.6	7.0	58.5	24.4	6.0	89.9
1975–79	0.6	7.8	59.5	23.0	5.3	90.3
1980–84	0.6	7.6	54.6	27.0	6.8	89.2
1985–89	0.5	6.7	52.6	29.1	8.0	88.4
1990–94	0.8	9.5	54.1	26.2	6.1	89.8
1995–99	0.7	9.9	56.8	24.2	5.5	90.9
2000–04	0.8	9.7	54.8	25.6	6.3	90.1
2005–09	1.0	10.4	54.1	25.7	6.7	90.2
2010–12	0.9	12.0	55.1	24.7	5.7	91.8

Notes: Calculations are based on Cabinet Office 2012c. The figures are the mean average of the years covered in each period. Since 'do not know' cases are not listed in the table, the total of each period does not amount to 100.

(disparity society) has come into being. Chiavacci spells out three dominant models of class analysis of Japan – the class struggle model immediately after World War II, the general middle class model during Japan's growth and prosperity period, and the divided society model during the nation's economic stagnation in recent decades.[5]

Interestingly, despite the claim of the emergence of *kakusa shakai*, an overwhelming majority of Japanese continue to regard themselves as belonging to the 'middle class', a pattern that has persisted for decades, as Table 2.1 shows. Moreover, as Table 2.2 shows, comparative studies of class affiliation in a number of nations found that 80–90 percent of people identify themselves as 'middle class', which suggests that this phenomenon is far from unique to Japan. The notion that Japan is a highly egalitarian society is palatable for overseas *soto* consumption, but it does not accurately reflect the *uchi* reality of Japan's material and cultural inequality.

The sense of inequality is quite marked in many dimensions of stratification, including those of income, assets, education, gender, and ethnicity. Although the nation may be the third-largest economy in the world, many individual Japanese do not feel that they themselves are well off, suspecting that a privileged fraction must be reaping the increasing wealth. Reliable nationwide surveys indicate that a significant proportion of respondents deem Japan a society of inequity and unfairness,[6] a

---

[5] Chiavacci 2008.

[6] *Yomiuri Shimbun* conducted a survey in collaboration with the BBC and found that 72 percent of respondents thought of Japan as a society of *fukōhei* (inequity), while 16 percent did not. YM, 22 September 2009.

Table 2.2   International comparison of 'middle-class consciousness' (%) (2005–06)

| | | Class identification | | | | |
Country	Upper	Upper middle (A)	Middle middle (B)	Lower middle (C)	Lower	Middle total (A)+(B)+(C)
Japan	0.8	14.1	44.0	28.5	8.6	86.6
Australia	0.7	27.0	32.7	31.5	3.3	91.2
China	0.3	4.9	38.5	27.9	18.7	71.3
Finland	1.2	21.6	36.1	33.0	3.0	91.7
Germany	0.7	20.0	36.4	32.2	4.0	88.6
Italy	0.7	26.1	27.3	33.4	4.4	86.8
Korea (South)	0.7	23.7	54.2	15.8	5.7	93.7
Sweden	1.8	33.9	33.4	14.6	4.3	81.9
USA	0.9	26.4	33.0	28.3	6.0	87.7

Source: Adapted from the Fifth World Values Survey conducted by the World Values Survey Association based in Stockholm, Sweden, in 2005–06. See Dentū Sōken and Nihon Research Center 2008, p. 218.

Note: The national total of each country does not amount to 100, because 'no answer' and 'don't know' cases are not included in this table.

pattern similar to other major countries. They also regard *migatte* (self-ishness), *fukōhei* (inequity), and *jiko sekinin* (self-responsibility) as the attributes that best characterize contemporary Japanese society.[7] The widespread notion that Japan is *gakureki shakai* (a society oriented inordinately to educational credentialism)[8] testifies to the popular belief that it is unfairly stratified on the basis of educational achievement. Moreover, unlike the United States and the United Kingdom, Japan has a relatively strong Communist party which often polls about 10 percent of total votes in national elections and some 20 percent in its strongholds like Kyoto, suggesting that some sections of the community harbor a strong sense of class inequality. These observations suggest that the '90 percent middle class' thesis may be losing sight of the *honne* side of Japan's social stratification structure.

There is an abundance of data on class in Japan. A group of Japan's class analysts have conducted a Social Stratification and Mobility (SSM) Survey every ten years since 1955, the most recent being in 2005, and have thereby amassed systematic time-series data over five decades.[9]

---

[7] According to the regular survey of the *Asahi Shimbun* on the consciousness of the Japanese (*Teiki kokumin ishiki chōsa*), at the end of 2006, the largest proportion of people (21 percent) saw 'selfishness' as the term that best describes Japanese society. 'Inequality' and 'self-responsibility' (18 percent) rank equal second. AM, 5 January 2007, p. 29.

[8] Amano, I. 2011.

[9] Hara and Seiyama 2005 and Hashimoto 2003 are based on the 1995 survey. See Kosaka 1994 for a summary of the 1985 survey.

Government agencies, newspaper organizations, and private research institutions have also published a large amount of quantitative data on the ways in which resources, values, and behavior patterns are distributed among different strata in Japanese society. Taken together, these resources provide ample material for understanding internal stratification.

Studies of class and stratification have long been a battleground between those who follow Marx and various non-Marxists and anti-Marxists, most notably those who favor a framework that originates in the work of Max Weber. The Marxian tradition tends to define social class as a grouping of people who share a common situation in the organization of economic production. Those who disagree with this framework are inclined to take the structural-functional approach and to classify individuals into statistically defined strata according to income, power, and prestige.

This chapter tries to provide preliminary signposts to issues covered in subsequent chapters. To these ends, it:

- presents some quantitative studies by Japanese sociologists of the ways in which classes and strata are formed;
- schematizes the ways in which economic and cultural resources are distributed;
- examines the extent to which inequality is reproduced from one generation to another;
- discusses several points about which one has to be cautious in examining the 'disparity society' thesis; and
- investigates a number of Japan-specific concepts related to class and stratification.

I   Classification of Classes and Strata

Exactly how many classes or strata are there in contemporary Japan? Researchers on social stratification have failed to come up with a definitive answer to this elementary question. Marxian analysts apply conventional class categories to the Japanese situation, but sometimes do so dogmatically, while non-Marxists tend to rely mainly on standard occupational classifications and engage in highly sophisticated statistical analysis without necessarily producing a clear overall portrayal of the class situation. In both camps, analysts tend to borrow, and sometimes refine, Western concepts and theories, and methodological techniques first developed in the United States and Europe.

Some Marxian researchers have produced empirical representations of class distribution in contemporary Japan on the basis of Marxian

Table 2.3   Class distribution based on Marxian categories (1950–2005)

| | % of population, by year | | | | | | | | | | | |
Class	1950	1955	1960	1965	1970	1975	1980	1985	1990	1995	2000	2005
Capitalist	2.2	2.8	4.4	7.1	6.3	7.3	8.2	8.3	8.8	9.8	8.7	8.4
New middle	11.2	11.7	11.2	12.8	14.0	15.8	16.2	18.0	19.1	19.3	19.6	19.0
Working	28.1	33.8	41.0	44.7	47.4	49.6	50.8	53.0	54.4	55.4	57.7	59.3
Old middle	58.5	51.7	43.3	35.3	32.4	27.3	24.7	20.8	17.6	15.5	14.0	13.3
Farming	45.2	38.0	30.3	22.9	18.3	12.9	10.0	8.4	6.3	5.3	4.4	4.0
Self-employed	13.3	13.7	13.0	12.4	14.1	14.4	14.7	12.4	11.3	10.2	9.6	9.3

Source: Adapted from Hashimoto 2011, p. 55, calculated initially from Census data.

categories.[10] For example, using SSM data, Hashimoto identifies four classes with distinct characteristics and estimates Japan's changing class composition, as displayed in Tables 2.3 and 2.4.

The capitalist class consists of corporate executives and managers. They have high incomes, considerable assets, and many durable consumer goods. Their political orientation is conservative and, by and large, they regard the status quo as impartial and fair.

The working class comprises mainly blue-collar workers, both skilled and unskilled, plus temporary and part-time workers. This is by far the largest class in Japan today. A majority of working class members have only the lowest levels of education and income and express the highest level of discontent with the existing situation. However, they remain apathetic and pessimistic about political change. As discussed in Chapter 1, the major line of demarcation in the working class is drawn between 'regular workers' (type I) whose employment status is relatively safe and 'non-regular workers' (type II) whose job security is precarious. The latter group can be called Japan's underclass[11] and shows distinctive characteristics, as Table 2.4 demonstrates. In 2013 the proportion of non-regular workers soared to approximately 40 percent of the workforce, a trend that shows an increasing level of job uncertainty in the labor market.[12]

In both small and large enterprises, the culture of blue-collar workers differs significantly from that of office employees. Generally, blue-collar workers view their work as a means of livelihood and not as a source of gratification and fulfillment. They see themselves as holding ignominious and inglorious positions on low rungs of the social ladder. On the whole, blue-collar workers begin each working day early and prefer to leave their

---

[10] For example, Hashimoto 2003.

[11] See Aoki 2006; Gill 2000; and Iwata and Nishizawa 2008 for life conditions of the underclass.

[12] Ministry of Internal Affairs and Communications 2013a.

Table 2.4 Characteristics of major classes

	Capitalist class	New middle class	Working class I: Regular workers	Working class II: Non-regular workers (underclass)	Old middle class
% of class members in the workforce[a]	5.0	20.2	35.7	24.3[d]	14.8
Average income of households (in 10,000 yen)	1,027[e]	824	592	407	640
% of households with no assets	3.4	5.8	12.4	23.8	7.3
Relative poverty rate[f]	3.3	3.3	10.0	34.8	16.6
% of married persons (35–54 years of age)	87.4	85.2	73.0	32.5	86.9
% of university graduates[b]	41.1	70.8	32.9	25.2	21.2
% of individuals identifying as 'higher than middle'[g]	35.0	13.1	7.8	4.7	11.3
% of individuals who are satisfied with their jobs[c]	40.2	25.1	16.9	16.6	29.3
% of individuals who feel that they may potentially be unemployed[c]	7.7	14.8	17.6	40.8	11.6

Sources: Adapted from calculations provided by Kenji Hashimoto. All the data are based on SSM 2005 except:

[a] 2007 Employment Status Survey (Ministry of Health, Labour and Welfare 2007d).

[b] 2001 Employment Status Survey (Ministry of Health, Labour and Welfare 2007d).

[c] 2003 JGSS (Japanese General Social Surveys) data. See Tanioka, Nida, and Iwai (eds) 2008.

Notes:

[d] The underclass section of the working class (type II) includes housewife part-timers who constitute 11.5 percent of the entire workforce. However, for technical reasons, this group is not included in the calculations of the figures below in this column.

[e] Those members of the capitalist class who work for companies with 30 or more employees earn 1,410 on average.

[f] See Chapter 1, Section 3 (b) and Table 1.5.

[g] The proportion of those persons who feel that they belong to the 'upper middle' section of the population or above.

working environment as early as possible.[13] They find more satisfaction at home and in community life than do white-collar employees. Generally, they value family life and take an active part in community affairs. In community baseball teams, after-hours children's soccer teams, and other sports clubs, blue-collar workers are prominent. They pursue these leisure activities to compensate for their *honne* sense of cynicism, alienation, and dissatisfaction with their workplace.[14]

The middle class is divided into two groups: the old middle class, composed mainly of farmers and self-employed independent business people, and the new middle class, which is made up of white-collar employees, including middle managers, professionals, and clerical office workers.

The old middle class comprises two groups: the farming population, whose numbers have consistently declined as a consequence of industrialization and urbanization, and independent small proprietors, classified as *jieigyō*, whose numbers have not significantly changed over time. Many of the latter run the small and medium-sized stores that line the streets of shopping areas (called *shōten-gai*) throughout the country. Running greengroceries, liquor stores, barber shops, pharmacies, fish shops, confectioneries, and so on, within or adjacent to residential communities, these independent business people make up a formal association in each shopping area with executives and other office-holders and play lively and leading roles in community affairs. Owners of small family factories and backstreet workshops comprise another important group of independent proprietors. Some have highly specialized manufacturing skills and others serve as subcontractors, and they buttress Japan's economy and technology. The old middle class, some members of which are cash-rich, is generally conservative, both politically and socially, low in educational credentials, and not inclined to engage much in cultural or leisure activities.

The model figure in Japan's new middle class is (in the Japanese English phrase) a 'salaryman', a white-collar, male company employee in the private sector. He embodies all the stereotypical images associated with the Japanese corporate employee: loyalty to his company, subservience to the hierarchical order of his enterprise, devotion to his work, a long and industrious working life, and job security in his career. The new middle class, which salarymen typify, constitutes less than a quarter of the labor force but is an ideological reference group for the working population. In literature, the genre of 'salaryman novels' focuses on the joys and sorrows of Japanese organization men. In the world of *manga*, 'salaryman manga', such as *Salaryman Kintarō* and *Kachō Shima Kōsaku*, attract a substantial readership. In housing, 'salaryman dwellings' are simple units with three small rooms and a kitchen. In money management, the 'salaryman finance' system enables financially ambitious corporate

---

[13] NHK 1992, pp. 82–3.   [14] Hamashima 1991, p. 362.

Table 2.5 Occupation-based social strata (1955–2005)

	% of males, by year						% of females, by year		
	1955	1965	1975	1985	1995	2005	1985	1995	2005
Professional	6.8	6.7	7.3	9.7	12.1	12.8	10.5	12.4	17.6
White-collar									
Large	8.7	14.2	14.7	17.2	17.3	17.5	10.3	12.7	11.4
Small	5.0	8.4	11.1	12.3	12.8	12.4	19.2	21.7	22.7
Self	10.0	12.1	11.5	11.4	13.0	9.4	11.0	16.4	9.9
Blue-collar									
Large	7.8	11.3	10.3	9.8	9.0	8.3	4.9	4.7	9.9
Small	8.9	15.9	19.1	21.2	19.3	23.1	24.4	19.4	23.4
Self	12.1	10.7	10.2	10.6	10.2	9.9	7.1	5.2	4.2
Agricultural	40.8	20.6	15.8	7.9	6.2	6.5	12.5	7.4	5.5

Source: SSM 05b, 1, p. 78.
Notes:
1. Data on women were not collected before 1985.
2. Large, Small and Self mean workers respectively in large corporations, and small companies, and the self-employed.

employees to borrow substantial amounts at high interest rates without the need to mortgage property. In psychoanalysis, 'salaryman apathy' refers to white-collar employees' psychological state of work rejection, in which they display psychosomatic symptoms every morning when they have to leave for work. Members of the new middle class are generally well educated but dissatisfied with their income.

Non-Marxian sociologists are inclined to use occupational categories as the classificatory basis for stratification analysis. For example, in the 2005 SSM study analysts identified eight occupational categories as representative of the fundamental stratification groups, as displayed in Table 2.5:

1 professionals;
2 white-collar employees in large corporations with one thousand or more employees (white-collar large);
3 white-collar employees in small businesses (white-collar small);
4 white-collar self-employed;
5 blue-collar workers in large corporations (blue-collar large);
6 blue-collar workers in small businesses (blue-collar small);
7 blue-collar self-employed; and
8 farmers and others in the primary sector of the economy (agricultural).

These classifications point to at least three significant trends.

First, Table 2.5 reveals that blue-collar employees in small enterprises have grown to become the largest group for both males and females. The self-employed remain a stable and durable group, while the agricultural population has declined sharply over time. Males are represented more than females in the relatively high-ranking white-collar group in large corporations. It is also obvious that a sizeable professional female group has emerged and expanded.

Second, non-Marxian researchers maintain that the types of aspirations and rewards that Japanese workers desire have qualitatively changed, with the society as a whole exhibiting more and more postmodern characteristics. Specifically, a considerable number of people whose basic daily needs are fulfilled now attach more importance to lifestyle values in their priority map. To capture such a value shift one can make a conceptual distinction between two types of status positions: 'achieved' status, based upon the attainment of high income, occupation, educational credentials, and material possessions; and 'relational' status, derived from active participation in volunteer work and community activity, leadership in hobby and leisure clubs, and civic activities in the community.

It is argued that the overall affluence of the nation has offered an ample breeding ground to 'class transcendentalists', people who give a high priority to values other than class betterment. Gratified by their current level of consumption, they now seek satisfaction in less material aspects of life. Some individuals increase their quality of life through the pursuit of hobbies, creative expression, or spiritual fulfillment, while others engage in volunteer work, environmental protection, and forms of socially meaningful or relationship-oriented activities that earn them respect and esteem in their family. According to some surveys,[15] one-third of Japanese people are oriented to this expressive, 'relational' form of status, with the remaining two-thirds continuing to focus on the attainment of instrumental, 'achieved' status within the class structure. One may suggest that most Japanese lead a schizophrenic existence. On the one hand, they are forced to deal with the market economy, yet on the other, they yearn for a more satisfying and fulfilling mode of life.

Third, non-Marxian and Weberian analysts posit a multidimensional framework and attempt to identify several class groups using the concept of status inconsistency. They define an individual as status inconsistent when he or she ranks high on one scale of social stratification (for example, occupation) but low on another (for instance, school background). A Korean female doctor in Japan, for example, would be a status-inconsistent person in the sense that she is high on the ladders of income and educational qualifications but low on those of gender

---

[15] SSM 95a, V, pp. 19–25.

	A	B	C	D	E
Status variables	E O I	E O I	E O I	E O I	E O I
Cluster %	15.4	13.6	8.0	56.9	6.1
Occupants of managerial posts (%)	68.5	49.2	82.2	31.3	7.5
Average household income (10,000)	989.0	700.1	701.7	663.4	234.0
High class identification (%)	39.7	27.4	23.8	14.7	8.3

Figure 2.1 Status-consistent and -inconsistent clusters (2005)
Source: Adapted from Hayashi 2008, pp. 159–66.
Notes:
1. E, O, and I respectively stand for educational background, occupational prestige, and income level.
2. The income figures are in 10,000 yen.
3. High class identification indicates proportion of individuals in the relevant cluster who identify themselves with either upper class or middle class.

and ethnicity because of prevailing prejudice and discrimination. Using the notion of status inconsistency and the 2005 SSM data, Hayashi dichotomizes the population into two groups – high and low – according to three criteria:[16] (1) in terms of *educational background* between four-year university graduates and those who have completed junior college, high-school, or middle-school education only; (2) according to *occupation* between professionals/managers and those who are not; and (3) in terms of *income* between those above and below the relative poverty line.[17] This method identifies eight analytical categories, three of which are empirically small in number and practically negligible, with five groups constituting major classes in contemporary Japan, as Figure 2.1 demonstrates. Two of these (A and E) are status consistent and form the upper and lower ends of Japan's class structure, consistently showing high or low scores respectively on all three measures. Three other groups are status inconsistent, exhibiting different patterns of incongruence across the three ladders of stratification.

Class A mostly comprises individuals whose positions are high in all three dimensions – with a good educational background, prestigious job, and sizeable income. Between their thirties and fifties, at the height of their occupational careers, most of these individuals have four-year university degrees or postgraduate qualifications, occupy either managerial or professional posts, and enjoy the highest levels of household income

---

[16] This section is based on Hayashi 2008.
[17] See Table 1.5 and the explanation associated with it.

and assets. Members of this class can afford to relish ample cultural lives, possessing high-tech goods and studying foreign languages. They visit museums, art galleries, and libraries, enjoy sporting activities, travel overseas, and read books more frequently than any other class. They form the top layer of Japan's stratification hierarchy.

Class B is mostly made up of relatively young university graduates with reasonably good incomes but without managerial or professional positions. They are status inconsistent in the sense that their positions are high on education and income scales but low on occupational attainment. While they are still in the early phase of their careers and in their twenties and thirties, they strive to move up to Class A. Many are employees of large corporations or public servants and form the middle layer of these large organizations. Their income and asset levels are lower than those of Class C, with their house ownership rate being the second lowest among the five classes.

Class C is another status-inconsistent group in the sense that its members are high in terms of occupation and income but low on education. Most are not university educated but have managerial or professional positions and earn good incomes, second only to Class A. Most are in their forties or older, a pattern that suggests they are at the height or towards the end of their careers, having achieved good occupational and income status with only high school education. The members of this class have the highest house ownership ratio among all the classes and tend to participate in volunteer work and other civic activities more actively than any other class.

Class D is the largest class in Japan today, constituting more than half of the working population, and is status inconsistent in the sense that its member income exceeds the subsistence level (namely, the relative poverty line), while their educational background and occupational status are on the lower side of the scale. More than two-thirds of this class are either blue-collar or agricultural workers and are employed by or own small businesses. With some three-quarters of this group having completed high-school education only, their positions are neither managerial nor professional, while the proportion of self-employed people is relatively large. The house ownership rate of this class is the second highest among the five, but their cultural and leisure activities are quite limited. An overwhelming majority of the members of this class regard themselves as belonging either to the lower middle class or the upper lower class, a perception that perhaps correctly reflects their position in the nation's stratification structure.

Class E represents the lowest class in Japan, consistently low on all three dimensions. This is the only class whose average income is below the poverty line. Compared with other classes, workers in their thirties and below, as well as in their sixties and above, are disproportionately represented in this class, an indication that poverty prevails mainly among the young and senior citizens. A majority of the members of Class E are employed by small businesses, with blue-collar and agricultural workers being predominant in this class. They constitute Japan's working poor, who hardly enjoy cultural activities in their leisure time and rarely travel overseas, let alone learn foreign languages. A majority of this group see themselves as belonging to the lower class.

Notably, the share of status-inconsistent individuals steadily increased from 48.2 percent in 1955, to 59.5 percent in 1965, 65.2 percent in 1975, and 70.6 percent in 1985, while the trend was reversed when the percentage declined to 61.8 in 1995.[18] Although based on a different method of measurement, the 2005 data show that the proportion was 78.5 percent, as Figure 2.1 demonstrates.

Boundaries between classes were generally blurred during the second half of the twentieth century, with a definite majority of persons leading a split-level existence, high in one dimension of social stratification and low in another. Status-inconsistent individuals tend to find it difficult to share coherent class-based interests and class solidarity. Analysts who regard Japan as relatively free of sharp class awareness attribute such 'class-unconscious' tendencies to the rise of status-inconsistent conditions.

However, a more recent study based on data collected in 2010 shows a different picture, in which the Japanese are divided more or less equally between status-inconsistent and status-consistent persons. Using four key variables – education, occupation, income, and assets – and performing 'latent class analysis', Fujiwara, Itō, and Tanioka identify four groups and explore the patterns of their class identification.[19] Table 2.6 exhibits the two status-consistent clusters (I and IV) at the upper and lower ends of the class hierarchy and the two status-inconsistent classes (II and III) between them. Cluster II comprises those who are high in education (university graduates) but low in occupation, income, and assets dimensions. Those in the other inconsistent group (III) are low in education and occupation but high in monetary terms, namely, income and assets. Although this study employs a different method of analysis from the previous analysis, it is notable that status-consistent groups (I and IV, some 47 percent) are very close in size to status-inconsistent groups (II and III, approximately 53 percent).

As the table shows, whereas persons in the two inconsistent clusters are inclined to see themselves as members of the lower middle class, status-consistent individuals tend to identify as members of the upper middle class and the upper lower class. The contrast, the study finds, is

[18] Hara 2000, p. 31.   [19] Fujiwara, Itō, and Tanioka 2012.

Table 2.6   Status-consistent and -inconsistent classes (2010)

Class	Education	Occupation	Income	Assets	Consistency	%	Identification
			Characteristic				
I	High	High	High	High	Yes	25.7	Upper middle
II	High	Low	Low	Low	No	22.9	Lower middle
III	Low	Low	High	High	No	30.5	Lower middle
IV	Low	Low	Low	Low	Yes	20.8	Upper lower

Source: Adapted from Fujiwara, Itō, and Tanioka 2012, pp. 53–5.
Notes: Specific categories are ranked from high to low as follows:
Education: (1) University graduates, (2) Other.
Occupation: (1) Upper white-collar (professional and managerial), (2) Lower white-collar (clerical and sales), (3) Blue-collar (Skilled, semi-skilled, unskilled, and agricultural).
Income: (1) High (nine million yen or more per annum), (2) middle (five to nine million), (3) low (less than five million).
Assets: Three categories from high to low.
Class identification: (1) Upper, (2) Upper middle, (3) Lower middle, (4) Upper lower, (5) Lower lower.

pronounced, with the recent advent of *kakusa shakai*, a condition strongly indicative of rising and acute class-consciousness.

The profile of Japan's class structure differs depending on whether it is analyzed according to a Marxian class framework or a multidimensional stratification approach. Whichever method is employed, however, the fact remains that a comprehensive examination of Japanese society can neither ignore nor avoid an analysis of class and stratification and the inequality and disparity in Japan's distribution of social rewards. This remains true whether one's theoretical orientation is towards positivism, constructionism, postmodernism, or cultural studies.

II   Distribution of Economic and Cultural Resources

The foregoing studies make no analytical distinction between two aspects of social stratification. The first concerns various societal *resources* that one acquires as a consequence of occupying a position in a stratified hierarchy. They include economic, political, and cultural resources. The other relates to the *agents* of stratification, those variables which determine individuals' differential access to societal resources. These agents include occupation, education, gender, ethnicity, and place of residence.[20] While Chapters 3 to 7 are organized around different agents of stratification, it might be helpful to draw a schematic picture of how

---

[20] For more details, see Mouer and Sugimoto 1986, part 4.

Table 2.7 Four types of economic and cultural resources

	Economic resources	
Cultural resources	High	Low
High	A	C
Low	B	D

two key types of resources – economic and cultural – are distributed among the Japanese.

Economic resources can be classified into two types. On one hand, income such as salaries and wages constitute flow-type resources.[21] On the other hand, a variety of assets form stock-type resources, including immovable assets (such as houses and land) and movable assets (such as shares and bonds).

Cultural resources cover knowledge- and information-based prerogatives, which some sociologists call cultural capital.[22] These resources in Japan tend to derive from educational credentials and are determined overwhelmingly in teenage years according to whether youngsters win or lose what Japanese media call the 'education war'. In a finely graded rank-ordered system of high schools and universities, the amount of prestige that they earn derives from the status of the school or university they attended and graduated from. Japanese leaders in bureaucracies and large firms tend to place excessive emphasis upon their members' schooling backgrounds, and this pattern has filtered through other social strata. The dominant definition of cultural resources in Japan is extremely education-based in this sense. One can also enhance one's cultural resources through receipt of honors, awards, and titles from established institutions, by winning popularity as a sportsperson or entertainer, and by acquiring fame through the mass media.

As the status-inconsistency model suggests, the levels of one's economic and cultural resources do not necessarily coincide. A rich store owner might not be a graduate of a prestigious university. A well-educated female graduate might not have a high-paying job. Academics at universities of low standing tend to receive higher salaries than those in high-ranking institutions. The very notion of status inconsistency points to such incongruity.

Cross-tabulation of the dimensions of economic and cultural resources produces a four-fold conceptual chart like Table 2.7.

---

[21] 'Incomes' in this chapter refers to flow-type resources, not stock-type resources.
[22] Bourdieu 1986.

Cell A represents the upper class, which possesses great quantities of both resources: executive managers of big corporations, high-ranking officials in the public bureaucracy, large landowners and real-estate proprietors, and those who own large amounts of movable assets. Generally, they have university degrees, usually from top institutions.

Some of these people may not have education-based cultural resources but acquire their functional substitutes by obtaining an honor or decoration for distinguished services, for establishing and managing a school or university, or for starting an endowment or foundation in their name for charitable work or to support various cultural activities.

Cell B comprises those who have considerable economic resources without a commensurate level of cultural assets. Many belong to the above-mentioned old middle class, including independent farmers and petty-scale manufacturers and shop owners.

The self-employed business class has remained a self-perpetuating stratum which is more or less free of the influence of educational qualifications. These self-employed business owners tend to hold both traditional and authoritarian views and, in this respect, resemble farmers in their value orientations. They generally find it desirable to follow a conventional way of life and look askance at those who question existing traditions and practices.[23] Many well-educated children of these independent people who succeed to their parents' businesses move into the upper class in Cell A with relative ease.

A television drama heroine called Oshin, a figure who moved many Japanese to tears in the 1980s, arrived at Cell B in the later phase of her life. Born in an impoverished family, she worked as a live-in nanny, maid, and in many other jobs in her childhood and adolescence with remarkable patience and perseverance. Without formal education, she succeeded as a businesswoman in establishing and managing a chain of supermarkets.

Given that educational credentials are the most significant cultural resource for upward social mobility, one should not lose sight of the fact that the majority of high school students do not advance to four-year university and have little choice but to establish themselves through the acquisition of economic resources, abandoning cultural prestige.

Cell C consists of those with high cultural credentials, who lack corresponding income and wealth. The major group in this category comprises well-educated salaried employees, 'organization men', who include administrative, clerical, sales, and non-manual employees, as well as corporate professionals. High-circulation weekly magazines that target this group have many stories of their discontent and disillusion. Many

---

[23] SSM 85 I, p. 57.

Japanese organization men with good cultural resources feel frustrated by the present institutional order precisely because their earnings do not appear to match their cultural privilege; it seems to them that more uneducated people, such as those in Cell B, lead more monetarily rewarding lives. Many new PhD holders teach as lowly paid casual instructors at one university after another and stay in the C category without being able to find stable, well-paid positions. Some people in the higher substratum of Cell C eventually move up to Cell A as they climb to the top of their occupational pyramid, becoming directors of large companies, high-ranking officials of the public bureaucracy, or professionals with handsome earnings.

Cell D represents the underclass, which lacks both economic and cultural capital. Most blue-collar workers, female workers in the external labor market, minority workers, and immigrant foreign workers fall into this category. This group is numerically quite large and will be the focus of analysis in subsequent chapters.

III   Reproduction of Inequality

How are economic and cultural resources transmitted from one generation to another? Occupation and education are the most visible factors that perpetuate inequality inter-generationally across social classes. Chapters 4 and 5 deal with these areas in some detail, but here we will briefly look at two processes. On the economic side, the degree to which assets are handed down from one generation to another has consequences for the continuity of inter-class barriers. Furthermore, the cultural continuity of different class groups is affected by the ways in which people are socialized into certain values and whether marriage partners come from a similar class background. Although often less conspicuous and more latent, these variables are fundamental to the processes of inter-generational economic and cultural reproduction of classes.

1   Asset Inheritance

The differentials of land assets have invariably been twice as much as those of income differentials, as Figure 2.2 displays. To examine inequalities in contemporary Japan, therefore, one must investigate its land ownership pattern, in view of the fact that land assets constitute about 45.2 percent of national wealth.[24] Although land prices declined

[24] Calculated from Cabinet Office 2006.

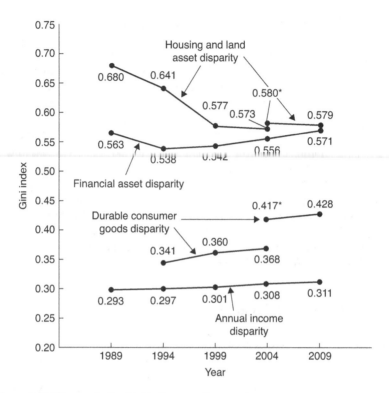

Figure 2.2   Changes in the Gini indices over time
Source: Ministry of Internal Affairs and Communications 2009a.
Note: The figures with asterisks are the 2004 scores adjusted on the basis of the calculation
method used for 2009.

in the 1990s and the early 2000s and property-based inequalities shrank
during the period, they constitute the most crucial dimension of social
disparity in Japan today.

Shimono and Ishikawa estimate that 57 percent of net household asset
holdings are inherited and argue that bequests constitute 39 percent
of national wealth.[25] Moreover, the highest level of inheritance tax has
been lowered since the 1990s. All this suggests that the asset owners
of Japan have largely sustained and even expanded their holdings inter-
generationally through inheritance. Asset disparities have not only produced but also *reproduced* two subcultural groups that show distinctly
different consumer behavior patterns in Japan today: a small number
of spenders who have resources to pay for costly luxury commodities,
and a large group of those who cannot afford to do so. Those who

[25] Shimono and Ishikawa 2002.

have considerable financial assets and large property incomes form a minority stratum at the top, and only they can enjoy extravagant lifestyles, purchasing expensive houses, bearing inordinate social expenses, and spending lavishly on fashion goods. The remaining majority, whose livelihoods are constrained by housing mortgages and bank loans, must carefully calculate their expenditure and cannot assume such profligate lifestyles.[26] However, there is very little difference between the asset 'haves' and 'have nots' in their purchasing of more ordinary commodities, including cars, bicycles, medical services, musical instruments, sports goods, audio equipment, and education.

High land prices, in particular, have given rise to a situation where the level of inequality between property owners and renters is so stupendous and so predetermined that those without properties to inherit cannot catch up simply by working hard and attempting to save. It is notable, as Figure 2.2 shows, that social disparities based on such financial assets as stocks and savings are also much more substantial than those based on income. Accordingly, one's income as measured in terms of salary and wage levels does not directly represent one's power to purchase commodities. The point is obvious when one compares, for instance, two company employees (Yamada and Suzuki) who have the same annual net salary of five million yen. Yamada inherited his parents' house and apartment and leases the apartment at two million yen a year, thereby enjoying a net annual disposable income of seven million yen. Suzuki has not yet been able to purchase a house and rents a condominium at two million yen a year, having therefore a net yearly disposable income of three million yen. One can imagine that, though their corporate salaries are identical, their purchasing power is substantially different.[27] Purchasing power and consumption capacity are determined chiefly by size of property and financial assets rather than wage income, and this pattern is transmitted from one generation to another mainly through asset inheritance.

2 Socialization and Marriage

More broadly, cultural capital appears to be passed on through highly stratified channels. Kataoka and others[28] have explored the extent to

---

[26] Though the groups that are called the 'neo-rich', *shin-fuyūsō* (new affluent class) and 'celebs' have attracted attention in mass media and popular publications in recent years, some analysts identified them as early as the 1980s. See Hakuhōdō 1985.

[27] For a similar illustration, see Ozawa 1989, p. 177.

[28] Kataoka (1998) devotes an entire volume to the studies of social stratification and cultural reproduction and, on the whole, sustains the claims of Bourdieu and Passeron developed in the French context. See also Kataoka 1992 and 2000.

which the amount of inherited cultural capital of individuals in their childhood affects the amount of cultural capital that they possess in adulthood. To generate a quantitative indicator of cultural capital in childhood, Kataoka examines the cultural environment of individuals in their pre-school and primary school days and uses a combined index that takes into account how frequently they listened to classical music at home, made family trips to art galleries and museums, and had family members read books for them, and whether they had collections of children's literature at home and played with building blocks. She also looks at the types of cultural activities of individuals in their adulthood and classifies them into 'orthodox' culture and 'mass' culture. 'Orthodox' cultural activities include writing poems, visiting art galleries, museums, and exhibitions, and appreciating classical music, while 'mass' cultural activities include going to concerts of popular music, rock-and-roll, and jazz, singing *karaoke* songs, and playing *pachinko* pinball. For both males and females, the study demonstrates very significant connections between cultural environment in childhood and participation in 'high' cultural activities in adulthood. The cultural capital available before one's teenage years influences one's style of cultural activity more strongly than do other variables, such as one's occupational prestige, household income, and even educational background. The cultural resources of a family condition and even determine its children's cultural lives after they reach adulthood.

In an empirical study of family socialization in Osaka, Kataoka[29] observes that parents of high social standing tend to inculcate the values of social conformity in their children, while those of low social status generally attempt to orient their children to individual integrity and family obligations. Specifically, fathers of high occupational position and mothers of high educational background are inclined to train their children to acquire proper etiquette and language, and well-educated mothers in particular try to discipline their daughters to behave decorously. The children of parents (especially mothers) of high educational background feel burdened by intense parental expectations of conformity.

In contrast, fathers with less education place more emphasis on the honesty of their children than do university-educated fathers. Compared with children from wealthy families, those from poor backgrounds are taught to refrain from being dishonest, and daughters of worse-off families are instructed not to break their promises. Parents with only compulsory education try to educate their daughters to avoid disgracing family members and to attend to family chores.

---

[29] Kataoka 1987.

Table 2.8 Intra-class marriages in terms of partner's educational backgrounds

Husband's education	Wife's education			Total
	I	II	III	
I University or college	**701 (68.9)**	*607 (24.2)*	*29 (4.1)*	1,337
II High school	304 (29.9)	**1,621 (64.6)**	*227 (31.8)*	2,152
III Middle school	12 (1.2)	283 (11.3)	**457 (64.1)**	752
Total (Percentage)	1,017 (100)	2,511 (100)	713 (100)	4,241

Intra-class marriage ratio = (701 + 1,621 + 457)/4,241 = 0.655
Source: Calculated from Shirahase, p. 73.
Notes:
Bold figures: Marriages between a man and a woman who share the same educational
      qualifications (intra-class marriages).
Italic figures: Marriages between a woman and a more highly educated man (women
      marrying upwardly).
Roman figures: Marriages between a man and a more highly educated woman (men
      marrying upwardly).

In the main, families of higher status appear to concern themselves with the outward appearance of their children's behavior. In contrast, parents of low status tend to stress internal probity and family responsibilities. These findings appear to run counter to the observations of Western studies[30] which suggest that middle class socialization stresses the formation of a non-conformist, individualistic self while working class families socialize their children into collective values.

The process of choosing marriage partners is neither random nor unstructured. The extent to which people find partners from the same occupational and educational backgrounds has always been great.[31] Intra-class marriages within identical occupational and educational categories remain predominant, and in that sense 'ascriptive homogamy' persists as an entrenched pattern.

This is most robust among university graduates, and inter-generational class continuity endures most firmly in most educated strata of Japanese society. On the basis of data from the SSM study, Table 2.8 shows the extent to which married couples share the same educational qualifications, a pattern indicated by the numbers in bold characters. The total number of educational intra-class marriages amounts to about two-thirds of the total sample. The table also demonstrates that marriages between a woman and a more highly educated man (shown in italics) are more prevalent than those between a man and a more highly educated woman (in roman characters). This not only suggests that, in

[30] Kohn 1977. See also Kohn and Schooler 1983.
[31] Shirahase 2008, especially pp. 73–7.

Table 2.9   Intra-class marriages in terms of partner's occupational backgrounds

Husband's occupation	Wife's occupation				
	I	II	III	IV	Total
I Professional and managerial	**88 (33.8)**	143 (14.1)	22 (6.7)	2 (2.7)	255
II Clerical and sales	106 (40.8)	**495 (48.7)**	64 (19.6)	7 (9.6)	672
III Manual	61 (23.5)	358 (35.2)	**224 (68.5)**	23 (31.5)	666
IV Agricultural	5 (1.9)	20 (2.0)	17 (5.2)	**41 (56.2)**	83
Total	260 (100)	1,016	327	73	1,676

Intra-class marriage ratio = (88 + 495 + 224 + 41)/1,676 = 0.506
Source: Calculated from Shirahase, p. 74.
Notes:
Bold figures: Marriages in which the occupations of husbands and those of wives belong to
     the same category (intra-class marriages).
Roman figures: Marriages in which the occupations of husbands and those of wives belong
     to different categories (inter-class marriages).

general, men attain higher levels of education than women, but also that
marriage remains one means by which women acquire upward social
mobility.

Table 2.9 displays the degree to which husbands and wives share similar
occupational backgrounds. Intra-class marriages, where the occupations
of the couple's fathers belong to the same category (shown in bold characters), constitute more than 50 percent of the sample. Although this is
a smaller proportion than the similarity rate of educational backgrounds
(66 percent), occupational backgrounds remain a significant force in the
formation of marriages.

Relatively independent of occupational background, the educational
environment appears to influence the choice of marriage partners. The
popular perception, then, that Japan is a society based on educational
credentialism seems correct – at least as it relates to the marriage market.

At the top end of the highest class, a complex web of elite-school old-
boy networks, hereditary successions, marriage connections, and uxorial
nepotism stretches among political, bureaucratic, business, and media
elites, who are interconnected to form a 'class of privilege'. In most
elections, approximately one-quarter of the members of the House of
Representatives have inherited their constituencies from their parents
or relatives, with the current and four recent prime ministers all falling
into this category.[32] In late 2013, some 40 percent of Cabinet ministers,

---

[32] Takarajima Henshūbu 2007, pp. 26–31. In this calculation, 'inheritance members' of
the House of Representatives are defined as those who have or had Members of the
Parliament among their relatives within the third degree of consanguinity or among their
spouse's relatives within the second degree. Some 82 percent of 'inheritance candidates'
were successfully elected in the 2005 general election.

senior vice-ministers, parliamentary secretaries, and prime ministerial aides inherited the constituencies of their parents or relatives.[33] So did 26 percent of the parliamentarians who are the members of the ruling Liberal Democratic Party.[34] Many elite diplomats come from the families of high-ranking diplomats and inherit their status, having moved from one country to another in their childhood with their parents and accumulated linguistic skills and personal networks.[35] Pedigree and lineage play significant roles in preserving the inter-generational continuity of the nation's establishment.

IV   Debate and Caution about the *Kakusa* Society Thesis

Although gaining broad acceptance, the so-called *kakusa* society thesis – the view that Japanese society is socially divided and fraught with class disparities – is subject to much debate and must be examined with caution. First, the assertion that Japanese society has *suddenly* become a *kakusa* society raises much skepticism. There is much well-founded argument that Japan has always been a class-divided and stratified society and never a unique 'middle-class society' as described by the *Nihonjinron* model. From this perspective, an abrupt shift took place in public awareness and sensitivity, not in empirical substance and reality. Even at the prime of the 'uniquely egalitarian society' argument, a considerable number of studies demonstrated that such claim may represent only the *tatemae* side of Japanese society. Some comparative quantitative studies suggest that Japanese patterns of socioeconomic inequality show no systematic deviance from those of other countries of advanced capitalism.[36] Income inequality is higher in Japan than in Western countries.[37] The overall social mobility rate in Japan is basically similar to patterns observed in other industrialized societies.[38]

The second proviso bears upon the optical illusion that appears to have persisted during the high economic era. There is no doubt that the high-growth economy of postwar Japan led to changes in the occupational composition of the population and shifted large numbers from agriculture to manufacturing, from blue-collar to white-collar, from manual to non-manual, and from low-level to high-level education.[39] However, this transfiguration left a false impression – that industrialization was

---

[33] *Shūkan Posuto*, 25 October 2013, p. 34.

[34] AM, 20 January 2014, p. 3.   [35] Takarajima Henshūbu 2007, pp. 70–3.

[36] For instance, Ishida 1993 and Seiyama 1994.   [37] Tachibanaki 1998.

[38] Ishida, Goldthorpe, and Erikson 1991.

[39] The total index of structural mobility records a consistent upward trend throughout the postwar years. The agricultural population provides the only exception to this propensity,

conducive to a high measure of upward social mobility. In reality, the *relative* positions of various strata in the hierarchy remained unaltered. For example, the educational system which produced an increasing number of university graduates cheapened the relative value of degrees and qualifications. To put it differently, when everyone stands still on an ascending escalator, their relative positions remain unaltered even though they all go up. A sense of upward relative mobility in this case is simply an illusion. When the escalator stops or slows down, it becomes difficult for the illusion to be sustained. The occupational system cannot continue to provide ostensibly high-status positions, and eventually it must be revealed that some of the social mobility of the past was in fact due to the inflationary supply of positions. This is exactly what many in the labor force began to feel when Japan's economy came to a standstill, recording negative growth and entering into a deflationary spiral in the early 2000s. The reality of class competition began to bite only when the economic slowdown failed to discernibly enlarge the total available pie.

Third, a widening gap between haves and have-nots may be exaggerated because of the increase in the proportion of the aged in the population. Since social disparities are the largest among senior citizens, an aging society tends to show a greater chasm between the rich and the poor. The demographic transformation towards a graying society overstates the general levels of class differentiation of the total population. Similarly, the increase in the number of single households (which Chapter 6 details) also tends to inflate the household-based Gini index scores, because these households generally sit at the low end of the class structure.

Fourth, Japan's socioeconomic disparities were accelerated not only by unorganized structural transformations but by deliberately engineered policy changes in the taxation system. They have decreased the rate of progressive taxation with the result that its redistribution functions have been weakened. For one thing, the consumption taxation scheme was put in motion in 1989, making it necessary for each consumer to pay 5 percent of the price of purchased goods as sales tax. The rate changed to 8 percent in 2014 and is expected to rise to 10 percent in 2015. This system benefits the wealthy and harms the poor, because the consumption tax is imposed on all consumers in the same way regardless of incomes and assets. Further, the reduction of the inheritance tax rate in 2003 has lessened the burdens of asset owners in the intergenerational

showing a consistent downward trend. The total index arrived at its peak in 1975, reflecting a massive structural transformation which transpired during the so-called high-growth period starting in the mid-1960s.

transfer of ownership. The tax reform in 2013 has not altered the basic pattern.

Finally, one would have to see the perception shift in class structure in Japan from the perspective of the sociology of knowledge. Apparent or real, recent changes in class situations took place close to the everyday life of opinion-makers and data analysts. Even when economic hardship and class competition were daily realities in the lower echelons of Japanese society, many of these commentators paid little heed to the issue, because they occupied privileged positions distant from the lower levels of social stratification. However, their perceptions began to alter with the shifting class structure affecting their acquaintances and friends in their networks as a consequence of the economic stagnation and downturn in the 1990s and 2000s. The job security of full-time employees in the elite track of large companies is now at risk.[40] The upper white-collar employees, a category that comprises managers and professionals, are an increasingly closed group, which the younger generations of other social strata find it difficult to break into.[41] A decline in scholastic achievements even among the pupils of the upper middle classes and above has aroused concern among parents.[42] There are grounds to suspect that the class position of 'class observers' influences their sensitivity to stratificational divisions in Japanese society.

V   Japanese Emic Concepts of Class

How do the Japanese conceptualize dimensions of social stratification? The Japanese equivalents of class and stratum, *kaikyū* and *kaisō*, are both terms translated from English. As such, they do not constitute part of the everyday folk vocabulary of ordinary citizens in Japan. Yet anyone familiar with the Japanese language would attest to the wide circulation of such Japanese terms as *jōryū kaikyū* (upper class), *chūsan kaikyū* (middle class), *kasō shakai* (lower-stratum society), and *shakai no teihen* (bottom of society). The Japanese have a clear conception of stratification in their society even if their notions may not be conceptually identical to their Western counterparts.[43]

One can easily list several Japanese emic terms that describe the dimensions of stratification. *Kaku* denotes a finite series of ranks. As a generic term, it can be applied to a wide range of ranking systems. *Mibun* implies

---

[40] Morioka 2009.

[41] Satō 2000. Some experts dispute this thesis. See, for example, Hara and Seiyama 2005, pp. xxiii–xxvi.

[42] Chūō Kōron Henshūbu and Nakai 2003.   [43] Befu 1980, p. 34.

a status position into which one is born. Although used more loosely at times, the term connotes ascriptive characteristics and points to caste-like features. In feudal times, a samurai's *mibun* clearly differed from a peasant's *mibun*. Even today, 'blue-blood' families are supposed to have higher *mibun* than that of the masses. The term *kakei* (family line) has a similar connotation, with a more explicit emphasis upon lineage and pedigree. In contrast, *chii* means a status position that one achieves over time. One's *chii* moves up or down in an occupational hierarchy. A company president occupies a higher *chii* than a section chief of the company. The most common word for rapid social mobility is *shusse*. It applies to successful promotion to high positions accompanied by wide social recognition. When one moves from a low *chii* to a high *chii*, one would achieve an appreciable level of *shusse*.

With regard to the concept of the middle class, different imagery under-lies each of the three terms used by survey analysts to indicate a middle position in a pyramid of ranks.[44] The first of these, *chūsan*, tends to point to the dimensions of property and income and to the middle to upper positions in the economic hierarchy. The second category, *chūryū*, has connotations of a middle domain of social status, respect, and prestige, rather than straight economic capacity. In interpreting this term, respon-dents primarily think of their occupational ranking and of such things as their family status, educational background, and friendship network, situating themselves in the middle on the basis of a combination of these criteria. A white-collar company employee might see himself as located below small business owners and skilled blue-collar workers economi-cally but would still describe himself as middle with regard to educational qualifications and occupational prestige. In contrast to the first two con-cepts, the third yardstick, *chūkan*, carries somewhat negative implications and suggests a middle location of insecurity, uncertainty, instability, and ambivalence between high and low positions. Survey results have shown that the largest percentage of the population classifies itself as *chūryū*, followed by a considerable proportion assessing itself as *chūsan*. The smallest segment identifies itself as *chūkan*.

Although the Japanese may not define stratification in precisely the same way as other nationalities, there is little doubt that people in one of the most competitive capitalist economies on earth live with their own sense of class and inequality, as subsequent chapters will reveal in greater depth. Chapter 3 examines geographical and generational varia-tions and inequalities as two basic sets of demographic diversities. Chap-ters 4 and 5 investigate the worlds of work and education, in which people compete in an attempt to optimize their resources and rewards through

[44] Odaka 1961.

achievement. Chapters 6 and 7 shift the focus onto such ascriptive modes of stratification as gender and ethnicity, attributes which are determined at birth and determine one's life opportunities and lifestyle in a fundamental way. These five chapters also probe the institutional and ideological apparatuses which sustain and reproduce the patterns of inequality and stratification.

3 Geographical and Generational Variations

The Japanese have different lifestyles depending on their place of residence and their age or generation. Their eating habits, type of housing, language, style of thinking, and many other aspects of their everyday life hinge upon where they live and how old they are. This chapter examines both geographical and generational variations in Japanese society with a view to assessing the ways in which these demographic characteristics condition the options and preferences of various Japanese persons.

I Geographical Variations

1 Japan as a Conglomerate of Sub-nations

A total of about 127 million people live in the 378 thousand square kilometer Japanese archipelago. In terms of territorial size, Japan is larger than Great Britain, similar in size to Germany, and considerably smaller than France and Italy. But being mountainous, with only about one-third of its land habitable,[1] Japan is more densely populated than any of those countries.[2] Not surprisingly, the strain of population density affects the lifestyles of the Japanese. In a crowded environment, urban dwellers in Japan learn early in life how to cope with the pressure of many people living in limited space. On station platforms in urban centers, passengers line up in two or three rows in an orderly manner. During rush hours, Tokyo subways and railways use 'pushers' to push workers into over-packed trains. Most city dwellers live in small houses, tiny condominiums, and meager flats, a situation that is the source of

---

[1] According to the estimate of the Bureau of Statistics of the Management and Coordination Agency in 1996, the proportion of habitable land (*kajūchi*) in Japan is 32.8 percent. Mountains, forests, and wilderness constitute the rest. See Ministry of Internal Affairs and Communications 2013c.

[2] Even in terms of conventional measures of population density, Japan (338 persons per square kilometer as of 2013) is ahead of the United Kingdom (260), Germany (229), Italy (202), and France (117). International Monetary Fund 2013.

widespread dissatisfaction among urban residents. Although the housing and furnishing qualities have greatly improved and are generally better than those in other Asian countries, many city inhabitants justifiably feel that their houses are not commensurate with the nation's status as an economic superpower. In the narrow streets of Japanese cities, drivers and pedestrians struggle to make their way through.

The Japanese archipelago comprises four major islands. The largest, Honshū, which stretches from Aomori prefecture in the north to Yamaguchi prefecture in the southwest, has the principal metropolitan centers. The four largest Japanese cities – Tokyo, Yokohama, Osaka, and Nagoya – are all on this island, as are other well-known cities such as Kyoto, Kobe, and Hiroshima. Hokkaidō, the second largest island, lies in the north and has the lowest population density. Traditionally the territory of the Ainu, this island came under the full jurisdiction of the Japanese government only in 1879. For centuries, the Ainu had not considered themselves to belong to the Japanese nation. In northern Honshū and southern Hokkaidō, an autonomous area had long existed in which the Ainu and the Honshū islanders enjoyed unique lifestyles. In the southwest is Kyūshū island, which used to serve as the corridor of contact with the Korean peninsula, the Asian continent, and the southern Pacific islands. Shikoku, the smallest of the four major islands, has been closely connected with the Kyoto–Osaka–Kobe nexus in the western regions of Honshū and served as its hinterland for centuries.[3]

In addition, Japan has nearly seven thousand small isles. The Ryūkyū islands, in the southernmost prefecture of Okinawa, maintain a distinctive regional culture. Near Hokkaidō, a group of islands under Russian occupation – Habomai, Shikotan, Kunashiri, and Etorofu – has been subject to territorial dispute between Japan and Russia for decades. The Sea of Japan is studded with such sizeable isles as Okushiri, Sado, Iki, and Tsushima. The Inland Sea area, between Honshū and Shikoku, is also dotted with numerous tiny isles and the sizeable island of Awaji. Even Tokyo comprises not only urban centers and suburban communities but also many small inhabited islands in the Pacific, including Ōshima, Toshima, Niijima, Shikinejima, Kōzushima, Aogashima, Miyakejima, Mikurashima, Hachijōjima, and the group of Ogasawara isles. The total number of people who live outside the four major islands is close to two million. Although numerically few, these islanders maintain lifestyles that are dominated by the marine environment, a reminder

---

[3] The archipelago's climate differs greatly from region to region. While southernmost Okinawa is semi-tropical, northernmost Hokkaidō is snow covered in winter and cool even in summer.

that the population of the nation's rural areas is by no means restricted to rice-growing farmers.

Japan is conventionally divided into eight regional blocs according to climatic, geographical, and cultural differences. These eight are Hokkaidō, Tōhoku, Kantō, Chūbu, Kinki (also called Kansai), Chūgoku, Shikoku, and Kyūshū. The nation is divided into forty-seven prefectures, the largest government units below the national level. Within each prefecture are numerous municipalities – cities, towns, and villages – which form local governmental units, each with a government office and a legislative body. Prefectures were first established in 1871, corresponding to several dozen regional units called *kuni* (nations) which had existed for more than ten centuries. Throughout Japanese history, these sub-nations were sources of regional identity and local distinctiveness. Even today in major cities there exist *kenjin-kai* (prefectural associations) organized by emigrants from each prefecture who wish to maintain social ties among themselves. Some observers[4] find it profitable to examine *kenmin-sei* (prefectural character) rather than Japanese national character. They maintain, for example, that people in Kyūshū and Shikoku are generally stubborn, authoritarian, and uncompromising. Residents of Kyoto are regarded as schizophrenic in sticking to traditional norms while introducing radical reforms. Inhabitants in Hokkaidō are said to enjoy relaxed lifestyles, take an open-minded attitude towards outsiders, and have a sense of independence of other areas of the nation. Although these descriptions may be speculative, impressionistic, and stereotypical, the point remains that these prefectural character-types are so diverse, and often contradictory, that one can hardly speak of the national character of the Japanese as though it were cast from a single mold.

Although Japan is often described as an internally homogeneous island nation, it has never been a stable territorial unit with consistent cultural uniformity. In reality, Japan has had fluctuating national boundaries and changing constituent regions. The territorial boundary of Japan as we see it today is a post–World War II concept. Even in the early twentieth century, it colonized Korea, Taiwan, northeast China, and Saghalien, with their populations constituting about 30 percent of 'imperial Japan'.[5]

The independent Ryūkyū kingdom endured in Okinawa, the southernmost prefecture of Japan today, for about four centuries during Japan's

---

[4] Sofue 1971.

[5] Oguma 2002, pp. 133–8. Prewar school textbooks, published by the Ministry of Education, stated unequivocally that the Japanese nation was multi-ethnic.

feudal period, until the central government formally absorbed it as a prefecture in 1879. Before its full incorporation into Japan, Ryūkyū enjoyed close trade relationships with China and South-east Asia, maintained its own autonomous culture, and identified only to a limited extent with main-island Japan. After the end of the Allied occupation of Japan, which followed its defeat in World War II, Okinawa remained under the occupation of the United States to serve as the American bulwark against communist nations and was not part of Japan until 1972 when the United States returned it to Japan. This is why about three-quarters of American military bases in Japan are in Okinawa, a situation which Okinawans regard as unfair and which, the national government admits, must be rectified. As a geographical unit, Japan should thus be seen as a variable, not as a constant.

Furthermore, throughout Japanese history, many people living in the area which is now known as Japan did not have the consciousness that they were *Nihonjin* (Japanese). Even in Honshū this consciousness has fluctuated. At the time of the establishment of the Japanese state in the late seventh century, the term *Nihon* (Japan) emerged as a description. Yet the concept then covered mainly the Kinki region, as evidenced by the fact that nobles and officials sent outside it regarded their assignment as a posting to a foreign area or a land of foreigners.[6] At the time, ordinary people dwelling outside the Kinki region hardly conceived of themselves as belonging to the nation of Japan.

Several territorial blocs, which initially were almost nations in themselves,[7] were identifiable during the formation of the Japanese state. Far from being a uniform nation, Japan has developed as a nation with multiple internal sub-nations. From the establishment of imperial rule, based in Nara and Kyoto in the seventh century, until the Meiji period, in the nineteenth century, these sub-nations engaged in bitter warfare in a bid to defend or expand their respective hegemony. In the initial phase, the Kinki sub-nation gradually conquered other blocs, placing them under its control. The feudal period, from the end of the twelfth century to the middle of the nineteenth century, eventually shifted the seat of real power to the samurai class of the Kantō sub-nation, but the Kinki area remained the seat of imperial power and the most dynamic hub of Japan's commercial activity.

These spatial variations of Japanese society have crystallized into two major dichotomies: competition between eastern and western Japan, and domination of the center over the periphery.

---

[6] Ōtsu 1985.   [7] Amino 1990, pp. 59–69.

Table 3.1 Relative characteristics of village structures in eastern and western Japan

Characteristic	East	West
Relationships within households	Vertical	Horizontal
Relationship of branch family to parent family	Subordinate	Independent
Inheritance	First son (or first daughter)	First son (or last son)
Retirement of house head	Absent	Present
Rank difference between first son and other sons	Strong	Weak
Relationships among relatives	Patriarchal	Matriarchal
Status of bride	Low	High
Control of hamlet community over households	Strong	Weak
Family lineage	Broadly defined kinship groups	Direct lineal descendants

Source: Summarized from Izumi and Gamō 1952, Table 21.

2   Eastern Versus Western Japan

The cultural styles of residents in the Kinki area are distinctively different from those in the Kantō area.[8] During the feudal period, Edo (present-day Tokyo and the heart of eastern regional culture) was the seat of samurai regimes, and Osaka was the center of commercial activities. The vestiges of their different pasts are still pervasive. Comparatively, Tokyo maintains a warrior-style local culture with the marks of formality, hierarchy, and face-saving, while Osaka retains a merchant lifestyle with an emphasis on practicality, informality, and pragmatism.

Community studies have found that vertical authoritarian relationships between landlords and tenants prevailed in eastern Japan, while horizontal egalitarian networks among rural households were stronger in western Japan.[9] On the whole, the family and kinship structures were more patriarchal and less democratic in the eastern region than in the western region. Comparatively, the status of women was higher in western Japan than in eastern Japan. Each household had a higher degree of independence in the village community in the west than in the east. These and other differences in village structures between east and west Japan are displayed in Table 3.1. Some analysts[10] suggest that the widely held view that Japan is a 'vertically structured society'[11] derives more from observations of eastern Japan than from those of western Japan, which is more horizontally organized.

---

[8] Tanigawa 1961.   [9] Fukutake 1949, pp. 34–48 and 69–115.
[10] For example, Yoneyama 1971.   [11] Nakane 1967 and 1970.

Kyoto the capital of the nation for more than ten centuries until 1868, represents the culture of western Japan in an acute way: the interpersonal relationships of Kyotoites are based upon the principles of non-intervention, partial commitment, and mutual freedom, rather than those of total loyalty and obligation.[12] In this sense, Kyoto has developed a more refined and 'modern' style of group dynamics than those in Tokyo and eastern Japan. This is why some observers contend that Japan is divided into two areas: Kyoto, and the rest, the latter of which adores and hates the former. From the Kyotoites' point of view, Tokyo is simply a local city which embodies the deep-seated inferiority complex of all non-Kyoto areas towards Kyoto.[13]

The regional distributions of minority groups display a distinct pattern. *Buraku* communities are concentrated in the western region, which contains nearly 80 percent of the *burakumin* population.[14] In particular, the Kansai district (Hyōgo, Osaka, Kyoto, Nara, Wakayama, and Mie prefectures in particular), the Chūgoku area (Okayama and Hiroshima), the Shikoku region (Kōchi and Ehime), and Fukuoka prefecture all have large urban *buraku* communities. In eastern Japan, *buraku* communities are generally small and scattered in agricultural and mountain villages. This distribution reflects the historical background. Western Japan differed from eastern Japan in its attitude to animal slaughter. In the east, where hunting and fishing played significant roles, the killing of animals and fish was accepted as a routine part of life. In the west, where farming was more important, there developed a tradition in which blood-related trades and activities were held in abhorrence.[15] To the extent that discrimination against *buraku* communities originated from attitudes to ancestors' alleged engagement in animal slaughter, butchery, and tanning, this divergence sheds some light on the comparative abundance of *buraku* communities in western Japan and their relative absence in eastern Japan.

Permanent Korean residents in Japan are also more concentrated in the western region than in the eastern areas, though major eastern cities such as Tokyo and Yokohama have large numbers. Osaka is the population center of resident Koreans, with about a quarter of them residing in this prefecture. Other areas of concentration include Hyōgo, Kyoto, Fukuoka, and Hiroshima prefectures. This geographical distribution reflects the fact that Koreans came, or were brought, to Japan during the colonial period as cheap labor to work for the construction, mining, and

---

[12] See Nagashima 1977, pp. 199–211; Yoneyama 1976.
[13] For instance, Umesao 1987, pp. 252–5.
[14] Buraku Kaihō Jinken Kenkyūsho 2001, p. 736. See also Aoki 2009, pp. 191–2.
[15] Amino 1990, p. 61.

shipbuilding industries, which flourished during the prewar and war years in western Japan.

The two regions differ even in food taste. While Tokyoites use heavily colored, strong soy sauce, Kansai residents prefer a lighter colored and weaker one. *Soba* noodles in Tokyo are generally saltier than *udon* noodles in Osaka. The patterns of health and illness are also regionally diverse. The adjusted prefectural death rates[16] suggest that, with regard to the three major causes of death in Japan, western Japan records more cancer deaths and eastern Japan more deaths caused by stroke (cerebral apoplexy), and central Japan shows the highest concentration of deaths by heart attack. Traditional methods of pain relief and alleviation of stiffness are more popular in the west than in the east. On a per capita basis, prefectures in western Japan have larger numbers of acupuncturists, masseurs, and moxa treatment specialists.[17]

Many new businesses were first established in Osaka. For example, a variety of distribution franchises originated from that city and spread across the nation. They include department stores attached to private railway terminals, public and private retail markets, consumers' cooperatives, and supermarkets. Some major media organizations also began in the Kansai area. Three of the five national dailies, *Asahi*, *Mainichi*, and *Sankei*, originated in Osaka. The first commercial radio station, Shin-Nippon Hōsō, commenced its broadcasting in 1951 in Osaka.

Osaka is also the breeding ground of popular culture. On national television, comedians who speak the Osaka dialect dominate entertainment programs. *Manzai*, dialogue shows in which two comedians exchange a series of uproarious jokes, are a form of entertainment in which performers from Osaka overshadow those from Tokyo. Yoshimoto Kōgyō, the entertainment production house which established itself in the 1910s in Osaka, has continued to produce the nation's most popular comedians, who have introduced a fresh current into this hilarious comic genre. *Karaoke*, do-it-yourself vocals performed with a backing track, which spread across the nation and became popular overseas, started in Kobe, adjacent to Osaka.

The residents of the Kansai region, which includes Osaka, Kyoto, and Kobe, do not hesitate to speak openly and publicly in their own language, and Kansai is the only language region which challenges the monopoly of the Tokyo dialect in the electronic media. This contrasts with the linguistic behavior of other non-Tokyo Japanese, who attempt to hide their accents when outside their own dialect area. Whereas the status of

---

[16] See Ministry of Health, Labour and Welfare 2012b.

[17] Ministry of Health, Labour and Welfare 2013b. Moxa treatment is a traditional pain-relieving method in which moxa is burned on the skin of the painful part of the body.

western Japan has declined in the postwar years, Osaka remains the most vibrant counterpoint to the dominance of Tokyo.

3   Center Versus Periphery

Economic, political, and cultural power concentrates in the industrial belt that stretches along the Pacific coast between three key areas. The long-standing contest between the Tokyo–Yokohama metropolitan area and the Osaka–Kyoto–Kobe metropolitan area is a competition between the two major centers of the nation. A third center, the Chūkyō metropolitan area, whose focus is the city of Nagoya, sits between these complexes. The world-famous *Shinkansen* (bullet-train line) commenced operation along this coastal route in 1964, consolidating the region's position as the nucleus of Japan's economic development. Half of Japan's population resides in these three urban centers, but one should remember that the other half lives in the peripheries, which depend very much upon the activities of the core.

The process of population concentration was expedited by the national bureaucracy, which sought to make Tokyo the center of centers. Under ministerial instructions, each industrial sector established its national headquarters in the capital. Numerous industrial associations mush-roomed in Tokyo, ranging from the Japan Automobile Manufacturers Association to the Japan Iron and Steel Federation. Other professional groups, such as the Japan Medical Association and the Japan Writers Association, also operate in the capital. High-ranking officials of the national bureaucracy are given executive positions in these industrial and professional federations after their careers in the public sector. With the intention that governmental programs and policies should be trans-mitted from these national associations to every member firm in Japan, the national bureaucracy has succeeded in establishing a government-controlled, Tokyo-centered industrial hierarchy. Large companies which previously had their headquarters in Osaka have gradually shifted them to Tokyo, thereby accelerating the concentration of economic power in the capital. Demographically, some thirty-five million people, or more than a quarter of the national population, reside in Tokyo and three sur-rounding prefectures, Kanagawa, Saitama, and Chiba. Yokohama, the prefectural capital of Kanagawa, has a population greater than Osaka's and has become the second most populous city in Japan.

Individuals move to these centers mainly because they provide more job opportunities, higher incomes, and more entertainment venues. As people continuously migrate into Tokyo with such motives, the capital has become the largest megalopolis, with accompanying functions and dysfunctions. On the positive side, the concentration of offices, firms, and stores makes communication between organizations less costly and time-consuming, and promotes efficiency in inter-organizational networking and coordination. For corporate negotiations, business people from various companies can organize meetings without needing to travel far. Government officials and company managers can meet face-to-face at short notice. However, organizational productivity and efficiency of this kind is accompanied by negative effects on individual life: poor housing conditions, congested environment, and extended commuting time. The weekday commuting time of the average employee in the Tokyo metropolitan area, for instance, amounts to one hour and thirty-seven minutes, with many travelling more than two hours each way.[18] For those who choose to live near their workplace, a well-equipped but small condominium is an option, a situation that prompted Western observers to describe the Japanese as 'workaholics living in rabbit hutches'.[19]

Although Japanese industrialization from the middle of the nineteenth century consistently absorbed the rural population into city areas, the high-growth economy from the 1960s onward accelerated the tempo of urbanization, giving rise to extreme population congestion in some urban centers and depopulation in some rural villages. Japan's complications lie not so much in the ratio of the total population to the amount of habitable land as in the skewed demographic distribution across regions.

Residents in extremely depopulated areas are alienated both economically and culturally. With youngsters leaving their villages for work in cities, older people find it difficult to sustain the agricultural, forestry, and fishery economies of those areas. With the liberalization of the agricultural market, the farming population has gradually lost government protection and competitive morale. Negative images of agricultural work make it difficult for young male farmers to attract spouses; an increasing number of them resort to arranged marriages with women from the Philippines, Sri Lanka, and other Asian countries.

At the national level, a series of legal measures have been introduced to promote public works projects such as road construction and resort development in the depopulated areas to stem the tide of rural emigration. At the provincial level, such localities have taken initiatives to organize the so-called *mura okoshi* (village revitalization movement) to develop agricultural products unique to each village, form networks for their nationwide distribution, and organize events and resorts attractive to city dwellers.

[18] NHK 2011, p. 13.

[19] This comment, made by an OECD observer, has attracted much media attention in Japan, together with the phrase 'the Japanese economic animals', which Asian leaders attached to Japanese business activities in the region in the 1970s and 1980s.

Admittedly, the per capita *kenmin-shotoku* (prefectural income) indicates that Tokyo, Osaka, Kanagawa, and Aichi, the central regions of the nation, top the list, while peripheral areas score lower.[20] However, on statistical happiness measures, such rural prefectures as Fukui, Toyama, Ishikawa, Tottori, and Saga rank highly, and Osaka, Hyōgo, and Kyoto prefectures (major urban centers in western Japan) are graded at or near the bottom of the ladder.[21]

On the whole, residents in peripheral areas enjoy a higher quality of life in many ways: they live in more spacious houses, commute to work in less time, and dwell in a more natural environment with fresher air and more trees. In these peripheral areas goods are also cheaper and residents enjoy more free time. These are among the factors which have brought some emigrants back to their home towns and villages, the so-called U-turn phenomenon that has been in motion since the 1980s.

4   Other Dimensions of Regional Variation

The plurality of Japan's domestic geo-political structure gave rise to various dimensions of internal variation in the nation. Three of these are described below.

(a)   Local Industries

In the economic sphere, each locality in Japan has *jiba sangyō*, unique local industries which use local resources and merchandise their products nationally or even internationally. These commodities range from ceramic ware, handicrafts, and special produce to luxury cloths. Many of these goods have a history of several centuries. *Yūzen-zome*, silk kimonos printed with gorgeous colorful patterns, have long been known as Kyoto's refined local product, manufactured with sophisticated dyeing techniques developed in the seventeenth century. Hakata textiles in northern Kyūshū, which originated in the thirteenth century, made much progress during the feudal period. Other well-known examples of local industries with long histories include Arita ware in Saga, Aizu lacquer ware in Fukushima, Ōshima fabrics on Amami island, and family Buddhist altars in Kyoto. Many regions produce unique kinds of *sake* rice wine (*jizake*) which are marketed across the nation. Small-scale but often innovative in product marketing, *jiba sangyō* enterprises have survived

---

[20] Prefectural accounts are calculated annually by the Economic and Social Research Institute of the Cabinet Office.

[21] Sakamoto 2011.

the challenges of mega-corporations based in Tokyo and other major metropolitan centers and have established themselves as the bastions of their regional economies.

(b) Popular Culture

Popular culture is also regionally diversified. Local folk songs called *min'yō* are distinctively provincial in their content and tunes, which have developed over time. Among the best known nationally, 'Tankō bushi', a coal miners' song, originated in the coal mining region of Fukuoka prefecture, in northern Kyūshū. 'Yasugi-bushi' is a song from Shimane prefecture, on the coast of the Japan Sea; it is accompanied by the loach-scooping dance, which imitates the scooping up of iron-rich sand in the area. A type of song called *oiwake* derives from travelers' chants in Nagano and Niigata prefectures, in north-central Japan. In the Ryūkyū islands, at the southern end of the Japanese archipelago, folk songs accompanied by the long lute called the *jabisen* have a special scale structure. Northern Japan abounds with such unique regional songs as the *obako* of Akita prefecture and the *okesa* of Niigata prefecture.

Traditional local festivals are also rich in regional variation, with sharp differences between village and city areas. In rural communities, festivals are generally linked with agricultural rites held in connection with spring seeding and autumn harvesting, and oriented to the communion between gods and humans. In urban localities, festivals take place mostly in summer and emphasize human bonding.

Grassroots sports culture also appears to differ regionally. Traditional sumo wrestling is popular in relatively peripheral areas such as Tōhoku, Hokkaidō, and Kyūshū regions, which produce the top-rated wrestlers. In contrast, most well-known baseball players come from more urban districts, such as the Kantō, Tōkai, Kansai, and Seto Inland Sea areas. Most teams that win the All Japan National High-school Baseball Tournament also come from these districts, reflecting the popularity of baseball at the community level there.[22]

Regional differences in popular food culture are obvious to long-distance train travelers. *Ekiben*, box lunches that are sold at stations or on trains, contain a variety of foods from land and sea, reflecting the distinct tastes particular to each locality. Japanized Chinese *ramen* noodles have different local styles and flavors, ranging from Sapporo *ramen* in Hokkaidō to Hakata *ramen* in Kyūshū.

[22] AM, 19 July 1992, p. 1.

(c)   Language

Although the Japanese language is divided broadly into the eastern type and the western type with regard to both accent and vocabulary, such a complex variety of dialects exists that a person from Iwate prefecture (one of the northernmost areas of Honshū Island) would not be able to communicate with someone from Okinawa prefecture (the southernmost district of the nation) if they spoke in their respective dialects. Since the vocabulary, pronunciation, and accent of radio and television announcers reflect those of middle-class Tokyoites, those who live outside the Tokyo metropolitan area hear the so-called standard Japanese form, but they speak their own dialects among themselves. Those raised outside the Tokyo region are thus bilingual, being competent in two types of Japanese. Most Japanese lead a dual life with regard to language.

5   Ideological Centralization

The concentration of the information industry in Tokyo lessens the visibility of the extensive regional diversity of Japanese society. In the world of electronic media, both the public broadcaster NHK (Japan Broadcasting Corporation) and commercial television networks televise an overwhelming majority of programs from Tokyo, transmitting them through local stations. Throughout Japan, most commercial television stations are associated with one of the five 'key stations' in Tokyo and relay the programs made in the capital. Very few locally produced programs have a chance of being broadcast nationally. In the print media, three major national dailies have a total circulation amounting to some twenty million, and most pages of national dailies are edited in Tokyo. Thus, the Japanese public is constantly fed views of the world and the nation that are constructed, interpreted, and edited in Tokyo. Outside the capital, local situations draw attention only as sensational news stories or as provincial items satisfying the 'exotic curiosity' of the Tokyo media establishment.

The centralization of the dissemination of information is accompanied by Tokyo control of Japanese 'language correctness'. The curriculum set by the Ministry of Education dictates that pupils should be taught to speak standard Japanese. Dialects of the periphery are often disparaged. For example, the dialect spoken in the Tōhoku district is regarded as rustic, and some schools in the region go so far as to force pupils to speak standard Japanese at school and to avoid using the Tōhoku dialect in the classroom. Thus, the dominance of the Tokyo subculture in media and language often obscures the reality of regional diversity in Japan.

In socio-geographic terms, Japanese society can perhaps be seen as being subjected to both the forces of centralization and the persistence of decentralized cultural order. Although there is little doubt that the ruling power of Tokyo has homogenized the nation, distinctive local cultural configurations have also endured. In many ways, this tug-of-war between the centralizing and decentralizing dynamics ends up making various areas similar in many ways. At the same time, it frustrates the domestic process of convergence of practices and values across regions. In this respect, Japanese society appears to be neither peculiar nor exceptional among advanced capitalist societies.

II   Generational Variations

The rapidity of change in the Japanese social structure has produced distinct generational subcultural groupings. Different age groups underwent different family socialization and educational training. They also encountered different social and political circumstances in their childhood, adolescence, and early adulthood. Accordingly, the outlooks of contemporary Japanese differ depending upon whether they experienced in their youth the three fundamental phases of Japan's recent history. The first of these was World War II and its aftermath during the 1940s and 1950s; the second was the relative stability and affluence from the 1960s and the 1980s, consequent to the nation's rapid economic growth; and the third began in the 1990s and marked the unprecedented stagnation and recession of the Japanese economy.

In relation to these three stages of recent history, the Japanese can be classified into four generations. The oldest of these is the *wartime* generation, which comprises those born in or before the early 1930s, who grew up before and during wartime and who have become a tiny minority because of their age. Next is the *postwar* generation, born between the late 1930s and the early 1950s, whose childhood occurred during the nation's recovery from postwar devastation and impoverishment through the rapid economic growth of the 1950s and early 1960s. The third group is the *prosperity* generation, born between the late 1950s and the early 1970s, which has no recollection of Japan's wartime activity or postwar poverty and which grew up during the period when Japan achieved economic prosperity and high status in the international community. Now in their forties and fifties, many of then occupy leadership positions. Finally, the youngest group, which might be called the *global* generation, was born in the mid-1970s and later. This group grew up in a period when the waves of globalization crashed upon Japan's shores, when the information revolution was in full swing, and when the Japanese economy began showing signs of serious stagnation.

The socialization experiences of these four generations reflect the changing patterns of social constraint on the everyday life of the Japanese. Over the decades, disciplinarian, repressive, and stoic styles of sanctions and control have given way to manipulative and permissive forms. Concurrently, the key elements of generational subculture have shifted away from perseverance, patience, and diligence towards indulgence, relaxation, and leisure.

Speaking generally, it could be said that the wartime generation embodies pre-modern characteristics, the postwar generation exemplifies modern ones, the prosperity generation increasingly displays postmodern tendencies, and the global generation personifies global culture. Table 3.2 presents the characteristics of the four generations.

1   The Wartime and Postwar Generations

The wartime generation went to school under the prewar and wartime education system, which placed an emphasis upon emperor worship, jingoism, and austerity. Many men in this group fought in battle and still justify aspects of Japan's wartime aggression. Others carry feelings of remorse, guilt, and shame for their actions and have committed themselves to pacifism. Although politically split, the wartime generation has little choice but to collectively face the realities of post-retirement life.

Those of the postwar generation had their childhood in the most turbulent years of change in the past century. In their primary and middle school years they witnessed the breakdown of their value system and became skeptical of the wartime generation and the insecurity and inconsistency of its militaristic philosophy.

The oldest of the postwar generation began school life during the war. City pupils in this group were evacuated to the countryside under the supervision of their teachers, grew up separated from their parents, and at the end of the war were primary school children. They remember a time when their teachers, who previously had preached imperialistic, militaristic, and totalitarian values, suddenly began to lecture on the importance of democracy, equality, and freedom.

The middle group of the postwar generation comprises those who were born in 1939 and commenced their primary schooling in April 1946 as the first batch of pupils to receive postwar education without exposure to wartime state propaganda. Members of this group have memories of their

Table 3.2 Relative characteristics of four generations

Characteristic	Generation			
	Wartime	Postwar	Prosperity	Global
Date of birth	The early 1930s and before	The late 1930s to the early 1950s	The late 1950s to the 1970s	The mid-1970s and thereafter
General lifestyle aspirations	Pre-modern	Modern	Postmodern	Global
Experience of postwar hardship	As adults	As children	None	None
School life experience	Breakdown of the wartime value system	Social anarchy; emphasis on democracy and freedom	Growing control and regulation	Both bureaucratization and commercialization
Economic situation at their entry into the job market	Recovery from war devastation	High-growth economy	'Bubble economy'	Recession and rising unemployment
Work ethic	High	High	Low	Low
Exposure to the information revolution in adolescence	No	No	Increasing	Full
Environment of social movements in early adulthood	Rise of labor movements	Rise of citizens' movements	Rise of environmental movements	Rise of non-governmental organizations, non-profit organizations, and volunteer groups
Attitude to the monarchy	Respectful	Ambivalent	Indifferent	Indifferent
Attitude to sexuality	Closed and strict	Relatively open	Permissive	Liberal

teachers telling them to blot out militaristic and nationalistic sentences from their textbooks.

The final group of the postwar generation was born in the so-called baby boom period of the late 1940s. They faced intense competition at all stages of their lives – entrance examinations to schools and universities, job applications, and promotions – because of sheer numbers. The media have popularized the phrase 'clod and lump generation' to describe the great size of this group.[23] Following the social anarchy that prevailed immediately after the war, this age group was brought up in a milieu of reaction, when school life began to show signs of increasing rigidity and control.

The postwar generation grew up in an environment in which every traditional value was questioned, liberal values were encouraged, and democratic principles were inspired. When members of this generation reached their late teens and early twenties, they spearheaded the nation-wide protests against ratification of the United States–Japan security treaty in the late 1950s and 1960s and the social movements against the Vietnam War in the late 1960s and early 1970s. The baby boomers also led campus protests around the country, which challenged all forms of academic and cultural authority.

When the tide of these movements subsided, however, most of the activists became company employees and public bureaucrats seeking to climb the occupational ladder, with some turning into 'corporate soldiers' devoted to the dictates of their firms. With regard to their internal value system, those of the postwar generation are skeptical of collective dedication to organizational norms and bureaucratic mandates. In their actual behavior, however, they have inherited the style of the wartime generation and work hard as 'working ants', 'workaholics', and 'economic animals' who toil for their organizations at the cost of personal pursuits. This discrepancy is perhaps partly attributable to a variety of powerful sanctions imposed upon individual employees against lazy work styles, as delineated in Chapter 4: employers and managers tightened control over workers under devastated conditions in postwar years. Employees also had strong incentives to work hard because Japan's economy could provide tangible rewards in return for their toil during the high-growth period until the early 1970s and during the bubble economy period in the 1980s.

The wartime and postwar generations remember how penurious the whole country was during and immediately after the war. Some experienced food shortages, even acute hunger, and shortages of cloth and other basic daily necessities. Others recall the days when people burned

[23] Sakaiya 1980.

wood to cook rice and heat baths, warmed their hands and rooms in winter with charcoal braziers, and used newspapers as toilet paper. These generations witnessed – and were themselves the engine of – the spectacular transformation of Japanese life into the one in which satiation, oversupply of automobiles, and over-consumption of paper posed national problems.

2 The Prosperity Generation

The Japanese economy recovered fully in the 1960s from wartime and postwar destruction, bringing new affluence to the young. The prosperity generation that emerged in this economic environment has become increasingly open in expressing self-interest and defending private life. This generation has been brought up in the context of three trends resulting from Japanese economic success: information revolution, consumerism, and postmodern value orientation.

First, the prosperity generation grew up in the beginning phase of the information revolution. The Japanese now live in a highly advanced information environment, which is dominated by such devices as smart phones, vending machines for food and tickets, satellite and cable television networks, MP3 players, the internet, emails, and personal computers. With Japanese electronics and information technology companies dominating international and domestic markets, the lifestyle of the Japanese is increasingly automated, their social relations being influenced by electronic media and their mass culture being presented through the medium of electronic devices. As high-tech manufacturing and knowledge-intensive industries have come to occupy a central position in Japan, the prosperity generation has taken it for granted that incessant innovations in the information environment constitute part and parcel of their daily reality. They diversify their approach to media. Social media plays a major role in the lives of this generation as a means of acquiring news and assessing social issues. They have not abandoned print media in general but devote attention to a wide range of information sources, including the internet.[24]

Second, the prosperity generation matured after Japanese society underwent a fundamental change of economic motivation, from production orientation to consumerism. Sociological analysts maintain that what drives affluent Japanese is not the 'deprivation motive' of people who work to free themselves from economic hardship, but the 'difference motive', which prompts them to purchase luxury goods and services

[24] NHK 2011, p. 69.

that give them a sense of being different from other people.[25] In this respect, Japan has attained a level beyond the stage of development in which consumer conformism dominated. In post-postwar Japan, it is argued, consumer preference is diversified, and the distribution market is segmented in such a way that a wide range of individual consumer demands can be met. The consumer conformity of indus-trial Japan has been transformed into consumer diversity in post-industrial Japan.

A third aspect of the subculture of the prosperity generation concerns a decline in both progress orientation and political radicalism, a trend which is said to characterize postmodern societies. Unlike older gener-ations, the prosperity generation is not interested in pursuing knowl-edge for the progress of society or in succeeding in the corporate world. Nor is it interested in organizing a revolutionary movement to fight the injustice of the existing order. For this generation, the domi-nant themes are playfulness, gaming, escape, tentativeness, anarchy, and 'schizophrenic differentiation', in contradistinction to the rigidity, cal-culation, loyalty, fixity, hierarchy, and 'paranoic integration of modern society'.[26]

The prosperity generation shows a marked departure from the work ethic of preceding generations, the cornerstone of Japan's economic 'mir-acle'. Far from being loyal to corporate imperatives, those who belong to this generation are willing to change from one job to another. In their youth, this generation could afford to have little interest in 'organization man' careers in large corporations and chose to work for corporations only if they provided good salaries and sufficiently long paid holidays. Some members of this generation enjoyed being 'free casuals' working at a specified task for a short period, moving from one temporary job to another with no clear direction in life and with a strong sense of ten-tativeness and uncertainty. Their primary aim was to lead a playful life (traveling abroad, mountain climbing, enjoying marine sports, and so forth) after saving a certain amount of money. Observers of the prosper-ity generation have characterized it as the *shin jinrui* (new race), which has qualitatively different values from the old, or as the 'moratorium' generation, which hesitates to make long-term decisions or life-plans.

Now in their middle age and in the middle of their occupational life, however, members of the prosperity generation have family responsibil-ities and cannot enjoy the kinds of lifestyles that they used to relish in their youth. Compared with younger age groups, they spend the largest amount of time working and commuting and have the least amount of 'leisure time'.[27] Yet, their priority is not devotion to the company but

[25] Imada 1987.   [26] Asada 1983.   [27] NHK 2011, p. 174.

open pursuit of their individual self-interest, with some people attracted to the performance-based workplace model while others see work as a way to facilitate a fun-loving existence outside the world of production and service. This generation continues to enjoy *manga* even in their middle age and sustains the playful visual culture that pervaded their childhood and adolescence. These tendencies are further enhanced in the cohort that follows the prosperity generation.

3   The Global Generation

Japan's youngest age group, the global generation, has inherited and retained many characteristics of the preceding prosperity generation, sharpening and expanding them in three key areas. First, the global generation grew up after the information revolution had begun and Japan's economy had been integrated into the global market. Hence, they take it for granted that their everyday lives are connected with those of others in different parts of the world. Some have traveled extensively overseas, often while still only teenagers. Since their adolescence, this generation has made it a daily routine to send and receive information via the internet and mobile phones and to watch cable television. This has resulted in a decline in their sense of geographical distance and an increase in their acceptance and appreciation of the notion of a borderless world. Activist elements within this age group now constitute the backbone of Japan's NGO activities overseas.

Second, this generation does not have a coherent and dominant narrative that governs their values. They grew up during and after the collapse of international socialism following the fall of the Berlin Wall in 1989 and the mass murder committed in 1995 by believers in the Aum cult with the release of sarin gas in the Tokyo subway lines, two dramatic events which marked the end of ideals for political progressivism and spiritual reformism and created a vacuum for firm belief and fervent conviction. To fill the void, the global generation increasingly lives in the virtual world, where the line between reality and fiction is blurred. Some become sexually aroused by the fabricated characters and images created on the virtual plane. Others find satisfaction not in socializing with persons in the flesh but in interacting with purely fictitious, adorable and life-sized figures. Still others see the world from the perspective of computer games as parallel internet data-base configurations with real-life social structures and regard internet-based interactions as more real than reality. These attributes are most fully embodied in the *otaku* groups of this generation, who are obsessed with internet products, both imaginary and physical, as detailed in Chapter 9.

Third, with a high proportion of casual employees becoming a regular feature of the Japanese workforce, the global generation is pessimistic about the job market. This contrasts starkly with the older generations, whose boundless optimism was based on what then seemed a reasonable expectation that the economy would continue to expand and that every prospective worker would be employed. Those now in their twenties and thirties see themselves as belonging to a 'disposable generation' and the 'lost generation',[28] because many companies are no longer able or willing to guarantee their job security into the future. This bleak employment situation has encouraged many young people to delay their marriage plans and to remain at home with their parents as 'parasite singles',[29] with a consequent increase in the degree of sexual liberalism. Although some of them have abandoned any hope of establishing a career within the corporate structure, they find gratification in pursuing independent lives of self-actualization. Some move from one enterprise to another without expecting or displaying corporate loyalty, others attempt to establish small-scale businesses, while still others work as casuals in the job market in order to support their own hobbies and pastime activities.[30]

Finally, as a product of small families and bureaucratized schools, the global generation is one of internal privacy and external caution. Its members are inclined to draw a line of autonomy and isolation around themselves and are sensitive to the intrusion of outsiders into their personal lives. Born in the period of the declining birthrate and raised with no or few siblings, many of this generation are used to intensive parental attention and protection and to having their own private room, their own autonomous space. Meanwhile, having received a much more structured, controlled, and commercialized education than preceding generations, they tend to be carefully conformist in face-to-face situations and fail to openly express opposing views.

The wartime and postwar generations followed the traditional principle of placing the public good before self-interest. With the emergence of the prosperity and global generations came the advent of what a perceptive observer has termed the 'neglect of the public and indulgence of the self'.[31] Table 3.3 shows the changing value orientations of the Japanese at different points in time. It indicates an almost unidirectional trend in which an increasing proportion of Japanese prioritize private interests and individual comfort over public commitments, such as propriety and civic spirit. Despite this change, the work ethic and wealth

[28] AE, 7 March 2011, p. 12.
[29] Yamada 1999 and 2001; *AERA*, 21 December 2009, p. 70.
[30] Kosugi 2008.   [31] Hidaka 1984, pp. 63–78.

Table 3.3 Changing value orientations of the Japanese: Responses to the question, How would you describe the most congenial lifestyle? (1930–2008)

Response	% of respondents giving answer, by year													
	1930	1940	1953	1958	1963	1968	1973	1978	1983	1988	1993	1998	2003	2008
To do what you find interesting, regardless of money or honor (interests)	12	5	21	27	30	32	39	39	38	41	40	41	39	39
To lead an easy life in a happy-go-lucky fashion (comfort)	4	1	11	18	19	20	23	22	23	23	26	23	23	27
To work hard and make money (wealth)	19	9	15	17	17	17	14	15	18	15	17	15	17	15
To lead a pure and upright life, resisting the injustices of the world (propriety)	33	41	29	23	18	17	11	11	9	9	6	8	7	5
To live a life devoted entirely to society without thought of self (civic spirit)	24	30	10	6	6	6	5	7	5	4	4	4	4	5
To study seriously and establish a reputation (honor)	9	5	6	3	4	3	3	2	2	3	3	3	4	5

Source: Adapted from Institute of Statistical Mathematics 2009, Table 2.4, and Hidaka 1984, p. 66.
Note: Columns may not add to 100% due to other answers and 'do not know' cases.

orientation have fluctuated only slightly and remain more or less constant.

In combining the regional and generational dimensions, it may be useful to visualize two Japanese: a retired farmer in a village in eastern Japan and a young casual worker in the city of Osaka, the center of western Japan. With a matrix of demographic variables affecting their life patterns, it is only natural for their value orientations and behavior patterns to display many differences.

III   Demographic Crisis

The age profile of the Japanese population is rapidly changing because of the declining birthrate and increasing life expectancy. The changing demography of age distribution in Japan has brought about crises both in the labor market and in the social welfare sector.

1   Aging of the Population

The life cycle of the Japanese changed dramatically during the twentieth century. In prewar Japan, the average life expectancy was less than fifty years, and each family produced a number of children. In 2012 the average life span was 86.41 years for women, the longest in the world, and 79.94 years for men, the fifth longest in international comparison.[32] In 2013 the number of persons of one hundred years and up exceeded fifty-four thousand, and 88 percent were female.[33] The size of the average household was a little over five persons between 1920 and 1950 but began to decline sharply from around 1955. It was 2.57 in 2012.[34]

As with most Western European countries, Japan has become an aging society, with an increasingly aged population and a decreasing number of people in the workforce. The proportion of those who are sixty-five years of age or older in the entire population came close to one-quarter in 2013, compared with 5 percent in 1950.[35] It is estimated that this will have increased to 40 percent by 2050.[36] Hence, the continuous supply of young, active labor that underpinned the postwar expansion of Japan's economy no longer exists.

[32] Ministry of Health, Labour and Welfare 2013a.   [33] AE, 13 September 2013, p. 17.

[34] Ministry of Health, Labour and Welfare 2013b.

[35] Ministry of Internal Affairs and Communications 2013a. The proportion of those who are seventy-five years of age or older exceeds 10 percent.

[36] The statistical estimate in 2009 of the National Institute of Population and Social Security Research.

Table 3.4   Average remaining years of life at the age of twenty by occupation (males) (1980–1990)

Occupation	No. of years remaining in given year			Above- and below-average consistency
	1980	1985	1990	
Professional and technical	55.64	58.85*	59.79	
Managerial and administrative	57.23*	59.64*	61.01*	+
Clerical	56.05*	59.01*	61.72	+
Sales	55.11	57.23	59.51	−
Service	53.76	55.46	55.37	−
Security	56.84*	59.85*	62.38*	+
Agriculture, forestry, and fishery	54.00	55.77	57.74	−
Transport and communication	55.37	58.59*	58.92	
Skilled workers and production operatives	56.69*	60.40*	63.18a*	
The unemployed	39.59	40.73		
Mining	46.83	42.21		
Labor force average	55.65	58.35	60.02	

Source: Ishikawa 1985 and National Institute of Population and Social Security Research 2001.

Notes: Asterisks indicate the figures that are higher than the labor force average. The right-most column shows the above-average groups (+) and the below-average groups (−) consistently at three time points.

[a] The 1990 data combined the categories 'Skilled workers...' and 'Mining'.

The increasing life expectancy of the Japanese has altered the retirement age of workers and the job market for the aged. The retirement system in Japan, which started in large firms at around the turn of the nineteenth century and became widespread in small businesses after World War II, used to set the mandatory retirement age at fifty-five, but with the advent of an aging society, companies were legally required to raise the age to sixty-five before 2013. In reality, many firms have changed internal corporate work rules to enable those over sixty years of age to continue their employment under reduced work arrangements. Many workers find jobs in subsidiary companies or through personal networks, and remain employed until their mid-sixties or even into their seventies, with diminished income and shorter working hours.

As Table 3.4 demonstrates, Japanese people's life expectancy differs depending on the occupational group to which they belong. The number of years a man is likely to live after the age of twenty is low among the unemployed and those engaged in farming, forestry, fishery, sales, and services when compared to those who are employed as managers, administrators, clerks, and security workers. Although the Ministry of

Health's broadly defined occupational classifications do not straightforwardly reflect class categories, variations in the life expectancy of different occupational groups prompt speculation regarding possible links between the length of someone's life and their social standing.

2 Declining Birthrate

The statistics of population dynamics that the Ministry of Health compiles annually show that the average number of children that a woman bears declined to 1.26 in 2005, the lowest figure ever recorded in Japan and one which shows a substantial decline from 4.53 in 1947. Japan's recorded birthrate was 1.41 in 2012 but still remains among the lowest in the industrialized world. Although higher than South Korea (1.22) and comparable to Germany (1.32), the Japanese figure (1.27) based on United Nations data available for cross-national comparison is below Australia (1.83), the United Kingdom (1.84), Sweden (1.87), France (1.89), and the United States (2.09).[37] Since the rate needs to be at least 2.07 to maintain the present population level, this trend heralds a long-term decline in Japan's population. If the present trend continues, the population of Japan will be half the present level in about 2080.[38]

The dwindling birthrate is attributable to the changing attitudes of women to marriage and family life. There appear to be at least two factors underlying the transformation. First, an increasing number of women feel that they cannot afford to raise many children when education costs are an immense burden. Second, women increasingly prefer to marry later, as more and more job opportunities become available to them. In 2012 the average age of first marriage for women was more than twenty-nine years of age,[39] which contrasts sharply with previous decades, when women married much younger. In 1950, for instance, women were an average age of twenty-three years when first embarking upon marriage.

3 Pressure on the Welfare Structure

The pension system in Japan consists of three state-administered programs that cover nearly all pension policy holders. The National Pension

---

[37] Estimates for 2005–10 prepared by the United Nations 2008.

[38] According to an estimate made by the National Institute of Population and Social Security Research in December 2006, the most likely population of Japan in 2100 is 4.8 million, about 38 percent of the present population.

[39] Ministry of Health, Labour and Welfare 2012b. The male age was nearly thirty-one years.

scheme, to which every adult between twenty and sixty years of age is supposed to belong, is the most basic layer of Japan's pension system. Started in 1961, the scheme was initially intended to look after individuals not covered under any other pension program. It provides a system in which all persons in the workforce, particularly those in agriculture, forestry, and fisheries, as well as independent proprietors and their families, can expect to receive pensions. It is compulsory for students aged twenty years or older to join the National Pension scheme. Generally, members of this program start receiving pensions at sixty-five years of age.

The other major schemes are Welfare Pension Insurance, designed to cover company employees in the private sector, and Mutual Benefit Pension Insurance, secured primarily for employees in the public sector. There are several mutual benefit associations for national bureaucrats, local public servants, employees of public corporations, those employed in the agricultural, forestry, and fisheries industries, and teachers and staff of private schools. There is also a special pension program for sailors. A portion of the contributions made by members of these schemes is transferred to the National Pension program for all Japanese. To equalize the two different arrangements for private-sector and public-sector employees, in 2010 the government gradually began to unify the contribution/payment criteria of the Mutual Benefit Pension scheme with those of the Welfare Pension scheme, with the process to be completed in 2015.

Table 3.5 shows four major patterns of post-retirement pension payment, consisting of three layers: National Pension payments made equally for all contributors (Level 1), contribution-based returns for Welfare Pension and Mutual Benefit Pension members (Level 2), and additional benefits for some groups (Level 3). Full-time housewives (or househusbands) of company or public-sector employees receive National Pension payments, provided their spouses arrange in their working life to have the required contribution deducted from their salaries.

Only people who have contributed to a pension insurance program during their working life receive pensions in Japan. Their monthly entitlement after retirement depends upon the sum of their contributions. Since many find the pension insufficient to cover the cost of living after retirement, some privileged few contribute to additional pension funds during their working lives so as to have a third-level pension income after retirement. For this purpose, Welfare Pension Foundations operate for private-sector employees and National Pension Foundations operate for the self-employed. Many large corporations have their own enterprise pension schemes which provide participating employees with handsome sums after retirement. In addition, post offices and life insurance

Table 3.5 Japan's pension structure

Characteristic	Pension type			
	Welfare	Mutual Benefit	National	National for full-time home carers
Main occupation	Company employees	Public servants	The self-employed	Full-time housewives (or househusbands)
No. of members (millions)	34.5	4.4	19.0	9.8
Pension payments				
Level 3: Special arrangements	Enterprise pension (privileged few)	Occupational Area Additions (to be phased out)	Private pension (contributors to personalized plans only)	None
Level 2: Returns proportionate to contributions to Welfare/Mutual Benefit scheme during working life	Welfare pension	Mutual Benefit pension (to be integrated with Welfare Pension in future)		
Level 1: Returns to all contributors	National pension	National Pension	National pension	National pension

Source: Adapted from Ministry of Health, Labour and Welfare 2012d.

companies sell personalized pension plans on an individual basis; install-
ments made to these plans are tax-deductible.

Public servants long enjoyed extra pension payments called Occupational Area Additions, comparable to the third-level pensions in the
private sector. This privilege was removed in 2010, although those who
were in the system before this time will be paid these additional amounts
on a pro-rata basis.

Two in five people failed to make contributions to the National Pension
system in the 2010s,[40] either because they could not afford to or because
they chose to manage personalized funds instead. No doubt, the increase
of non-regular workers is a major contributing factor. This trend poses a
challenge to the long-term viability of the national program.

Thus, the lifestyles of elderly Japanese differ substantially depending
upon which combination of these three levels of income they receive.
Using a house metaphor, one might say that those with the National
Pension can live only in single-story dwellings, while most retirees with
the Welfare/Mutual Benefit Pension reside in double-story houses. Those
public servants who are entitled to Occupational Area Additions and
those private-sector workers who could afford to make additional contributions in their working lives are able to enjoy luxurious three-story
houses. This reality explains in part why income disparity is greater
among senior citizens than in any other age group.

To cope with the labor crisis caused by the aging of the workforce,
and to bring cheap labor into the job market, the Japanese establishment
has two options. One of these solutions focuses upon women as the chief
source of additional labor. An alternative strategy involves using foreign
workers to resolve the problem. Although these solutions are not mutually
exclusive, the predicament must inevitably force the Japanese leadership
to abandon the predominantly male and Japanese-only labor market and
to manage the labor system on the basis of a more heterogeneous working
population. Chapters 6 and 7 discuss these issues at some length.

[40] Ministry of Health, Labour and Welfare 2012d; AM, 9 August 2013, p. 4.

4   Forms of Work in Cultural Capitalism

I The Numerical Dominance of Small Business

1 Small Business as Majority Culture

Popular overseas *soto* images of Japanese society are colored by the notion that it is a country of mega-corporations. These perceptions have been engendered by Japanese products and associated with such household names as Toyota, Mitsubishi, and NEC. However, the *uchi* reality is that, although powerful and influential, large corporations constitute a very small minority of businesses in Japan, both in terms of the number of establishments and the size of their workforce. An overwhelming majority of Japanese enterprises are small or medium in size, and it is these that employ the bulk of the workforce. While small may or may not be beautiful, 'it certainly is bountiful, and thereby deserving of its fair share of attention'.[1] Small- and medium-sized companies are the mainstay of the Japanese economy.[2]

In the Japanese business world they are known as *chūshō kigyō*, medium and small firms. For brevity, one may lump both types together and call them small businesses. The Small Business Standard Law defines *chūshō kigyō* as those companies that employ not more than three hundred persons or whose capital does not exceed three hundred million yen.[3]

As Table 4.1 shows, nearly nine out of ten employees work in businesses with fewer than three hundred workers. Furthermore, more than

---

[1] Granovetter 1984, p. 334.

[2] This pattern is not unique to the Japanese situation but universal across advanced capitalist economies. The observed reality contradicts the long-held view that the development of capitalism would annihilate small-scale enterprises to pave the way for monopolistic domination by large companies, although oligopolies do dominate and control small businesses.

[3] Some areas in tertiary industry are exceptions to this general definition. For the wholesale sector, the employee and capital ceilings decrease to one hundred persons or one hundred million yen respectively. For the retail sector, the cut-off figures are much smaller: fifty employees or fifty million yen. For the service sector, they are one hundred employees or fifty million yen.

Table 4.1 Distribution of establishments and employees in the private
sector by firm size (2009)

Firm size (no. of employees)	Establishments (%)	Employees (%)
1–4	59.5	12.9
5–9	19.6	12.9
10–29	15.1	24.5
30–99	4.5	22.3
100–299	0.9	13.5
>300	0.2	13.8

Source: Calculated from Ministry of Internal Affairs and Communications 2009b, vol. 1, p. 33.

half of private-sector establishments employ fewer than thirty workers.
Large corporations with three hundred or more workers employ less than
15 percent of the labor force in the private sector.[4]

Even in the manufacturing sector, small businesses employ three-
quarters of workers, with the overwhelming majority in the textile, furniture, ceramics, and fittings industries. Numerically, small businesses also
dominate the parts-production sectors of the export-oriented car and
electronics industries. In the construction industry, more than nine out
of ten employees work in small businesses.[5] Since large firms and their
employees occupy only a small segment, the so-called Japanese management theories based on *omote* observations of this minority section lose
sight of the *ura* dynamics of the great majority of Japanese enterprises.

Macroscopic data analysis shows that one of the most fundamental
divisions of stratification in the male population of Japan lies between
those employed in large corporations and those in small ones,
although their respective internal variations are increasingly discernible.
Table 4.2 shows key differences between large and small businesses.
Notably, the so-called lifetime employment system does not operate in
the small business sector. This is the system under which employees are
expected to remain with the same company or enterprise group for their
entire career; the enterprise in return provides a wide range of fringe benefits. The system applies only to regular employees in large companies,[6]
although there are signs that it has weakened due to the prolonged recession during the 1990s and thereafter. In general, job mobility between

---

[4] These patterns do not change even if one eliminates agriculture, forestry, and fisheries
from the calculations.

[5] Based on Ministry of Internal Affairs and Communications 2009b.

[6] There is a debate over whether the lifetime employment system has been a unique
Japanese structure. Koike 1988, for example, contends that long-service workers are so
numerous both in Europe and in the United States that Japan is not unique.

Table 4.2 Relative characteristics of large and small Japanese firms

Characteristic	Firm size	
	Large	Small
Inter-company mobility	Low	High
Separation of corporate ownership from management	Strong	Weak
Labor union organization ratio (proportion of unionists as employees)	High	Low
Working hours	Short	Long
Educational background of employees	High	Low
Salary levels	High	Low
Employees' involvement in community affairs	Low	High
Decision-making style	Bureaucratic	Entrepreneurial

firms is considerably higher in small enterprises. It is often claimed that Japanese companies have accomplished the managerial revolution so fully that their top managers are usually not their owners. This generalization holds true for large companies, but owner-managers abound in small businesses.

2   Plurality of Small Business

Japanese economists who have debated the nature of Japan's small enterprises fall into two broad categories. The first group expands on the dual-structure thesis, which holds that big businesses accumulate their capital by exploiting and controlling small businesses which have little choice but to offer workers low pay under inferior working conditions.[7] The second position emphasizes the vitality, dynamism, and innovation of small businesses that have responded flexibly to the needs of clients: small firms have adapted themselves effectively to the changing environment by developing their own technology, know-how, and service methods, thereby leading both domestic and international markets. The phenomena identified by both positions do exist in the world of Japanese small business. Its internal variation is partly determined by the extent to which small businesses are controlled by large companies at the top of the corporate hierarchy.

At the highest level, Japan has three major financial groups: the Mitsubishi UFJ Financial Group, the Mizuho Financial Group, and the

[7] For example, Yoshitani 1992.

Mitsui-Sumitomo Financial Group. These 'mega-banks' were formed and reshaped after a series of alignments and realignments at the beginning of the twenty-first century in an attempt to rationalize the banking sector, which was over-burdened with bad loans accumulated in the 1990s, and to head off challenges from foreign financial institutions eager to gain a foothold in the world's third-largest economy. More broadly, Japan's industrial sector has a few major conglomerates: Mitsubishi, Mitsui, Sanwa, and Sumitomo. With a major bank at its center, each of these groups includes diverse, large-scale companies ranging from manufacturing to trading. The Mitsubishi group, for example, comprises approximately forty major companies specializing in a range of enterprises, including banking, the car industry, the chemical industry, the metal industry, construction, real estate, life insurance, the electrical industry, forestry, warehousing, and aluminum refining. Most of these companies' names carry the prefix 'Mitsubishi'. In addition to these conglomerates, some big business combinations dominate particular industrial areas. These include the Toyota, Toshiba, Nippon Steel, AEON, and Kintetsu groups. Positioned at the helm of the business community, these groups each have a string of subsidiary companies and subcontracting firms organized hierarchically in a structure known as *keiretsu* (enterprise grouping). Within each group, the subsidiary companies mutually support each other, arranging reciprocally profitable finances, the cross-ownership of stocks, and long-term business transactions. This business structure is modeled on that of a family and normally requires each company to belong to a single *keiretsu* group. In a sequence of subcontracting arrangements, higher-level companies give contract jobs to companies lower in the chain, who may in turn give contracts to still lower companies. Generally, the lower the subcontractor, the smaller its size.

Importantly, a significant part of the small-business community remains reasonably free of the intervention and influence of the *keiretsu* network. Although these relatively independent small firms differ in size, they are comparatively autonomous, self-reliant, and maverick in their behavior. Cross-tabulation of the two dimensions – firm size and the extent of *keiretsu* intervention by large companies – is shown in Table 4.3, which represents four kinds of small businesses.

(a)   Medium-sized Subsidiaries in Keiretsu Networks

Type A comprises medium-sized firms belonging to a grouping of enterprises under the immediate direction of large companies. These *keiretsu* companies can rely upon finance, expertise, and other support from their parent companies. In return, parent companies appoint their own employees as directors, managers, and executives of the main businesses

Table 4.3 Four types of small business

Company size	*Keiretsu* intervention	
	High	Low
Medium	(A) Subsidiary companies	(C) Venture businesses; maverick high-tech firms; entertainment promoters
Small to petty	(B) Low-ranking subcontractors; franchise shops	(D) Independent proprietors; neighborhood retail shops; professional offices

under their direct control in the *keiretsu* network. Large companies regard these positions as suitable postings for management staff that are close to retirement age.

(b)   Low-level Subcontractors under Keiretsu Control

Many of the small businesses that fall into Type B are petty subcontracting factories. At the bottom rungs of the subcontract hierarchy are ultra-small enterprises called *reisai kigyō*, which employ fewer than ten workers. This type includes firms run by self-employed individuals with the assistance of family members. Vulnerable to the manipulations of large corporations, this group is the most deprived zone of Japan's economy.

Subcontracting companies find it difficult to reduce the working hours of their employees, since they operate at the whim of their parent corporations. Many subcontractors, occasionally or frequently, receive orders before a weekend or a holiday and must deliver goods immediately following it. To meet this requirement, subcontractors have little choice but to operate during weekends and holidays. At times, they receive orders from their parent companies after normal working hours with the requirement that the goods be delivered the following morning. For these subcontractors, overtime remains the norm, and as long as parent companies wield such power, their working conditions are unlikely to change.

At the bottom of the chain of subcontractors are daily laborers, in such flophouse quarters as Sanya in Tokyo and Kamagasaki in Osaka, who mainly sustain the construction industry. They find jobs on a daily basis through recruiters, many of whom have gangster connections. These laborers work on construction sites and engage in demanding physical tasks. They inevitably compete in the labor market with foreign workers.

(c)   Maverick and Venture Businesses

Type C companies are characterized by their relatively large firm size and their management's capacity to make decisions without much interference from big business. Many of these companies have made independent innovations in product development, production technology, and marketing, thereby establishing significant shares in markets which large corporations failed to develop. As medium-sized enterprises, these innovation-oriented firms maintain superiority over rival companies, not only in capital procurement, plant, and other hardware areas, but also in technical know-how, human-resource development, and software spheres. Increasingly, enterprises in this category include venture businesses that depend on knowledge-intensive technology and new service businesses that rely upon the diversification of consumer interests.

Small enterprises of this type can adapt to changes in market demands more flexibly than large bureaucratic corporations. Some expand by developing 'crevice businesses', business opportunities that big companies have left open and which have much potential. Others commit themselves to speedy, entrepreneurial styles of decision-making and to flexible responses to clients' requests.

The entrepreneurs in this sector may lack social prestige and the status which large-company businessmen relish, but they possess confidence and find satisfaction in their work. Independent and highly motivated, the leaders of this group seek self-actualization rather than organization dependency, thereby developing a lifestyle and value orientation different from that of people working primarily within the *keiretsu* system. These small-business elites generally possess higher levels of assets than career employees of large firms and tend to be the *chūsan* type middle class rather than the *chūryū* type, into which big-business white-collar elites tend to fall.[8] Panasonic, Honda, Sony, and Nintendo, which have become household names around the world, emerged from this sector.

(d)   Independent Small Proprietors

Type D businesses are mainly those of independent small proprietors such as neighborhood retail shop owners, snack-bar managers, barbers, hairdressers, rice dealers, public-bathhouse operators, liquor merchants, stationers, dry cleaners, and the like. This sphere also includes some professionals who manage small offices, including general medical practitioners, lawyers, and tax accountants.

---

[8] See Chapter 2, Section V, for the distinction between the two types.

The subculture of small business proprietors differs considerably from that of 'organization men' in large firms. On the whole, non-professional self-employed people do not place a high priority on university education and find vocational training more relevant to achievement of their occupational goals. Many have gone through high schools specializing in vocationally oriented teaching for industry or commerce. In recent years, special vocational schools for high-school graduates (see Chapter 5) have offered further education for those who aim at managing small businesses of their own. Many who seek to manage such small-scale establishments as barber shops, beauty parlors, and restaurants often go to these special vocational schools with a view to succeeding to the management of their parents' independent businesses.

A further difference between small proprietors and company employees is that the former tend to pass on their businesses from one generation to another. Approximately two-thirds of self-employed business people inherit the businesses of their parents or parents-in-law, a pattern that suggests that this group has its own process of class reproduction. The overwhelming majority of this group lives in city areas, and a high proportion of these people appear to live with their parents upon marriage, another reflection of inter-generational continuity in this sphere. In comparison with their counterparts in Korea and Taiwan, the sector of Japanese independent proprietors has a smaller proportion of outsiders from different class backgrounds.[9]

Self-employment is institutionalized as a desirable occupational career path. Typically, those who choose this track initially work for a company, to acquire skills for the future, then establish independent businesses either on their own or with their family members. In other words, many small proprietors themselves used to be workers employed by small independent businesses.[10] During their time as employees, they acquire special knowledge, skills, and personal connections while working in inferior conditions as trainees or apprentices. Upon completing high school, a person from this group might first work as an attendant at a gasoline station, then as an auto mechanic at another station, and thereafter learn how to manage such a business. Having amassed considerable savings and successfully negotiated a bank loan, he or she may later establish a gasoline station of his or her own and become an independent proprietor. In traditional urban Japan, it was an established practice for such an apprentice to serve under an independent merchant for a long period from his or her teens, become the head clerk, and finally set up his or her own shop with the blessing of his or her master. This practice, known as *noren wake* (splitting a shop sign curtain), is less common today in its original form but persists in transformed shape as an arrangement for establishing a solid career route for those who start without educational credentials or material resources.

Small business owners who are not necessarily connected with *keiretsu* networks work longer hours than their employees. Some are willing workaholics who enjoy their company life above all things and have very limited communication with family members.[11] Others, particularly owners of small enterprises in the service and entertainment industries, cannot afford to employ many staff and are forced to work long hours in order to economize on labor costs.

Independent small business people are prominent in community organizations and events. In particular, those who manage small shops have a stake in maintaining good relations with their communities and are frequently involved in community festivals, district events, and local fundraising. This group produces many leaders and active members of the neighborhood associations that make political and social decisions about community affairs. Unlike salary employees, who normally work in firms distant from their homes, these community-based independent shop owners, who live and work on the same premises, combine business with pleasure in promoting the social cohesion of their localities.

The variety that exists in the small business community suggests that the value orientations and lifestyles of its workers differ greatly depending on firm size and the degree to which firms are free of the control of large companies. Some are submissive, passive, and evidently exploited. Others are innovative, participatory, and openly entrepreneurial. These facets manifest themselves in different circumstances in different ways. One must be cautious about stereotyping Japanese small business employees, especially as they constitute an overwhelming majority of the labor force.

II   The 'Japanese-style' Management Model

The work practices of Japanese firms have long influenced and shaped the overall images of the nation. For the past few decades, the so-called *Nihon-teki keiei* ('Japanese-style' management) model has attracted disproportionate attention in labor studies in Japan, where the three treasures of Japanese work organization – lifetime employment, seniority-based wage structure, and enterprise unionism – are said to prevail, although the model derives mainly from the observations of white-collar employees in large companies, a tiny minority in the workforce. Because of the economic slowdown since the 1990s, 'Japanese-style'

---

[11] Nippon no Shachō Kenkyū-kai 1994.

Table 4.4 Two management models

Characteristic	Management model	
	'Japanese-style'	Performance-oriented
Guiding principles	Employee loyalty to company	Employee contribution to company
Corporate responsibility for employees	Ensuring job security	Substantial rewards to high achievers; low achievers as disposable
Ideological metaphor	Company as a family based on 'Japanese culture'	Company as each employee's tool for achieving individual wellbeing
Employment practice	Lifetime employment	Contractual
Wage structure	Seniority-based; years of service	Performance-based; individual output
Labor unions	Enterprise unionism	Insignificant
Mid-career recruitment	Rare	Frequent (head-hunting)
Skill formation	In-house training, un-portable	In-house training, plus acquisition of portable qualifications
Primary aim of management	Optimization of company profit	Maximization of shareholder dividends
Source of work motivation	Team work	Individual initiative
Main labor market	Internal labor market	External labor market
Applicable employee sectors	Core employees in large firms, in manufacturing in particular	Employees in small firms; non-regular employees; highly paid professionals with special skills
Social disparity	Undesirable; to be limited	Inevitable; good incentive

management, once lauded as the driving force of the nation's economic boom, is now under critical review and under threat by the performance-based and output-oriented management model which resembles the Anglo-American style of management. The key characteristics of both paradigms are contrasted in Table 4.4.

1   Firm-based Internal Labor Markets

The first model, the *Nihon-teki keiei* system, is predicated upon firm-based internal labor markets which function in conjunction with the lifetime employment system. According to this model, typically, a company will recruit a batch of new graduates every year, conduct intensive in-house on-the-job training, and rotate employees laterally from one department to another to make them multi-skilled and versatile. For instance, a fresh employee may be assigned first to the accounting department, then to the sales division, and switched after a few years to the advertising section. The employment arrangements are based not so much on formal contracts as on informal agreements; a new recruit may be given a statement that he or she has been hired, but not an explicit covenant which spells out job specifications. Employees have a strong incentive to work hard and improve enterprise performance since the bonus system is built into salary structure to distribute corporate gains among them. Based on the *nenkō chingin* (seniority-based wage) structure, salaries are generally determined by length of service in the firm and are structured in such a way that inter-company movement would not pay off in the long run.

Large corporations take initiatives to provide their employees with corporate welfare facilities ranging from company housing to recreation facilities. By establishing themselves as acceptable workers within the corporate framework, employees qualify for long-term low-interest company loans so that they may purchase houses or fund their children's education. To gain access to these schemes, however, employees must demonstrate resolute commitment to their corporate lives, and thus strong corporate allegiance. Once established, such an arrangement ties them more firmly to their company and increases their dependence upon it. Japan's white-collar employees are often sarcastic about their controlled lives, likening them to *miyazukae,* the unenviable lifestyles of officials in the service of the court in ancient Japan, who had to put up with various kinds of humiliation to survive in highly bureaucratic government organizations. To a considerable extent, the ways of life of today's 'salarymen' resemble those of samurai warriors, who devoted themselves to their feudal lords and to the expansion of the privilege and prestige of their house and fief. The paradigm has long served as a role model for many sectors of the Japanese labor force.

The top management of large companies is composed of long-serving successful ex-employees who have risen through the ranks; stockholders have little influence in the decision-making processes of their company, giving rise to a sharp distinction between corporate ownership and management. Furthermore, because large companies have chains of subsidiary and subcontract firms based upon *keiretsu* and other arrangements, they can function with relatively small bodies of employees in relation to their scale.

These features of large corporations have prompted many observers to argue that Japan's capitalism differs from its Western counterpart.[12] Some analysts maintain that Japanese firms have developed corporationism (*kaishashugi* or *kigyōshugi*), in which employees are completely

---

[12] For example, Johnson 1990.

tied to the company.[13] Others propose a distinction between stock-holder capitalism (*kojin shihonshugi*) and corporate capitalism (*hōjin shihonshugi*) and maintain that the latter predominates in Japan.[14] In stockholder capitalism as it is found in Western societies, companies function as incorporated bodies formed to maximize stockholders' returns. In corporate capitalism, each corporation becomes a substantive and personal entity as though it had a personality of its own, with its interests overriding those of individuals connected with it.[15]

Since companies are thus anthropomorphized and deified, they become omnipotent and omnipresent in the lives of their members, executives, managers, and regular employees alike, compelling them to dedicate themselves to the companies' 'needs' and 'commands'. Thus, these 'corporate warriors' are expected, in an almost military fashion, to devote themselves to the requirements of the enterprise at the expense of individual rights and choices. In return, virtually all Japanese companies pay bonuses to their regular employees in summer and winter, the amount depending upon company performance in the preceding term. Many firms also arrange and pay for company excursions and conduct company funerals when managers and directors die. Some firms even maintain company cemeteries.

To maintain these semi-totalistic characteristics, Japan's large companies use diffuse and nebulous rhetoric in evaluating employees' ability in terms of their personal devotion to the company, and likening the firm to the family.

2   Manipulative Definition of Employee Ability

Large Japanese companies evaluate their employees, both white-collar and blue-collar, annually or biannually throughout their occupational careers. These appraisals, which determine employees' wage levels and promotion prospects, take a range of abilities into account. In this regard, the Japanese vocabulary distinguishes three types of ability: *jitsuryoku*, manifest ability which one demonstrates in a particular project or undertaking; *soshitsu*, latent ability that one possesses in relation to a particular domain of activity; and *nōryoku*, latent, undifferentiated, general, and

---

[13] Sataka 1992a, 1993a, and 1993b; Matsumoto 1991.   [14] Okumura 1991.

[15] The Japanese legal system selectively adopts these assumptions in favor of anthropomorphizing corporations as juridical persons. Like individual persons, they are allowed to make political donations and to engage in political activities. Japan's criminal law does not subject enterprises to criminal charges, on the grounds that they are fictitious, impersonal entities.

overall ability that one has as a person. The third element is imprecise and comprises vague ingredients of 'human character', 'personality traits', and 'psychological makeup', but it plays a crucial role in personnel evaluation in the firm-based internal labor market.[16] This market presupposes the production of generalist employees who can cope with multiple job situations, and therefore each employee is expected not only to display a job-specific manifest ability but to possess a wide range of attributes that are not necessarily connected with his or her job but are consistent with the broad goals of the firm. This means that the expected attributes encompass such nebulous components as *hitogara* (human quality) and *jinkaku* (personhood) that go beyond the specific requirements of one's occupational duties. Workers are aware that they are assessed in terms of the extent to which they are cooperative, obliging, and harmonious in their interpersonal relations.

When personnel evaluation places a significant emphasis upon these ambiguous areas of *nōryoku*, employees have to compete with each other to demonstrate that they have general qualities compatible with corporate goals. This is why some employees arrive at the office every morning earlier than the stipulated starting time to clean their desks and office furniture. For the same reason, many office workers stay after normal working hours until their boss leaves the office. Somewhat similarly, subordinates often assist with the preparation of the funeral of a relative of their superior. Employees engage in these tasks because they know that their human quality and personhood outside their job specifications are constantly subject to corporate appraisal. In this sense, their behavior springs not from altruism but from calculations regarding the presentation of personality traits that might affect their chances of promotion and salary increases. Their *tatemae* has to be unqualified loyalty to corporate norms, but their *honne* lies in the maximization of their interests in the system.

Meanwhile, their superiors are far from being free of similar compulsion. They cannot expect to lead their subordinates smoothly without exhibiting their own human quality and personhood beyond the call of job-specific duties. Thus, at their own expense, Japanese middle managers take their subordinates to pubs and restaurants after work, not only to listen to their complaints and troubles, but also to moralize on the importance of devotion to company work. Managers visit their subordinates' relatives in hospital and act as go-betweens for their subordinates' marriages. In so doing, managers can expect to count on the support and dedication of the employees of their department in tasks beyond their designated responsibilities.[17] Managers play the role of corporate socializer

---

[16] The discussion here follows Iwata 1981, pp. 117–45.   [17] Befu 1990b.

in this way because their chances of promotion partly hinge upon their success in this area. Managers who can command their subordinates in this extra-duty realm are regarded as competent and as having the above-mentioned third element of ability, *nōryoku*.

Employees' levels in large companies rise in accordance with the length of their service to the company, moving up sharply towards the end of their careers (generally in their fifties). The seniority-based wage structure makes employees reluctant to move from one company to another in the middle of their careers; they can maximize their salary benefits by staying in the same firm.

In the face of the prolonged recession, increasing off-shore corporate operations, and gradually rising unemployment in the 1990s, some large companies started to examine their salary and promotion structures and began to introduce a system which places more emphasis on employees' manifest abilities and concrete achievements. Head-hunting is not unusual, and some middle managers now receive annual salaries on the basis of their performance in the previous year. In some sections of big business, there are signs the lifetime employment system and seniority-based salary scheme are collapsing.

3   The Family Metaphor as a Socialization Device

Japanese corporate leaders have used the family metaphor to inculcate the norm of total commitment in their employees. The key formula of this strategy is to liken a company to a family. An enterprise expects its employees to cultivate close internal relationships, develop family-like warmth and order, and regard the company as a center of their lives, more important than their own families. Intriguingly, when speaking of their company to outsiders, many employees call it *uchi* (our house or home) and when speaking of competitor firms use a suffix, *san*, normally attached to a family name. Toshiba, for example, is referred to as Toshiba-san, and Nissan as Nissan-san. This approach is based upon the clear sense of *uchi–soto* distinction and immerses individual employees in their work without an overt sense of alienation, although it does not work fully for blue-collar workers. Whether one calls such immersion complete commitment or total exploitation, this Japanese management technique focuses on moralistic indoctrination and introduces expressive symbols to accomplish instrumental processes.

It goes without saying that a business is a complex organization engaged in profit-making and capital accumulation. The firm has to compete, expand, and exploit to achieve these goals. It is far from being altruistic, compassionate, and empathetic. In contrast, the presumed principles of the family are based upon self-sacrifice, mutual assistance, and harmonious affection. It is supposed to be the prototype of communal organization. The *tatemae* of the firm being the family manipulatively conceals the *honne* of corporate operations. The Japanese management method has shown that it is effective to use communal symbolism to attain the goals of business organization; it may well be more effective than the legalistic, impersonal, and bureaucratic vocabulary which some Western companies appear to prefer.

Within this framework, corporations invest heavily in socialization programs for their employees. They normally have morning sessions, not only to prepare for the day, but in many cases to cite company mottos and sing company songs. At a formal level, major companies hold intensive training sessions for several weeks for new employees, in an endeavor to infuse company policies and practices into their minds. Some of these sessions even attempt to rid the corporate rookies of their sense of self and ego. In extreme cases, some companies require them to sing songs in a busy street without feeling shy. Others compel them to perform physical exercise to the point of near exhaustion. These training programs have no bearing on the substance of the trainees' future work. Instead, the drills are designed chiefly to mold the newcomers into selfless and egoless employees who are willing to subject themselves to company orders, no matter how unreasonable they may be. Many firms organize resocialization sessions of these and other kinds for low and middle managers. In German sociological language, Japanese companies put up a façade of being *Gemeinschaft* (community) although they are *Gesellschaft* (association) in reality.

Thus, application of the family metaphor to a corporation has played havoc with the family itself, which has increasingly become subject to the imperatives of the corporate world. In this twisted sense, the corporation is a family and the family is a corporation in many sectors of contemporary Japan.[18]

III   Job Market Rationalization

While this familial and paternalistic 'Japanese-style' model remains entrenched in Japan's work culture, the prolonged recession of the 1990s and the concomitant penetration of globalizing forces into the Japanese

---

[18] The situation generated many popular expressions referring to the inability of company-first men to fit into the family environment. They have been sarcastically called huge garbage of no use to family life. Also, a popular saying has been in circulation in the mass media: 'it is best for the husband to be healthy and not at home'.

economy have seen two fundamental shifts in the system of work – the casualization of the workforce and the introduction of performance-based employment.

1   Casualization of Labor

The first distinctive trend is the casualization of the labor force, a development that has been deemed a major factor that has contributed to the widening inequality between social classes, as discussed in Chapter 2. The restructuring that many companies launched in the face of the sluggish economy produced a growing number of part-time and casual workers and sharpened the line of demarcation between *seiki shain* (regular employees) and *hi-seiki shain* (non-regular employees). Regular employees encompass the full-time salaried workers who enjoy various company benefits, with many relishing the privilege of lifetime employment. Non-regular employees include a variety of impermanent workers with disposable employment status and an unstable wage structure. With economic rationalism forcing managers to minimize the costs of employment, 38.2 percent of all employees fall into the category of non-regular employees in 2012.[19] It is estimated that 57.5 percent of working women belong to this group. Many of these non-regular workers form the 'working poor', a class of individuals who attempt to work hard in vulnerable jobs but are unable to break the cycle of underemployment and under-subsistence. Because of their unprotected positions, many of them submit themselves tamely to this condition and fail to demonstrate their dissatisfaction openly for fear of their employers refusing to renew their existing contracts.

These marginalized employees comprise a few subcategories, some of which overlap. The first of these is made up of the so-called part-time workers. Although classified as part-timers, many in this group work more than thirty hours a week and differ little from full-time regular employees in terms of working hours and the substance of the jobs they perform. Married women who work to help support family finances far outnumber other types of part-timers. Generally, these 'full-time part-timers' receive low hourly wages, stay in the same position for years without career prospects, and rarely have the privilege of joining the employee Welfare Pension system, to which employers make contributions.

The second subcategory consists of those who engage in *arubaito* (side jobs), a Japanese term derived from the German word *Arbeit* (work). Many students do after-school or vacation jobs to cover the costs of their

[19]   Ministry of Internal Affairs and Communications 2013a.

school life. 'Moonlighters' who earn extra money from casual jobs also belong to this category. Although 'part-time workers' normally describes those who work less than full-time, most of the workers who perform *arubaito* are regarded as having full-time work (including schoolwork).

In popular parlance, the term *freeter* is an established classification that combines these two subcategories (though it excludes married female part-timers) and signifies those young workers who are ostensibly willing to engage in casual work of their own volition. The term comes from the English word *free* combined with part of the German term *Arbeiter* (people who work) and invokes the image of free-floating and unencumbered youths who work on and off based on their independent will, though the reality behind this image is highly complex.[20] Many are the so-called moratorium type youths who are buying time against the day when they could obtain better employment status, after dropping out of either school or other work without clear plans for their future. Some set their sights on being hired as regular employees despite the lessening number of these posts over time. Others accept casual work in the hope of obtaining 'cultural' jobs in the arts or doing skilled craftwork, although paths to long-term employment in such areas are narrow and limited. Still others simply drift in the casual job market, living week by week or month by month, with no aspirations for their future life course.

There are also other forms of non-regular workers, including contract employees (*keiyaku shain*), who are employed in the same way as regular workers for only a specified contract period; temporary workers (*haken shain*), who are dispatched from private personnel placement agencies; and part-time employees who work for a few years after retirement under a new contract (*shokutaku shain*).

These non-regular workers are now firmly embedded in the Japanese economy, which cannot function without their services. They are quite noticeable in Japan's highly efficient and fast-paced urban life, at the counters of convenience shops and petrol stations and in fast-food restaurants, some of which are open twenty-four hours a day. One can also observe many non-regular workers among middle-aged female shop assistants in supermarkets, elderly security guards at banks, and young parcel-delivery workers from distribution companies.

The casualization of employment poses a particularly serious problem for workers in the prime of their working lives. Without having much hope for the future, some drift into the life pattern of the so-called NEET, youth who are never educated, employed, or vocationally trained. It is telling that among males in their early thirties (thirty to thirty-four years

---

[20] For details, see Kosugi 2008.

of age) only 27 percent of non-regular workers are married – less than half the rate of regular workers (60 percent).[21]

2   Performance-based Model

The second emerging trend that departs from the conventional internal labor market model is the rise of new work arrangements, in which short-term employer evaluations of an employee's market value and job performance form the key criteria determining remuneration and the continuation of employment. Some enterprises have started to offer large salaries to employees with special professional skills and achievements while not ensuring job security.

These companies no longer take years of service as a yardstick for promotion and wage rises and have thus opened ways for high achievers to be rewarded with high positions and exceptional salaries regardless of age or experience. Under this scheme, many employees opt for the annual salary system and receive yearly sums and large bonuses subject to their achievement of pre-set goals. Their job security is at risk if they fail to meet the set targets. It has been argued that this system provides good incentives to ambitious individuals and motivates them to accomplish work in a focused and productive manner. Although not representative of a large majority, a few bright success stories of high-flyers who have chosen this path are splashed in the mass media from time to time. Head-hunting and mid-career recruitment have become rampant among high-flying business professionals in the elite sector.

Although a majority of large corporations adopt the performance-first principle in one way or another, the number of employees who elect the annual salary system remains a minority. On the whole, this form of employment is more popular in the service sector than in the manufacturing industry.

The performance model has been subject to criticism in many respects. The system, in reality, requires employees to work inordinately long hours without overtime for the attainment of set goals and thereby enables management to pay less per unit of time and reduces the total salary costs of the company. It has also been pointed out that the introduction of the annual salary system not only creates two groups of employees in an enterprise but also enhances the level of intra-company social disparity and reduces teamwork and morale. At issue also is the transparency of the evaluation process regarding the degree to which pre-arranged goals have been attained. While advocates of the performance model contend that

---

[21] Ministry of Internal Affairs and Communications 2013a.

the scheme is in line with globally accepted business practice, 'Japanese-style' management proponents maintain that it is predicated upon the principle of the survival of the fittest, a doctrine detrimental to the general wellbeing of employees. Even in the late 2000s, in the sphere of value orientation, the paternalistic 'Japanese-style' management model appears to have robust support among Japanese workers: national random surveys conducted by the Institute of Statistical Mathematics have consistently shown for more than half a century that 'a supervisor who is overly demanding at work but is willing to listen to personal problems and is concerned with the welfare of workers' is preferred to 'one who is not so strict on the job but leaves the worker alone and does not involve himself with their personal matters'.[22] Likewise, a larger proportion of the Japanese populace would prefer to work in a company with recreational activities for employees such as field days and leisure outings despite relatively low wages, rather than in one with high wages without such a family atmosphere.

The debate over the performance model flared up because it started affecting the elite sector; 'Japanese-style' management has never fully applied to small businesses, which adjust their employment structure according to economic fluctuations, with workers moving from one company to another with considerable frequency. An increasing number of non-regular workers, those part-timers and casuals with no long-term employment base, are hired and fired depending upon performance and output. One should, therefore, examine the debate over the competing models of work with a conscious focus on the lower end of the labor-force hierarchy. The extent to which the current trend gives credence to the convergence hypothesis discussed in Chapter 1 remains to be seen.

IV   Cultural Capitalism: An Emerging Mega-trend

Culture has become big business around the world, with advanced economies increasingly dominated by the information, education, medicine, welfare, and other cultural industries that specialize in the world of symbols, images, and representations. Japan's capitalism has been at the forefront in this area by producing fresh value-added commodities in the face of growing competition from Asian countries to which the centers of industrial production have shifted. No longer the manufacturing powerhouse of the world, Japanese capitalism has carved

---

[22] Institute of Statistical Mathematics 2009, Table 5.6. In the 2008 survey, 81 percent supported the former type and 15 percent the latter.

out new markets through expertise in the worlds of software technology, visual media, music, entertainment, hospitality, and leisure. In these fields, Japanese companies continue to hold comparative advantage and claim international superiority, thereby releasing a constant stream of cultural products into the global market and reshaping the Japanese economy.

One may argue that Japan has now developed *cultural capitalism*, which relies upon the production of symbols, knowledge, and information as the guiding principle of wealth creation and focuses upon cultural attractions and activities as the primary factors motivating consumption. The debate over Cool Japan and soft power, as discussed in Chapters 1 and 9, has arisen in this context. To provide a map of the comparative features of emerging cultural capitalism as distinguished from conventional industrial capitalism, Table 4.5 contrasts the modus operandi of the two types of capitalism in existence today. It should be stressed that the features in the cells do not denote exclusive properties of each type but exhibit the relative points of emphasis of the two for comparative purposes.

As early as the 1980s, market analysts were quick to point out that the patterns of Japanese consumer behavior were becoming diversified in a fundamental way. Previously, manufacturers sold models standardized for mass consumption, successfully promoting them through sales campaigns and advertisements. Recently, however, this strategy has become ineffective as consumers have begun to seek products in tune with their personal preferences. They have become more unpredictable, selective, and inquisitive. The notion of the Japanese as uniform mass consumers does not effectively account for their consumer behavior patterns today. A consumer behavior study[23] suggested the emergence of *shōshū*, individualized, divided, and small-unit masses, as opposed to *taishū*, the undifferentiated, uniform, and large-scale mass. The research institute of Hakuhōdō,[24] a leading advertising agency, also argued that the notion of *bunshū* (segmented masses) would account for the behavior of consumers more effectively than the conventional view of them as a homogeneous entity. In short, cultural capitalism thrives with mass customization, the production of many different commodities tailored for specific focus groups, unlike industrial capitalism, which is built on the mass production of a small number of standardized goods. If industrial capitalism survives on the relative homogeneity of consumer lifestyles, cultural capitalism founds itself upon their differentiation. Mobile phones, for instance, are frequently revamped with different functions, designs, and colors, fashioned to fulfill the distinct desires of particular and shifting

[23] Fujita 1984.   [24] Hakuhōdō 1985.

Table 4.5   Patterns of two types of capitalism

Characteristic	Capitalism type	
	Industrial	Cultural
Major goods for production	Physical, material commodities	Symbols, knowledge, information
Predominant economic sector	Secondary	Quaternary
Major worker type	Mass production worker	Knowledge and information worker
Employee relationship to workplace	Fixed, location-bound	Mobile, location-free
Market structure	Standardized	Segmented
Output mode	Mass production	Mass customization
Means of consumption	Dedifferentiated	Differentiated
Consumer motivation	Practical use, best price	High 'added value', luxurious brand
Cyberspace dependency	Medium	High
Corporation structure	Bureaucratic, organized	Entrepreneurial, disorganized
Inter-company mobility	Considerable	High
Job security	High priority	Low priority, casualization of labor
Reward structure	Mixture of company loyalty and performance	Primarily performance-based
Labor unions	Pervasive	Insignificant
Means of wage protection	Collective worker solidarity	Individual employee resourcefulness
Sources of anxiety	Subsistence and freedom from poverty	Loss of identity and existential angst
Psychiatric tendencies	Paranoiac	Maniac, schizophrenic
Origin	Industrial revolution	Information revolution
Japanese notion of consumers	*Taishū* (mass consumers)	*Bunshū* or *shōshū* (segmented /or divided consumers)

demographics. Contents of takeout box lunches sold to office workers at convenience stores are highly varied to satisfy the diverse tastes of youngsters, women, middle-aged men, and other socioeconomic groups.

Such differentiation of consumer motivations mirrors alterations in the criteria of class formation. Hara and Seiyama, leading experts in social stratification, argue that inequality has been removed in contemporary 'affluent' Japan as far as 'basic goods' are concerned, while the nation is increasingly stratified in pursuit of what they call 'upper goods'.[25] Absolute poverty was eradicated when the population's subsistence needs were

---

[25] This is a major theme of Hara and Seiyama 2006. See pp. 164–7 in particular.

met. Almost every household can now afford a television set, telephone, car, rice cooker, and other essential goods for a comfortable daily life. Virtually all teenagers advance to senior high school and fulfill their basic educational requisites. In the meantime, community perceptions of social stratification are becoming multidimensional. The different sectors of the Japanese population are increasingly divergent in their respective evaluations of status indicators. Some attach importance to asset accumulation, while others regard occupational kudos as crucial. Still others would deem quality of life the most significant dimension. In each sphere, what Hara and Seiyama call upper goods are scarce, be they luxury housing, postgraduate education, or deluxe holidays, with these expensive commodities being beyond the reach of many people. Thus, social divisions in Japanese society today derive not so much from the unequal distribution of commonplace and mundane industrial goods as from that of prestigious and stylish cultural goods.

It is an established convention to divide economies into three sectors of activity: the primary sector (including agriculture, forestry, and fisheries), which transforms natural resources into products; the secondary sector (comprising manufacturing and construction), which produces finished goods from the output of the primary sector; and the tertiary sector, which offers services or intangible goods and encompasses industries ranging from retail, wholesale, finance, and real estate to the public service. Given that some three-quarters of workers in Japan's private sector are now employed in the tertiary sector,[26] this sector needs reclassification according to internal varieties. Specifically, the recent expansion of areas that make knowledge-based, informational, and value-added products forms what may be categorized as the quaternary sector, which branches off from the conventional tertiary sector. Although no governmental statistics are based on such a category, on a rough and conservative estimate, more than one-third of Japan's workforce operates in this sphere, ranging from employees in the information and telecommunications industries, medical, health care, and welfare sectors, restaurants, hotels, and other leisure businesses to education and teaching support staff, and academic and specialist workers. As Table 4.6 suggests, the number of employees engaged in the quaternary sector far exceeds the number of employees in the manufacturing and construction industries that are typically classified as the secondary sector. These figures are admittedly very crude approximations.[27] Nevertheless,

---

[26] Ministry of Internal Affairs and Communications 2012.

[27] Some researchers of the quaternary sector – such as Kenessey 1987 – include real estate in this sector. The approximation here is quite conservative and simply shows that the quaternary sector now forms an independent, expanding, and sufficiently large sector in its own right.

Table 4.6 Distribution of employees in four Japanese mega-sectors

Sector	% of employees
Agriculture, forestry, and fisheries*	0.6
Mining	0.0
Primary	**0.6**
Manufacturing	16.6
Construction	6.9
Secondary	**23.5**
Wholesale and retail	21.0
Transport and postal services	5.9
Electricity, gas, heat, and water supply	0.4
Real estate	2.6
Compound and other services	8.7
Tertiary	**38.6**
Information and communication	2.9
Finance and insurance	2.8
Medical, health care, and welfare	11.1
Restaurants and hotels	9.6
Education and learning support	3.1
Academic research and specialist technical services	3.0
Daily life services and entertainment	4.6
Quaternary	**37.1**

Source: Calculated from Ministry of Internal Affairs and Communications 2012.

Note: Asterisk indicates the figure does not include privately run household businesses.

broadly speaking, cultural workers undoubtedly predominate as much as industrial workers in the landscape of Japan's workforce today.

In tandem with these domestic shifts, Japan is now seen internationally as a superpower in marketing a variety of products around the world in various areas of popular culture, including computer games, pop music, fashion, and architecture, not to mention *manga* and *anime*. In the field of education, Kumon, which uses special methods to tutor children in a variety of subjects, has spread across at least forty-four countries and territories. In music, the Suzuki method is marketed as a unique and special approach to enhance musical talents. Even in sushi restaurants, Japanese cuisine techniques constitute the core of business activity. Nintendo is now a household name around the world, and computer games made in Japan enjoy immense popularity. So do sudoku puzzles – initially actively commercialized in Japan. These developments reflect the sharp edges of the emerging international division of labor in which the production of cultural goods occupies a crucial position in advanced economies in general and in Japanese capitalism in particular, a point which the last section of Chapter 9 analyzes in some detail.

It is worth noting that an increasing number of workers in the cultural sector, if not all, can produce commodities without being bound to a particular physical place of work. If industrial capitalism originated from the industrial revolution in the late eighteenth and early nineteenth centuries, cultural capitalism exploded with the information revolution in the late twentieth century and was accompanied by the sudden expansion of the internet and the proliferation of mobile phones. Cyberspace technology enables cultural workers to be de-localized, and this tends to facilitate the above-mentioned casualization of employment. At the same time, the creative expertise of cultural products can easily be copied without authorization and pirated inter-territorially. To confront this situation, the 'Basic Law of Intellectual Properties' was enacted in 2002 to safeguard not only Japanese patents but also the nation's contents industry, which produces original texts, images, movies, music, and other creative data, although strict state regulation of cyberspace continues to be a near impossibility.

In this environment, workers become fragmented, with their work–life becoming increasingly compartmentalized. Labor unions, once the bastion of worker solidarity, have gradually lost membership and power, and individual employees attempt to defend themselves by being self-centered, resourceful, and entrepreneurial. At the beginning of the twenty-first century, the Japanese are concerned less with the survival and subsistence issues that govern industrial capitalism and more with the precariousness of their sense of identity and reality, the existential issues that characterize cultural capitalism. This trend forms a backdrop against which people attempt to carve out a new form of community in expanding civil society, a theme that will be examined in Chapter 10.

V   Social Costs of Japanese Work Style

The ideological framework of work practices in Japan, particularly of the 'Japanese-style' management type, has had both positive and negative consequences. No doubt it has greatly contributed to the *omote* dynamism and achievements of Japanese economic institutions. However, it has also produced a number of social costs on its *ura* side, impinging not only on individual rights but also on the health of many workers.

1   Service Overtime

The Labor Standards Act, amended in 1993, stipulates that the statutory norm for working hours in Japan is forty hours per week. Any work performed over this limit is supposed to be treated as overtime, with an additional payment at a higher rate. In reality, however, Japanese companies maintain the practice of 'service overtime', whereby employees work after hours without receiving overtime allowances. On average, it is estimated that less than half of workers (46.9 percent) are fully paid for overtime work.[28] Although this practice contravenes the Labor Standards Act, it prevails in many firms, which take advantage of vulnerable employees who are conscious that their devotion to the corporation's requirements is under constant assessment. Those who do unpaid overtime do so, on average, for more than twenty hours per month.However, paid overtime can constitute an important part of workers' lives today. They tend to build overtime payments into their household budgets to cover housing loan repayments and education costs and thereby compel themselves to work beyond normal working hours.

Although Japanese workers are entitled to paid annual leave of up to twenty days, they take about half of their entitlement.[29] Employees also normally use part of their annual paid recreation leave as sick leave, as most Japanese companies do not have clearly defined provisions for paid sick leave. When employees suffer long-term ailments, it is generally at the company's discretion whether and how long they are paid during their illness.

Article 36 of the Labor Standards Act stipulates that a company's management can require employees to work overtime or on holidays, as long as it has a written agreement with a labor union representing more than half of its employees and has submitted it to the head of the labor standards supervision bureau concerned. The conclusion of such an agreement enables employers to avoid criminal prosecution even if they impose overtime on unwilling workers. However, legal scholars disagree over the extent to which employers may demand overtime of workers. At one end of the spectrum, it is argued that the signing of an agreement binds all unionists to corporate overtime requirements. At the other end, it is maintained that each worker has a right to refuse to work overtime even after an agreement has been reached between management and labor. The reality is that many Japanese employees find it difficult to leave the office before their bosses, because they are under constant pressure to demonstrate their loyalty to the company by staying late.

2 Karōshi

With long working hours established as a norm of corporate life, a significant number of employees have shown symptoms of chronic fatigue;

[28] Rengō Sōken 2012.

[29] In 2011, the average annual entitlement was 18.3 days, but the average annual leave actually taken was 9.0 days (49.3 percent). Ministry of Health, Labour and Welfare 2013a.

some have worked themselves to death. The term *karōshi* (which literally means death caused by excessive work) has been coined to describe sudden deaths brought about by extreme exhaustion and stress resulting from overwork. Heart attacks, cardiac insufficiency, cerebral or subarachnoid (membrane) haemorrhage, and other heart and brain malfunctions top the list of causes of *karōshi*.

Legally, *karōshi* falls into the category of work-related casualty which industrial injury insurance is supposed to cover. In reality, however, it is difficult to prove *karōshi*. In 2012, 842 families lodged applications for death benefits, but government labor authorities recognized only 338 as cases of *karōshi* – an approval rate of about 40 percent, with much regional variation.[30] The low percentage is attributable to the general reluctance of corporate management to release crucial data. The Industrial Injury Insurance Law requires that applications for worker compensation be accompanied by detailed reports on the work schedule of the relevant employee prior to his or her death. The bereaved family must submit the reports to the government Labor Standards Inspection Office, which assesses and authorizes claims for industrial injury compensation. However, companies tend to deny access to full information about the working hours of the deceased for fear of the corporate reality of inordinate hours of labor becoming public. Instead, the company management often provides the family with a gift of money in token of their sympathy and pays part of the funeral expenses in an attempt to cover up the circumstances leading to *karōshi*.

Initially, *karōshi* occurred among such front-line workers as truck drivers, migrant workers from rural areas, and local government employees, but it became increasingly frequent among middle managers of small enterprises and more recently at top management level. *Karōshi* occurs in almost every industry, particularly in the manufacturing sector and in the service sector, where working hours remain extraordinarily long. Volunteer lawyers organized the National Council against Karōshi and established *karōshi* hotlines across the nation to provide workers and their families with legal advice.

3   Tanshin Funin

The firm-based internal labor market system assumes that the firm constantly conducts on-the-job training to develop the skills of its employees. They are required to be rotated from one job to another, from one department to another, and from one office to another. Lateral and diagonal job

---

[30] Ministry of Health, Labour and Welfare 2013d. In a majority of cases, those deceased worked overtime for more than one hundred hours per month on average.

rotation forms an essential component of the development of employees with diverse skills. This system, however, has not only economic benefits but social costs.

Approximately nine hundred thousand married Japanese employees – approximately one in fifty workers – live away from their families because they have been transferred to branches or factories far from their family homes. About one in five companies adopts this practice, known as *tanshin funin* (single posting).[31] It is most prevalent among large corporations and national and local governments. These have about half the *tanshin funin* population, two-thirds of whom are between thirty-five and fifty-four years of age, and about half of whom are white-collar employees occupying managerial, professional, technical, and clerical positions. Among those dispatched to overseas branches, about one-third are *tanshin funin* postings.[32] The Supreme Court and lower courts have ruled that *tanshin funin* is legal as long as it is arranged 'because of corporate requirements'.[33] The judiciary takes the position that employees should endure the disadvantages caused by *tanshin funin*, which is 'not illegal even if it vitiates the stability of the family'.[34]

In some cases, employees accept *tanshin funin* because it involves promotion. But difficulties regarding education, housing, and family health stand out as the major reasons for their acceptance of this practice.[35] The largest proportion of *tanshin funin* employees attribute their acceptance to problems concerning their children's education. High school students, in particular, often face difficulty in transferring from one school to another, because admission to a high school is normally granted to those who have successfully passed an entrance examination in the final year of middle school. Transfer procedures and requirements are often cumbersome and complicated. Moreover, many pupils in elite institutions, even at elementary and middle school levels, are reluctant to move to a different prefecture for fear of having to study at a school of lower standard and possibly losing in the race to enter a prestigious university. These problems mean that when the father takes up his new position, he leaves his family behind.

The second major reason for company bachelorship concerns housing problems. In many cases, house-owning employees would have to let their houses if their families moved with them, but the Tenancy Law gives much protection to tenants, to the extent that they can continue to claim occupancy unless landlords have 'justifiable reason' to reoccupy their

[31] Ministry of Internal Affairs and Communications 2013a.
[32] Japan Institute of Labor 2001.
[33] The Supreme Court's reasoning on 17 September 1999.
[34] The Tokyo District Court's ruling in September 1993.
[35] Institute of Labour Administration 2003.

properties. Because of frequent disputes between tenants and landlords, house owners who are ordered to transfer are often disinclined to let their houses and choose to temporarily separate from their families.

The third reason for *tanshin funin* relates to the health problems of family members. Many middle-aged salarymen live with their aging parents, some of whom are seriously ill or even bedridden. When transferred to a distant office, these employees choose to leave the task of nursing ailing parents with their spouses and move to the place of their new assignment alone.

These dark sides of Japan's economic development are partly attributable to the docility of Japan's labor unions, which often put corporate business imperatives ahead of workers' rights.

VI   Enterprise Unionism and Labor Movements

By and large, Japanese labor unions are enterprise unions which do not cut across company lines. Each enterprise union draws its membership from the non-managerial employees and some lower-level managers of a firm, regardless of their job classifications, and independently of whether they are blue-collar assembly-line workers, clerical office workers, engineers, or company accountants. About nine in ten unionists in Japan belong to enterprise unions of this kind.

1   Decline and Skewing in Union Membership

A majority of workers in Japan, particularly those in small businesses, are not unionized and have no organized way of defending their rights against management. The proportion of the workforce that joins labor unions has declined to less than one in five. As of June 2013, the unionization rate was about 17.7 percent, less than one-third of its peak of 55.8 percent in 1949, as Figure 4.1 shows.

The unionization rate declines with the size of the firm; more than 45.8 percent of workers in corporations with one thousand or more employees are labor union members, but only 1.0 percent in small companies with fewer than one hundred employees are unionized, as Table 4.7 indicates. Labor movements in Japan are essentially a large-corporation phenomenon. They tend to defend the interests of large-corporation employees who enjoy full-time employment status, often at the expense of their small enterprise counterparts and non-regular workers.

The internal structure of organized labor is not uniform. To be sure, the 'all-member-entry' type enterprise unions, where company employees of

Table 4.7   Unionization rate by firm size (2012)

Firm size (no. of employees)	Unionization rate (% of employees)
<100	1.0
100–999	13.3
1000+	45.8

Source: Ministry of Health, Labour and Welfare 2012a.

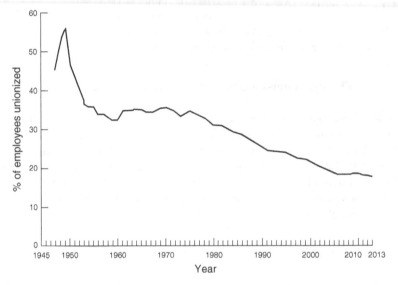

Figure 4.1   Changes in the Japanese unionization rate (1947–2013)

Source: Ministry of Health, Labour and Welfare 2013e.

all classifications are supposed to be union members, form the core of Japan's unionism. However, there are two other types of unions.[36] One type consists of 'plural-type' unions, which co-exist separately within an enterprise and compete with each other as majority and minority unions. In many cases, one tends to be anti-management and the other pro-management. These plural-type unions account for a substantial portion of labor dispute cases in the private sector, handled by the Central Labor Relations Committee (*Chūrōi*). The other type consists of 'new-type' unions, which operate mainly in the margins of the workforce and tend to be craft unions based on occupational similarities and to transcend enterprise lines. Cases in point include unions of temporary and part-time workers, of the mentally ill and physically handicapped, and of

[36] Mouer and Kawanishi 2005; Kawanishi 1992.

female workers. These unions attract membership mainly from workers in medium, small, and petty firms and represent interests vastly different from those of workers in the core sector.

These union activities, however, remain peripheral, as mainstream organized labor tries to find its way into the Japanese establishment and to acquire influence in national decision-making. Increasingly conciliatory and yielding, unions resort less and less to strikes and other forms of industrial dispute. In addition to 'corporationism' making inroads into workers' lives, the strategy of the national leadership of organized labor has contributed to the decline in union militancy.

An overwhelming majority of enterprise unions are organized under the umbrella of their industrial national centers, such as the All Japan Prefectural and Municipal Workers' Union, the Confederation of Japan Automobile Workers' Unions, the All Japan Federation of Electric Machine Workers' Unions, and the Japanese Federation of Textile, Garment, Chemical, Mercantile, and Allied Industry Workers' Union. These industrial unions are further centralized into the Japan Trade Union Confederation, popularly called *Rengō*. It came into existence in 1987 with the amalgamation of separate national federations of unions in the private sector, such as *Sōhyō* (the General Council of Trade Unions), *Dōmei* (the Japanese Confederation of Labor), *Chūritsu Rōren* (the Federation of Independent Unions of Japan), and *Shinsanbetsu* (the National Federation of Industrial Organizations). With the incorporation of public-sector unions, mainly under *Sōhyō* in 1989, *Rengō* has a total membership of 6.7 million as of 2012, accounting for two-thirds of all unionists in the nation.[37] A competing national union federation, *Zenrōren* (the National Confederation of Trade Unions), which is more politically oriented and closely associated with the Japanese Communist Party, has a much smaller membership, amounting to about six hundred thousand (6 percent of all unionists).

Management groups at all levels have consistently attempted to weaken organized labor throughout the postwar years, but at least three additional factors, all of which represent aspects of emerging cultural capitalism, have contributed to its downfall. The first of these is the change in the industrial structure of the Japanese economy. The manufacturing sector, particularly the textile and shipbuilding industries, where the unionization level was high, went through intensive rationalization programs and lost a considerable number of workers. Concomitantly, the service sector, where unions had traditionally been weak, expanded rapidly, and the number of part-time and casual workers increased dramatically. These changes stood in the way of union attempts to maintain

---

[37] Ministry of Health, Labour and Welfare 2012a.

membership. The second negative factor was the implementation of privatization and deregulation programs, which the government brought into effect in the 1980s. These programs attenuated, fragmented, or abolished public-sector unions, which had formed the bastion of postwar Japanese labor movements. In this process, the Japan Railways Union and the Japan Telecommunications Union, which had engaged in numerous nationwide militant labor disputes in the past, vanished from the forefront of the labor movements. The third catalyst for the decline in union membership was the increasing apathy of the younger generation towards political causes, reformist activities, and organized protests. Once a potent political force pertinent to the interests of a large proportion of the working population, most labor unions in Japan have become increasingly irrelevant to a majority of their former constituencies.

2   Capital–Labor Cooperation

The union militancy, which swept the nation immediately after World War II and before the high-growth period, is now a thing of the past. At the firm level, the enterprise union structure makes it difficult for workers of the same job classification to form an inter-company alliance. At the national level, labor has often acquiesced in management's call for controlled wage increases and long working hours in the name of defending the international competitiveness of the Japanese economy. Behind these conciliatory styles of Japan's labor lies a union structure in which only a tiny fraction of union leaders remain labor advocates throughout their careers. A significant proportion of union officials at the enterprise level assume their posts as a stepping-stone to managerial positions. Within the framework of enterprise unionism, union leaders, who know that their term of office is limited, often cultivate connections with high-level executives when dealing with management. This experience gives an advantage to ex-union officials who seek promotion within the company. In a considerable number of companies, the head of the personnel department or the labor division is an ex-union leader. This makes it difficult for union members to lodge serious complaints against managers with union leaders, who might secretly communicate with the management. In most cases, the company management provides union offices and pays union officials' wages. Thus, in many large corporations, enterprise unions often act as the 'second management' to pacify the labor force.

Enterprise unionism presents a major obstacle to the reduction of working hours. Each enterprise union engages in decentralized, firm-based negotiations with company management, but no firm can find it easy to shorten working hours without knowing what competing firms might decide about the issue, since a one-sided reduction may weaken the company's competitive edge. In contrast, Germany, Sweden, Norway, Denmark, and the Netherlands have been able to shorten working hours, because these countries have institutionalized centralized collective bargaining systems.[38] Within this structure, agreements that unions and employers' organizations make at the center bind all firms in the relevant industry and ensure that uniform practice prevails. With regard to working conditions, and specifically working hours, then, the centralized system of bargaining frees both employers and unionists from the anxiety of inter-company competition that is embedded in Japan's enterprise unionism makeup.

In the world of blue-collar workers, Japan's large corporations successfully reorganized the system of management and supervision throughout the 1960s and 1970s. As the core of the rearrangement, they attempted to open an avenue for promotion for blue-collar workers beyond the level of foreman and thereby lower the wall between them and white-collar workers.[39] In the steel industry, for instance, management instituted the rank of *sagyōchō*, operation managers responsible for the overall administration of production lines. Placed between the plant manager and foremen, these blue-collar middle managers were placed in charge of production control and personnel surveillance. As the factory-floor level proxies of high-level managers in corporate headquarters, they were fully authorized to make performance evaluations, attitude assessments, and bonus appraisals of the rank and file in their unit. The operation manager system paved the way for a new career structure in which blue-collar workers could expect to be able to move up not only to middle-management level, but also eventually to the rank of plant manager. The scheme gave a fresh sense of direction to the newly appointed operation managers, who had lost respect and influence as foremen because technological innovations had made their production skills outmoded. They emerged as workplace figures of authority embodying the directives of the company. Furthermore, with enterprise unionism in place, operation managers were union members, and often union officials. This virtually closed off the possibility of unions taking up blue-collar grievances and frustrations as the central issue of labor–management negotiations.[40]

In fact, the posture of most labor unions has been compatible with the ideology of competition. Invoking the principle of equality, they have

---

[38] Deutschmann 1991.   [39] Watanabe 1990, pp. 87 and 189–90.

[40] See Ihara 2007, based on the author's experience as a blue-collar worker in one of the best-known companies in Japan.

pressed for implementation of a structure in which blue-collar workers have the opportunity of promotion beyond the demarcation line between blue- and white-collar workers. When the barrier was removed, or at least obscured, unions approved and even encouraged competition among blue-collar workers seeking those opportunities; in that sense, labor and capital have been in accord.

On the whole, unions of large companies have accepted the management's reasoning that an increase in productivity would lead to the enlargement of the 'size of the pie', which would eventually lift wage levels and improve the living standard of workers. This argument gained credibility among union officials at the time of the high-growth economy, and since the 1960s unions have generally cooperated with management in productivity increases, technological innovation, and organizational restructuring.

Notwithstanding their general partnership with management, *Rengō* and other industrial federations try to represent labor interests, combat managerial interests, and orchestrate labor demands every March and April in their 'Spring Offensive', in a bid to win national benchmarks of annual wage and bonus increases for each industry. During this season, the national industrial unions, with varying success, negotiate with their national counterparts in industrial management in an attempt to gain as high an increase as possible.

The Spring Offensive has established the system in which all participating enterprise unions in the same industry come to agreements with their management, in such a way that the annual salary increase is set to virtually the same figure. Although this used to help unions form a united front against management groups during the high-growth period, the across-the-board figures tended to be settled at the level of low-performance firms in the stagnating or recessionary economy in the 1990s and thereafter. Also, this style of bargaining became counterproductive in the context of growing diversity in the labor composition, salary structure, and working hours requirements of firms in the same industry. The Spring Offensive used to be accompanied by acute industrial action, but this is no longer the case. The overall level of serious strikes has declined so much that strikes have virtually been contained. Japan has become practically a strike-free society.

With the downturn of the economy in the 1990s and the 2000s, cooperation between capital and labor intensified, with unions prioritizing job security over wage increases and most employer groups willingly complying with their demands. With individual workers fearing job cuts, job-sharing and the curtailment of overtime income, along with other forms of salary stagnation or reduction, have become the centerpieces of a labor strategy which has only increased the workers' docility.

VII   Distribution of Corporationism

In response to the oil crises of the 1970s, Japan's large firms implemented a scheme of lean management, a strategy which minimized the number of employees who had well-paid and well-protected jobs with numerous fringe benefits. This program involved shifting some of these workers to small businesses under the control of the large corporations, the expansion of the external labor market of part-timers and casual workers, and an intensification of the work of the employees who retained the privilege of remaining in the internal labor market.

The lengthy recession further eroded the treasured lifetime employment system in large firms and allowed them to justify corporate restructuring. With the strong yen and the concomitant increase in off-shore operations, many firms began to suffer from the oversupply of career-line white-collar employees who had expected to occupy managerial positions. Economic imperatives overshadowed the cultural rhetoric of companies as families, resulting in redundant employees being dislodged from their positions or simply fired. The alleged Japanese culture of group harmony has little substance in this context.

The restructuring of Japan's large firms also entails the partial collapse of the seniority-based wage structure and the introduction of a wage system which uses the achievement of tasks as the prime criterion of assessment. As discussed in the section on the performance-based model above, some employees are now given a set annual salary, depending more upon their performance in the previous year and less upon length of service to the company.

The changing values among youngsters coincided with the degeneration of the lifetime employment ideology. The younger generation is less willing to identify itself with the doctrine of achieving one's position in an organization through long-term patience and perseverance. Thus, the workforce that exemplifies the allegedly distinctly Japanese business practice, the lifetime employment arrangement, has declined in size. The fact that this elite group of employees was a small minority to begin with corroborates the hypothesis that Japan's work culture is much more diverse than that of workaholism, job dedication, company loyalty, and group orientation.

Although corporations wield relentless power over the everyday lives of many Japanese, there is considerable difference in the way in which individuals are linked to the corporate world. In pondering such variation, it may be useful to consider two analytical dimensions. One is the situational dimension, which gauges the extent to which an individual occupies a career-line position in an established enterprise. The other is the ideational dimension, which measures the degree to which

Table 4.8   Distribution of corporationism

Socialization into corporationism	Career prospects in corporation structure	
	High	Low
High	(A) Corporate soldiers	(C) External aspirants
Low	(B) Internal skeptics	(D) Latent escapees

an individual is socialized into the values of the corporate community. Correlation of these two dimensions yields four profiles corresponding to four possible types of Japanese workforce, as Table 4.8 indicates.

Cell A represents the corporate soldier type who holds a promising position in a major company and believes in corporate reasoning. Elite salarymen who are committed to the expansion of their company belong to this group. They are the stereotype of Japanese businessmen. Industrious workaholic owner-managers of small enterprises have similar corporate commitments.

Cell B exhibits the internal skeptic type who is employed in an internal labor market and occupies a post with good income and security but does not accept the ideology of corporationism at the *honne* level. An example would be a career-track employee who gives higher priority to activities outside his company and has little interest in devoting himself to corporate work. Another illustration might be an upwardly mobile department head who works slowly during business hours, stays late only to maximize overtime payments, and does not really care whether the company performs well or not.

Into Cell C falls the external aspirant type, who embraces the dominant values of large corporations but does not have a position within their structure. Cases include backstreet factory workers who want to let their children have a good education in order to acquire a job in a top company, and a non-career clerical worker with limited education who shows an extremely high level of company loyalty and devotion, in the hope of being recognized and promoted in the corporate hierarchy.

Cell D is composed of the latent escapee type, who has little to do with the elite course of the corporate world and has no sympathy with the dominant corporate values. Examples are blue-collar workers who are mainly interested in after-hours leisure activities. Many young female office workers who regard working in a company as a short phase of their life course before marriage also fall into this category. Also in Cell D are most non-regular workers, who have neither job security nor reasons to believe in the company-first doctrine. Given that they amount to nearly

40 percent of the labor force, Cell D's members comprise the largest number of workers among the four cells.

Although the description of Cell A type workers is given undue emphasis in images of Japanese workers, they actually represent only a small portion of Japan's labor force. Greater balance is required in studies of work in Japan.

5   Diversity and Unity in Education

I   Demography and Stratification

The postwar Japanese education system is patterned on the American model. At the age of six, children enter primary school, which has six grades. They then proceed to middle school, which comprises three years; completing it is mandatory. Some 98 percent of those who complete compulsory education then progress to three-year high school.[1] Thus, nearly all students complete twelve years of schooling, making high school education virtually semi-mandatory. An overwhelming majority of government schools are coeducational, but some private schools are single sex.

Beyond this level, four-year universities and two-year junior colleges operate as institutions of higher education. Nationally, about 47.4 percent of fresh high school graduates proceed to four-year universities.[2] The proportion of students enrolling in tertiary institutions has steadily increased, and those who possess university degrees amount to 19.9 percent of the entire population. Outside the sphere of universities and junior colleges, a large number of unregulated, private commercial schools called *senmon gakkō* (special vocational schools) run vocation-oriented courses for those who have completed high school but who are unable or unwilling to attend universities and colleges. Some full-time university students are 'double-schooled' in these vocational schools to strengthen their technical skills and qualifications. As Table 5.1 shows, Japanese who are university educated are a minority; the vast majority of Japanese have had little to do with university life.

The average formal education level of the Japanese is among the highest in the world. Parents and students in Japan are conscious both of the prestige associated with higher educational credentials and of the long-term pecuniary rewards that they bring. As Figure 5.1 indicates, the average level of lifetime salaries and wages of university graduates is much

---

[1] Ministry of Education and Science 2013a.   [2] Census 2010.

Table 5.1   Demographic distribution of final education levels

Final education level	No. of people (millions)	% of population
Elementary and middle school	16.8	18.9
High school[a]	41.4	46.4
Junior and technical college[b]	13.2	14.8
University and graduate school	17.7	19.9
Total	89.1	100.0

Source: Census 2010.
Notes: The figures are based on the entire population at the age of
    fifteen and above.
[a] Includes five-year middle schools in the pre-WWII system.
[b] Technical colleges are *senmon gakkō*.

higher than that of those who completed only high school education.[3] With the general rise of living standards, parents are increasingly prepared to invest in education in the hope of their children acquiring a comparative material advantage in future life.

The most visible class cleavages emerge at the level of entrance to high school. There are various types of high schools. Some are government funded and others are privately funded, the respective student numbers being in the ratio of seven to three. With regard to curricula, high schools are divided into two main groups: those providing general education with the expectation that a significant proportion of their students will advance to universities and colleges, and those specializing in vocational education (such as for agriculture, industry, and commerce) on the assumption that their students will enter the job market of their specialization on completion of their studies. The distinction between the two types is somewhat blurred; some general school students start working immediately after finishing high school, while some vocational students proceed to universities and colleges. A further significant proportion enters *senmon gakkō*.

It is widely believed that the Japanese educational structure is of a 'tournament' type in which losers who have failed in their teens are virtually unable to take up the same challenge in life. This propels students, particularly in elite schools, to make fervent preparations for university entrance examinations. On close inquiry, however, the Japanese system

---

[3] Some studies have cast doubt on the popular view that one's educational qualifications influence one's long-term monetary rewards more decisively in Japan than in Western societies. For example, Ishida 1993 shows that the relationship between the two variables is stronger in the United States and the United Kingdom than in Japan.

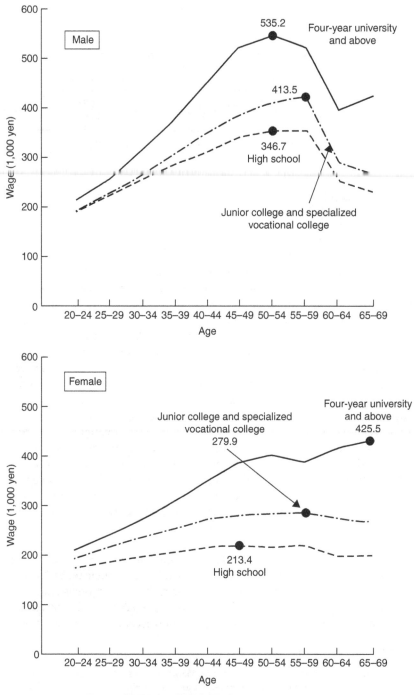

Figure 5.1 Disparities of age-based wages among male and female employees by educational background

Source: Ministry of Health, Labour and Welfare 2012c, volume 1.
Note: The black circles indicate the highest point in each group.

Table 5.2 Distribution of the high school student population

School type	Academic (universities)	Semi-academic and semi-vocational (junior colleges)	Vocational 1 (jobs)	Vocational 2 (private vocational schools)	Approx. % of students
	Destination path				
Government	A	C	E	G	70
Private	B	D	F	H	30
Approx. % of students	50	10	20	20	

Source: Ministry of Education and Science 2013a.
Note: Percentage figures are rounded to the nearest multiple of ten.

is closer to the 'league' type, where one defeat is not the end of the road, because a 'return match' is built into the system.[4] The framework induces many unsuccessful candidates to devote another year or even two or three years to prepare for the entrance examination of their desired faculty. These students, who are between high school and university levels, are popularly labeled *rōnin* (lordless samurai), as they are attached to no formal educational institution and are therefore regarded as 'masterless'. Many *rōnin* attend private cramming schools which train students specifically for university entrance examinations. This group constitutes some 5 percent of the total number of high school graduates.

1   Two Paths of Schooling: Academic and Vocational

The demography of the high school student population is given in Table 5.2, which shows four major options open to those who complete high school education.

The first is taken by about half of high school graduates who progress straight to universities with four-year degree courses, which are made up of three types. The first comprises national universities supported financially by the central government, including many of the most prestigious, for example, Tokyo and Kyoto universities. The second type comprises a small number of public universities funded chiefly by prefectural or municipal governments. The third group consists of private universities and colleges, including such well-known institutions as Waseda and Keiō

---

[4] Takeuchi 1991. He argues that the United States' system is closer than the Japanese system to the 'tournament' type arrangement.

universities. In 2012, of a total of 771 four-year universities, approximately three-quarters were private institutions.[5] Institutions of higher education differ greatly, not only in repute, but also in the nature and quality of the education they provide and the quality of their students.

The second path comprises 373 junior colleges that provide two-year degrees. The number of these colleges has declined over time since a peak in the mid-1990s when the number approached 600. Some 90 percent of students at this level are female, contrasting with four-year university courses, where the male/female ratio is around 1:1. With little academic motivation, many females regard their time in these institutions as a phase between high school and marriage. Though junior colleges are classified as academic institutions, most of them are private and similar to vocational schools in their educational substance, with much emphasis placed on training for home-making and domestic science.

The third available route is the employment track, which approximately 17 percent of high school graduates opt for. Most vocational or commercial high schools prepare their students for this path, and some students who have graduated from general high schools also choose it.

The fourth group, the 17 percent or so of high school leavers who do not succeed in taking any of the above three routes, go through the path of attending privately managed vocational colleges. These include schools for secretarial assistance, English conversation, cooking, sewing, bookkeeping, nursing, computer programming, flower arrangement, hairdressing, and so forth. Such vocational schools, which have thrived outside the formal education system, absorb potentially unemployed youth into a vocational training environment. To a considerable extent they mask the extent of latent unemployment.[6] These schools accommodate many of those who have completed studies at low-ranking general high schools but who cannot pass a university entrance examination or get a job; in this sense they provide a rescue mechanism for mediocre and low performers at high school. Mostly privatized, commercial, and profit-oriented, these institutions remain outside government regulations and subsidies, drawing their earnings almost wholly from students' tuition fees on the basis of a full-fee user-pays principle.

One should bear in mind that about one-half of Japan's youth do not advance to four-year universities, and most of the students outside the first track make no preparation for university entrance examinations. With clear vocational orientations, they are less achievement-driven and more practical. The well-publicized 'examination hell' belongs to a minority of Japanese youth.

---

[5] Ministry of Education and Science 2013a.   [6] Inui 1990, p. 230.

2   The Ideology of Educational Credentialism

The ideology of educational credentialism pervades Japanese society and spreads an examination culture across considerable sections of Japan's schools.[7] In the distribution of occupational positions in Japan, it is believed that educational background plays an exceptionally important role. At the level of higher education, universities are rank-ordered in terms of prestige and reputation in such a way that degrees from top-ranking universities are regarded as essential qualifications for high positions in the occupational hierarchy. Large corporations and the public bureaucracy in particular are believed to promote employees on the basis of the university from which they graduated. Such a belief induces many candidates for university examinations to choose prestigious universities rather than disciplines in which they are interested or departments which have good academic reputations. Thus, those who aspire to tertiary education are intensely competitive in preparing for the entrance examinations of reputable universities.

Extensive mass media coverage of these tendencies influences the normative framework of Japanese education, making its top layer the model to be emulated. The increasing severity of the competition at this level has filtered down through high school in such a way that middle school pupils struggle to get into high schools which produce large numbers of successful entrants to highly ranked universities. Pupils who begin this process early commence their preparations in primary school, so that they may gain admission to established private secondary schools which have systematic middle and high school education geared to university entrance examinations and high pass rates for entry into prestigious universities.[8] Students are expected to digest a considerable amount of material to reach the levels demanded by the examinations of high schools and universities.

Elite academic high schools, which constitute approximately the top 10 percent of all academic high schools, are imbued with examination-oriented culture, although there are fine variations between two types.

---

[7] See Amano, I. 2011 for the origins of educational credentialism in Japan.

[8] Though in comparative terms they are few, pupils who go through the so-called examination hell are over-represented in media stories and scholarly writings, partly because most journalists and academics themselves trod this elite path and tend to identify with those who follow it. Newspapers and magazines play up how hard these students work to pass a series of examinations – curtailing sleep, abandoning summer and winter vacations, and studying unceasingly during weekends. The public is accustomed to annual media hype over which high schools produced how many students successful in gaining admission to which universities. Each year, public commentators routinely lament the negative impact of examination hell on the psychological wellbeing of students.

On one hand, 'long-established schools', which were established before World War II, have room to maintain a 'legacy of cultivating well-balanced "enlightened" all-rounders'.[9] On the other, newer elite schools, many of which were established during the 1960s, are more focused on producing results.

The examination-oriented culture of Japanese education necessitates an elaborate system of criteria for assessing students' knowledge. On the pretext of avoiding subjective evaluation, these criteria give priority to the supposedly objective appraisal of pupils' capacities to memorize facts, numbers, and events and solve mathematical and scientific equations. This framework attaches little importance to the development of creative thinking, original problem formulation, and critical analysis in the areas of social issues and political debates. Thus, rote learning and repeated drilling are the predominant features of Japan's education, particularly at secondary-school level, where examination culture permeates deeply into the classroom. Consequently, Japanese students rank high in international comparisons of mathematical and scientific test results. Critics argue that the nation's school system produces an army of youngsters who have had excellent training in basic factual knowledge but limited education in critical social thinking.

Meanwhile, the degree to which educational credentialism actually prevails in Japanese society remains a moot point. Studies suggest that, in the private sector, promotion rates of graduates from prestigious national universities are in fact lower than those of graduates from certain less well-known private and local institutions.[10] This finding has been debated at length and points to the possibility that the promotion structure of Japanese companies may be based more on competition among individuals and on merit than on educational background, particularly the importance of the *alma mater*.

Practical attempts have been made to weaken the influence of university rank on status attainment in the occupational sphere. In recruiting fresh graduates, some companies have instituted the practice of refraining from asking the name of the university from which an applicant is graduating. Certain ministries within the national bureaucracy have made some attempts to reduce the proportion of graduates of the University of Tokyo in their career-track positions. Others have tried to lower the promotion barriers between elite-track and non-career bureaucrats. Whether these more egalitarian measures actually erode this bastion of elitism or have little bearing upon the overall trend, the fact remains that the upper echelon of the Japanese hierarchy is embroiled in a debate over

---

[9] Okano 2009a, p. 194.   [10] Koike and Watanabe 1979; Takeuchi 1981.

the definition, extent, and consequences of educational credentialism in Japan.

3 The Commercialization of Education

Education in Japan is expensive business. The system imposes a considerable financial burden on families. Although tuition fees were made gratuitous in public high schools from 2010, education is especially costly for those studying in private schools and universities.

University education in Japan is regarded as a private privilege rather than a public commodity. Public universities funded by national, prefectural, or municipal governments constitute only a quarter of higher education institutions. They charge their students tuition fees (approximately 536 thousand yen), which exceed 10 percent of the national average annual income of salary earners (some 4.09 million yen).[11] Although partially subsidized by national government, private universities and colleges have much higher tuition fees plus considerable entrance fees, which exceed the national average annual income at some institutions. Scholarships are few in number and low in value. Furthermore, since most tertiary institutions are clustered in major metropolitan centers, students from rural and provincial areas must pay considerable accommodation costs.[12] Accordingly, students depend heavily on their parents' financial support during their university years. Their support constitutes some 62 percent of students' tuition and living costs.[13] Thus, parents' capacity to support their children affects their advancement to the tertiary level.

Parents' willingness to invest in their children's education has paved the way for 'shadow education'[14] outside formal schooling. There is an examination industry which controls and makes profits from extra-school education. Most important in this industry are *juku* schools, after-school coaching establishments that thrive because of the intense competition over school and university entrance examinations. These schools range from large-scale private training institutions to small home-based private tutorial arrangements. In 2013, some 50 percent of primary school pupils and 60 percent of middle school pupils went to *juku* after

---

[11] Data based on 2011 figures. Ministry of Education and Science 2011b; National Tax Agency 2011.

[12] The average living cost (including tuition) of all university students in 2010 was approximately 1.83 million yen, nearly half the average income of salary earners. Japan Student Services Organization 2014.

[13] Japan Student Services Organization 2014.   [14] Stevenson and Baker 1992.

school.[15] Some attend to catch up with schoolwork, while others prepare for entrance examinations. Still others regard *juku* as a social place, somewhere for them to spend time with their friends. Whatever the motivation, the result of this mushrooming in *juku* attendance has been a decline in young people's after-school leisure time. The *juku* phenomenon also implies that schools have failed to satisfy students' educational needs. Some large *juku* chains have developed such examination know-how that a considerable number of minor universities and colleges commission them to formulate entrance examination questions.[16]

In response to the increasing trend for a five-day working week in industry, the Ministry of Education introduced a five-day week into the government school system in 2002. It was intended that this would provide pupils with more time outside school to play and enjoy individual freedom. Ironically, however, the system has provided the commercial education industry with the opportunity to compete intensely for the expanded Saturday market. With more and more students studying at *juku* and other after-school establishments, the new arrangement appears to have simply transferred a large section of the student population on Saturdays from the formal school system to the commercial sector.

The extent to which parents can invest in the education of their children depends very much on their resources, and those youngsters who finish their education in government high schools and start working at the age of eighteen (Cell E in Table 5.2) mostly come from families lacking economic resources. Some well-placed and well-resourced parents put their children into expensive elite private schools (Cell B) which have single-stream middle school and high school curricula. Some of these schools have links with private universities or track records of producing students successful in obtaining admission into prestigious universities.

In the overheated climate of examination fervor, commercial education firms developed a statistical formula to measure the test result of each student in a large sample with a view to predicting the probability of his or her passing the entrance examination of a particular school or university. This measure, called *hensachi* (deviation score), is designed in such a way that the mean of scores for a group of students taking a test is always fifty and the standard deviation ten. From time to time, commercial test companies organize prefecture-wide or nationwide trial examinations taken by a large number of students from various schools. Locating each applicant's *hensachi* score on the distribution curve, the companies measure the likelihood of success with high accuracy on the

---

[15] Estimated from Ministry of Education and Science 2013d. The samples were taken from grade six and nine pupils.

[16] AM, 25 January 2010, p. 28.

basis of past data on the minimum entry score for the school or university department in question. These scores have provided valuable information for applicants wishing to decide which institution they should apply to enter.

This system of measurement is so widely used that until 1992 most middle schools allowed commercial test companies to conduct *hensachi*-producing tests in their classrooms. The Ministry of Education banned this practice in 1993 in a bid to stem increasing commercialism in school precincts. However, students remain interested in obtaining pre-examination numerical data on their scholastic attainments compared with those of students from other schools. Consequently, firms in the examination industry have continued to conduct examinations outside schools. In the absence of interschool comparative data prior to high school entrance examinations, held in January and February, teachers as well as parents choose to rely on commercial tests that produce students' *hensachi*.

At the top end of the high school hierarchy in major metropolitan areas, reputable private high schools (Cell B in Table 5.2), which have a stake in the business of recruiting high-scoring middle school students, give them 'acceptance commitments' mid-year, well in advance of formal entrance examinations, on the basis of their early third-year marks. Although officially prohibited, this underhand practice continues unrestrained, appearing to emulate the corporate practice of firms which offer advance contracts of employment to promising university students who are to graduate the following year.

Hensachi arrangements are routine among high school students vying for university places. They sit for commercially organized trial examinations which provide candidates, both third-year high school students and *rōnin*, with fairly accurate ideas of their chances of getting into their preferred university department. These scores not only rank students but do so in relation to a numerical ranking of university departments.

Education culture within the elite school setting has gradually come to reflect corporate culture within the enterprise environment. Just as ability-based salaries increasingly represent the human worth of each employee, so too are the numerically calculated *hensachi* marks treated as though they were the sole indicator of the total value of each student. At the core of the examination culture of Japanese schools is a 'one-dimensional system of the rank ordering of abilities measured solely by *hensachi* scores'.[17]

---

[17] Inui 1990.

4   School–Business Interactions

Companies in Japan make a practice of recruiting fresh graduates through school guidance-counseling units. Therefore, Japanese schools interact intensely with the business community in providing job placements for students. In this nexus, many dedicated high school teachers devote themselves to finding jobs for their students. The teachers in relatively disadvantaged schools, from which most students enter the job market immediately after high school education, play a vital role in helping students secure jobs.[18]

Through the assistance of these school officers, high school students who wish to find work would normally start looking for a job and sit employment examinations for various companies in the summer or fall of their final year. New recruits complete high school in March and commence work en masse on 1 April, the first day of Japan's financial, school, and academic year. On this day throughout the nation, companies conduct formal ceremonies where new employees assemble in large halls to listen to pep talks given by their executive bosses.

The school-based recruitment system, which is legally supported by the 1949 revised Employment Stabilization Law, became a widespread practice in the 1960s and 1970s, allowing employers to choose the schools to which they would send job-application forms and related employment information. Students attending schools which companies do not approach have virtually no way of gaining an interview. If prospective employers are dissatisfied with the quality of students they hire from a given school, they can switch their preference to other schools. This situation causes guidance-counseling teachers to maintain and expand recruitment channels with companies in rivalry with their counterparts at other schools. In turn, corporate personnel officers compete with each other to secure a constant supply of quality students from quality schools. Locked into reciprocal transactions, schools and enterprises thus form a central nexus in the recruitment market. These school–firm interactions also shape the hierarchical ranking of schools in each area, and a school's ranking reflects its standing with companies as a supplier of quality job applicants, and the standings of the companies it deals with. Their dedication and commitment in this regard make the scheme work.

A similar system prevails at university level. Prospective graduates commence job-hunting early in their final year, but large corporations

---

[18] See Okano 1993; and Okano and Tsuchiya 1999 for detailed ethnographic studies in this area.

(prestigious ones in particular) consider applications only from students of the universities that they have designated in advance. Students from mediocre universities have no opportunity to be evaluated by these firms. This practice, which is known as the university designation system and which operates either openly or covertly, is the major reason for the stratification of tertiary institutions in the job market. Approximately half of all major companies target only a small number of top universities for the recruitment of fresh employees.[19] Corporations justify the system on the grounds that, in the absence of dependable detailed information about the quality of each student, the most reliable indicator is the level of the university which he or she has succeeded in entering: the more difficult it is to get in, the more ability the prospective employee must have.

From a corporate manager's point of view, the level of difficulty of entry to each department of each university can be measured most credibly by its entrance examination score as reflected by the *hensachi*. With the *hensachi*-based university designation system firmly established, high school students who wish to advance to higher education must pass an entrance examination of a university with a high *hensachi* standing in order to have the prospect of obtaining a good job after graduation. Given that employment opportunities with the best material rewards exist in the internal labor market, particularly in the large corporation sector, students' *hensachi* scores not only represent their chance of gaining admission to a reputable university but are constant reminders of their position in the race for good employment.

Superimposed on the four regular paths for high school graduates is the external labor market, composed of part-timers, casual workers, temporary agents, and other non-regular employees. This has grown as a consequence of the shrinkage of the internal labor market as discussed in Chapter 4. Although on-the-job training of an enterprise's regular employees is a concomitant of the internal labor market, the continual expansion of the external market raises the question of who should be responsible for training its workers and bearing the cost involved. Given the fact that vocationally oriented *senmon gakkō* produce many graduates who enter the external market, the numerical expansion of these institutions provides a partial solution to this problem.

5   Articulation of Class Lines

Educational institutions are, in principle, meant to provide avenues for upward social mobility and to perform equalization functions among

---

[19] *AERA*, 17 December 2012, p. 28.

different social classes. Provided sufficient educational opportunities are available, the bright son of a laborer in a rural area should be able to pursue higher education and to climb to higher positions in the social hierarchy. Most Japanese perceive that this is not really the case. They regard the education system as more unfair than other dimensions of inequality, such as wealth, occupation, and gender.[20] Education-based class lines are discernible in at least four areas: geographical distribution of high-achieving and underperforming schools, differences in family socialization processes, stratification in high school culture, and social backgrounds of students in prestigious universities.

(a) Class Ecology of Schools

Primary and middle schools which deliver compulsory education show different levels of student academic achievement depending upon where they are located. By and large, high-achieving schools are situated in middle-class communities where living space is plentiful, amusement centers are far away, crime prevention associations are few, and mis-behavior and deviant behavior are rare. Schools in lower-class districts show opposite characteristics, and their pupils are comparatively under-achieving.[21] The contrast reflects the class ecology of schools which teachers and education administrators prefer to ignore.

The publication of the results of national academic tests conducted annually by the Ministry of Education for grade six and nine students, for instance, has met strong opposition from some educators who fear that the revelation of school scores could lead to the public ranking of schools and inevitably unveil the class environment of each school – a visible, physical, and spatial reality of class differentiation of education which contradicts the ideology of egalitarianism at the compulsory edu-cation level. Facing this actuality, some parents choose to educate their children *outside* their school districts, a practice which some municipali-ties authorize.

(b) Family Socialization and School Culture

The ideology of achievement-oriented meritocratic competition in schools often veils who defines what is meritorious and who gains an advantage over whom on the basis of defined criteria. An example is the way in which class background affects the amount of study outside

---

[20] SSM 05b, 7, p. 95; SSM 95a, II, pp. 119–22 and 156–7; Kosaka 1994, p. 200, Table 10.1.

[21] Yoder 2004, pp. 28–9.

school, an indicator of students' motivation to learn.[22] The children of professionals and managers study after school far more than those whose parents are in other occupations. Both fathers' and mothers' educational backgrounds also influence the extent to which students study outside school hours. Pupils with disadvantaged backgrounds are generally deprived of motivations to develop academic skills after school hours.

High school students' interests differ significantly between high- and low-ranked schools. Examination hell in high-ranking schools provides merely a partial picture. Students on the bottom rungs of the school ladder find more significant meaning in their part-time jobs outside school, regarding them as enjoyable, useful, fulfilling, and relaxing. Many of them hardly study at home, distance themselves from class work and extracurricular activities at school, and self-actualize in outside work, where they willingly acquire a sense of responsibility and the qualities of perseverance and courtesy. These job-oriented students expect to live independently of their parents, to become self-supporting in their future full-time job, and to marry earlier than school-oriented students. In this sense, part-time jobs facilitate students' self-reliance, self-support, and independence. In comparison with students in schools at the top of the school hierarchy, those near the bottom acquire real-life experiences outside school and mature relatively quickly.[23]

At the bottom of the high school hierarchy are more than one thousand evening schools which operate throughout the nation. These schools cater for a wide range of students numbering more than one hundred thousand. Though little attention is given to this segment of the student population, these evening high schools accommodate a broad variety of disadvantaged students: underachievers at middle school level, so-called problem children, ex-sufferers of 'school phobia', dropouts from daytime high schools, and the physically handicapped. Other students include middle-aged and elderly adults who could not go to high school in their youth. Evening schools also cater for many 'new comer' youths and adults from foreign countries who want to acquire literacy and a high school graduation certificate. This group forms a majority in some schools, which are required to tailor their teaching practices accordingly.

(c) Patterns in Prestigious Universities

The class background of high school graduates continues to influence their likelihood of proceeding to prestigious universities. An

---

[22] Kariya 2008, pp. 78–85.   [23] Takeuchi 1993, pp. 120–1.

overwhelming majority of students who gained admission to the medical schools of major national and public universities graduated from private high schools in major cities which provide six years of integrated middle and high school education, while those who completed government schools constituted a tiny minority of admissions.[24] Highly selective medical schools are now almost monopolized by elite private school graduates whose parents had the resources to send them there in the first place. In these schools, students complete all the high school curricula by the end of the second year of high school and exclusively spend their third and final year preparing for university entrance examinations.

The social backgrounds of students at the University of Tokyo are concentrated in the elite sector. A majority of the students come from families in which the father is engaged in a professional, technical, managerial, or educational occupation. The average income of their parents exceeds 150 percent of the national average income of male wage earners in their late forties and fifties.[25] About half the students at this university come from the top thirty high schools, two-thirds of which are private high schools connected with their own middle schools; students in these schools are trained in a six-year continuous course.[26] With regard to parental occupation, income, and school background, there is little doubt that the children of those who occupy the higher echelons of the social hierarchy and possess greater economic and cultural resources comprise an overwhelming majority of the student population of Japan's most prestigious university. Class plays a major role in determining high school students' access to top institutions of higher education.

II   State Control of Education

The Japanese education system is characterized by a high degree of centralization and domination by the national government. This pattern derives from the fact that Japan's modern school system was developed in the last quarter of the nineteenth century at the initiative, and through the intervention, of the powerful Ministry of Education. Japan had an extensive community base in education towards the end of its feudal years, in the form of many grassroots temple schools run by priests and local intellectuals, as well as schools for youngsters of the samurai class, managed by feudal lords. But the strong leadership of the central government determined not only the tempo of the spread of schools as

---

[24] *Shūkan Daiamond*, 1 June 2013.   [25] Tokyo Daigaku 2012.
[26] *Sunday Mainichi*, 7 April 2013.

modern institutions, but also the shape and content of their curricula. And although the education system was decentralized and democratized immediately after World War II, the postwar liberalization process never overturned the dominance of the state in the management of schools. Even today, the Ministry of Education[27] controls the content and tone of all school textbooks, supervises curricula throughout the nation, and has considerable power over the administration of universities. The vestiges and legacy of prewar centralized education remain a potent force, which maintains a wide range of practices common to most schools in the country. Because of the concentration of power in the ministry of Education, its political and ideological stance has provoked heated controversy throughout the second half of the twentieth century. This structure counteracts the diversification of school culture and propels the unification of education in a number of ways.

1   Textbook Censorship

The Ministry of Education has the power to censor the contents of all textbooks used in primary and middle schools. In prewar years, it compiled its own textbooks and enforced their use at primary and secondary levels throughout the nation. After World War II, the system of state textbooks was abolished, and numerous commercial publishers began producing their own textbooks for various subjects. However, the Ministry retained the authority to modify the content and wording of any textbook and made it a legal requirement that no textbooks could be distributed without its authorization. Because of its power of censorship, the Ministry's policy on the contents of textbooks on social studies and Japanese history has often galvanized the public. By and large, the Ministry's textbook inspectors have sought to censor descriptions of Japanese atrocities during World War II, depictions of political dissent and social movements against the government, and discussions of individual rights and choices. They have tried to sway the writers towards emphasizing nationalism and patriotism, submission and obedience to social order, and duties and obligations to society.

The Ministry attracted international criticism in the 1980s for its directives that the textbook description of Japan's military activity in Asia in the 1930s and 1940s be changed from 'aggression' to 'advancement'. Similar emphatic disapproval was voiced when it was revealed that

[27] With the amalgamation of other government units, the Ministry is now officially called the Ministry of Education, Culture, Sport, Science, and Technology. For the ensuing discussion, it is simply called the Ministry of Education or Ministry of Education and Science.

textbook examiners insisted that Korea's independence movements during the Japanese colonial period be portrayed as violent rebellions and attempted to dilute the depiction of Japanese wartime activities. Section IV of Chapter 8, on the 'history war', will discuss these issues in more detail.

The constitutionality of the government textbook authorization system surfaced as a controversial issue with a series of lawsuits brought by Professor Saburō Ienaga, an eminent historian, against the Ministry of Education. The Supreme Court ruled in 1993 that the system was constitutional and maintained that the state had the right to control the substance of education.

The present system enables examiners to reserve judgment and to provide 'opinions for revision'. The writers cannot expect to pass further screening without complying with these 'opinions'. Authors of social studies textbooks cite instances where the Ministry advised them to change their wording from 'the rights of senior citizens' to 'the welfare of senior citizens' and from 'the rights of consumers' to 'the life of consumers' and also suggested they should include a sentence about the legality of the Self-Defense Forces.

Furthermore, approved textbooks are chosen for use in the classroom not by individual teachers or by schools, but by the education board at prefectural, county, or municipal level, and are bought and distributed en bloc. Because of the size and profitability of the textbook market thus organized, publishers cannot avoid making pecuniary calculations in dealing with Ministry textbook examiners. Thus, market-driven conformity prevails because of monetary considerations on the part of publishing houses.

2   Curriculum Guidelines

The Ministry exercises further control over the substance of education through its requirement that schools follow *gakushū shidō yōryō*, the detailed guidelines on what is to be taught and how it is to be taught at each grade from primary school to high school. For example, the 1989 guidelines (the sixth revised version since the first provisional guidelines of 1947) required all schools to hoist the Rising Sun flag as the national flag on ceremonial occasions and to sing the Kimigayo song as the national anthem, although the public is still divided over these requirements because the flag and song were used as symbols of nationalistic moral education during the war years. Although educators have debated whether or not these guidelines are legally binding for individual teachers, the reality is that the Ministry effectively uses them to force teachers to comply with the government's educational framework.

3   Conformist Patterns of Socialization

The fact that Japan's education structure has developed under the guidance and domination of the central government has left its mark on the way in which routines, conventions, and practices cut across regional lines. Several common patterns of socialization at school deserve attention.

(a)   Militaristic Ethics

Japanese schools invoke militaristic ethics for the 'personality formation' of students. These ethics have multiple layers, but all embrace the notion that some physical training is needed to produce a socially acceptable person.

At the mildest level, Japanese children are expected to follow various forms of military discipline in the classroom. It is part of Japanese classroom routine for a classroom leader to shout at the beginning of a session, '*Kiritsu!*' (stand up), '*Rei!*' (bow), and '*Chakuseki!*' (sit down) – calls that the entire class is expected to follow as a greeting to the teacher.

It is also customary for teachers to arrange their pupils by height order in classrooms and assemblies. Although this gives the external appearance of sequence and regularity, the underlying presumption is that the taller the better; students are always conscious of their physical location in the height order of their classmates.

The most standard school uniform for boys is still a semi-military style of black jacket with a standup collar, and black trousers. Some schools, and many school sports clubs, require male students to have their hair cropped close, a practice similar to that applied to soldiers in the Japanese military before and during World War II. The idea is that Spartan simplicity in school life will cultivate a strong, manly, and austere personality.

The system of quasi-military age-based hierarchy is ingrained at the interpersonal level. Commencing at secondary school, pupils are introduced to a pervasive student subculture in which junior students (*kōhai*) are expected to show respect, obedience, and subservience to senior students (*senpai*). Even outside school, *kōhai* students are expected to bow in greeting when they encounter *senpai* on the street. Inside school, the *senpai–kōhai* relationship is perhaps most intense and articulated in sports club activities; the new members, who are usually first-year pupils, are normally required to engage in menial tasks for the initial phase of their membership. At the instruction of older members, they must serve as ball boys or girls, clean the playing field and equipment, and even wash team members' clothes, without themselves being allowed to practice or train for the probationary period. This convention stems from the rationale that one can become a good player only after one has formed a submissive personality, willing to follow orders from a coach or captain. The belief is that one can develop a proclivity for subservience by being chastened by a series of humiliating tasks.

Every day after school, children must clean their own classrooms, school hallways, stairways, toilets, playground, and so forth. Behind this practice is the notion that pupils learn to be both humble and hard-working through sweeping with a broom, wiping the floor with a damp cloth, and getting their hands dirty. This routine is supposed to train pupils to be compliant, cooperative, and responsible citizens.

(b)   Psychological Integration

Schools in Japan have developed techniques to promote psychological uniformity and cohesion among pupils. It is standard routine in many subjects for a teacher to instruct an entire class to read a textbook aloud, in unison. This gives the class a sense of working together and makes it difficult for any child to deviate from the set pattern. Not only high and middle schools but all primary schools in Japan have their own school song, which pupils sing together at morning assemblies, sporting events, and other ceremonial occasions to promote emotional integration.

Every school has a few annual events for which pupils collectively prepare and which are designed to generate a sense of group cohesion and achievement. A sporting day (*undō-kai*), which all schools have in fall, is among those key events. On that day, every pupil competes in running, hurdle races, relays, and so on. By convention, pupils are divided into red and white groups, which vie with each other for a higher total score. Teachers and parents participate in some races, and *undō-kai* is usually an exciting community affair. A day for dramatic and musical performances is another important occasion on the school calendar. Before an audience of the entire school, each grade performs a drama, some classes sing several songs, and some clubs play music, traditional and Western. Every pupil is expected to take part in this occasion, for which a full day is reserved.

All children in Japan also learn standard gymnastic exercises in groups; these are practiced to the accompaniment of certain tunes broadcast by the Japan Broadcasting Corporation (NHK). The so-called radio gymnastics program has been broadcast every morning since prewar days, and schools across the nation adopted it as part of their physical education curriculum. As a result, most people in Japan know how to perform the exercises, which are expected to be performed not only in physical education classes, but also at athletic meets and many other sporting events. On such occasions every participant is expected to perform the exercises to a standard tune, generating an atmosphere of unity and solidarity.

Participation in school athletic clubs provides another mechanism for the psychological integration of students into school life. Compulsory in the majority of middle schools, such *bukatsu* (extracurricular activities) take place after formal school hours and often on Saturdays and Sundays as well. At middle-school level, three-quarters of boys and half of girls participate in sports-oriented *bukatsu* activities.[28] Generally, the participation rate is high in rural areas and low in the Tokyo and Osaka metropolitan regions. As part of interschool competitions and regional and national games, *bukatsu* both promote a sense of togetherness and decrease the amount of free time available to pupils, some of whom manage to attend *juku* in the evening after finishing school club activities late in the afternoon.

(c)   Check-ups and Self-policing

Japanese schools generally have excellent physical examination programs. Each school has a school doctor or doctors who conduct physical check-ups of all pupils on a regular basis. All schools in Japan keep good records of the height, weight, and vision of every pupil, measured at least once a year. No doubt this meticulous concern with pupils' physical condition contributes to early detection and treatment of their health problems.

A similar interest in the wellbeing of pupils extends to their attitudinal and behavioral 'correctness'. Slogans with such designations as 'goal for this week' and 'aim for this month' usually fill the walls of Japanese classrooms. These class aims are normally of a moralistic nature: 'Let us not run in the corridors', 'Let us try to answer teachers clearly', 'Let us keep our school toilets clean', and so on. In some cases teachers set the objectives; in other cases pupils are instructed to collectively formulate them in class discussions. These exercises, designed to keep pupils in line, are followed by 'soul-searching sessions' in which the entire class is expected to discuss whether the set objectives have been attained and, if not, what should be done in the future. In many schools, each class has pupils in charge of *fūki iin* (school discipline) or *shūban*

---

[28] Nippon Junior High School Physical Culture Association, 2012.

(students on weekly duty), who are expected to maintain class morals. These students assist teachers in ensuring that all pupils comply with school norms.

III   Regimentation and Its Costs

1   Excessive Teacher Control

Rigidity, stringency, and regimentation have increasingly dominated Japanese education since schools increased teacher control of pupils in the 1970s and 1980s. This trend reflected the response of educators to the rise of political protests in secondary schools in the late 1960s and to the growth of school violence in the late 1970s and early 1980s. To suppress potential deviance from school norms, school administrators and teachers tried to tighten their grip on students by shaping their outward behavioral patterns into a uniform mode. This tendency gave rise to what many commentators call *kanri kyōiku*, the regulatory style of education that underscores control of students' bodily expressions and tries to standardize their appearances and personal effects.

School teachers are not a uniform body which supports this trend unreservedly. Many resisted the moves and attempted to maintain the relatively decentralized, liberal structure of education established immediately after the end of World War II. This was most visible in a series of confrontations which the Japan Teachers Union mounted against the Ministry of Education. The union took a firm stance in the name of democratic education against almost every move to reverse postwar educational reform and tighten state control. Though the union gradually lost ground to the Ministry, and lost membership as part of the overall decline in unionization, some teachers still maintain a genuinely progressive spirit. More importantly, many teachers are sincerely concerned about the wellbeing of their pupils, anxious to see them develop their potential fully, and eager to introduce innovative methods of teaching. Accordingly, one must look at the cost aspects of Japanese education in some perspective. Nonetheless, the price of regulatory education is highly visible in many aspects of school life.

(a)   Corporal Punishment

It is illegal in Japan for teachers to use force against pupils. However, in reality some teachers resort to *taibatsu* (physical violence), occasionally inflicting serious injuries. In 2012, 6,721 cases of corporal punishment were reported in primary, middle, and high schools, with 14,208 students subjected to teacher violence and 1,116 cases resulting in physical injuries.[29] Despite frequent media reports on specific cases, the practice has not abated.

In some cases, corporal punishment has led to students committing suicide. In 2013, in a high school in Osaka, as a training method a male teacher coaching basketball repeatedly hit and kicked the captain of the school team, who killed himself in despair. In 2009, in a high school in the same city, a male teacher in *kendō* (Japanese fencing), infuriated by a female student's behavior, punched her in the face and clubbed her with a bamboo sword several times, resulting in her suffering a sprained neck and a ruptured eardrum.[30] A male high school teacher in Gunma Prefecture who coached a female volleyball team inflicted similar violence on a student who later suffered from such severe depression that she could not attend school.[31]

These are not incidents that occur in Japanese schools every day. Nonetheless, teachers' violence against students is not a rare occurrence, and many cases remain unreported for obvious reasons.[32] Some Japanese educators, particularly many teachers of physical education, believe that the military style of training is necessary to make pupils face the world.[33] They see education as a way of fostering in pupils what they call *konjō*, the fighting spirit, tenacity, and doggedness. These teachers rationalize the use of violence as necessary to achieve this goal.

To make matters worse, a considerable number of students, as well as parents, encourage or connive in the imposition of illegal corporal punishment.[34] Some discipline-oriented parents go so far as to praise violent teachers for their zeal and enthusiasm and see the violence as an important means of motivating their children. The behavior of such teachers is predicated on this sort of community attitude.

[29] Ministry of Education and Science 2013b.

[30] AM, 27 November 2009, Osaka edition, p. 35.

[31] AM, 17 July 2009, Gunma edition, p. 29.

[32] Some four hundred teachers were penalized in 2011 for perpetrating violence against students. Ministry of Education and Science 2011a.

[33] According to a survey carried out by the *Asahi Shimbun* in 2013, some 10 percent of high school teachers in charge of their school baseball teams consider corporal punishment as a necessary form of correction. AM, 2 July 2013, p. 18.

[34] An *Asahi Shimbun* survey of 510 students belonging to sports clubs at three universities found that more than 60 percent of respondents regarded corporal punishment by coaches and other leaders as an acceptable form of discipline. AM, 12 May 2013, p. 16. A citywide survey conducted in 2001 by the city office of Kita Kyūshū showed that more than three-quarters of parents believed that in some circumstances teachers should be allowed to inflict physical punishment on their pupils. AM, 28 March 2002, Seibu edition, p. 32.

(b)   School Regulations

Another area of national controversy is the extensive application of detailed school regulations. These rules include a range of trivial restrictions on the length and color of hair, mode of dress, size and type of school bags, type of shoes, and so forth. In many schools, teachers stand near the school gate every morning to ensure that pupils wear the correct items in the correct way, in accordance with school regulations. The prevalent school uniform for girls in Japan is a sailor suit, with a middy blouse and skirt. The idea is that female students should not show too much individuality and must wear plain, quiet, and modest clothes without dressing in gaudy or bright colors. For similar reasons, some schools impose strict rules on girls about ribbons, eyebrows, socks, accessories, hair styles, and so on and check these from time to time.

The Japanese education system displays patterns contrary to trends in other industrialized societies, where a style of learning shaped by permissive choice-oriented guidance is favored over authoritarian training. Ironically, since commercialism and consumerism dominate the world outside school, the very discrepancy between these two spheres of life induces some students to indulge in deviant behavior.

2   Costs of Regulatory Education

The regimented style of education leads to student frustrations, which are often translated into the gloomy situation which some observers call the 'desolation of school culture'. Its two aspects have formed the focus of national debate.

(a)   Ijime

Ijime (bullying) has become rampant in schools since the mid-1980s, the very time when Japan's economic performance became the envy of other industrialized nations. *Ijime* is a collective act by a group of pupils to humiliate, disgrace, or torment a targeted pupil psychologically, verbally, or physically.[35] In most cases of *ijime*, a considerable portion of pupils in a class take part as supporting actors. In this sense, it differs from other types of juvenile delinquency whose actors are restricted to a few individuals. In *ijime*, a majority brings ignominy upon a minority of one, a strong group gains satisfaction from the anguish of a pupil in a weak and disadvantaged position, and a large number of spectator pupils

---

[35] For a detailed analysis of *ijime* in Japanese schools, see Yoneyama 1999; and Naitō 2009.

acquiesce in such harassment for fear of being chosen as targets themselves. School bullying remains a constant feature of Japan's school life, with one hundred and forty thousand reported cases during the six months from April to September 2012.[36] Some children victimized by acts of *ijime* have committed suicide.

Bullying often takes a 'soft' form, in damaging victims psychologically rather than physically, and even presents the appearance of being playful rather than manifestly violent. To the extent that the world of children reflects that of adults, the *ijime* phenomenon appears to mirror the way in which the pressures of conformity and ostracism operate in work environments and the community at large.

(b)   School Phobia, Dropouts, and 'Rehabilitation'

The regulatory education system that emphasizes corporal control produces students who suffer from *tōkōkyohi* (school phobia), *futōkō* (truancy), and *hikikomori* (social withdrawals).[37] Refusing to attend school, they stay at home in their own rooms and often take on autistic tendencies, not even communicating with their parents. Some of these children become violent, inflicting injuries on family members. The number of primary and middle school children who attended school for no more than thirty days a year exceeded one hundred and ninety-one thousand in 2012, with more than 3 percent of middle school pupils falling into this category.[38] Cases of school refusal are, in a sense, children's body language or body messages in response to school attempts to control their bodies.[39]

The frequency of violence that pupils commit in school against teachers, classmates, and school properties suddenly increased from the late 1990s, with the total reported number of cases in primary, middle, and high schools amounting to fifty-six thousand in 2011.[40] Although violence is most prevalent in middle schools, some primary school teachers are forced to deal with so-called classroom disruptions, where recalcitrant pupils pay them no attention and eventually rob them of their confidence, rendering them incapable of running a classroom.

Against this backdrop, unofficial and unlicensed 'rehabilitation schools' have thrived. These are organized by individuals with no formal teaching qualifications, who claim that they have special techniques

---

[36] AM, 23 November 2012, p. 1, based on an emergency survey by the Ministry of Education and Science.

[37] For *hikikomori* cases, see Zielenziger 2006.

[38] Ministry of Education and Science 2013a.

[39] Imazu 1991, pp. 80–8.   [40] Ministry of Education and Science 2013a.

to retrain problem children. Some parents turn to these as a last resort. In reality, many of these rehabilitation schools confine children in accommodation in a remote area and subject them to violence, which their trainers regard as an essential component of the rehabilitation program. These trainers contend that they can change the children by putting them through a series of severe physical tests. As a consequence, some cases of serious injury and death have resulted. These self-appointed educators vigorously attempt to mold pupils and students into a narrowly defined confine of acceptable behaviour, either manipulatively or by force. Such action meets only a limited challenge and finds considerable acceptance in the community.

Violence, dropouts, and other 'problems' in schools are not unique to Japan, but no firm comparative data in this area are available. The cost aspects of Japanese education must be examined against what it has attained. In fact, Japan can take pride in its achievement in high literacy and numeracy. The OECD conducted a survey based on the Programme for the International Assessment of Adult Competencies in 2011–12 to compare the academic abilities of adults in twenty-two member countries and found that Japan ranked first in both literacy and numeracy and tenth in problem-solving competence in information technology.[41] No doubt, the Japanese educational system has produced a highly intellectual and skilled adult population. Despite a complicated system of writing, virtually everyone who has gone through Japanese compulsory education can read and write, making Japan almost free of illiteracy. Japanese shop assistants rarely make calculation errors, an indication that Japanese schools teach pupils numeracy skills with meticulous precision. The regulatory-style education system has made youngsters responsible and cooperative; stations, trains, and other public areas in Japanese cities are generally clean and free from graffiti, unlike some cities in Western countries. These observations formed the background against which rival orientations to Japanese education emerged, as discussed in Section VI below.

IV   Continuity and Change in University Life

One irony of Japan's education scene lies in the sharp contrast between stringent schools and slack universities. Although primary and secondary education in Japan produces highly trained pupils, Japan's universities tend to remain a resting space or 'leisure land' for many youngsters.

---

[41] Organization for Economic Cooperation and Development 2013; AM, 9 October 2013, pp. 1 and 34.

Exhausted, both mentally and physically, by examination hell, some students seek relaxation, enjoyment, and diversion in their university life. Others take advantage of the permissive and non-competitive culture of their institutions. University students spend an average of only half an hour per day studying outside the classroom, while middle and high school pupils in their final years spend more than one hour on average.[42] Japanese students can afford to be lazy, because Japanese firms hire university graduates not so much on the basis of what and how much they have studied as on the *hensachi* ranking of their university. The employment race is more or less over after the university entrance examinations, and grades achieved in university subjects do not significantly alter the situation. University students are aware that employers are not interested in what students have learned in university and rely on on-the-job training and other intra-company teaching techniques to train their new university graduates.

It is true that ambitious students who intend to pass competitive state examinations for the legal profession or for elite public service jobs study hard. The same is true of medical, engineering, and some other science students. But on the whole, Japanese students do not see their university life as a value-adding process for enhancing their qualifications but as a moratorium period to be enjoyed, prior to their entry into the job market. Higher education has come to mean less a productive pursuit of knowledge than a consumption phase of relatively uncontrolled leisure time.

Because of the high expenditure that university life requires, most students engage in so-called *arubaito* (casual or part-time jobs), ranging from private tutoring of primary and secondary pupils to various kinds of manual work: working in restaurants, serving as shop assistants, delivering goods by truck, cleaning offices after working hours, and so on. Although university students all around the world work as part-timers and casuals, such work is almost built into Japanese student life, and the Japanese economy depends heavily on the external labor market filled by university students' *arubaito*, as discussed in Chapter 4.

By and large, university teaching staff members are prepared to pass most students without a strict evaluation of their academic performance. They are allowed to cancel their classes a few times a year without arranging substitute sessions. Students take this for granted and are often delighted to see class cancellation announcements on campus notice

---

[42] Ministry of Internal Affairs and Communications 2011. These figures also suggest that the so-called examination hell phenomenon in middle and high schools is limited to the privileged sector.

boards. A significant number of faculty members in non-science, arts-based departments are derelict in their duty to seriously assess their students, and it is more or less assumed that, once one is admitted to a university, one will likely graduate from it.

The hierarchical structure of Japanese academia resembles that of Japan's business community in several respects. A system of *keiretsu* akin to the corporate world is widespread among institutions of higher education, with low-ranking universities being affiliated with established high-status universities. Professors of major prestigious universities have informal power to transfer their postgraduate students and junior staff for appointment to minor universities under their control, just as large companies relocate their employees from time to time to smaller enterprises under their command. In universities of repute, 'inbreeding' remains the governing norm, with alumni occupying the high tiers of faculties. Upon the retirement of a full professor holding a chair, it is usually the case that his or her associate professor is promoted to the chair. In top-ranking universities, very few outsiders who have graduated from other institutions are appointed to high-status posts, although this pattern has been relaxed in recent years. Just as large corporations maintain a system of lifetime employment, so do universities of high standing fill their positions with their own graduates. In both cases, long-term insiders occupy the executive or professorial posts, and outsiders even of high merit find it difficult to make inroads.

In the climate of globalization, deregulation, and privatization, however, national and other public universities have been transformed since the early 2000s into independent corporate bodies and are expected to display the flexibility, productivity, and accountability required of a business enterprise. This means that universities cannot remain complacent and must prove innovative, efficient, and responsive to the demands of both the student market and the broader community.[43] Universities now normally publicly advertize vacant positions which were once, in most cases, filled through internal deliberations on candidates recommended through personal networks of high-ranking academics. Yet, whether each appointment is based on merit-based open competition or 'horse-trading' behind the formal process is still the *ura* reality remains debatable.

At the top of the hierarchy of higher education institutions, universities are under pressure from the business world as the tide of globalization escalates transnational competition for top-rate students. To recruit talented students from around the world and to produce internationally

---

[43] See Eades, Goodman, and Hada 2005 for the consequences of the institutional reforms of universities, which were set in motion in 2004.

competitive graduates, high-ranking universities offer courses conducted in English. Many Japanese students on these campuses are expected to study in English, so that, upon graduation, they are competent and at ease in transnational communications, although the number of professors who are fully capable of delivering lectures in English is limited. To be in tune with European and American university calendars, these institutions have introduced some flexibility in accepting overseas and domestic students at multiple time points, relaxing the system of April admissions only.

Meanwhile, the declining birthrate (discussed in Chapter 3) has inevitably led to a gradual decrease in the student population. Hence, universities and colleges at the bottom end of the hierarchy are finding it increasingly difficult to attract prospective students and to meet their enrollment quotas. Confronting the prospect of losing out in the struggle for survival, these institutions lower the criteria for student selection or accept applicants virtually without entrance examination.

Under these circumstances, three tiers of tertiary institutions are formed. The old, prestigious universities maintain the culture of elite institutions, while low-ranking universities are increasingly job market–oriented and show little difference from junior colleges and vocational schools. In between the two, middle-level universities mix both orientations to maintain their positions in the university pyramid. Tertiary institutions are not a uniform entity.

V English: Means of Status Attainment?

English-language learning constitutes a focus of debate about how Japan should 'internationalize' and represents an activity that goes beyond formal school education. At one end of the spectrum, some opinion leaders argue that, given that English is the *lingua franca* of global communications, it should be the second official language in Japan to enable future generations of Japanese to manage international dealings without difficulty.[44] English is the transnational communication tool in Asia on which Japan's economy increasingly relies. At the other end of the spectrum, critics maintain that the Japanese should be mindful of what they see as English-language imperialism, in which English is the cultural arm of Anglo-American dominance in the world.[45] They argue that the allocation of excessive amounts of time for English teaching at school will not only reduce hours allocated for Japanese reading and writing but also lead to the virtual colonization of Japanese culture.

[44] Funabashi 2000.   [45] Tsuda 2003; Ōishi 2005.

A hypothetical picture reveals the cultural power of the English language. If Japanese were the dominant language of international communication, Japanese pupils and students would not have to learn English, and non-Japanese would need to study Japanese. Viewed from a different perspective, however, non-native learners of English, under many circumstances, might relish the bilingual and bicultural experiences that are largely unavailable to native English speakers.

Either way, in reality, business firms with global interactions implement programs to compel their employees to communicate in English. Some, including UNIQLO (a casual clothes shop chain) and Rakuten (an internet mall management company), go so far as to make it a corporation rule for staff to speak English within the company setting. Most large companies rely on an English-language test, the Test of English for International Communication (TOEIC), initially developed in the United States (for non-native speakers, with a focus on business English) at the request of the Japan Business Federation and the Japanese Ministry of International Trade and Industry. In 2012 more than 205 million people took the test in Japan. There is every indication that the number will keep rising, because an increasing number of enterprises use the TOEIC score for employment and promotion.

Career-track bureaucrats must acquire practical English. From 2015, applicants for employment examinations for national bureaucracy elite paths must take the Test of English as a Foreign Language (TOEFL), which is used internationally to assess a person's ability to study at universities in the United States and other English-speaking countries.[46] This is a move away from examinations that focus on English reading ability towards more balanced appraisals that include speaking, listening, and writing.

In schools, English teaching faces a challenge. English classes at secondary schools have long focused on book learning, with an emphasis on grammar and translation, to enable high school students to prepare for university entrance examinations which tend to test their grammatical and vocabulary knowledge rather than communication skills in English. Under the initiative of the Ministry of Education, elementary English is introduced at the primary school level in an attempt to immerse children into the conversational English environment at early ages. Since 2011, all pupils around the nation in grades five and six have been taught English at least once a week.

Many school teachers are not competent enough to teach spoken English. In their school and university days, an overwhelming majority of them were brought up in 'bookish' English and have not mastered

[46] AM, 5 May 2013, p. 1.

Table 5.3 Participation rate in learning English by occupation and income

(a)

Occupation	% of population
Professional, engineering	16.8
Managerial	12.3
Clerical	10.6
Sales	8.2
Transport, cleaning, packing	3.5
Delivery, machine operation	2.1
Construction, mining	1.9
Agriculture, fishery, forestry	1.4

(b)

Annual income (10,000 yen)	% of population
1500+	22.6
1000–1499	25.8
900–999	21.1
800–899	16.7
200–249	6.2
150–199	4.8
100–149	5.0
No income	4.0

Source: Ministry of Internal Affairs and Communications 2011, volume 2, pp. 64, 66.
Note: Only the occupational and income categories which show the four highest and four lowest percentage scores are listed.

communicative English. To meet the classroom demand, the government-initiated Japan Exchange and Teaching Program, in operation for nearly three decades, has increased the number of young teaching assistants recruited from English-speaking countries to help Japanese teachers in English sessions. Thus, a wide range of Japanese business and education leaders are galvanized to improve the level of English proficiency in companies and schools.

The dominance of the English language in international communication has drastically expanded with the development of information technology–based global communication. Information sharing and opinion exchange via the internet are increasingly carried out in English between non-native speakers. In Asia, where Chinese is the most widely spoken language, cross-border communications are conducted mainly in English, the unrivaled elite language in the region.

Public enthusiasm for English learning appears to reflect the unsubstantiated proposition that those with a good command of English can achieve higher status positions. Among the Japanese labor force, people who study English as part of their self-education are patterned along class lines, as Table 5.3 shows. Individuals with high levels of occupational prestige and annual income are far more engaged in English learning than those who are less privileged and worse off. By and large, the former are more exposed than the latter to the world outside Japan and find it necessary to study English to meet the daily requirements of their business lives. In other words, English requirements are dictated by the working environment. In fishery, for example, competence in English communication is generally unnecessary and, therefore, would not form a class line in the fishing community. At the forefront of the global trading industry, however, one's English fluency would determine one's promotion prospect and serve as a stratification agent among employees.

It remains to be seen if English-language fluency will serve as a significant agent of social stratification in Japan at large, drawing a class line between those who are English savvy and those who are not. Unsurprisingly, the level of English fluency among Asians correlates with the degree of their exposure to the global environment: the AsiaBarometer survey,[47] conducted by a team of social scientists across Asia, suggests that in virtually all countries in Asia, including Japan, those who consider themselves to have a good command of English are likely to have a family member or relative who lives abroad and to have friends from foreign countries. They also tend to make international trips frequently, watch television programs produced overseas, and communicate globally via the internet, for their work or in their private lives.

Focusing on the Japanese and South Korean situations, Piller, Takahashi, and Watanabe examine English-language learning (ELL) in economic rather than educational terms.[48] They see it as an economic commodity whose availability differs depending upon the social positions of the learners. Privileged students can afford to pay for private tuition in English to improve their access to higher education and to higher status, whereas the underprivileged cannot. The consumption of ELL is encouraged as a means of self-transformation, and ELL is conducive to increased social stratification in the context of neoliberal ideology.

Based on the Japanese General Social Surveys,[49] Koiso suggests that there is every indication that the 'English divide' in the population – the discrepancy between the haves and have-nots of English fluency – is taking shape.[50] On the whole, upper white-collar employees have the highest level of command of English, followed by lower white-collar employees. Blue-collar workers and those engaged in agriculture, forestry, and fisheries are at the lower end of the scale. The level of education also affects the level of proficiency. In terms of generational differences, younger people are more likely to be fluent, because they have more opportunities to use English. Those who enjoyed a higher level of parental income at the age of fifteen have a better command of English, a pattern which suggests that family resources available in one's mid-teens are crucial.

English-language competence, however, may not necessarily serve as all-powerful linguistic capital that enables its acquirers to attain

---

[47] Inoguchi, Tanakah, Sonodah, and Dadabaev 2006, pp. 417–19.
[48] Piller, Takahashi, and Watanabe 2010. See also Piller and Choi 2013.
[49] Osaka University of Commerce, JGSS Research Center, 2003.
[50] Koiso 2009. The level of English proficiency in this study is self-defined.

high socioeconomic status. Arguably, English proficiency is not the key expertise required for upward mobility but simply an auxiliary skill which does not ensure a successful career by itself. English users without other, more significant professional abilities or certificates – whether in legal, medical, engineering, information technology, administrative, sales, or accounting fields – would remain handy translators only. Meanwhile, if individuals are equipped with one or more of these qualities *plus* English competency, the combination would put them in a stronger position. To that extent, English fluency could be seen as a supplementary, not the principal, determinant of social stratification.

VI Competing Educational Orientations

Japanese education appears to be both first class and uncreative. It looks pre-modern in some areas and postmodern in others. This somewhat contradictory picture of Japanese education has given rise to a variety of scholarly and policy-oriented debates about the overall quality of the Japanese education system. At one end of the debate, some observers point out that Japanese education is geared to producing students who are good at answering multiple-choice questions but who lack creativity and originality in thinking.[51] These analysts maintain that Japanese schools suppress spontaneous behavior and enforce discipline so harshly that bullying and other forms of deviant behavior darken school life. For these analysts, Japan's education system represents a case not to be emulated. At the other end, ethnographic researchers tend to point out its high standards, egalitarianism, and meritocratic orientation, while acknowledging its problematic features as well.[52] Some take a positive view of what they regard as the harmonious, group-cohesive, and collectivist emphasis of Japanese education. Others are explicit in suggesting that American schools must learn from Japanese schools.[53] The two competing perspectives reflect fundamental ideological differences among researchers regarding the extent to which educational institutions should perform functions that legitimize the existing order and transmit social values and basic skills from one generation to another or should liberate students from past conventions and traditions.

Against this backdrop, from the 1990s onward, a strong lobby group of business people and academics have successfully pressed for what they call the liberalization of education, in line with the philosophy of

---

[51] Ambaras 2006; McVeigh 2000; Schoolland 1990.
[52] Cave 2007; Fukuzawa and LeTendre 2001; Sato 2003.
[53] Stevenson and Stigler 1992; Vogel 1979.

Table 5.4 Four competing educational orientations

Institutional focus	State control	
	Curtailment	Preservation
Incentive-based variety	(A) Market-oriented neoliberals	(B) Regulatory pluralists
Structural equality	(C) Anti-government democrats	(D) Developmental conservatives

privatization and deregulation, and for the reduction of government control and the operation of the free market within the education system. They maintain that overly obedient workers without much initiative are counterproductive to the increasingly internationalized Japanese economy, which now requires diverse, innovative, and creative human resources to confront global competition. Moreover, it is argued that the egalitarianism which Japan's school culture has embraced in the second half of the twentieth century has had negative effects on student motivation. Because schools attempt to ensure equal treatment of all pupils regardless of their academic abilities and achievements, the degree to which students are motivated to study depends more on their family background than on any school-based incentives. In this sense, it is argued, 'parentocracy' rather than meritocracy has prevailed.[54]

Proponents of the market-oriented education system, often referred to as neoliberals, have set the stage for a series of debates for the past couple of decades. Although few would disagree with the importance of students' academic achievements and creative skills, educators differ on two fronts as to how to achieve these broad goals: first, the degree to which the state should control education is under contention; and second, the extent to which Japan's education should focus on incentive-based variety or structural equality is at issue. As shown in Table 5.4, four models compete with each other, exhibiting different positions vis-à-vis these two issues.[55]

Cell A represents the neoliberal approach to education, which favors market-driven elite education. This stance has gained ground against the backdrop of the globalization of the economy and with the support of major business organizations and the urban middle class. The exponents of this position maintain that the Japanese economy requires individuals

---

[54] Kariya 2001 and 2008 argue that ideological egalitarianism in schools has served only to intensify a family-based, inter-generational consolidation of stratification and inequality in the educational process.

[55] See Okano 2009b for a different typology.

who can adapt themselves to the increasingly internationalized business environment with individual initiative, flexibility, and cultural skills. This approach takes the view that Japan's educational system must introduce more student-centered, innovation-oriented, and problem-solving programs to produce a labor force which can meet the challenge of the rising tide of knowledge-intensive and high tech–focused capitalism.

Neoliberal thinking has influenced a number of areas. Since the beginning of the twenty-first century, an increasing number of individual teachers and schools have been given the freedom to introduce a new 'interdisciplinary' subject. To provide a wide range of choices, strict school zoning was relaxed in some prefectures to enable students to enroll in schools of their preference. Some schools now recruit principals from the business world to bring in management methods to make teaching efficient and productivity based. English classes, which used to be taught at middle-school level and beyond, are now offered at many primary schools in the belief that the younger generation should be more literate and fluent in the contemporary *lingua franca* of the global economy.

Cell B represents the orientation of what one might call regulatory pluralists who support some liberalization in education while maintaining that state control should remain intact. Policy-makers in the Ministry of Education appear to be headed towards this direction in terms of both meeting the neoliberal challenge and maintaining their vested interests. Since the late 1980s, they have encouraged more liberal education aimed at the formation of the whole person and free from excessive pressure to rote learn. They argued that Japanese children lack both individual autonomy and interpersonal sociability and should develop broader skills for social activities and contributions in the age of internationalization in a more relaxed and pluralistic environment. In 2002, the Ministry of Education revised its official national guidelines to promote so-called *yutori kyōiku* (pressure-free education), which led to the reduction of educational curricula and class hours and the introduction of 'interdisciplinary' classes. Instead of assessing a school child's ability relative to others, the system instituted an evaluation scheme based on an absolute scale. It was emphasized that pupils' achievements should be measured not only in terms of 'results' but also 'processes' so that the efforts of pupils who work hard but still attain only low marks can be properly rewarded.

With no classes now held on Saturdays, a five-day week was adopted in a bid to give pupils more time to play, socialize, and enjoy work outside the formal school system, to encourage the development of fully fledged personality and individuality. Some primary and middle schools combined to become integrated schools to provide students with a more diverse social environment.

The scheme of special educational zones (*kyōiku tokku*), introduced in 2003, entitles schools in particular areas to prioritize specific programs. Although many schools take advantage of teaching English beyond national benchmarks on the basis of this new system, it also makes it possible for interested groups to set up schools for alternative education and for underachievers in specified localities. Many of these schools operate as companies. Civil NPOs can now establish schools for students with special needs or from underprivileged backgrounds to meet their special needs. Some of these schools occupy the facilities of closed schools. Others encourage their students to learn in direct contact with the natural environment in the countryside. Still others run correspondence schools which pupils physically attend on a flexible basis.

Cell C comprises a 'democratic' model shared by those who are concerned with what they regard as increasing inequalities in education while remaining critical of state regulatory power, favoring the deregulated, relaxed education that allows latitude for a variety of choices and options. This framework claims to inherit the educational ideals of 'postwar democracy', which underscored the spirit of egalitarianism and social justice. The Japan Teachers' Union remains committed to this line of thinking, together with such left-leaning political parties as the Japan Communist Party and the Social Democratic Party of Japan, which have taken anti-government positions over decades. Disapproving of the state control of education and the examination-focused practices in schools, those in this camp, who often label themselves as 'progressive educators', are concerned with prevailing structural inequalities that afford different opportunities to different social classes.

Generally inclined to be anti-government, 'progressive educators' direct their criticism at educational credentialism, rote learning, competitive university examinations, and extra-school educational providers (such as *juku*) and argue for a curriculum that develops students' originality, creativity, and problem-solving skills. Although neoliberals use similar language, democrats depart from this group in stressing that these attributes be encouraged equally among all students and not reserved for the elite.

Democrats point out that the introduction of market-oriented liberalism in education has enabled elite private schools, ambitious government schools, and *juku* to offer excessive inducements to allow students to compete successfully in examinations. Many top private schools that conduct six-year integrated middle and high school education teach required materials over five years and reserve the final, sixth year exclusively for preparations for high-ranking universities. Some government schools hire *juku* instructors and organize evening and weekend classes to equip their students with the skills and techniques that help them to pass the entrance examinations of prestigious universities. The democrats maintain that the relaxation of national curricula enables the private-sector examination industry to expand its influence on the formal school system.

Cell D represents the conventional state-led uniform education with an emphasis on national homogeneity and equality. This approach is in harmony with the discourse that governed the high-growth economy of the 1960s to the 1980s when Japan underwent rapid development under the powerful national bureaucracy. The advocates of this model argue that it ensured relatively egalitarian and uniform education across regions and classes, a pattern now eroded by neoliberal and pluralist policies. Influential in the Liberal Democratic Party and the interest groups that represent rural residents and independent small business owners, this view tends to attribute the ills of Japanese society today to the failure of the excessively liberal and democratic styles of education that post–World War II educational reforms brought about. Its proponents are also adamant that forms of education that give children too much freedom and too many choices have lowered the level of their academic ability.[56] The supposed decline in students' scholastic outcomes paved the way for the introduction of the nationwide achievement test in 2007 which measures the distribution of academic scores across areas and schools.

Attaching importance to the nation's tradition, national pride, and patriotism, champions of the conservatives argue that stricter control and discipline should be introduced into schools to educate pupils to 'love Japan' and to respect the national flag and anthem. Hostile to the school culture that these proponents believe the Allied Occupation Forces imposed on Japan immediately after the surrender in 1945, they have successfully managed to require schools to hoist the flag and have students sing the anthem on ceremonial occasions. On the right wing of the conservative spectrum, a group of academics which had criticized Japan's history textbooks as 'excessively masochistic' in 2001 produced a textbook of their own which glorified Japan's past and whitewashed the darker aspects of its history. Despite arousing severe criticism from domestic civic groups, teacher organizations, and the governments of South Korea and China, the Ministry authorized the book after insisting on a number of amendments. However, even with this authorization, most government schools remain reluctant to adopt the text.

In some respects, the four models overlap and the lines of demarcation between them are blurred, because they often employ the same

---

[56] Tose, Okabe, and Nishimura 1999 and 2000.

language, although they may have different motives. Yet, the complex interrelations and interactions between educational liberalism and academic attainment, student motivation and family background, and ideological egalitarianism and structural stratification form intricate matrices, the interpretation of which will continue to dominate Japan's pedagogical debate in the coming decade.

6   Gender Stratification and the Family System

The rise of feminism outside and inside Japan has sensitized observers to gender stratification in Japanese society and has directed attention to a wide range of questions. In what ways are Japanese women subjected to a Japan-specific system of gender control? What kinds of gender barriers exist in Japan's labor market? How is female sexuality regulated in Japan? How are women disadvantaged in the Japanese family structure? This chapter examines these issues as the most fundamental problems of stratification, arguably more pivotal than other forms of inequality in contemporary Japan. Specifically, this chapter examines the patriarchal family registration system, which is embedded in gender relations and the family system in Japan, women's employment situation in the labor market, issues of sexuality and reproduction, marriage and divorce, and various types of family life.

I   The Family Registration System and *Ie* Ideology

Beneath Japan's gender relations and family system lies an elaborate system of registration which penetrates into the life of every Japanese and controls it in a fundamental way. The *koseki* (family registration) system is the cornerstone of the scheme, representing the usually veiled *ura* aspect of Japanese family structure. The basic unit of *koseki* is not an individual, but a household. The records of each individual's gender, birthplace, date of birth, parents' names, position among siblings, marriage, and divorce are kept in detail in each household *koseki* and filed in the local municipal office.

The concept of family lineage is built into the *koseki* system. Technically, one can remove one's name from the current register and establish an independent *koseki* at any time, but most people do this at the time of marriage. Up to two generations, typically a couple and their children, can be included in a *koseki*. A three-generation register is legally unacceptable; for example, if grandparents, a married couple, and their children live under the same roof, the grandparents must keep their own *koseki* and the two younger generations keep a separate one. How each individual branched off from a previous *koseki* register is an important piece of information in the current register.

In the hands of organizations, the *koseki* has become a powerful instrument that provides full personal information about members, as it has become widespread practice for organizations to require potential members to submit a copy of their *koseki* when they seek membership. *Koseki* data are required for many other crucial occasions. In the past, companies required job applicants to submit their *koseki* papers. Minority groups, particularly the *buraku* activists, vehemently opposed this practice, because the companies were able to discriminate against *burakumin* whose minority backgrounds were indirectly identified by the papers showing their birthplace and permanent address. Although this convention was gradually abolished in the 1970s in response to the protests of *buraku* movements, the system works as a powerful deterrent to deviant behavior, because 'stains' in *koseki* negatively affect the life-chances of all family members. As each *koseki* is organized on a household basis, those who acquire a copy can examine the attributes not only of an individual, but also of his or her family members.

Supporting the family registration system, a *jūmin-hyō* (resident card) system requires each household to register its address and membership with the municipal office of its current place of residence. Accordingly, when a family moves from area A to area B, it must remove its old residence status from the municipal office of area A then report its new address and other family information to the municipal office of area B. In this way, the Japanese government secures detailed information about each household and its history through local governments. The resident card previously contained information identifying the gender, sibling order, and legitimacy status of each child, but the scheme was revised in 1995 so that each child is now listed simply as 'child', a change which feminist groups had long demanded.[1]

Behind the twin institutions of the family registration system and the resident card system lies the ideology of *ie*, which literally means house, home, or family but signifies something much more than these English words imply. *Ie* represents a quasi-kinship unit with a patriarchal head and members tied to him through real or symbolic blood relationship. In the prewar civil code, the head was equipped with almost absolute power over household matters, including the choice of marriage partners for his family members. The headship of *ie* was transferred from one generation to another through primogeniture, whereby the first son normally

---

[1] In the *koseki* system, the sibling order of each child constitutes an essential piece of information.

inherited most of the property, wealth, and privilege of the household, as well as *ie* headship. As a general rule, the second and younger sons established their own branch families, which remained subordinate to the head family. For the continuation of *ie* arrangements, it was not unusual for a family without a son to adopt a boy from a different family. Each *ie* unit was expected to provide fundamental support for the imperial system. The postwar civil code considerably dismantled the patriarchal elements with the introduction of the general principle of gender equality. However, the ideology associated with the *ie* system still persists as an undercurrent of family life in Japan, and some key ingredients of the *ie* practice survive at the beginning of the twenty-first century in the maintenance of the *koseki* system, which disadvantages women in a number of ways.

1   The Notion of Household Head

The system makes the household the source of information and requires each household to nominate its head.[2] In reality, nearly all heads are male: some 96 percent of couples who marry nominate the husband as head of the household.[3] The head is listed at the beginning of the register, separately from his individual entry as a member of the household. His *honseki* (permanent address) becomes that of his household, requiring its members to assume the same *honseki* as long as they remain listed in the same register. When the household head changes his surname for some

[2] The Ministry of Home Affairs defines the concept of household head in some detail on the basis of patriarchal principles:

1   In the case of the father and his first son both earning a living for the household, the father should be deemed its head in accordance with commonly accepted ideas, even if the father's income is less than that of the first son.
2   In the case of the father being his first son's dependant in terms of income tax law and his first and second sons both earning a living for the household, the first son should be deemed its head even if his income is less than that of the second son.
3   In the case of neither the father nor his first son having any income and the second son being chiefly responsible for earning a living for the household, the first son should be deemed its head in accordance with commonly accepted ideas, so long as he is regarded as only temporarily unemployed.
4   The wife becomes the household head when the husband has no income and the wife earns a living.

'Questions and answers concerning the Law on Basic Registers of Residents', a notice dispatched by the head of the Administration Department of the Ministry, cited in Satō 1991, pp. 138–9.
[3] Ministry of Health, Labour and Welfare 2006b, Table 13.

reason, the members of the household must change their surname in the *koseki* to match his. Even when the household head dies, his headship continues in his household register as long as other members of the household remain listed in it. Accordingly, in many cases, a widow remains in her husband's *koseki* even after his death.[4] Furthermore, Article 772 of Japan's civil code stipulates that a baby born within three hundred days of a formal divorce is entered into the *koseki* of the household head, who is the ex-husband in nearly all cases. This requirement applies even if he is not the baby's biological father. Thus, the *koseki* scheme deters women from divorcing, preserves the male advantages of the patriarchal order, and protects the *ie* system in a fundamental way.

2   Children Born out of Wedlock

The *koseki* system makes a status distinction between children born in lawful marriage and those born out of wedlock. This has serious implications for inheritance, because Japan's civil code stipulates that the spouse of the deceased is entitled to half the estate, with the remaining half to be distributed equally among the children of the deceased. This is a big change from the prewar code, in which the first son inherited the property and wealth of the household almost exclusively. However, children born out of wedlock are entitled to only half the entitlement of legitimate children. The Supreme Court ruled in September 2013 that this provision of the civil code violates Article 14 of Japan's Constitution, which guarantees equality under the law.[5] Reflecting the diversification of family values, more than twenty-three thousand babies were born out of wedlock in 2012, amounting to some 2.2 percent of babies born in that year,[6] a situation the judiciary could not ignore. Although the ruling makes it necessary for the civil code to be amended, the proportion of children born outside formal marriage remains very low in comparison with other countries (Sweden, France, Denmark, the United Kingdom, the Netherlands, and the United States all exceed 40 percent[7]), an indication that the *koseki* system serves as a disincentive to de facto relationships and keeps consolidating the norm that formal marriages should be the only form of union.

The *koseki* system requires a birth to be recorded on the mother's family documents even if the child is given up for adoption. Since the system records illegitimate births as a matter of public registration, women often opt for abortion to avoid the social stigma of having an illegitimate

---

[4] Sakakibara 1992, pp. 88–90.   [5] MM, 5 September 2013, p. 1.
[6] Ministry of Health, Labour and Welfare 2013f.
[7] Ministry of Health, Labour and Welfare 2013f.

child officially recorded. Doctors are prosecuted for encouraging women who became pregnant out of wedlock to give birth and for making arrangements for childless couples to adopt and register as their own children the babies thus born. These doctors' actions are illegal under the family registration law, although they could arguably be morally justified given the large number of unwed pregnant women who want neither to have an abortion nor to keep a baby born outside marriage. There are also numerous childless families desperate to adopt a baby. The family registration system thus socially penalizes single mothers and their children, thereby serving as a powerful apparatus to preserve 'traditional' family structure and values.

3   Deterrence to Divorce

The family registration system has been an important deterrent to divorce. The divorce rate in Japan has progressively increased since the 1960s, reaching a peak at the beginning of the twenty-first century. However, it has never matched the level recorded in the last quarter of the nineteenth century, when couples freely chose to marry or divorce in conformity with their local customs. The highest recorded divorce rate (divorces per one thousand persons) was 3.4 in 1883, while the postwar peak was 2.3 in 2002.[8] With the enactment of the nationally uniform civil code at the end of the nineteenth century and the national consolidation of the *koseki* system, marriages and divorces became a matter of government regulation and official registration, and the divorce rate in the first half of the twentieth century declined sharply. Although the annual total of divorces has increased in postwar Japan, the divorce rate remains close to the same level as at the end of the nineteenth century, and is among the lowest recorded in industrially advanced nations.

Economic considerations are, of course, the predominant reason why many women stay in marriages; those who depend on their husbands financially have little choice but to continue to live with them. In addition to this major constraint, the *koseki* system puts another restraint on the possibility of divorce. Divorce requires two separate family registers to be established; if the couple have children, each child must be moved to one of the new registers, in most instances the mother's. Because copies of these papers are often required on such crucial occasions as employment,[9] passport acquisition, marriage, divorce, and inheritance,

---

[8] Yuzawa 1987, pp. 166–7; Ministry of Health, Labour and Welfare 2013f.

[9] Although in *tatemae* (see Chapter 1) companies are not allowed to require job applicants to submit their *koseki* papers (to protect private information), there are many reported cases in which job applicants were asked to do so immediately after employment. It is usually

the children of divorced parents can be stigmatized through this public documentation. Fearful of a 'stain' being placed on their children's registers, many married couples, particularly women who are deeply involved emotionally in their children's wellbeing, vacillate over divorce even when that option is a sensible one. On the whole, the system serves as an impediment to divorce and thus buttresses the patriarchal marriage structure.

4   Surname after Marriage

The *koseki* system requires that on marriage wife and husband take the same surname, which must be one of their former surnames. Legally, a married couple are not allowed to keep different surnames. When Ms Toyota and Mr Suzuki marry, they must both become either Toyota or Suzuki, and one of them must abandon their pre-marriage surname. In virtually all cases the woman abandons her surname and is entered into the register of her husband, who is usually listed as the household head.

Some women, mainly professionals, choose to use their maiden name as a *tsūshō* (popular name) or promote the practice of *fūfu bessei* (different surnames despite formal marriage) and thereby challenge the rigid requirements of the family registration system.[10] In response to calls from women's groups for a more liberal approach to the surname issue, governmental administrative councils have been making recommendations to change the *koseki* requirements, although no legislation has eventuated. A national survey conducted by the Cabinet Office in 2012 revealed that public opinion was almost evenly divided over whether to amend the civil code so that couples could assume different surnames. A considerable majority of those who opposed an amendment believed that it would affect children negatively.[11]

5   The Family Tomb

Japan's conventional funerals exhibit the endurance of *ie* principles. The common practice is for the body of the deceased to be brought back home, even if he or she died in hospital. A wake is held nearly all night

the case that successful applicants are required to submit certified copies of selected items on their *jūmin-hyō* (resident card) to the hiring company.

[10] Some feminists call this the trap of separate surnames. See Ueno 2009, pp. 199–205.

[11] Cabinet Office 2013b.

beside the body at the house where the person lived. Memorial services are also normally held at home, before the body is taken to a crematorium.

Following the convention of ancestral lineage, most families have family tombs where their ancestors are believed to be entombed. By convention, 'descendants' include women who have married male offspring of the family genealogy. Because the *koseki* system is predicated upon the patriarchal logic that the wife belongs to her husband's family line as his subordinate, she is usually buried in his family tomb with his ancestors. Nevertheless, increasing inter-regional mobility, diversified family structure, and land price inflation have induced a substantial number of people, particularly women in urban areas, to reconsider the traditional methods. They object to the custom of family-tomb burial, with its close links with *ie* ideology. Although the family registration system does not dictate where one should be buried, it provides a framework in which the patriarchal system governs women even after death.

6   *Seki* and *Ie*

In a broader context, the Japanese social system is supported by the notion of *seki*, the view that unless one is formally registered as belonging to an organization or institution, one has no proper station in society. As *seki* pervades Japanese life fundamentally, most Japanese are greatly concerned about which *koseki* they are registered in and the form their entry takes. *Nyūseki* (entry into a register) and *joseki* (exit from a register) are cause for anxiety. The notion of *seki* also manifests itself in *gakuseki* (school registry), which is a national student dossier system. After death, one is supposed to be registered in *kiseki* (the registry of those in the posthumous world).

The *ie* system survives in community life in a visible way. Almost every Japanese household has a *hyōsatsu* (nameplate) on or near its gate or front door. The plate displays the surname of the household, often with the given name of its head. In some cases, the names of all household members are exhibited, with that of the household head first and in slightly larger characters. While aiding postal workers, newspaper deliverers, and visitors, these plates serve as a constant reminder that the *koseki*-style ideology permeates the psyche of most Japanese. Those who do not possess Japanese citizenship cannot establish their own *koseki* and are thus clearly distinguished from Japanese nationals.

Although every society has some system of registration – such as electoral rolls, social security numbers, and birth and marriage certificates – Japan's family registration system differs from others in using the household as the unit, packaging a range of information into each *koseki*, and socially ostracizing those who do not fit into the male-dominated conventional family structure promoted by the *koseki* system. This is why de facto relationships are often kept hidden, although de facto couples, as well as sexually alternative groups, have become more vocal in recent years (see Chapter 9). The small number of de facto relationships occur mainly among professional women who relish economic independence and good career prospects, and among lower-class women who have little to lose from negative public perceptions. Thus, the understanding of gender relations in Japan requires an in-depth knowledge of the working of the family registration system, which affects all Japanese at every turn of their lives, functioning as an often invisible, but highly effective, way of maintaining patriarchal order.

II   The Labor Market and Women's Employment Profiles

1   The M-shaped Curve of Women's Employment

Japan's female workers in 2013 constituted more than 40 percent of the total paid workforce. The workforce participation rate of Japanese women has shown a steady upward trend, and more than 60 percent of all women between fifteen and sixty-five years of age are engaged in waged labor. Married middle-aged women from forty-five to fifty-four years of age have the highest labor-force participation rate among women in various age groups, with three in four being employed in one form or another.[12] With regard to industrial classification, women are concentrated in the tertiary industry, in particular in the service, sales, restaurant, finance, and insurance sectors. In the manufacturing industry, women are conspicuous in light industries, such as textile and food production, rather than in heavy industries. On the surface, these statistics suggest that women do not regard domestic labor as their only option and play a highly significant role in the labor market.

Unlike most men, however, the majority of women who explore the possibility of entering the job market solve complex equations involving many variables. From a life-cycle perspective, women must generally make decisions at three different times: at marriage, following childbirth, and when their last child commences schooling. Figure 6.1 demonstrates that the younger generation, which has produced fewer children and has an increased life expectancy, has a far longer post-childrearing period of life compared with preceding generations. Furthermore, only about

---

[12] Ministry of Internal Affairs and Communications 2013b.

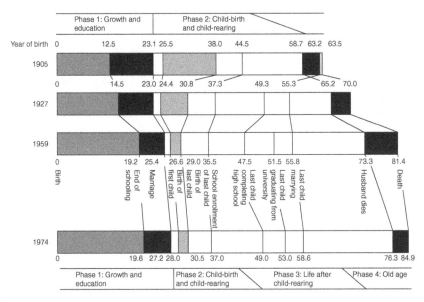

Figure 6.1   Lifecycle model of married women

Source: Adapted from Inoue and Ehara 2005, p. 3.

one-quarter of them remain in the workforce throughout their married life. When the initial childrearing phase is over, about three-quarters of those women who left work to have children return to the labor market. Although most women aspire to work, the reality is that their careers are constrained in ways foreign to most men.

The strength of these pressures manifests itself in the so-called M-shaped curve of female labor-force participation (see Figure 6.2). The curve ascends to the mid-twenties, descends in the early thirties, and swings steadily upward to the late forties, when it finally begins to decline. The valley between the two peaks represents the phase in which women leave the labor force for childrearing. The valley has become less steep over time, although the situation of Japanese women lags behind other industrialized societies where the M-shaped curve for women's participation in the workforce has almost disappeared, replaced by a reverse U-shaped curve with no visible drop in the arch. The *latent* female labor participation rate in Figure 6.2, which includes women who wish to work, suggests that there is a substantial gap between the two rates, actual and latent.

The M-shaped curve began to emerge in Japan with the consolidation of fast economic growth in the 1960s, and part-time work has dominated as an option for women who wish to return to work after childrearing.

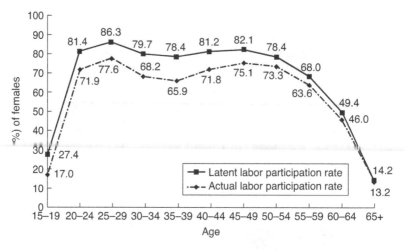

Figure 6.2   Age-based female labor participation rates (2010)

Source: Kokuritsu Josei Kyōiku Kaikan 2012, p. 37.

In the late 2000s, approximately seven out of ten part-time and casual workers were women,[13] and housewives constituted an overwhelming majority of this category, thereby creating a large 'housewife part-time labor market'.

This process has been occurring in tandem with the overall casualization of labor, as discussed in Chapter 4. In Japan, the label of part-timer covers not only those employees with limited working hours, but also those who work as long as regular full-time workers but who are hired on a fixed-term basis and paid hourly rates without fringe benefits. Of the part-timers belonging to the latter category, a majority are women.

In other words, to cope with the chronic labor shortage of the past five decades, Japanese capitalism has sought to recruit women, chiefly as supplementary labor, at low wages, and under unstable employment conditions.[14] Feminist sociologists regard this as the second compromise between capitalism and patriarchy.[15] The first was the so-called Victorian compromise, which assigned men to production roles and women to the reproductive function. The second compromise differs in that it generates a new gender-based division of labor, which makes many women part-time wives and part-time workers. These women work not to secure economic independence but to supplement their household income. On average, the contribution a woman makes to the family income remains

[13] Ministry of Internal Affairs and Communications 2009b.
[14] See Kimoto 2006 for the way Japanese management has dealt with women.
[15] Ueno 2009, pp. 138–57.

less than a quarter of the total, an amount too small to achieve economic equality with her husband in their household. To the extent that the second compromise keeps women in deprived positions in wage labor as well as in domestic labor, it subjects women to the imperatives of both capitalism and patriarchy.

The proportion of married women who were housewives with part-time work surpassed that of full-time housewives in 1983. Part-time housewives can be divided into two groups.[16] In the first group, domestic work precedes outside waged work. The housewives of this category tend to suspend full-time work, dedicate themselves to childrearing, and resume outside work later in life as part-time employees. The second group gives priority to waged work at the expense of domestic work. Those in this group do not generally interrupt their careers, and they end up with higher positions and better salaries in their middle age. In contrast with Euro-American and other Asian societies, where the second group of housewives dominates, the Japanese pattern indicates a predominance of the first group in the part-time housewife population. To the extent that this tendency persists, the interdependence between capitalism and patriarchy is entrenched rather than eroded. In 2012 those who supported the proposition that 'men should work outside and women should stay home' amounted to 51.6 percent, while 45.1 percent opposed it.[17]

2   The Two-tier Structure of the Internal Market

To consolidate this process, Japanese business leaders have split female labor into several tiers. At the level of regular full-time employees, they have implemented programs which attempt to classify female workers into two categories. For women in the category of *sōgō shoku* (all-round employees), companies arrange career paths in the same way as those for male career employees. These female employees are expected to accept the same conditions as male corporate soldiers. *Sōgō shoku* women must be willing to work overtime on a regular basis, to be dispatched to an office distant from their home for a few years (a practice known as *tanshin funin*, as discussed in Chapter 4), and to continue work without interruption during the childrearing phase of their life-cycle.[18]

Outside this small group of elite female employees is a larger category called *ippan shoku* (ordinary employees), who play less important roles in their workplace. They remain peripheral and subordinate workers with low wages, and management does not expect them to perform demanding

---

[16] Ueno 1990, pp. 263–5.   [17] Cabinet Office 2012a.
[18] See Suzuki 2008 for women's overall career issues.

functions or to follow a career path. Most women who prefer to give priority to family life opt for this category.

The Japanese business establishment justifies this two-tier system from a human-capital point of view. This perspective focuses on the way in which management invests in the formation of company-specific skills in internal labor market structures. Japanese corporations place emphasis on intensive on-the-job training and socialization, which commence immediately after employees enter an organization. This practice disadvantages female employees who leave the labor force in the middle of their careers. To optimize the returns of company spending in this area, employers target their investment at male employees, who are statistically more likely to provide continuous service than female employees. When women return to the workforce after a long break, they are far behind men of the same age bracket with regard to acquired skill. Employers therefore vindicate their position on the grounds of economic investment in human capital and find it economically rational to implement a system of statistical discrimination against women.[19] With the implementation of the two-tier system, however, the business establishment has no economic reason to eliminate women from career paths if female employees are willing to work as *sōgō shoku* in the same way as male career employees in acquiring company-specific skills.

Nonetheless, Table 6.1 shows the harsh realities of gender inequality at the apexes of occupational pyramids. A majority of those who have attained managerial positions have not borne children, and most of the female managers who have borne children have relied on the support of their parents or parents-in-law in caring for them. The boards of directors of major corporations listed on Japan's eight stock exchanges are the least open to women. Of public servants in the top levels of the national bureaucracy, women comprise a very small fraction. The worlds of the judiciary and labor unions also have dismal records in this respect. The World Economic Forum, which annually produces the Global Gender Gap Index, a measure of gender-based disparities in economic, political, and education- and health-based criteria, ranks Japan 105th out of one hundred and thirty-five countries surveyed in 2013.[20]

Women in the *sōgō shoku* career path tend to come from a particular background. They must hold a degree from a four-year university, preferably a reputable one, and this means that their parents must have both the financial and the cultural resources to support their education. Most of these elite women marry men within the elite track and receive financial and other support from their parents, who in many cases own substantial personal and real assets. This means that the cream of working

---

[19] Brinton 1992, Chapter 3.   [20] World Economic Forum 2013.

Table 6.1 Proportion of positions of power held by women

Position	% of positions held by women
Members of the Parliament[a]	
House of Representatives (2013)	7.9
House of Councilors (2013)	16.2
Members of prefectural and municipal legislatures (2012)[b]	11.4
Business managers	
at *jūyaku* (director and above) level (2011)[c]	1.2
at *buchō* (department head) level (2011)[d]	4.5
at *kachō* (section head) level (2011)[d]	5.5
at *kakarichō* (subsection head) level (2011)[d]	11.9
Union leaders in *Rengō* (Japanese Trade Union Confederation) (2010)[e]	
National industrial unions (*tansan*)	7.3
Prefectural unions (*chihō rengō*)	6.2
High-ranking officials in the national bureaucracy (2012)[f]	
at the top five grades, the so-called designated posts (*shiteishoku*)	1.9
at the section head (*kachō*) level or above	2.6
Judges (2011)[g]	20.9
Prosecutors (2011)[g]	19.7
Lawyers (2012)[g]	17.4
School principals (2012)[h]	
at primary school level	18.7
at middle school level	5.6
at high school level	6.5
Full professors in universities (2012)[h]	13.4
Presidents in universities (2012)[h]	8.7
Journalists in newspapers (2012)[i]	16.5

Sources:
[a] Compiled by the Secretariats of the Houses of Representatives and Councilors.
[b] Compiled by the Ministry of Internal Affairs and Communications at the end of 2013.
[c] Nikkei Digital Media 2011. The figure covers major companies listed on Japan's main stock exchanges.
[d] Ministry of Health, Labour and Welfare 2011.
[e] Japanese Trade Union Confederation 2010.
[f] National Personnel Agency 2012.
[g] Nihon Bengoshi Rengōkai 2012.
[h] Ministry of Education and Science 2013a.
[i] Japan Newspapers Publishers and Editors Association 2012.

women enjoy three income sources – their own and their spouse's salaries, plus their parents' contributions.[21]

In particular, women in the labor force above the age of forty are highly diversified in terms of income. Wage differentials between female

---

[21] Ueno 1991, p. 153.

workers in this age group are greater than those between male workers.[22] For women of the same age and length of service, the difference between wages in small firms and big companies is greater than for their male counterparts. Likewise, wage differences between section heads and above on one hand and the rank and file on the other are greater for women than for men, as are the differences for those with university degrees and those without. In their forties and fifties, female university graduates earn nearly twice as much as those with only middle school education.

The increasing demand for female labor and the declining birthrate have caused law-makers and business leaders to institutionalize two provisions to enable women to stay in the workforce. One is the Equal Opportunity Law, enacted in 1985, and the other is the Child-care Leave Law, put into effect in April 1992. Neither has a penalty clause.

The Equal Opportunity Law holds up an ideal of equality between men and women in the workplace, but it has no sanction clause and lacks the teeth to force employers to comply with its terms. Further, the principle of equality of opportunity operates among those with equal educational qualifications and therefore legitimizes discrimination between different educational backgrounds. In 2012, on completion of high school education, 45.8 percent of girls advanced to universities with four-year courses, while 9.8 percent went to two-year junior colleges. In contrast, 55.6 percent of boys proceeded to four-year universities and almost negligible numbers to junior colleges.[23] In this context, the law has consolidated rather than broken down the practice of relegating women to the peripheral labor market. In 2008, women who were on the *sōgō shoku* career track comprised merely 6 percent of all career-track employees, with some 17 percent of newly hired career employees being women in the same year.[24] With the diversification of work, an increasing number of companies have established other semi-elite-track job categories, such as semi–*sōgō shoku* and *chūkan shoku* (middle positions), the occupants of which are not required to be relocated to distant offices or to work beyond specified hours.

The Child-care Leave Law requires all companies to allow female or male employees to take parental leave without pay for up to one year to enable them to care for a newborn child. After the leave period, companies must allow the employee to resume work in the same job, or a position of equivalent standing. This law, like the Equal Opportunity Law,

---

[22] Ministry of Health, Labour and Welfare 2007e. An important study in this area is Tachibanaki 2010.

[23] Ministry of Education and Science 2013a.

[24] Ministry of Health, Labour and Welfare 2010.

Table 6.2   Who nurses bedridden
senior citizens at home in Japan?

Carer's relationship to senior citizen	% of carer's
Husband	14.3
Wife	36.8
Son	12.0
Daughter	15.6
Daughter-in-law	17.2
Other	4.1

Source: Ministry of Health, Labour
and Welfare 2010.

has no penalty clause, and companies that fail to comply with it do not face legal prosecution. In 2012, some 83.6 percent of female workers who have given birth took parental leave, while only 1.9 percent of males did.[25]

Most companies in Japan do not allow their employees to take leave to nurse aged relatives. However, it remains the convention that the family, rather than institutions, must care for the infirm elderly. Once an old person falls seriously ill or becomes completely bedridden, family members or relatives are expected to attend to them personally. Only a minority of families are willing and able to use nursing homes, hospitals, and other medical institutions. This places a heavy burden on women, who care for bedridden senior citizens in more than seven in nine cases.[26] While some sons do look after their ailing parents, the task is more frequently forced on a daughter-in-law or a daughter (see Table 6.2). A married working woman, typically in her mid-forties, who lives with her parents-in-law or parents faces the dilemma of choosing between her job and family obligations.

3   Four Types of Married Women

Women outside the primary labor markets are partially connected with the corporate world but certainly are not socialized into its values as fully as full-time male employees. For example, women opt for more flexible work arrangements than men, and in comparison with male workers, female workers give conspicuous priority to activities outside work. In this sense, women's lifestyles appear to foreshadow the future work patterns of the Japanese labor force.

[25] Ministry of Health, Labour and Welfare 2013a.
[26] Ministry of Health, Labour and Welfare 2010

Table 6.3   Permeation into the lives of married women by the capitalist and patriarchal orders

Patriarchal order	Capitalist order	
	Strong	Weak
Strong	(A) Family-supporting part-time workers and part-time housewives	(C) Full-time housewives accepting the status quo
Weak	(B) Career women, many in *sōgō shoku*	(D) Community activists and networkers not in workforce

These observations suggest that the degree of structural penetration of corporate norms into individual life orientations differs between men and women: women are less indoctrinated with corporate logic than men. On the whole, women are at the periphery of capitalist production, and from this vantage point they can more critically examine and remodel the existing system. Some Japanese feminists argue that women should make men more 'feminine' in every sphere of life instead of attempting to 'catch up' with men.[27]

The life of women can be seen in terms of the extent to which it is integrated into two types of social order. One of these is the capitalist order, which concerns the way in which the system of economic production and distribution is organized. Whether one engages in paid employment or not is the most conspicuous indicator of the extent to which one is involved in this order. The strongest factors influencing a married woman's decisions in this matter are her husband's income and her access to inheritable assets.[28]

The other dimension is the patriarchal order, in which male power controls women in family and community life. The more gender equality women achieve in this sphere, the freer they are from this control and the less enmeshed are their lives in the patriarchal order. Married women in Japan could perhaps be classified according to the degree of their incorporation into these two orders (see Table 6.3).

(a)   Part-time Workers and Part-time Housewives

Cell A includes part-timers who are content with a family situation where the husband is the breadwinner and the wife plays a supporting role both financially and with regard to household chores. Women who choose to

---

[27] Ueno 1988, pp. 183–4.   [28] Ozawa 1989; Ueno 1991.

work as part-time or casual workers see their work mainly as a supplement to the household budget. Furthermore, two institutional disincentives actively discourage part-time working housewives from earning more than a certain amount. A housewife who earns less than 1.03 million yen per annum is not required to pay income tax.[29] She can also remain her husband's dependant, enabling the husband to claim a dependant's allowance. Similarly, as long as her earnings do not exceed 1.30 million yen, she is classified as a dependant on her husband's pension and medical insurance policies. Such structural constraints encourage women to work only casually or on a part-time basis. In daily life, one encounters such women working at cash registers, as hostesses at snack bars, and as sales assistants in shops and stores. Some women, however, adopt different approaches to their employment.

One alternative is to register with a 'temp' (*haken*) company which sends specialist workers on a fixed-term basis to firms that request them. These workers work in a range of areas, including computer programming, interpreting, secretarial work, bookkeeping, drafting, and cleaning buildings. Women in their late twenties with some occupational experience make up most of the female *haken* workers. Work in this area is attractive to them partly because they are assessed on their ability and performance rather than seniority and partly because they are not bound to a single company. However, the prime reason for women choosing this type of work arrangement is its flexibility, which allows them to adjust their working hours and select their work environment to suit their personal situations and preferences.

Another option open to women in the external labor market is to start small businesses of their own. Some run *juku*, after-school private tutorial classes, in their homes. Others form groups that own small shops selling a wide variety of goods, ranging from women's clothing or accessories to crockery. Some groups manage various food-related operations, ranging from coffee shops to confectioneries. These businesses sometimes operate as part of a franchise network. Most women who take this alternative appear to be motivated by its compatibility with childrearing and other home duties and, in particular, by its allowing them to arrange their working hours flexibly and independently. Many in this category are in their mid-thirties or older and their children have reached school age.

Some women choose to work in the evening as hostesses in the bar and restaurant business. Called *mizushōbai*, this type of work is widely available in pubs, night clubs, saloons, taverns, high-class restaurants,

---

[29] This amount corresponds to about one-quarter of the national average annual income of regular employees.

and other entertainment venues. Women in this business are expected to amuse male customers who eat and drink in these quarters before going home. While bordering on the sex industry, the *mizushōbai* world provides high wages for women who are prepared to work irregular hours. Although many of them are unmarried young women, married women and divorcees who want quick cash also work in this sector. A small minority of them even aspire to own such venues of their own and make their careers in this world.

Generally, women's work styles are constrained by differences in the ways in which men and women structure their non-working hours. On average, in 2010, a man spends fifty minutes per day on weekdays on such household tasks as cooking, cleaning, washing, shopping, and child-minding, while a woman devotes four hours and twenty-five minutes to household tasks.[30]

Feminist studies suggest that the reference group for women in the part-time labor market is not career women (in Cell B) but full-time housewives (in Cell C). They want to be women of leisure but cannot, because of their family's financial situation. Because they go out to work in order to be a 'good mother', they feel some role strain but do not really find fundamental role conflict in their dual existence; they are satisfied to give priority to their family life rather than their work, and in that sense they are the women who, in conservative reckoning, 'unfortunately failed to become full-time housewives'.[31]

(b)   Career Women

Cell B comprises career women who compete with men at work and who have a largely free hand in the management of their family lives. Most of the above-mentioned *sōgō shoku* types fall into this category. The political push for gender equality in recruitment and promotion in the workplace comes from this group.

(c)   Full-time Housewives

Cell C comprises full-time housewives whose lives are subordinated to the requirements of their husbands. This type accepts the trade-off between freedom from paid work and toleration of male-dominated family life.

At best, the power of full-time housewives remains equivocal. Banks in Japan do not allow married couples to establish joint accounts. To purchase daily necessities, it is not uncommon for a housewife to carry

[30] NHK Hōsō Bunka Kenkyūsho 2011, pp. 88–93.   [31] Ueno 1991, pp. 154–5.

Table 6.4 Decision-makers in Japanese households

Decision type	Decision-maker (%)			
	Husband	Wife	Both	Other
Purchase of land or house	48.6	5.7	35.7	10.1
Savings and investments	25.0	47.7	23.8	3.5
Control of daily household budget	13.4	69.8	14.2	2.6
Overall decision-making power	53.4	16.2	23.8	6.6

Source: Cabinet Office 2002, Chapter 4, Section 2.

her husband's cashcard to use an automatic teller machine to withdraw money from his bank account (into which his company pays his salary). This pattern is routine for couples in which the husband is the full-time breadwinner and the wife is the full-time housewife. Furthermore, ordinary families do not have checkbooks but pay their monthly bills in cash through banks or internet banking, a task usually performed by the wife. Accordingly, when it comes to living expenses, the wife generally controls the household purse. Despite this, the husband takes the leadership in making major family decisions. A national government survey shows that in only a small proportion of households the wife makes decisions on the purchase of such large items as land, houses, cars, and furniture; these decisions are usually made either collectively by the couple or mainly by the husband, as Table 6.4 indicates. Most people feel that the overall household decision-making power rests with the husband, not the wife. This suggests that the power of the wife in household matters in Japan may be exaggerated, although the trend is towards more equality between spouses.

(d) Networkers

Cell D of Table 6.3 consists of those who choose not to work in the business world but who at the same time pursue gender equality in the household. Many female community activists and networkers fall into this category.[32]

Some women choose to work in community-based organizations. These include, for example, workers' collectives which aim to establish alternative work structures, where employees can participate in decision-making processes on the basis of democratic principles.[33] These collectives do not regard profit-making as their prime goal and attempt to provide communal networks among members. Some collectives organize community colleges or culture centers for adult education. Others

[32] See Ueno 2009, pp. 56–7.   [33] Amano, M. 2011, pp. 133–65.

establish recycling shops, and still others operate as links of a larger cooperative chain. In a variety of family service clubs, members help each other in such household chores as cleaning, shopping, washing, and infant nursing, for a nominal fee. Participants in these organizations receive remuneration for their work, but their interest in these activities centers on the establishment and expansion of autonomous women's networks in the neighborhood and beyond. These organizations tend to form a kind of horizontally structured society, based on linkages cutting across community lines. Women in their late forties and fifties, who have been liberated from the time and expenditure required for childrearing and child education, play a major role in these activities. With their husbands still working, they have plenty of time and sufficient financial resources to become heavily involved in these ventures. With little access to the established labor market at their age, these women have become a new type of proprietors in pursuit of self-realization through work.

Some networkers play major roles in reformist political groups at the community level. Some of these activists are involved in protest activities against development projects which would negatively affect residents' interests. Others object to the construction of high-rise condominium buildings in densely populated urban centers. Still others take part in movements against the extension of highways and roads, which cause noise and air pollution. Networkers oriented to environmental issues organize distribution networks of organically grown vegetables and fruit, selling them directly to consumers from farmers without intermediary dealers. The demands of these women are connected with community issues and family needs directly enough to affect local politics. With time available and good networking skills, these activists represent significant political voices in grassroots Japan.

III   Sexuality and Control of the Female Body

1   Contraception and Abortion

The Japanese health authorities legalized the use of the contraceptive pill in 1999, more than three decades after it became available internationally. In general terms, these authorities are stringent in regulating available means of contraception and lenient in allowing abortion as a method of birth control. This diverges from the pattern in most other industrialized societies, where a wide range of contraceptives, including the pill, are openly available and the issue of abortion remains contentious. Although Christianity has played a significant role in shaping the abortion debate in the West, the *ie* ideology of the Japanese government, combined with the stance of the medical profession, had, until recently, prevented the pill from being generally available in Japan.

Another factor in this has been the prevalence of misinformation and disinformation regarding the 'side effects' of the pill, so much so that even now condoms remain the most widely used method of contraception in Japan. About 85.5 percent of couples who practice birth control use condoms to prevent pregnancy, with pill users totaling only 3.7 percent.[34] This situation can be traced back to the chemical poisoning argument which led to the official banning of the pill as a contraceptive in 1972. Before then, Japanese were able to purchase it freely in drugstores without a prescription, officially not as a contraceptive but as a medicine for hormone- and menstruation-related problems. However, a series of chemical poisoning scandals in the 1960s led the Ministry of Health and Welfare to be concerned about the pill. The scandals (none related to the pill) included deformed babies born to women who had taken thalidomide during early pregnancy, and babies poisoned by arsenic in milk powder. The Ministry became extremely cautious, and in 1967 it prohibited Japanese pharmaceutical companies from producing the pill. Between 1972 and 1999, the Ministry classified the pill as a medicine available solely by prescription, and not as a contraceptive.

To complicate matters, the threat of Acquired Immune Deficiency Syndrome has enabled critics of the pill to take a new stance and argue that its liberalization would discourage the use of the condom, which is the most effective preventive method against the spread of AIDS. In 1992 this argument swayed the Central Pharmaceutical Affairs Council, the advisory body of the Ministry of Health and Welfare, against recommending the legalization of the pill. The council, composed of medical experts, met regularly to discuss the pill issue and made a negative recommendation despite the demands of feminist and civic liberalization pressure groups.

More importantly, the Ministry had long taken a moralistic stance regarding the pill, contending that if it were legalized it would foster promiscuity and corrupt women's morals. The implication was that, having freed women from the fear of unwanted pregnancy, the pill would encourage them to liberally engage in sexual activity and thereby undermine the 'respectability' of the Japanese family system. It is ironic, though perhaps not surprising, that while it took three decades for the contraceptive pill to be legalized, the pill for curing male impotence, Viagra, was authorized and freely marketed in 1999, after only half a year of deliberation and debate.

[34] Japan Family Planning Association 2012.

The sexual revolution occurred and had an important impact in Japan despite such moralizing policies directed towards women. Hence, more than 80 percent of unmarried people approve of premarital sex, and nearly one-third of unmarried teens have experienced sexual intercourse. Approximately two-thirds of the unmarried population have sexual experiences before their mid-twenties.[35] A survey of fourteen thousand people conducted in 2013 by a major condom manufacturing company shows that the average age of first sexual experience for women in their twenties is 18.5 and for men in the same age bracket the average age is 18.9, while the national figure, which includes all the respondents, is 20.3,[36] a pattern that confirms that premarital sex is an accepted and established norm today.

Mass media in Japan present private sex lives openly and without much restraint. In a popular television entertainment program entitled *Welcome Newly Weds*, a *rakugo* comedian (traditional Japanese comic storyteller) and his assistant interview newly married couples about their initial encounters, sexual experiences, and love lives so hilariously and humorously that the show has been successfully running for more than four decades.[37] Many popular magazines are full of nude pictures and sexual descriptions. Adult books and videos are readily available. Still, sex education is often a taboo at home and underdeveloped at school, with both parents and teachers reluctant to have open discussions in this area.[38] An increasing gap between the moral pretenses of the adult community and the behavioral realities of their adolescent children has created a social atmosphere conducive to unwanted pregnancies and abortions.

Abortion is established as a legal means of birth control in Japan. The reported number of abortions is approximately two hundred thousand per year.[39] These are regarded as conservative figures; women normally pay abortion costs in cash because National Health Insurance does not cover them, and for taxation purposes many doctors do not report all cases of abortion. Japan's Eugenic Protection Law allows women to have abortions for economic reasons.[40]

The abortion industry has a peculiar concomitant on the religious front. Some temples have an area which accommodates hundreds of

---

[35] These figures are based on National Institute of Population and Social Security Research 2011b.

[36] Sagami Gomu Kōgyō 2013.

[37] On the popularity of this program, see AE, 22 October 2013, p. 1; AE, 21 January 2011, Osaka edition.

[38] See, for example, Nihon Seikyōiku Kyōkai 2013.

[39] Ministry of Health, Labour and Welfare 2013b.

[40] On the advice of the Public Hygiene Council in 1989, the Ministry of Health, Labour and Welfare changed the period within which abortion is allowed from the first twenty-four weeks of pregnancy to the first twenty-two weeks.

small, doll-like stone statues called *mizuko jizō*, some covered with baby bibs and caps, others with toys beside them. Feeling guilty and contrite, some women who have had abortions have dedicated these costly stone carvings to the souls of their aborted fetuses. With the sizeable market in mind, some temples openly advertise the availability of this service in newspapers and magazines, specifying costs and fees.

2   Domestic Violence

Violence at home takes many forms. In prewar Japan, a husband's violence against his wife was accepted. The practice still persists, although it is more concealed, and in recent years the English term *domesuchikku baiorensu* (domestic violence) has often been used rather than the original Japanese phrase *kateinai bōryoku* (literally meaning intra-family violence). The National Police Agency reports that in 2012 more than four thousand people were arrested over the most extreme cases of domestic violence – murder, manslaughter, injurious assault, or assault – and 93.1 percent of victims were female.[41]

A nationwide government survey conducted by the Cabinet Office in 2011 indicates that 32.9 percent of women experienced physical violence or psychological attack from their husbands or partners.[42] In most cases, the man had hit his spouse or girlfriend with a fist, slapped her face, kicked her body, or twisted her arm. A considerable number of women reported being partially strangled, or hit with a baseball bat, a golf club, or a belt. A significant proportion of victims of physical violence suffered injuries; the worst injuries included bone fractures, burns, and burst eardrums. Violent men are not restricted to any particular class lines; they include doctors, university professors, and public servants in significant numbers. Despite this reality, only a small number of community shelters for women operate in Japan, primarily on the basis of volunteer support with very limited government subsidies.

It is important to note that the same government survey shows that some 18.3 percent of male respondents were subjected to either physical or psychological violence from their wives or partners.[43] Although the male proportion is about half of the female rate, domestic violence is not confined to males using force against women. This remains one of the unexplored areas of gender studies in Japan.

Court data show the extent of domestic violence which women suffer. When a wife files a divorce request, the husband's domestic violence is

---

[41] Cabinet Office 2013a, pp. 99–101.   [42] Cabinet Office 2011.
[43] Cabinet Office 2011.

usually cited as a major reason for the action, second only to 'personality incompatibility'.[44] Although the exact extent of violence of this kind remains unidentifiable, in all probability it is much more widespread than is commonly believed. The nature of the problem makes it less visible than other social issues.

The phrase *kateinai bōryoku* also includes the kind of domestic violence that children direct against their parents. Those children who are violent towards their parents are mostly in the middle school age bracket, and most cases involve a boy kicking, beating, or punching his mother. The family type that produces most domestic violence of this kind typically has a father who pays no attention to the children and a mother who tries to control and protect the children excessively. To a considerable extent, these incidents reflect the predicament of many Japanese families in which the father works long hours and spends little time at home, and the lonely mother finds emotional satisfaction in excessive expectations of the children's success. In this respect, children's domestic violence indirectly represents injuries that Japan's corporate system has inflicted on Japanese families.

3 Sexual Harassment

The notion of sexual harassment has recently been imported into Japan from Western countries, although the practice has a long history. The shortened and Japanese version of the concept, *sekuhara*, has gained wide circulation from court cases that women have brought against men's behavior in workplaces. With the rise of feminist consciousness the government has taken steps to address the issue of sexual harassment as part of a national agenda to establish a gender-equal society. To this end, two types of sexual harassment have been targeted:

1 the 'retaliation' type, in which women who have resisted and/or reported male sexual approaches are dismissed, demoted, or subjected to pay cuts; and
2 the 'environment' type, in which photographs of nude females, sex jokes, and sexual innuendo in the workplace adversely affect the morale of female employees and de-value their achievements.[45]

Because of power relations in workplaces and ambiguities in the legal framework, many cases remain unreported, although a considerable

---

[44] Kokuritsu Josei Kyōiku Kaikan 2012, p. 27.
[45] The Ministry of Labor Notice 20, 1998.

number of cases have surfaced since the concept of *sekuhara* gained public currency. In Tokyo, approximately one in five working women has reported that she has been subjected to sexual harassment at work.[46] Some women have charged that they were transferred or fired when they rejected their male superior's sexual advances. Others have complained that they experienced *sekuhara* during business trips, company excursions, or drinking parties. Still others have pointed out that their male colleagues have touched their breasts or hips, causing them an acute sense of unease that negatively impacts on their business performance.

In metropolitan areas, working women complain about sleazy sexual harassment in packed commuter trains. A national survey conducted by the Management and Coordination Agency published in 2000 revealed that 48.7 percent of women surveyed stated that they had been sexually harassed either in a crowded train or in the street.[47] To deal with the situation, some railway companies in Tokyo, Osaka, and other major city areas introduced 'women only' carriages for morning peak hours and late evenings in the 2000s, although the view that this represents 'reverse gender discrimination' persists.

Stalking has also become a nationwide issue, with an increasing number of women being followed or watched, or receiving unwanted telephone calls or emails. After a few 'stalker crimes' attracted national media attention, the National Diet legislated against stalking in 2000.

IV Marriage and Divorce

1 Marriage

A considerable number of Japanese couples marry through family arrangements, with a go-between serving as intermediary. In the past century, a majority of all married couples in Japan were united in this way.[48] Love marriages have increased, however, and only 5.3 percent of couples who married at the beginning of the twenty-first century (2006–10) married through family arrangements.[49] Nonetheless, arranged marriages not only remain a practical alternative for some sections of the community but provide a normative model for many types of marriages.

Preparation for an arranged marriage commences with the parents of a child of marriageable age circulating his or her photograph and

---

[46] Tokyo Metropolitan Government 2006.
[47] Management and Coordination Agency, Office for Gender Equality 2000.
[48] SSM 85, IV, p. 129.
[49] National Institute of Population and Social Security Research 2011b.

personal history through their network of friends and acquaintances. When two parties in the arranged-marriage market become interested in exploring the possibility of a match, they have an intermediary organize a *miai* session, a meeting where prospective marriage partners are introduced, normally in the presence of their parents, who leave shortly afterwards. Although there is no standard procedure from this point, the prospective partners usually arrange another meeting if they are mutually interested. This may or may not progress to marriage.

Even in love marriages, procedures can take forms similar to those of arranged marriages. Marriage ceremonies are conducted in the presence of a go-between couple, and on the understanding that the marriage represents a union between House A and House B.[50] *Ie* ideology surfaces on these ceremonial occasions, attaching importance to family pedigree, lineage, and consanguinity. Outside the venue of the wedding reception, a sign is normally displayed to indicate that a marriage is to occur linking the two houses. Prior to a wedding ceremony, they exchange betrothal presents as a kind of engagement ritual. These presents (*yuinō*) symbolize an agreement that the houses have entered a special relationship. The centerpiece of the exchange is the betrothal money that the parents of the groom are expected to give to the bride or her parents to enable her to purchase household goods and make other preparations for their married life. Other presents, which include food and sake, elaborately wrapped, reflect the traditional village custom in which members of the two households eat and drink together to mark the beginning of the special relationship of mutual assistance between them during harvest and other busy seasons.

Most marriage partners initially encounter each other either through the friendship networks of their siblings or at work or school.[51] Therefore, the process of choosing a marriage partner is class-dependent; people are apt to find partners from the same educational and occupational background, as Table 2.8 and Table 2.9 of Chapter 2 show. In this sense intra-class homogamy persists as an entrenched pattern.

The marriage market in Japan shows a dramatic surge of inter-ethnic marriages in recent years. In 2006, some 6.1 percent of all marriages in Japan were between Japanese and non-Japanese nationals, although the rate declined to 3.2 percent in 2012.[52] The overall upward swing resulted from a range of interlaced factors. The influx of foreign workers,

---

[50] See, for example, Edwards 1989.

[51] The survey by the National Institute of Population and Social Security Research in 2005 shows that the 'sibling network' type is numerically the largest group.

[52] Ministry of Health, Labour and Welfare 2013f. The ratio was less than 1 percent in 1980.

as well as students, into Japan since the 1990s has increased the chances of Japanese developing relationships with them. A large number of Japanese youths travel overseas or work for NGOs in developing countries as activists or volunteers and find their partners there. More recently, similar international marriages have been arranged for urban factory workers.

These marriages have made it clear that Japan's *koseki* system is organized for Japanese nationals only. Non-Japanese spouses cannot be recorded in the system and therefore must go through a complicated process to obtain official papers that show that they are formally married.

2 Divorce

The divorce rate in Japan remained low compared with major Western countries before the 1980s but has risen steadily to a level comparable to some European countries.[53] In 2011 there was one divorce for every three marriages: the divorce rate calculated this way is about one-third.[54]

Most divorces in Japan occur by mutual consent of the couple without intervention by the family court. Only about one in ten divorces involves judicial arbitration, judgment, or ruling. Divorces by consent prevail among the young, whose divorce rate is high. Those in the middle aged and elderly bracket, where the divorce rate is relatively low, tend to rely more on the family court. For older couples, divorce involves a wider range of conflicts over asset ownership, inheritance, and access to children.

Most divorce cases in postwar years have involved couples married for less than two years. Although this pattern persists to some degree, the trend since the 1970s has been an increase in divorces among couples married for more than ten years. This means that the number of children affected by divorce has increased. It is not uncommon now for a couple with several children to divorce.

In cities, particularly among the educated middle class, the gradual spread of feminism has weakened the stigma of divorce. With an increasing number of women in the labor market, women are more financially capable of leading independent lives and looking after their children following divorce. Moreover, women see divorce in a more positive light

[53] The divorce rate, measured as the number of divorce cases per thousand people, was 2.0 in Japan in 2007; it was 3.6 in the United States (2007), 2.8 in Britain (2003), 2.0 in Sweden (2006), 2.3 in France (2006), and 2.6 in South Korea (2006). (Kokuritsu Josei Kyōiku Kaikan 2009, p. 26).

[54] Ministry of Health, Labour and Welfare 2012b shows that six hundred and sixty-two thousand couples married and two hundred and thirty-six thousand divorced in 2011.

than men; while women tend to regard it as an act of courage and autonomy, men generally find it an occasion of unhappiness, rashness, and failure.

Both cultural and institutional factors conspire to suppress the divorce rate, which could become higher. The lack of economic independence on the part of some women makes it difficult for them to take steps to pursue the divorce option.

Divorced women in Japan are penalized in many spheres of life. To begin with, a housewife who does not have a regular income is not likely to have joint ownership of the house or flat where she lives with her husband. Because banks do not make housing loans to those without a steady income, a full-time housewife normally does not jointly hold the title to the property with her husband. This means that a housewife who wants a divorce or a separation has no place to go and must look for new accommodation at her own expense. This is why some Japanese women put up with quasi-divorce, where the wife and husband live under the same roof despite the virtual collapse of their marriage, a practice known as *kateinai rikon* (divorce within marriage).

After divorce, only one parent can have legal guardianship over children in Japan; joint custody is not a widely recognized practice. Although the mother obtains custody of her children in more than three-quarters of all divorce cases,[55] she cannot realistically expect her ex-husband to share the cost of childrearing. Legal authorities have limited the enforcement of any judgments of the family court, and it is a statistical reality that an overwhelming majority of divorcees raise their children without the financial support of their former husband.

Communication gaps between couples are accepted realities in Japan. In this context, those who regard conjugal love as the essence of married life are not an overwhelming majority. Marriages of convenience are widely condoned in order to maintain family stability. Approximately half of all women favor the proposition that 'if one is dissatisfied with one's marriage partner, one is free to divorce',[56] with the largest proportion of those likely to agree with the statement being in their forties. Many Japanese women still tend to refrain from divorce out of consideration for their children and parents, and at the expense of their own connubial satisfaction.[57]

---

[55] Ministry of Health, Labour and Welfare 2012b; Yuzawa 1995, pp. 182–3.

[56] The Cabinet Office's opinion survey on gender equal society conducted in 2007 finds that 47.2 percent of women agree with the proposition and 45.8 disagree. Cabinet Office 2007.

[57] See Ueno 2009, pp. 192–5, on 'wives at the mid-life crisis stage'.

V   Types of Family

Single households are now the largest household group in Japan. In 2010, for the first time in modern Japanese history, their proportion (32.4 percent) exceeded that of nuclear families (27.9 percent).[58] The idealized nuclear family – a household with a married couple with a child or children – can no longer be imagined as the most 'typical' form of Japanese household. The diversification of the Japanese household system is irreversibly underway, as Table 6.5 shows.

Table 6.5   Distribution of household types (%)

Type	Year	1960	1980	1990	2005	2010
Single		16.1	19.8	27.6	29.5	32.4
Couple with children		38.2	42.1	31.9	29.9	27.9
Couple only		7.3	12.5	18.9	19.6	19.8
Extended family		30.5	19.7	13.6	12.1	10.2
Mother and children		6.4	4.9	6.5	7.1	7.4
Father and children		1.1	0.8	1.2	1.3	1.3
Other		0.3	0.2	0.4	0.5	0.9

Source: 2010 Census data and Kokuritsu Josei Kyōiku Kaikan 2012, p. 18.

1   Dominance of Single Households

The numerical dominance of single households stems partly from the surge of youngsters who choose alternative lifestyles: life-time singles, cohabitants without formal marriage, and homosexuals who have 'come out'. Single male households outnumbered single female households in all age brackets except at or above the age of sixty-five, an indication that many casually employed men find it difficult to form families.

This situation does not mean that the Japanese are becoming more single-oriented. A national survey suggests that only 7.1 percent of men and 5.6 percent of women have 'no intention to marry throughout their lives'.[59] These percentages roughly correspond to the proportions of unmarried people in their forties and indicate that no fundamental inter-generational value change has taken place with respect to intention to marry. White-collar employees are more eager to marry than blue-collar workers or self-employed or unemployed people. Contrary to popular

[58] The 2010 Census.
[59] National Institute of Population and Social Security Research 2006.

belief, university-educated career women are eager to have a married life and are more intent on marrying than those with high school or middle school education. On the whole, the institution of marriage remains the most 'desirable' form of male–female relationship, although community acceptance of other forms appears to be gradually spreading.

2   Nuclear Family Patterns

The declining birthrate brought about a sudden drop in the size of families in postwar years. The average household size hovered at around five people until 1955 but declined to 2.42 people in 2010,[60] a change that took closer to a century in major Western countries. Nuclear families with few children have dramatically increased during this period, with most families with children choosing to have only one or two.

On the whole, nuclear families enjoy a high degree of autonomy and independence; the wife does not have to worry about the daily interventions of parents-in-law. These nuclear families typically settle down first in a small but well-equipped apartment or condominium. They then move to a detached house, if their financial and social conditions allow. Condominium buildings that sprawl across and around major cities reflect the spread of small families with one or two children. Their self-contained, partitioned, and rather comfortable lifestyles became consolidated with the wide availability of reasonably priced household electric appliances such as refrigerators, vacuum cleaners, and washing machines. Freed from manual family chores, housewives in these circumstances have been free to raise a small number of children the way they like without interference from the older generation.

On the negative side, however, many city-dwelling women in nuclear families, particularly full-time housewives, lead solitary and alienated lives. This is not just because their husbands devote themselves to their companies, rarely attending to family matters, but also because the numbers of children are fewer, the woman's parents may live far away, and interaction with other families in the neighborhood is rare. Consequently, full-time housewives find themselves directing all their energy to child-rearing and develop fervent expectations regarding the future of their children in an attempt to obtain the psychological gratification that they cannot get from their spousal relationship. Some analysts[61] call this predicament 'mother–child adhesion', a situation that sometimes has pathological consequences.

---

[60] The 2010 Census.   [61] Kimura and Baba 1988.

A majority of childrearing mothers have some support system and can avoid the extreme forms of isolation often associated with secluded nuclear families. Despite the expansion of the number of conjugal families, parents or parents-in-law continue to assist in caring for their grandchildren, especially if the grandparents live nearby. In the absence of such grandparental support, women in the infant-rearing phase develop neighborhood groups for mutual assistance. They organize play groups, get together at a member's home on a rotational basis, and enjoy conversation while their children play together. Some even organize a voluntary association of mothers in need of mutual support for baby care. Those who live in the atomized urban environment must look for a non-kin support system in their neighborhood. Thus, grandparental backing and neighborhood-group support are two practical alternatives for young mothers.

3   Decline in Extended Families

The proportion of extended families with two adult generations living under the same roof has rapidly declined to a little more than 10 percent.[62] In *ura* reality, most two-generation families make this arrangement for pragmatic rather than altruistic reasons. Given the high cost of purchasing housing properties, young people are prepared to live with or close to their parents and provide them with home-based nursing care, in the expectation of acquiring their house after their death in exchange.[63] Even if the two generations do not live together or close, aged parents often expect to receive living allowances from their children, with the tacit understanding that they will repay the 'debt' by allowing the contributing children to inherit their property after death.[64] This is why aged parents without inheritable assets find it more difficult to live with their children or receive an allowance from them.

In extended families, the most traditional norm requires that the family of the first son reside with his parents. This often leads to bitter and malicious tension between his wife and her mother-in-law. Because of rapid changes in values between generations, such tension frequently becomes open conflict. The old mother-in-law expects submission and subservience from the young wife, who prefers an autonomous and unconstrained lifestyle. Soap operas on Japanese television abound with tales of discord and friction of this kind, reflecting the magnitude of everyday problems in this area. These programs are popular because

[62] The 2010 Census data.   [63] Ōtake and Horioka 1994, pp. 235–7.
[64] Horioka 1995.

many in the audience can identify with the characters and their predicaments.

In the countryside, where three-generation families are prevalent and kinship ties are well established, full-time housewives can rely on parents or parents-in-law and so participate in social activities outside home during their infant-raising period.

Children living in extended families appear to enjoy interactions with a wider range of people, such as grandparents and neighbors.

4   Schematic Summary

To compare the nuclear family with the extended family in relation to family norm, it may be helpful to consider two dimensions of classification: type of residential arrangement, which ranges from extended family to nuclear family; and family norm, ranging from lineage orientation to conjugal orientation. Combining these two dimensions, one can envisage four family types, as displayed in Table 6.6.

Table 6.6   Four types of families in Japan

	Residential arrangement	
Family norm	Extended family	Nuclear family
Lineage orientation	A	C
Conjugal orientation	B	D

Source: Adapted from Mitsuyoshi 1991, p. 141.

Cell A represents the most traditional type, in which the *ie* principle predominates and the married couple lives with the husband's parents. Cell D consists of autonomous, modern nuclear-family types where the conjugal ideology prevails. Between these two extremes are two intermediate mixed varieties.

Cell B includes families where two adult generations live in the same house but value conjugal relations more than lineal ones and lead mutually independent lives. Because of high property prices, city families, particularly in the Tokyo metropolitan areas, choose this lifestyle by building a two- or three-story residence with self-contained floors for each conjugal unit.

Cell C includes nuclear families that believe in lineage-based relations between generations. These families may live apart for occupational and other reasons, but closely follow traditional conventions governing marriage ceremonies, funerals, festivals, ancestral worship, family tomb management, and gift-giving among kin, and interact intimately with each other.

The past few decades have witnessed many drastic changes in Japan's family structure. The number of women and men who have chosen not to marry or have children has grown. So has the number of those who marry later in their lives. One also observes a rise in cases of divorce, single mothers and fathers, stepfamilies, international marriages, and gay and lesbian couples. Although some of these trends figure less conspicuously in Japan than in other advanced societies, they point to the growing diversification and relativization of the Japanese family system. These tendencies have revealed not only the structure of power relations between the sexes, but also internal differentiation *within* the world of women.

'Japaneseness', Ethnicity, and
     Minority Groups

I Japanese Ethnocentrism and Globalization

Japan has frequently been portrayed as a uniquely homogeneous society both racially and ethnically.[1] For decades, the Japanese leadership
inculcated in the populace the myths of Japanese racial purity and of the
ethnic superiority which was supposed to be guaranteed by the uninter-
rupted lineage of the imperial household over centuries. In the years of
rapid economic growth since the 1960s, many observers have attributed
Japan's economic success and political stability to its racial and ethnic
homogeneity. Conscious of the extent of support for racist ideology of
this type, the Japanese establishment has often resorted to the argument
that mono-ethnic Japanese society has no tradition of accepting outsiders.
Exploiting this, the government accepted only a small fraction of refugees
from Vietnam and other areas of Indochina into Japan in the 1970s and
1980s, although the nation had brought millions of Koreans and Chinese
into Japan as cheap labor before and during World War II. The ideology of mono-ethnic Japan is invoked or abandoned according to what
is expedient for the interest groups involved in public debate. Since the
ratification of the Convention Relating to the Status of Refugees in 1981,
Japan accepted only 616 refugees in the three decades up to 2012.[2]

Analysts of the social psychology of the Japanese suggest that the inferiority complex towards the Caucasian West and the superiority complex
towards Asian neighbors have played a major role in Japanese perceptions of other nationalities. The leadership of modern Japan envisaged a
'ladder of civilizations' in which Euro-American societies occupied the
highest rungs, Japan was somewhere in the middle, and other Asian countries were at the bottom.[3] Also notable is the persistence of the doctrine
of *wakon yōsai* (Japanese spirit and Western technology), the dichotomy
which splits the world into two metaphorical hemispheres, Japan and
the West, and assumes that the spiritual, moral, and cultural life of the

---

[1] See Befu 2001; Oguma 2002.   [2] Ministry of Justice 2013b.
[3] See Tsurumi 1986, pp. 5, 53, and 62.

Japanese should not be corrupted by foreign influences no matter how much Japan's material way of life may be affected by them.[4] Borrowing some elements of imported Western imagery, the Japanese mass culture industry has portrayed black persons in derogatory ways in comics, television programs, and novels. Popular among business elites, books which perpetuate anti-Semitic stereotypes based upon the old propaganda of the 'international Jewish conspiracy' hit the bestseller chart from time to time.[5]

At the same time, Japanese society is exposed to the international community on an unprecedented scale. With the appreciation of the Japanese yen, many Japanese firms have no choice but to move their factories off-shore and interact directly with the local population. The Japanese travel abroad in numbers unparalleled in history. Satellite television technology brings images of the outside world into the living rooms of many Japanese. The information revolution has propelled an increasing number of internet-savvy individuals to interact with people beyond Japan's national boundaries. Both cities and rural areas witness an increasing flow of foreign students, overseas visitors, and long-term residents from abroad. The Japanese demand for both manual and skilled labor has brought phenomenal numbers of foreign workers into Japan. Grassroots Japan is undergoing a process of irreversible globalization. This has sensitized some sectors of the Japanese public to the real possibility of making Japanese society more tolerant and free from bigotry.

Thus, contemporary Japanese society is caught between the contradictory forces of narrow ethnocentrism and open internationalization. Intolerance and prejudice are rampant, but individuals and groups pursuing a more open and multicultural Japan are also active, challenging various modes of racism and discriminatory practices.

A nationwide time-series survey conducted by Japan's Institute of Statistical Mathematics over more than half a century includes a controversial yet thought-provoking question: In a word, do you think the Japanese are superior or inferior to Westerners? It is intriguing that a prestigious research institute has kept asking the question for more than five decades, a pattern that in itself reflects the degree to which the Japanese are ethnically conscious of their location in the international rank order. The long-term survey results, shown in Table 7.1, indicate that Japanese national self-confidence fluctuates in accordance with the economic performance and achievements of the country. During the period of national humiliation and devastation in the 1950s, following the defeat in World War II, a majority accepted the notion of Japanese being mediocre and ordinary in comparison with those vaguely referred to as Westerners.

[4] Kawamura 1980.   [5] For racial representations in Asia, see Takezawa 2011.

Table 7.1   Time-series survey results on the superiority of the Japanese to Westerners. In a word, do you think the Japanese are superior or inferior to Westerners?

Year	Superior (%)	Inferior (%)	Same (%)	Cannot say in a word (%)	Other (%)	Don't know (%)	Total
1953	20	28	14	21	1	13	99 (2,254)
1963	33	14	16	27	1	9	100 (2,698)
1968	47	11	12	21	1	7	99 (3,033)
1973	39	9	18	26	0	7	99 (3,055)
1983	53	8	12	21	2	5	101 (2,256)
1993	41	6	27	20	0	5	99 (1,833)
1998	33	11	32	19	0	6	101 (1,339)
2003	31	7	31	24	1	6	100 (1,192)
2008	37	9	28	22	0	4	100 (1,729)

Source: Institute of Statistical Mathematics 2009, Table 9.6.
Notes:
1. The question was not asked in 1958, 1978, and 1988.
2. The figures in brackets in the total column indicate sample sizes (based on random sampling).

With the resurgence of the Japanese economy in the 1960s and 1970s, the Japanese appeared to regain self-esteem and pride, which culminated in the decade of self-glorification in the 1980s, when Japan's economy enjoyed a wave of unprecedented prosperity and the nation attained the status of economic superpower. As Japan entered the period of stagnation and recession and struggled under the weight of a sluggish economy in the 1990s and thereafter, the public perceptions became sober, although the 'superiority' group far outnumbers the 'inferiority' group. Notably, those who tend to see no difference between the Japanese and Westerners have risen in numbers in recent years, a tendency possibly reflecting a gradual decline in competitive race consciousness and a steady rise in global identity. In the age groups in and below the thirties, the 'no difference' respondents outnumber the 'superior' respondents. These trends form the backdrop to the competing ethnic paradigms discussed in Chapter 1.

II   Deconstructing the 'Japanese'

Japan has a variety of minority issues, ethnic and otherwise, which the proponents of the homogeneous Japan thesis tend not to address. As discussed in Chapter 1, some 5 percent of the Japanese population can be classified as members of minority groups, a conservative estimate which rises or falls depending upon how the category of minority groups is defined. In the Kinki (Kansai) area, the center of western Japan, the

Table 7.2   Characteristics of minority groups

Group	Population	Geographical concentration	Cause of minority presence
Burakumin	2,000,000	Kansai region	Caste system during the feudal period
Resident Koreans	400,000	Kansai region	Japan's colonization of Korea
Ainu	24,000	Hokkaidō	Honshū inhabitants' aggression in northern Japan
Foreign workers	2,250,000	Major cities	Shortage of labor

proportion exceeds 10 percent. The term 'minority' is deliberately used in a conventional fashion here in order to highlight the *ura* and *uchi* realities of contemporary Japanese society.

This chapter will survey the contemporary situations of four main minority groups in Japan, as shown in Table 7.2: the Ainu, *burakumin*, Koreans, and foreign workers. Their minority status results from different historical circumstances, as sketched in Chapter 1 and detailed in later sections: the Ainu situation derived from the Honshū race's attempt at internal colonization of the northern areas since the sixth century; the *buraku* problem stems from the caste system in the feudal period; the Korean issues originated from Japan's external aggression into the Korean peninsula in the first half of the twentieth century; and the foreign workers' influx began with Japan's economic performance in the 1980s and 1990s.

These minority groups bring to the fore the fundamental question of who the *Nihonjin* (Japanese) really are. One may consider at least seven aspects of Japaneseness – nationality, ethnic lineage, language competence, place of birth, current residence, subjective identity, and level of cultural literacy – as Table 7.3 indicates. While each dimension is in some respect problematic,[6] the main objective of the table is to show that there can be a number of measures of Japaneseness and multiple kinds of Japanese. In combining the presence or absence of their attributes, one can analytically classify the Japanese into numerous types.

If we do not define who the Japanese are solely on the basis of citizenship, on which bureaucrats make decisions, a number of questions occur.[7] The distinction between Korean Japanese, who differ only in terms of citizenship, seems in many cases to be rather artificial. Should naturalized sumo wrestlers, who have acquired Japanese passports, be

[6] For example, the conceptual boundary of the Japanese race remains an unresolved question, though this table relies on the conventional racial classification. Language fluency is also a variable. Here it is defined as native or near-native competency in Japanese.

[7] The following discussion follows Sugimoto and Mouer 1995, pp. 296–7; Mouer and Sugimoto 1995, pp. 7–8.

Table 7.3 Various types of 'Japanese'

Specific examples	Nationality (citizenship)	'Pure Japanese genes'	Language competence	Place of birth	Current residence	Level of cultural literacy	Subjective identity
Most Japanese	+	+	+	+	+	?	?
Korean residents (not naturalized)	-	-	+	+	+	?	?
Japanese businessmen posted overseas	+	+	+	+	-	?	?
Ainu and naturalized foreigners	+	-	+	+	+	?	?
First-generation overseas who forfeited Japanese citizenship	-	+	+	+	-	?	?
Children of Japanese overseas settlers	-/+	+	+/-	+/-	-	?	?
Most immigrant workers in Japan	-	-	-/+	-	+	?	?
Third-generation Japanese Brazilians working in Japan	-	+	-/+	-	+	?	?
Some returnee children	+	+	-	+	+	?	?
Some children of overseas settlers	+	+	-	-	-	?	?
Children of mixed marriage who live in Japan	+	+/-	+	+/-	+	?	?
Third-generation overseas Japanese who cannot speak Japanese	-	+	-	-	-	?	?
Naturalized foreigners who were born in Japan but returned to their home country	+	-	+	+	-	?	?
Most overseas Japan specialists	-	-	+	-	-/+	?	?

Source: Expanded from Fukuoka 2000, p. xxx; Mouer and Sugimoto 1995, p. 31.

considered more Japanese than expatriate Japanese who have forfeited Japanese citizenship? What about two Japanese who work in similar situations overseas and who consider themselves Japanese, but one retains his or her citizenship while the other takes up citizenship in the country in which he or she resides? What about Japanese-born children growing up abroad, for whom English or some other language might be considered their first language? What about Japanese Brazilians who have come to live in Japan? Who has the right to decide who the Japanese are?

The notions of biological pedigree and pure Japanese genes are widespread but controversial and questionable. Especially important is the ill-defined criterion labeled simply as Japanese cultural literacy. Depending upon which culture of Japan one refers to, the amount of cultural literacy one has differs greatly. For instance, many foreign workers in Japan lack polite Japanese and know nothing about the tea ceremony, but are probably more knowledgeable than middle-class housewives about the culture of subcontracting firms in the construction industry. Some returnee school children from overseas may not be fluent in Japanese but may be more perceptive than their teachers about the culture of Japanese education observed from a comparative perspective.

There may be different interpretations of the rules which distinguish Japanese from other peoples. One can be exclusionist and define only those who satisfy all the seven criteria in Table 7.3 as Japanese. One can be inclusionist and argue that those who satisfy at least one criterion can be regarded as Japanese. There are also many middle ground positions between these two extremes.

Figure 7.1 presents the expansion and contraction of the definition of 'the Japanese' in a pyramid form. In climbing the pyramid (Arrow A), we rigorously and restrictively apply all the criteria in Table 7.3 and make each a necessary condition for being 'pure Japanese'. The higher we ascend, the smaller the numbers who qualify as Japanese. Those occupying the base of the pyramid can become 'Japanese' only through monocultural assimilation. In contrast, in descending the pyramid (Arrow B), we regard fewer criteria as a sufficient condition for being a 'multicultural Japanese'. The further we descend, the larger the number of people defined as 'Japanese', so that this term becomes inclusive and multicultural and allows for the coexistence of many ethnic subcultures.

Empirical studies, particularly that conducted by Tanabe based on a national random sample,[8] appear to suggest that contemporary Japanese deem 'self-definition' the most important criteria for determining who the 'Japanese' are, as Table 7.4 shows. Citizenship ranks as the second

---

[8] Tanabe 2012 and 2013. The data are based on a random sample of 1,102 collected in 2003 for the project, which formed a part of the International Social Survey Program.

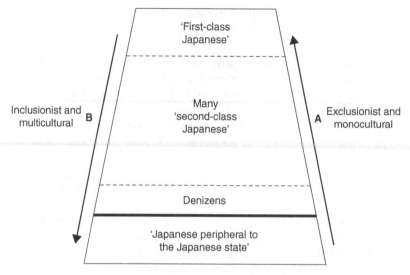

Figure 7.1   Pyramid showing definitions of 'the Japanese'
Notes:
1. Arrow A: The result of zealously applying all the criteria in Table 7.3 and making each a necessary condition to being a pure 'Japanese'. The 'Japanese' population thus defined, is small but increases through a process of monocultural assimilation. Demands cultural homogeneity.
2. Arrow B: The result of eschewing an overly exclusionist definition. Allows for fewer criteria to be viewed as a sufficient condition for being a multicultural 'Japanese'. The population is increased through a process of multicultural acceptance. Allows for many subcultures to coexist.
3. The bold line indicates the Japanese state barrier. Citizenship is the most significant factor that determines who is above or below the line.
4. See Mouer and Sugimoto 1995, p. 244, for a presentation of a similar idea.

most important yardstick, followed by language competence. The racial dimension ('pedigree') figures relatively low in its significance in comparison with other criteria.

Tanabe's research further endeavors to examine the distribution of national identities among the population. He classifies all respondents in terms of the extent to which (1) they are inclusive or exclusive in defining who the Japanese are, (2) they are proud of Japan politically, (3) they are proud of Japanese culture, and (4) they are prone to accept foreigners into Japan. As Table 7.5 demonstrates, the project then combines these four dimensions and shows that contemporary Japanese form four clusters with respect to their national identities.

The first cluster comprises those internationally oriented individuals who are highly open to and accepting of foreigners and inclusive in

Table 7.4   Importance attached to criteria for determining 'Japaneseness'

Criterion	% of respondents giving this answer	
	Important	Unimportant
Self-definition	84.8	12.4
Citizenship (*kokuseki*)	84.5	13.3
Language competence	76.4	21.4
Place of birth	74.4	23.2
Length of residence	71.3	25.9
'Pedigree' (*kettō*)	69.7	27.4
Adherence to the laws	61.4	31.0
Religion	23.1	69.1

Source: Adapted from Tanabe 2012, p. 267.
Note: The figures indicate the percentage of people who find the criteria 'important' or 'unimportant'. Since there are 'no response' cases, the total does not amount to 100 percent.

Table 7.5   Relative characteristics of four types of national identities

Characteristic	National identity type			
	(1) Globalist	(2) Culturalist	(3) Chauvinist	(4) Exclusionist
Definition of 'Japaneseness'	Highly inclusive	Inclusive	Highly exclusive	Exclusive
Political pride	Very low	Low	Very high	Very low
Cultural pride	Very low	High	Very high	Low
Anti–foreign immigration	Very low	Low	High	Very high
Average age	41.6	42.0	57.6	57.4
Educational level	High	High	Low	Low
% of population	15.2	28.1	31.5	25.1

Source: Adapted from Tanabe 2012, p. 276.

defining 'Japaneseness'. These globalists have lower levels of political and cultural pride in comparison with other clusters. The second cluster resembles the first except that its members have a high degree of pride in Japanese culture and can be labeled 'culturalists' or 'traditionalists'. People in these two groups are relatively young and well educated.

The third cluster is made up of fervent chauvinist nationalists who are infused with national pride and hold exclusive orientations to 'non-Japanese'. The fourth cluster is similar to the third in its strict definition of the 'Japanese' and is closed to receiving foreigners into Japan. Its members are generally xenophobic and exclusionist but not as confident about Japan's politics and culture as the third group. People in these two clusters are relatively old and less educated.

These observations exhibit diverse national identities in the Japanese populace and, in particular, cast doubt over the claim about the alleged nationalistic tendencies of Japanese youth. It appears that older people are more entrenched in ethnocentric orientations. More broadly, larger questions regarding who controls the criteria and the right to define the 'Japanese' frames the debate about minority and ethnicity issues in Japan today.

III The *Buraku* Problem

The largest minority group is that of *burakumin*, an outcast group which shares the racial and ethnic origin of the majority of Japanese. There are no biological differences between *burakumin* and majority Japanese, nor is there any means of distinguishing between them by sight. The *burakumin* have fallen victim to the bigoted belief that, since their ancestors belonged to a social category below ordinary citizens during the feudal period, they constitute a fundamentally inferior class. A wide range of nasty discriminatory practices against *burakumin* reflect an invisible caste system in Japanese society.

The term *buraku* means a settlement, hamlet, or village community, and *burakumin* denotes the residents of such units. Unfounded prejudice has forced *buraku* members to live in secluded communities under conditions of relative impoverishment. The exact size of the *burakumin* population remains unknown, because they are Japanese citizens by race and nationality, and discrimination is based upon elusive labeling. The latest official survey conducted by the Ministry of Internal Affairs and Communications gives the number of *buraku* communities as 4,442 and that of their residents as 2,158,789.[9] This survey focused upon localities which the government has designated as entitled to benefit from public projects aimed at the elimination of discrimination. There are at least one thousand localities whose status is the subject of dispute between the government and community groups. Taking these factors into consideration, informed guesses put the number of communities at six thousand and that of *burakumin* at three million,[10] but it remains a contentious issue, as discussed later, how to define who *burakumin* are.

Some *buraku* communities have existed for nearly four centuries. Segregated communities began to emerge around the sixteenth century and

[9] The survey was conducted in 1993. See Buraku Kaihō Jinken Kenkyūsho 2001, p. 736.
[10] Buraku Kaihō Jinken Kenkyūsho 2001.

were institutionalized by the strengthening of the class system of the Tokugawa feudal regime. This system classified the population into four recognized ranks – samurai warriors at the top, farmers in the second rank, artisans in the third, and tradespeople at the bottom – but placed the ancestors of present-day *burakumin* outside these ranks, even locating them in separate neighborhoods.

Two types of outcasts dwelt in these communities. The first, known as *eta* (which literally means the amply polluted or highly contaminated), comprised several groups: workers in the leather industry, including those who butchered and skinned cattle and those who produced leather goods; low-ranking craftsmen, such as dyers and bambooware and metalware makers; transport workers, including watermen and seamen; shrine and temple laborers; and irrigation workers and guards of agricultural fields. The second category was that of *hinin* (which literally means non-human people), comprising entertainers, beggars, executioners, and so forth. Although regarded as lower than *eta* in rank, those in the *hinin* classification were allowed to climb to non-outcast status (under limited circumstances), whereas those in the *eta* category were not.[11]

Prejudice exists against *burakumin* in marriage, employment, education, and many other areas. The marriage patterns of *burakumin* give an indication of persistent discrimination against them. A government survey of *buraku* communities[12] shows that three out of five marriages in the sample are between those who were born in these communities. Inter-community marriages between *burakumin* and non-*burakumin* are in the minority, and marriages between a *buraku* male and a non-*buraku* female are much more frequent than between a *buraku* female and a non-*buraku* male. There are numerous examples of non-*buraku* parents or relatives opposing marriages with *burakumin*, refusing to attend marriage ceremonies, or declining to associate with a couple after marriage. Discriminatory practices in marriage sometimes involve private detective agencies called *kōshinjo*. At the request of conservative parents, these agencies investigate the family background, friends, political orientation, and other private and personal details of a prospective bride or groom.

At the same time, there are signs that youngsters are gradually freeing themselves from entrenched prejudice and taking a more open stance. Inter-community marriages have increased among the younger

[11] A widespread myth is that *burakumin* are ethnically different from majority Japanese. A version of this fiction insinuates that the ancestors of *burakumin* came from Korea, an account that reflects Japanese prejudice against Koreans.

[12] A 1993 survey of 59,646 couples resident in *buraku* communities. Prime Minister's Office 1993. This is the only nationwide study conducted in the past quarter of a century.

generation, the survey[13] showing that they constituted more than 60 percent of the marriages in which the husband was less than thirty-five years of age. This appears to suggest that the attitude of the majority community is changing.

Several features of the employment patterns of *buraku* inhabitants are conspicuous. A significant proportion work in the construction industry; the proportion employed in the wholesale, retail, restaurant, and service industries remains relatively low. Compared with the labor force in general, workers from *buraku* are more likely to be employed in small or petty businesses at low wages. Yet a considerable improvement in work opportunities for young people is discernible, indicating that discriminatory practices in workplaces have gradually declined.

Discrimination against *burakumin* has been sustained in covert ways. It was revealed (mainly in the early 1970s) that some companies secretly purchased copies of clandestinely published documents which listed the locations of, and other data on, *buraku* communities. The companies engaged in such activities in an attempt to identify job applicants with a *buraku* background and to eliminate them at the recruitment stage. The companies were able to accomplish this by checking the lists against the permanent address that each job applicant entered on his or her *koseki* papers, which were normally required at the time of application. At least ten blacklists of *buraku* communities surfaced in the 1970s and 1980s. The resolute condemnation of this practice by *buraku* liberation movements revealed the way in which the *koseki* system was used to discriminate against minority groups. The protest led to the establishment of a new procedure requiring applicants to write only the prefecture of their permanent address on the application form, so that address details now remain unknown to prospective employers. Nonetheless, taking advantage of the anonymity of cyberspace, unidentified individuals upload the locations of *buraku* communities to the internet and post derogatory images and discriminatory language.[14]

The government has introduced special anti-discrimination legislation since 1969 in an attempt to counter discrimination against *buraku* communities. These laws ensure that the government provides financial support to projects that will improve the economic, housing, and educational conditions of *burakumin*. These legal steps enable *burakumin* to apply for special funds and loans to improve their houses, community roads, and business infrastructures, and to allow their children to advance beyond compulsory education.

Defining who *burakumin* are is made more complicated by the fact that the common prejudice against them stems from a belief that they all

---

[13] The same 1993 survey.   [14] Buraku Kaihō Jinken Kenkyūsho 2013, pp. 95–108.

Table 7.6   Five types of *buraku* communities

	Residence	Genealogy	Occupation
(1) Traditional	+	+	+
(2) Residential and genealogical	+	+	–
(3) Residential	+	–	–
(4) Occupational	–	+	+
(5) Dispersed	–	+	–

Source: Based on Noguchi 2000, pp. 106–17, and adapted from Aoki 2009, p. 193. A few possible analytical types are not listed here because they are nonexistent in empirical reality.

live in particular, geographically confined communities. Another public belief is that their ancestors engaged in unclean acts of animal butchery during the feudal period. Furthermore, it is also widely believed that all *burakumin*, even today, work in particular industries inherited from the past, mainly in the leather industry. The prejudice, then, contains three clear markers: residence, genealogy, and work.[15] Table 7.6 exhibits five types of *buraku* communities and shows the diversity of their real life situations. The first type represents the traditional communities with demarcated territories in which genealogically connected *burakumin* work in *buraku*-inherited industries. Although this prototype exists around the country, a majority of *buraku* communities today are of the second type, where the residents no longer engage in conventional *buraku* industries: their occupational structure resembling that of Japanese society at large. Anti-discrimination movements are strong in these two types of communities, although government authorities and *buraku* activists disagree as to which localities constitute *buraku* communities.

Furthermore, a significant number of other people settled in *buraku* after the Meiji Restoration, when the outcaste system was officially abolished. Forming the third type, they have no blood links with those who lived in *buraku* areas during the feudal period, and few of them work in *buraku*-inherited industries. Also, a considerable number of *burakumin* have moved out of *buraku* to live in mainstream communities. The fourth type comprises those who still work in the conventional *buraku* enterprises, while the fifth type does not, often deliberately obscuring their identities. All of this suggests that defining *burakumin* status is problematic in itself.[16]

The social movements of *buraku* organizations have been militant in pressing their case for the eradication of prejudice and the institutionalization of equality. Their history dates from the establishment in 1922 of

---

[15] See Noguchi 2000; and Aoki 2009.   [16] For more on this point, see Davis 2000.

Suiheisha, the first national *burakumin* organization committed to their liberation. Because of its socialist and communist orientation and radical principles, *Suiheisha* was disbanded during World War II but was revived in postwar years and became *Buraku Kaihō Dōmei* (the Buraku Liberation League). The largest *buraku* organization, it claims a membership of some two hundred thousand and takes the most radical stance, maintaining that *buraku* discrimination is deep-rooted and widespread throughout Japanese society. *Kaihō Dōmei* has adopted the strategy of publicly confronting and denouncing individuals and groups that promote discrimination either openly or covertly. This method, known as *kyūdan* (impeachment), has often been accompanied by the tactic of confining the accused in a room until he or she makes satisfactory self-criticisms. As the most militant *buraku* organization, the League has also mounted a number of legal challenges. The best-known case is the so-called Sayama Struggle, in which the League has maintained that a *buraku* man, who was sentenced to life imprisonment for having murdered a female high school student in 1963 was framed by police and the prosecution, who were prejudiced against *burakumin*.

As a means of combating prejudice against minority groups, activists have pressed hard for exclusion of biased words and phrases from print and electronic media. The Buraku Liberation League, in particular, has targeted newspapers, magazines, television and radio stations, and individual writers and journalists who have used expressions that it regarded as prejudicial. Under pressure of public accusation by the League, many have been compelled to offer public self-criticism and apologies. Other minority groups have followed suit and have effectively shaken the complacency of the Japanese majority. No doubt this tactic has contributed to the increasing community awareness of the deep-seated unconscious prejudice built into some expressions.[17] The physically handicapped, who also see themselves as a minority, are sensitive to the use of particular expressions and often publicly join the fray.

---

[17] As a consequence of these attempts to correct discriminatory language, self-discipline by major cultural organizations has often verged upon self-censorship. Some novelists, comic writers, and popular magazines voice concern over what they regard as the minority groups' nitpicking and witch-hunting tendencies. These critics maintain that minority charges regarding 'language correctness' have become so excessive and trivial that they now put freedom of expression in jeopardy. Some complain that they cannot use even such expressions as 'blind' and 'one-handed' for fear of being accused of prejudice towards the physically disadvantaged. Others complain that the language correctness argument suppresses various forms of humorous or comic conversation and writing. Countering these arguments, activists and representatives of minority groups maintain that freedom of expression exists not to defend the powerful and the status quo but to bolster the human rights of the weak and the deprived.

The anti-discrimination campaign waged by *buraku* movements has resulted in visible material improvements for *buraku* communities. With a shifting of emphasis to the software rather than the hardware aspects of *buraku* liberation in the 1990s, activists started reviewing the impeachment measures that terrified some sections of the majority Japanese. They now place emphasis on institutional solutions, campaigning for the legislation of the *buraku* Emancipation Basic Law, which would make it a national imperative to root out *buraku* discrimination and prejudice. They also promote broader issues of social justice and human rights in collaboration with minority groups who share similar problems.

IV Korean Residents

Resident Koreans, often referred to as *Zainichi* Koreans, comprise the largest long-term minority group with foreign origin. According to Ministry of Justice official figures, they number approximately three hundred seventy-seven thousand,[18] and an overwhelming majority of them are third, fourth, and even fifth generation residents who do not have Japanese citizenship but whose native language is Japanese. If one includes those Koreans who have taken Japanese citizenship and their descendants as *Zainichi* Koreans, their number would be far larger, depending upon how many generations one goes back.

Given that citizenship is not the only criterion to determine one's identity, it is a contentious issue who *Zainichi* Koreans are: even after taking up Japanese citizenship, many define themselves as Japanese nationals of Korean heritage, regard themselves as distinct from Japanese nationals of Japanese heritage, and form a part of *Zainichi* Koreans.

After the colonization of Korea in 1910, the Japanese establishment brought their parents and grandparents to Japan as cheap labor in mining, construction, and shipbuilding. In 1945, some 2.3 million Koreans lived in Japan, and about 1.7 million, nearly three-quarters, returned home during the six months after the end of World War II. The remaining six hundred thousand chose to settle in Japan, realizing that they had lost contact with their connections in Korea and would have difficulty in earning a livelihood there. As second-class residents, Koreans in Japan are subjected to discrimination in job recruitment, promotion, eligibility for pensions, and many other spheres of civil rights.

Because the Korean peninsula is divided into two nations, capitalist South and communist North, the Korean population in Japan is

---

[18] At the end of 2012, special-status permanent residents, the so-called *Zainichi* Koreans without Japanese citizenship, numbered 377,350 (Ministry of Justice 2013a).

also split into two groups: the South-oriented organization *Mindan* (the Korean Residents Union in Japan) and the North-affiliated *Chongryun* (the General Association of Korean Residents in Japan). Although an overwhelming majority are oriented to South Korea, increasing numbers have become non-committal and seek to establish new identities as hybrid *Zainichi* Koreans, not necessarily prioritizing their ancestral origins.

Political conflicts on the Korean peninsula are often translated into tensions in the Korean communities in Japan. During the Korean War, in the early 1950s, the two Korean organizations engaged in bitter confrontations at the community level. In more recent years, Japanese public opinion was agitated by North Korea's suspected nuclear development and missile launches over the Japanese archipelago, as well as the revelation that its secret agents had abducted Japanese nationals in the last quarter of the twentieth century, many of whom are still unaccounted for. Because of *Chongryun* loyalty to the North Korean government on these issues, the North-oriented Koreans received a serious setback, although remaining active in ethnic education and managing dozens of full-time ethnic schools across the country, including one university, in an attempt to maintain the Korean language and culture among young, now mainly fourth and fifth generation Koreans.

1   Nationality Issue

Japan's nationality law reflects the image of a racially homogeneous society. The law adopts the personal rather than the territorial principle of nationality – the *jus sanguinis* rather than the *jus soli* principle – in determining one's nationality according to that of one's parents rather than according to the nation of one's birth. Foreign nationals' children born in Japan cannot obtain Japanese citizenship, while children whose father or mother is a Japanese national automatically become Japanese citizens at birth regardless of where they are born. Therefore, the second and later generation children of Koreans born and resident in Japan can become Japanese only after they take steps towards naturalization and the Ministry of Justice approves their application. The nationality law still requires that applicants should be persons of 'good conduct', an ambiguous phrase which permits the authorities to use their discretion in rejecting applications.

From the Korean perspective, the Japanese government's position on the Korean nationality question has been inconsistent. During the colonial period, Koreans were made Japanese nationals, although a separate law regulated their family registration system. Accordingly, male Koreans had the right to vote and to be elected to national and local legislatures; some were in fact elected as national parliamentarians and city legislators. However, with the independence of South and North Korea and the enactment of a fresh election law immediately after the end of World War II, Korean residents in Japan were deprived of voting rights. On 2 May 1947, one day before the promulgation of the new postwar Constitution, the Japanese government put into effect the Alien Registration Ordinance, which virtually targeted Koreans in Japan, classified them as foreigners, and made them register as alien residents. Following the outbreak of the Korean War and the intensification of the Cold War in eastern Asia, the Japanese authorities hardened their attitude towards Koreans in Japan and enacted the Alien Registration Law upon the termination of the Allied occupation of Japan and the advent of independence, in 1952.

With the passage of time, a growing number of resident Koreans have chosen to take up Japanese citizenship. From the mid-1990s to the early 2010s, five to twelve thousand *Zainichi* Koreans forfeited Korean citizenship every year to naturalize as Japanese.[19] While deciding to change their nationality for complex and mixed reasons, they all appear to cherish the notion that they should now live as Korean Japanese, not as Koreans living in Japan, and share the same obligations and rights with Japanese citizens.[20] Although pragmatic and realistic in many respects, this position encounters criticism from within the *Zainichi* community as instrumental and expedient but might represent a future trend as fifth- and sixth-generation Koreans who have little knowledge about Korean culture and language come to the fore.

Housing discrimination against Koreans is widespread and often surreptitious. Some owners of flats and apartments openly require occupants to be Japanese nationals. Some real estate agents make it a condition for applicants to submit copies of their *koseki* papers and resident cards for identification purposes, a shrewd attempt to exclude non-Japanese because foreign residents do not have *koseki* and their resident cards show their nationality.

Another contentious issue is the names that naturalized Koreans may assume. The Japanese government long took the position that foreigners must officially assume Japanese-sounding names as a condition of naturalization. Those Koreans who acquired Japanese citizenship had to give up such Korean names as Kim, Lee, and Park for more Japanese-sounding names such as Tanaka, Yamada, and Suzuki. Although this requirement has been removed, the name issue is a particularly sensitive point among Koreans in Japan because of the historical

---

[19] Ministry of Justice 2013c.
[20] Asakawa 2003, especially Chapter 4 and concluding remarks.

fact that the Japanese colonial regime in Korea forced all Koreans to assume Japanese surnames and to officially register them with government offices. The program known as *sōshi kaimei* (creation and revision of names), which reflected the Japanese method of total psychological control, humiliated Koreans. Yet, a majority of *Zainichi* Koreans now use Japanese names, either always or usually for their daily living, with an increasing number of youths adopting this course of action.[21] One in three switches between Korean and Japanese names, depending on the situation. A small minority, just more than one in ten, keeps their Korean names, indicating that 'Japanization' appears to be an inevitable trend in this regard.

Within the *Zainichi* Korean community, a generation gap is discernible. The first generation, now a numerical minority that nevertheless retains considerable influence over Korean organizations in Japan, remains committed and loyal to their home country and government, some hoping to eventually return home. Second and third generation Koreans born and raised in Japan have little interest in living in Korea, but feel ambivalent towards both Korean and Japanese societies. Many had to struggle to learn Korean as a second language in the Japanese environment. An overwhelming majority have studied in Japanese educational institutions, have only limited knowledge of Korean society and history, and enjoy Japanese popular culture as much as the Japanese. Some have the traumatic experience of discovering their real Korean name only in their adolescence, because their parents used a Japanese name to hide their ethnic origin. Few have escaped anti-Korean prejudice and discrimination in employment, marriage, and housing. The younger generations, committed permanent residents with interests in Japan, increasingly put priority on the expansion of their legal, political, and social rights.

Despite the changing climate, marriage between Koreans and Japanese remains a sensitive issue. Many first and second generation Koreans who retained memories of Japan's colonial past and its direct aftermath felt that marrying Japanese was a kind of betrayal of Korean compatriots. Over time, however, the proportion of intra-ethnic marriages between Koreans has declined. After the mid-1970s, Koreans who married Japanese outnumbered those who married Koreans. The youngest Koreans, many of whom are the fourth and fifth generations and are in their twenties or are younger, do not accept the older generations' argument that Koreans should marry Koreans to maintain their ethnic consciousness and identity.[22] Incapable of speaking Korean and

---

[21] From a national survey conducted by *Mindan* in 2000. For details, see AE, 23 March 2001, p. 22.

[22] Min 1994, pp. 253–64. According to a report in the *Tōitsu Nippō*, South Korean newspaper published in Japan on 23 January 2008, 8,376 *Zainichi* Koreans married Japanese

Table 7.7   Four identity types of Korean youth in Japan

Attachment to Japanese society	Importance attached to Japan's colonial history	
	Strong	Weak
Weak	(A) Fatherland orientation (we are Koreans who happen to be in Japan)	(B) Individualistic orientation (we seek self-actualization privately)
	Bilingual	Mostly speak Japanese; eager to learn English
	Korean name	Not concerned about the name issue
Strong	(C) Multicultural orientation (we want to find ways of cohabiting with Japanese)	(D) Assimilation orientation (we want to be Japanese)
	Primarily Japanese	Japanese only
	Korean name	Japanese name

Source: Adapted from Fukuoka 2000, p. 49.

acculturated into Japanese styles of life, young Koreans find it both realistic and desirable to find their partner without taking nationality into consideration: an overwhelming majority of Koreans now marry Japanese nationals. Likewise, the younger generation is more prepared to seek naturalization as Japanese citizens.[23]

Overall, the passage of time since the end of Japan's colonization of Korea in 1945 has altered the shape of the Korean issue in Japanese society. An overwhelming majority of Korean residents now speak Japanese as their first language and intend to live in Japan permanently. With an increase in inter-ethnic marriages with Japanese and the rise of the South Korean economy, many Japanese Koreans are reluctant to take a confrontationist stance and are eager to establish an internationalist identity and outlook, taking advantage of their dual existence.[24] Against this background, young Koreans have become divided about the extent to which Koreans should remember and attach importance to the history of Japan's colonization and exploitation, and the degree to which they are attached to Japanese society as the environment where they have grown up. Combining these two factors, Fukuoka constructs a model of four types of Koreans, as shown in Table 7.7 above.[25] At the practical level,

nationals in 2006, quadruple the figure in 1971, accounting for approximately 1 percent of all marriages in Japan.

[23] Min 1994, p. 272.
[24] See Chapman 2008 for various forms of resident Koreans' identities.
[25] The discussion here is based on Fukuoka 2000, pp. 42–60.

young Koreans differ in terms of the language they use in everyday life, and whether they use a Korean or Japanese name.

The first type (Type A) of Koreans have a strong sense of loyalty to their home country and define themselves as victims of Japan's annexation of Korea; they reject any form of assimilation into Japanese society.[26] Many Koreans of this type were educated in ethnic schools and became bilingual. Generally, they take pride in being Korean, use Korean names, and hold membership in the North-orientated General Association of Korean Residents in Japan (*Chongryun*). Sharply critical of Japanese discrimination against Koreans and primarily reliant upon Korean business networks, they tend to form closed Korean communities, have close friends only among Koreans, and see themselves as foreigners in Japan.

In contrast, Koreans with an individualistic orientation (Type B) neither take much notice of the past relationship between Korea and Japan nor have strong attachment to Japanese society. They seek to advance their career in an individualistic way without depending on organizational support. Cosmopolitan, achievement-oriented, and confident of their ability, they are interested in acquiring upward social mobility by going to top Japanese universities or studying in the United States or Europe. Most of them are not concerned about the name issue, use Japanese in most situations, and are eager to learn English as the language of international communication.

The multicultural type (Type C) represents a new breed of Koreans who remain critical of the legacy of Japan's attitude to Korea, have a strong Korean identity, and use Korean names. However, unlike Type A, they regard Japanese society as their home base and establish a multicultural lifestyle in which they live with the Japanese without losing their sense of Korean autonomy and individuality. Many used Japanese names in the past to hide their Korean identities but became conscious and proud of their ethnic duality while taking part in anti-discrimination movements with Japanese citizens. Having studied in Japanese schools, most of them consider Japanese their first language, but some study the Korean language on their own initiative. These Koreans are politically conscious and reform-oriented while having a deep attachment to the Japanese local community in which they were brought up. The activists of this group work closely with Japanese groups to press for equal rights for Koreans and other foreign nationals in Japan.

Assimilationist Koreans (Type D) put the first priority on becoming Japanese in every way. Brought up in a predominantly Japanese

---

[26] This group (Type A) is cautious about the movement of the multiculturalist group (Type C) that demands voting rights for Koreans and other foreigners in Japan. Type A Koreans tend to regard such a move as assimilationist.

environment, they are totally Japanese, culturally and linguistically, and believe that what's done cannot be undone with regard to Japan's past colonial policy. Many attempt to remove their 'Korean characteristics', adapt themselves fully to Japanese society, and thereby seek to be accepted by the Japanese. Most of them become naturalized Japanese nationals.

Over time, the Japanese authorities have taken a conciliatory position, with local governments in particular assuming generally sympathetic stands towards Korean communities. In response to Korean residents' appeal, the Supreme Court ruled in 1995 that the Constitution does not prohibit permanent residents without Japanese citizenship from having voting rights in local elections. In 2002, Maibara City, Shiga Prefecture, became the first municipality to grant these rights to non-Japanese permanent residents. Reform-minded Japanese are vocal in their claim that Japan cannot be an internationalized society without cultivating genuine openness and tolerance towards the largest long-term ethnic minority in Japan.

Ethnic minority groups do not necessarily lack economic resources, nor do they always fall behind mainstream groups in educational and occupational accomplishment. A comparative analysis of the 1995 SSM data and the data on *Zainichi* South Koreans gathered in 1995 and 1996 casts doubt on stereotypical images of Koreans resident in Japan as being relatively poor and uneducated (see Table 7.8).[27] At the end of the twentieth century, Japanese Koreans enjoy higher levels of income than Japanese nationals and, as such, no longer form an economic minority. Neither their overall educational level nor their average occupational prestige score differs significantly from that of Japanese nationals. It is noteworthy, though, that Korean residents in Japan are predominantly self-employed small business owners, a fact which suggests that they continue to face employment and promotional discrimination in larger Japanese-owned corporations and enterprises. As independent business people, many *Zainichi* Koreans manage *yakiniku* restaurants and *pachinko* parlors and run small financial or construction-related enterprises. With the avenues of upward social mobility obstructed in large institutions, most Koreans rely on kinship networks within the Korean community in order to find work or establish their businesses. These informal webs of personal and ethnic connections have proven to be valuable social resources, given that the meritocratic route to class betterment in the broader Japanese society tends to remain largely unavailable to them.

The political and economic advancement of *Zainichi* Koreans has irritated ultra-nationalist elements. The group called *Zaitoku-kai*, an

---

[27] Kim and Inazuki 2000, pp. 188–9.

Table 7.8 Relative class positions of majority Japanese and *Zainichi* Koreans

	Japanese Majority	Zainichi Koreans
Class indicators (average)	Average	Average
Educational attainment (Years of schooling)	12.35	12.01
Occupational prestige score	47.32	48.02
Annual personal income (10,000 yen)	494.23	531.84
Occupational classification (%)		
Upper white-collar	22.4	14.2
Lower white-collar	20.2	12.4
Self-employed (*jieigyō*)	23.2	52.1
Blue-collar	28.3	21.0
Agriculture	5.9	0.3
Total percentage	100.0	100.0
Sample size	1,092	676

Source: Adapted from Kim and Inazuki 2000, p. 189.

Note: The *zainichi* sample does not include women, North Korean nationals, or Koreans who have naturalized as Japanese. The Japanese sample used for comparison comprises only male respondents.

association which challenges what it regards as the excessive privileges given to *Zainichi* Koreans, frequently wages noisy demonstrations on the streets of Tokyo and other major cities, chanting abusive, xenophobic, and chauvinistic language against Koreans and other minority groups. This group attracts mainly young and marginalized men who attribute their plight to the improvement of the conditions of Koreans in Japan.[28] Although there is mounting concern about the open and public 'hate speech' of *Zaitoku-kai*, its vocal and noisy presence is testimony to the fact that the deep-rooted anti-Korean discriminatory reality has not been wiped out of Japanese society.

V Indigenous Ainu

The Ainu race, the indigenous population of northern Japan, now comprises some twenty-four thousand persons and seven thousand households living in Hokkaidō.[29] No systematic survey of the Ainu population in Honshū and other parts of Japan has been conducted. At least a few thousand Ainu are thought to reside in the Tokyo metropolitan area. A

---

[28] Yasuda 2012; Higuchi 2014 questions the marginality of this group.
[29] Hokkaidō Prefectural Government 2006.

highly inclusivist estimate puts the number at some two hundred thousand throughout the entire Japanese archipelago.[30] For more than ten centuries, they have suffered a series of attempts by Japan's central government to invade and deprive them of their land, and to totally assimilate them culturally and linguistically.[31] In this sense, their history resembles that of Native Americans and Aboriginal Australians. Under pressure, the Japanese parliament and government formally recognized the Ainu as an indigenous people of Japan in 2008, although much still remains to be debated and reformed, including textbook contents, employment security, and heritage preservation.

Immediately after the Meiji Restoration, the Tokyo government took steps to designate Hokkaidō as 'ownerless land', confiscated the Ainu land, and established a governmental Land Development Bureau. The dispatch of government-supported militia paved the way for the assault of Japanese capital on virgin forests. Until recently, the national government regarded the Ainu as an underdeveloped and uncivilized race, took a high-handed assimilation policy, and demolished much of Ainu traditional culture. The land reform, which was implemented during the Allied Occupation of Japan in the late 1940s and equalized land ownership for the agrarian population in general, had the reverse effect for the Ainu community, because the Ainu land that non-Ainu peasants had cultivated was confiscated on the grounds of absentee land ownership. As a result, the Ainu lost approximately one-third of their agricultural land in Hokkaidō. Governmental and corporate development projects are still degrading the conditions of the Ainu community. The most contentious such project was the construction of a dam near Nibutani in the southwest of Hokkaidō, where the Ainu have traditionally captured salmon. The Sapporo District Court ruled in favor of the Ainu in 1997 and recognized their indigenous rights.

Occupationally, many Ainu work in primary industry or the construction industry, with a considerable number being employed as casual day laborers. Sharing a plight common to aboriginal people subjected to the commercial forces of the industrialized world, the Ainu have often been portrayed as leading exotic lives and made showpieces for the tourism industry. The Ainu community is increasingly cautious about the exploitation of the curiosity value of their arts and crafts. Nonetheless, the fact remains that Ainu culture differs in many respects from the culture of the majority of Japanese, bearing further testimony to the diversity of Japanese ways of life. Some ecologists and environmentalists

---

[30] Poisson 2002, p. 5.

[31] There are a number of place names of Ainu origin in the eastern and northern parts of Honshū island. This is testimony to the fact that the Ainu lived in these areas in ancient Japan and a reminder that Japanese military power pushed the Ainu to the north after a series of military conquests.

find fresh inspiration in the customary Ainu mode of life, which emphasizes 'living with nature'. Ainu culture is based on a world-view which
presumes that everything in nature, be it tree, plant, animal, bird, stone,
wind, or mountain, has a life of its own and can interact with humanity.
But only the very old remember the songs and folklore which have been
orally transmitted through generations, because the Ainu language has
no written form. With most Ainu being educated in Japanese schools and
their everyday language being Japanese, the preservation of Ainu culture
requires positive intervention, without which it might disappear entirely.

The continuance of discrimination and prejudice against Ainu
prompted the Hokkaidō Ainu Association to alter its name to the
Hokkaidō Utari Association to avoid the negative image of the Ainu label:
utari in the Ainu language means comrades, intimates, and kin. Against
the backdrop of the rise of ethnic consciousness around the world since
the late 1960s, Ainu groups became involved in international exchanges
with ethnic minority groups in similar plights in other countries, including Native Americans and Inuits. In 1994, the Year of Indigenous Peoples, Ainu groups organized an international conference in Nibutani, in
Hokkaidō, paving the way for increased international exchanges between
such groups.

After years of the *utari* groups' demands, in 1977 the Japanese parliament put into effect a new law governing the Ainu population, to
'promote Ainu culture and disseminate knowledge about the Ainu tradition'. This historic charter urged the Japanese public to recognize the
existence of the Ainu ethnic community and its distinctive culture within
Japan. The law also pressed for respect for the ethnic dignity and rights
of the Ainu population. At the same time, a century-old discriminatory
law called *Kyū-dojin hogohō* (Law for the Protection of Former Savage
Natives), which had been in force since 1899, was repealed.

An Ainu representative who ran on a socialist ticket gained a seat in
the Upper House of the Japanese parliament in 1994 – the first Ainu to
do so – and made a speech there partly in the Ainu language. Although
few high school social studies and history textbooks give an account of
the contemporary life of the Ainu, their voices at the parliamentary level
have both made them visible to the Japanese public and given some hope
for its better understanding of Ainu issues.

VI   Immigrant Workers from Overseas

Foreigners resident in Japan increased dramatically in the 1980s and
early 1990s. An influx of workers from the Philippines, China, Brazil,
Peru, Thailand, and other developing countries boosted the total number
of foreign residents in Japan to nearly 2.25 million at the beginning of

2013, nearly 2 percent of the total population.[32] The figure includes long-term Korean and Chinese residents, the so-called 'old comers', who are descendants of those who came to Japan during the Japanese colonization period in the first half of the twentieth century. In addition, nearly sixty-two thousand undocumented foreign workers are believed to be working in the margins of the Japanese economy.[33] This situation has produced a significant diversification in the composition of the foreign population, with new migrants forming another large minority group in Japan.

Numerically, the largest foreign population in 2013 was Chinese, followed by Koreans, Filipinos, Brazilians, Peruvians, and Americans.[34] The national background of foreigners in the workforce correlates with their occupational status.[35] A majority of foreigners are employed as production process workers and laborers, most of whom are Latin American and Asian. Some 7 percent work as professional and technical workers, many of whom are North American and British.

The unprecedented flow of foreign workers into Japan stemmed from the situations in both the domestic and the foreign labor markets. 'Pull' factors within Japan included the aging of the Japanese workforce and the accompanying shortage of labor in unskilled, manual, and physically demanding areas. In addition, the changing work ethic of Japanese youth has made it difficult for employers to recruit them for this type of work, which is described in terms of the three undesirable Ks (or Ds in English): *kitanai* (dirty), *kitsui* (difficult), and *kiken* (dangerous). Under these circumstances, a number of employers found illegal migrants, in particular from Asia, a remedy for their labor shortage. On the 'push' side, the strong Japanese yen is attractive to foreign workers who wish to save money in Japan in the hope of establishing good lives in their home countries after working hard for a few years.

The overwhelming majority of employers who hire foreign workers are themselves on the bottom rung of the subcontracting ladder in construction and manufacturing, or are in the most financially shaky sectors of the service industry. These employers generally manage very petty businesses which involve late-night or early-morning work, and which must weather economic fluctuations at the lowest level of the occupational hierarchy. Male immigrants who work as construction laborers usually perform heavy work at construction sites. Most of those who are employed in manufacturing work in metal fabrication, operate presses and stamping machinery, make car parts, or work for printers and binders. In the service sector, migrant workers are employed in restaurants and other establishments to do much of the dirty work. Many female foreign workers are hired as bar hostesses, stripteasers, and sex-industry workers.

---

[32] Ministry of Justice 2013a.   [33] Ministry of Justice 2013a.
[34] Ministry of Justice 2013a.   [35] The 2010 Census data.

Without Japanese language skills and knowledge of Japanese culture, these new immigrants form the most marginalized cluster within the marginalized population in Japan.

In addition to these unskilled workers, Japanese society requires highly skilled professionals at the higher end of the occupational pyramid. The nation's information technology industry, for instance, competes globally with its counterparts in post industrial economies to recruit highly qualified individuals from around the world to develop cutting-edge products and to facilitate international business. Well paid managerial and professional expatriates abound in prestigious quarters in Tokyo, which is dotted with expensive condominiums. Educational institutions are under pressure to acquire English-language teachers and academics who can teach in English. These trends should never abate, although elaborate bureaucratic systems, competing vested interests, and tenacious nationalist ideology decelerate the process of acceptance of foreigners into Japanese society even at this level.

The 'new-comer' migrants do not form a monolithic block. Many 'self-actualization' types exist alongside the stereotyped 'money-seekers', who come to Japan to earn Japanese yen.[36] Some are pseudo-exiles who left their countries of origin because they had grown dissatisfied or disillusioned with the political, economic, or social conditions there. Others are students – both secondary and tertiary – learning the Japanese language and other subjects while working as non-regular employees. More recently, a growing demand for nursing care workers has prompted a rise in qualified Asian women working in the nursing service sector in Japan.

Undocumented foreign workers face numerous institutional and cultural barriers.[37] They are not entitled to enroll in the National Health Insurance scheme and are therefore required to pay the full costs of medical treatment. In cases of work-related accidents, they can file applications for workers' accident compensation, but in doing so they risk being reported to authorities and deported back to their countries of origin. Japanese schools, where the children of migrant workers enroll, face the challenge of teaching Japanese to them with sensitivity to their linguistic backgrounds. The longer undocumented foreign families reside in Japan, the more firmly and extensively their children develop their networks of friends. Many acquire Japanese as their first language and cannot develop fluency in their parents' mother tongue. These families encounter a situation in which both staying and leaving present cultural and linguistic dilemmas.

In 1990 the Ministry of Justice instituted special treatment for the descendants of overseas Japanese, allowing second- and third-generation

[36] Komai 2001, pp. 54–64.   [37] Tanno 2013, pp. 63–72; Komai 2001, pp. 105–17.

Japanese from foreign countries to work as residents in Japan, regardless of skill level. Consequently, the number of young Japanese Brazilians, for instance, has increased drastically in Aichi, Kanagawa, and Shizuoka prefectures, where the car plants of Toyota, Nissan, Suzuki, and Honda operate. Observers attribute the preferential treatment of Japanese offspring to the Japanese authorities' ethnocentric belief that those of Japanese extraction are more dependable, trustworthy, and earnest than other foreigners.

In addition, a program to train foreign workers in Japanese firms was established to provide foreign workers with residence permits and enable them to learn techniques and skills and to gain experience which they would use in their home countries. For many small firms suffering labor shortages, the trainee program serves as a practical way of recruiting cheap labor because of ambiguities regarding the distinction between real training and disguised labor. For large multinational corporations with plants overseas, the program is a way to train future core employees for their branch firms and solve their labor problems within Japan. Furthermore, to deal with the traffic of migrant workers, complex webs of brokers, service contractors, and travel agencies have proliferated in both Japan and home countries and have developed into solid institutional structures for transnational migration.[38]

Two stances compete regarding the ways in which Japan should accept non-Japanese as part of the nation. One position contends that the country should admit only skilled workers, already well educated and well trained in their home countries. Underlying this argument is the obvious concern that unskilled workers will lower the standard of Japan's workforce, and that the nation will have to bear the cost of their training and acquisition of skills. There is also a tacit fear that, uneducated and undisciplined, they may 'contaminate' Japanese society, leading to its destabilization and disintegration.

The opposing position, which argues for the acceptance of unskilled workers, is partly based on the pragmatic consideration that the Japanese economy simply cannot survive without unskilled foreign workers filling the lowest segment of the nation's labor force. The pro-acceptance position also maintains that how Japan addresses its minority issues will perhaps prove the most critical test of its globalization; the nation can hardly claim to have a cosmopolitan orientation while it fails to accept ethnic and racial diversity within.

Grassroots community attitudes to foreign residents in Japan are varied and diverse.[39] Research has shown that blue-collar workers and low-income earners are likely to believe that Japanese society should remain monocultural and that there is neither race-based nor nationality-based

---

[38] Tanno 2013.   [39] For example, Nakazawa 2007; Tanabe 2013.

inequality. In contrast, multiculturalists who feel that Japan should accept foreign residents and believe that ethnic inequality is prevalent in Japan are well educated and are white-collar workers who occupy relatively high socioeconomic positions in Japanese society. They take an open-minded, egalitarian, and progressive stance, while enjoying a comfortable standing as the 'victors' of status competition.[40]

VII Problems and Pitfalls

The notion of internationalization propels some segments of the Japanese population towards more open, universalistic, and global orientations. A considerable number of citizens' groups devote themselves to assisting and protecting foreign residents in Japan. Across the country many individuals of various ages attend study sessions on Japan's ethnic issues, perform voluntary work in support of workers from overseas, and participate in political rallies for the human rights of minority groups. With the international collapse of Cold War structures and the domestic realignment of labor union organizations, minority movements too have shifted their ideological framework away from the orthodox model of class struggle in which links with the working class were given prime importance. Instead, minority-group activists have moved towards international cooperation with ethnic and other minority groups abroad.

There is perhaps much truth in minority groups' claims that their problems are the product of distortion and prejudice on the part of a majority of Japanese. Until 1995 Japan was among the few nations which had not ratified the International Convention on the Elimination of All Forms of Racial Discrimination, brought into effect by the United Nations in 1969. Even after the ratification, the Ministry of Foreign Affairs does not consider the *buraku* discrimination problem as an area covered by the convention, on the grounds that it is not a racial issue. Challenging this view, *buraku* liberation movements argue that their minority status derives from community prejudice based upon lineage or pedigree, precisely the realm of discrimination which the convention attempts to eliminate. Japan's peculiarity perhaps lies not in its freedom from minority problems, but in its lack of recognition and admission that it has such problems.

At the same time, minority groups face an awkward dilemma in defending their culture. On one hand, they take it for granted that they have every right to maintain and advocate their practices and values to challenge the assimilationist ideas of the mainstream majority à la *Nihonjinron*.

---

[40] Ōtsuki 2008, p. 119, and 2013.

This is why Ainu groups, for example, vigorously protest whenever leading Japanese politicians commit gaffes by claiming that Japan is a mono-ethnic and monocultural society. On the other hand, if one accepts the blurring boundaries of each minority group and its internal variations, one would have to avoid the pitfall of stereotyping it. When we say, for example, that *Zainichi* Koreans are entitled to uphold and expound Korean culture, we must ask, which Korean culture? Given that it is diverse, dynamic, and multiple, its substance would differ, depending upon class, region, gender, and other factors. In advancing the idea of a singular Korean culture, one would be formulating *Kankokujinron* (theories of Koreanness) that is concentric to *Nihonjinron*. To the extent that other minority groups – be they *burakumin*, Ainu or Okinawans – are internally variegated, they cannot avoid the same trap if they advance the illusion of their singularity, uniformity, and homogeneity.

VIII   Japan Beyond Japan

The globalization of Japanese society has produced considerable numbers of three types of Japanese who live *beyond* Japan's national boundary. The total number of Japanese nationals living overseas was approximately 1.2 million in 2012.[41] The first of these are Japanese business people and their families who are stationed abroad to manage company business under the direction of corporate headquarters in Japan. With ample financial backing from their head offices, these Japanese nationals enjoy lavish lifestyles far above those of the middle class of their country of residence. In most cases, they live in residences larger than their houses in Japan and relish the good living which the strong yen allows them. Since their lives are tied to Japanese corporate and state interests, their notion of internationalization is often coupled with a concern for maintaining smooth business relations with foreign countries and foreign nationals, to conduct peaceful diplomatic negotiations, and to present favorable images of Japanese society abroad. To that extent, the *tatemae* of internationalization advocated by these overseas business representatives is tinged with the *honne* of nationalism.

The second type comprises Japanese citizens who choose of their own volition to live overseas semi-permanently. Many are 'cultural refugees from Japan' who have expatriated themselves from the corporate world, the education system, or the community structure of Japanese society.[42] These people differ from previous Japanese emigrants who fled economic hardship. New emigrants attempt to establish themselves abroad

---

[41] Ministry of Foreign Affairs 2013.   [42] Sugimoto 1993, pp. 73–85.

to escape what they regard as Japan's rigid social system. They find satisfaction in living beyond the confines of the *uchi* world of Japan and interacting with the *soto* world in a liberated fashion. By and large, the new 'lifestyle emigrants' intend to stay in the country of their choice for a reasonably long period, although they may not plan to settle there permanently.[43] They have one foot outside and the other inside Japan and endeavor to find some balance between the two worlds. To that extent they live cross-culturally. Some go so far as to savor the pleasure of 'cultural schizophrenia'. Others choose to forfeit Japanese citizenship and become non-Japanese nationals, although their numbers are exceptionally small. In Australia, one of the most popular destinations of such lifestyle migrants, the citizenship acquisition rate of the Japanese is the lowest among all migrant groups. The 'strong loyalty of the Japanese to their nationhood and the notion of "we Japanese" appear to be deep-seated', even among those who have chosen to live abroad indefinitely.[44]

The third type consists of an increasing number of foreigners who reside outside Japan, have acquired fluency in the Japanese language and are 'Japan literate', being capable of understanding not only the *omote* side of Japanese society but the *ura* side as well. These people are 'Japanese' linguistically and intellectually, if not in terms of national citizenship (see the bottom row of the Table 7.3). Some readers of this book may regard themselves as belonging to this community of 'cultural Japanese'.

With an increasing number of Japanese going beyond Japan's geographical boundaries and more foreigners entering Japan, there are no simple answers to the vexed questions of who the Japanese are and what Japanese culture is. Although conventional analysis of the Japanese and Japanese culture focuses upon the comparison between 'straight Japanese' and 'straight foreigners', knowledge of globalized Japan will not improve without thorough investigation into the mixed categories, some of which Table 7.3 displays. Japan *beyond* Japan sensitizes one to the viability of conceiving of Japanese society both inside and outside the Japanese archipelago.

[43] Sato 2001.
[44] Sato 2001, pp. 156–61. The 2005 Census continues to confirm the pattern.

8   Collusion and Competition in the Establishment

Japan's establishment comprises three sectors – big business, parliament, and the national bureaucracy – which some commentators say are in a three-way deadlock. The economic sphere, overseen by the leaders of big corporations, is subordinate to the public bureaucracy, which controls the private sector through its power to license companies, regulate their activities, and decide upon the implementation of publicly funded projects. However, officials in the bureaucracy are subservient to legislators, especially those of the governing parties, who decide on the bills that bureaucrats prepare for the National Diet and whose ranks many officials join after they have climbed to a certain career level. Politicians, in turn, remain submissive to the leaders of the private sector, because they require pecuniary contributions to individual and party coffers to maintain their political machines. Figure 8.1 summarizes mutual dependence and competition among these three power blocs at the helm of Japanese society.

The three-way structure of Japan's establishment resembles the tripartism of politics, business, and labor, which collectively coordinates the policy-making processes in some European and Australasian countries. However, the Japanese pattern is characterized by the conspicuous absence of labor union representatives. Although the largest national labor confederation, *Rengō*, has some influence on the state decision-making process, its level of representation is hardly comparable to that of union organizations in other countries. The public bureaucracy enjoys strong influence over both the economy and the politics of the entire nation.

As Chapter 4 examined the operation of the business community, this chapter focuses on the bureaucracy and Japan's political circles, touching on the business world only when relevant and in terms of its relations to the other two power centers. The discussion also covers some aspects of establishment media, both print and electronic, which have significant influence over the formation of public opinion.

Japan's Constitution defines the parliament as the nation's highest decision-making body, which is made up of the House of Representatives

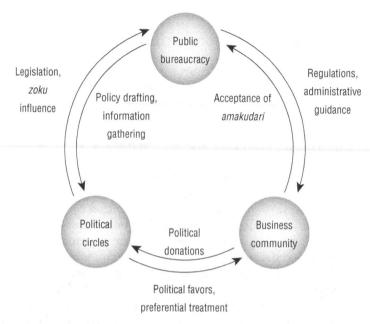

Figure 8.1   Three-way rivalry among power centers

(the lower house) and the House of Councilors (the upper house). Four
hundred and eighty parliamentarians constitute the House of Representatives, three hundred of whom are elected from single-seat constituencies. With the nation divided into eleven separate regional blocs, the
remaining one hundred and eighty members are chosen by the regional
proportional representation system where voters cast their votes for the
political parties of their preference. All political parties nominate and
rank their candidates, with successful candidates elected on the basis of
their party's share of total votes. The House of Councilors comprises
two hundred and forty-two members, whose term of office is six years,
with half of the seats up for election every three years. While ninety-six
seats are allocated to councilors elected through the national proportional
representation system, the remaining seats are filled by local representatives voted in through the conventional multi-member constituency
system.

As of April 2014, the House of Representatives comprises members of nine political parties, with the Liberal Democratic Party (LDP)
in government in coalition with New Kōmei. The Democratic Party
of Japan (DPJ) is the major opposition party. The Japan Restoration
Party, Your Party, the Japan Communist Party, People's Life Party,

the Social Democratic Party of Japan, and the Unity Party are minor parties.

The current electoral system was established in 1996 as part of the reform package designed to put an end to gerrymandering. Yet, at the 2012 national election, for the single-seat constituencies of the House of Representatives, the value of votes for the least populated area (the third district of Kōchi prefecture) was 2.42 times greater than that of the most populated area (the fourth district of Chiba prefecture). With respect to the House of Councilors, the discrepancy in the value of votes in the 2013 election between the least and most populated districts was as high as 4.77 (the gap has remained at approximately 5.0 for the past two decades with little change).[1] The judiciary has ruled that the current situation is in violation of the Constitution, with a few lower courts finding some of the latest elections invalid. At the highest level, however, the Supreme Court tends to prevaricate, ruling that the present condition is 'in a state of unconstitutionality', an equivocation that admits that the existing circumstances are far from constitutional but refrains from going as far as invalidating the past elections. Despite all this, the competing vested interests of the political parties involved have hindered the revision of the current electoral boundaries.

Japan's polity is based on the separation of powers between three mutually independent branches of government: the legislative (the parliament), the executive (the cabinet and the bureaucracy), and the judiciary (the court). Following the British Westminster system, the prime minister, who heads the executive branch, is elected by the Diet (the parliament), usually the head of its majority party. The judges of the Supreme Court are selected by the prime minister and subjected formally to a people's review conducted in conjunction with national elections. The bureaucracy is the only branch of government in which incumbents are never evaluated by formal popular vote.

This chapter first examines Japan's system of national bureaucracy as the deep-rooted and entrenched center of power. The second section then investigates the emerging political economy which downplays the bureaucracy-led developmental state. The new free market paradigm has not only encroached upon bureaucratic power but has altered the landscape of politics. As the third section explores, however, the sharpening conflict between the two political economies does not necessarily mean the fundamental transformation of the world of politics, with many issues left unresolved and sidestepped. After governing the nation for six decades almost uninterruptedly, the LDP, which was occasionally driven into opposition between the early 1990s and the early 2010s, eventually

---

[1] AM, 29 November 2013, pp. 1–2.

returned to power in the 2012–13 elections, clinching landslide victories in both Houses. The final section scrutinizes Japan's major media organizations as part of the establishment.

I   Dominance of the Public Bureaucracy

It is widely acknowledged that the state, particularly the government bureaucracy, holds supreme authority over private sector companies in Japan. Throughout Japan's industrialization, the central government was the engine of economic transformation. To optimize this process the national bureaucracy has recruited talented university graduates as career officials chosen for management ability and provided with high prestige and official status. Able, dedicated, and often arrogant, these bureaucrats are believed by many to be the real power-holders in the nation. The perception is consistent with some state practices relating to the private sector. Government ministries hold the power of licensing, permitting, authorizing, and approving a wide range of production, distribution, and sales activities, thereby regulating the private sector even in trivial details. Furthermore, without statutory grounding, public officials are empowered to provide relevant companies in the private sector with *gyōsei shidō* (administrative guidance) on levels of production, pricing, and quantities of imports and exports, in the name of national interests. Career bureaucrats often retire from officialdom in the late stages of their careers to take up executive positions in large corporations, a practice referred to as *amakudari* (landing from heaven). These three conventions exemplify the power and privilege of elite bureaucrats in Japan.

1   Control and Regulation

The public bureaucracy imposes legal controls on institutions and individuals in any society. Japanese officialdom, however, stands out in two respects.

(a)   Degree of Control

The Japanese bureaucracy exercises control over an extremely wide range of activities. It is estimated that approximately one-third of production activities are subject to state regulation.[2] National government ministries can restrict the number of producers and stores in certain spheres and

[2] Management and Coordination Agency 2000.

control the prices and shapes of some commodities. Regulation extends to individual lives. The Ministry of Land, Infrastructure and Transport, for instance, requires car owners to have their cars inspected annually. Because the inspection covers dozens of items, car owners must normally rely on the expensive and often excessive services of private car inspection firms which the ministry designates.

(b) Jurisdictional Sectionalism

Ministries compete with each other to maximize their spheres of regulation. Because different ministries try to place their domains of influence under their own jurisdiction, national economic activity is partitioned along ministry lines. Jurisdictional sectionalism impedes communication between different ministries and thwarts coordination.

In center–region relationships, the corresponding departments of prefectural and municipal governments serve as the local arms of national ministries, which delegate nationally funded projects to them while attempting to control them from above. Since prefectural and municipal governments have only limited rights to impose taxation, they must rely on subsidies from the national government. This provides national bureaucrats with the power to oversee and influence local governments. Furthermore, national career officials are routinely sent from their base ministry to serve terms in key posts in prefectures and municipalities. The Ministry of Internal Affairs and Communications, for example, may dispatch elite-track officials to head the general affairs department of a major city. The Ministry of Agriculture, Forestry and Fisheries might regularly fill a post in the livestock industry division of a prefecture with a career ministry bureaucrat. Most of these officials move between the two spheres of government several times as part of the promotion process. This vertically partitioned structure of sectionalism intensifies inter-ministerial competition and makes bureaucrats obsessed with their departmental vested interests.

2 Amakudari

The bureaucracy's power of regulation is linked with the ways in which elite officials secure posts in public corporations and private companies when their official careers have ended. High-ranking bureaucrats normally find executive positions in semi-government or private enterprises in the industries they once supervised. This practice is known as *amakudari* ('descent from heaven' appointment) and gives rise to collusive links between official circles and large companies.

The career track of elite bureaucrats has several phases. Initially, university students who aspire to the national public bureaucracy must pass a national examination before applying for admission to a particular ministry. The examination, which covers a range of subjects including some areas of law, is highly competitive, and the majority of successful applicants are from the University of Tokyo. For career bureaucrats selected in this way, year of entry to the ministry constitutes a prime index of promotion. Although they move across different sections and departments during their career, those who joined in the same year are promoted to positions at more or less the same time. However, because higher posts are fewer, a certain number must drop out of the race every year, and this elimination process continues until someone gets the position of administrative vice-minister, the highest position in a ministerial hierarchy. Officials eliminated in this process must retire from the ministry and find jobs outside government through the *amakudari* arrangement.

The business world finds it beneficial to have ex-bureaucrats in upper managerial positions because they have in-depth knowledge of, and personal networks within, the powerful national officialdom. The Japan Shipbuilding Industry Association, for instance, routinely imports high-ranking officials of the Ministry of Land, Infrastructure and Transport to fill its top positions. The Japan Pharmaceutical Manufacturers Association makes it a rule to have former officials of the Ministry of Health, Labour and Welfare as its leaders. These 'old boys' are valuable assets for the industry; through them the business world can maneuver officialdom in the directions it prefers. The other side of the coin is that the 'young boys' in the bureaucracy know that they will be likely to end up occupying important positions in the corporate world so see no harm in maintaining congenial relations with representatives of that world.

These posts assure former high-ranking national bureaucrats of high incomes, authority, and prestige in their fifties and sixties. Ex-bureaucrats occupy a majority of executive posts in government and semi-government corporations, such as the Highway Public Corporations, the Japan Finance Corporation for Small Business, and the Japan International Cooperation Agency. Many former officials move from one corporation to another, collecting large retirement allowances. A majority of the former Ministry of Finance officials who 'descend from heaven' find jobs in financial institutions in the private sector, in securities companies, banks, credit unions, and so on. Most of the ex-officials are in executive positions, and a considerable number are in charge of internal audit and inspection. Given that the financial sector provides employment for retired bureaucrats, it comes as no surprise that the Ministry of Finance often dithers about implementing a full investigation into financial scandals involving banking institutions in the private sector. This environment gives rise to a back-scratching alliance between the national bureaucracy and the business community.

Many executive members of the Institute of Cetacean Research, a non-profit organization which represents Japan's pro-whaling position both domestically and internationally, are ex-bureaucrats of the Fisheries Agency of the Japanese government, a pattern which environmental groups see as an *amakudari* arrangement.

Politics is another significant career route for high-ranking bureaucrats who leave the public service. Some enter national politics by standing as candidates for parliament. Approximately one-third of prime ministers after the end of World War II were ex-bureaucrats, although ex-bureaucrats have not produced a prime minister for the past two decades. Others end up winning governorships in prefectures. The Ministry of Internal Affairs and Communications is a breeding ground for top local politicians. Seconded to a prefectural government as section or department head from the ministry during their careers, many national bureaucrats cultivate ties in the political and business networks in the region and act as a pipeline between the locality and the national center. Some of these career officials are chosen for vice-governorships and make preparations for future gubernatorial elections. Such strong influence in prefectural politics stems in part from the prewar practice in which governors were appointed by the national government, not elected by popular vote. In recent years, candidates for gubernatorial and mayoral elections have often been chosen by a group of major political parties after horse-trading among themselves. The interparty collusion tends to favor candidates who have high technocratic skills and no direct prior party affiliations, conditions which national elite bureaucrats tend to satisfy.

3   Administrative Guidance

The practice of *gyōsei shidō* provides another illustration of the power of the national bureaucracy over the business world. Both institutionalized and amorphous, the practice takes the form of a ministry giving advice, suggestions, instructions, and warnings to business confederations; these are without statutory basis and are frequently made behind closed doors without written records being kept. In the absence of firm documentation, outsiders have virtually no means of acquiring detailed information concerning such activities.

The business world is often a willing partner to administrative guidance and benefits from it. The practice leaves the task of coordinating competing interests in the business world to the overseeing ministry, thereby minimizing the cost of such activities to the private sector.[3] Making use of the third-party mediation expertise of the public bureaucracy, the business community can rely on administrative guidance to inexpensively resolve its internal disagreements.

Moreover, many managing directors and other key figures in major industrial associations are themselves ex-bureaucrats. They have landed from heaven and been hired by industry to deal with the bureaucrats offering administrative guidance. Although administrative guidance has the appearance of bureaucracy instructing the private sector, it is often the case that officials and business representatives have thrashed out the substance of guidelines before they are officially proposed. In these instances, the industrial world, as the object of ministerial guidance, is involved in its formulation and therefore becomes the source of guidance to itself.[4] Collaborations of this kind raise the question of who in fact determines the content of administrative guidance.

On the whole, administrative guidance and other forms of government intervention rely on manipulation rather than coercion. To impose their recommendations and advice, government ministries dangle such carrots as preferential treatment with regard to taxation and finance, public works contracts, and government subsidies. Since companies must obtain authorization for licenses and registration from ministries, national bureaucrats can use this power to induce businesses to comply with ministerial policies.

Regulation, *amakudari*, and administrative guidance enable national bureaucratic elites to manage the state with enormous privilege and to run the economy with long-term planning of a bureaucratic nature. The webs of influence they weave are so extensive and entrenched that they are unwilling to abandon their vested interests even though politicians repeatedly attempt to implement administrative reform programs to downsize the bureaucracy. By definition, bureaucrats' positions are hardly affected by election outcomes. A change in government does not result in changes in the occupants of bureaucratic posts, whose own rules and conventions govern their promotions, transfers, and retirements, with only a very limited number of cases of intervention by politicians. Neither subject to popular elections nor responsive to changes in parliamentary situations, national bureaucratic elites operate in an empire of their own, far from being 'public servants'.

[3] Shindō 1992, p. 105.   [4] Shindō 1992, pp. 105–13.

II Two Competing Political Economies

Two competing political economies form the undercurrent of the dramatic shift in Japanese politics. The bureaucracy-led political economy that enabled Japan to achieve high growth and attain economic superpower status has become obsolete in the late twentieth century in the face of rapid globalization that affects every sphere of Japan's economic fabric. The information industry operates across national boundaries, rendering state control useless. Government intervention in the market of diversifying consumer preferences tends to be fruitless and often counterproductive. State imposition of standardization on the private sector reduces incentives for creative ideas and healthy rivalry for better rewards.

In this context, a new political economy that revolves around free market competition began to emerge, challenging the system of state regulation that obstructs its effective operation. The old political economy has been based on the developmental state model in which the national bureaucracy decides on the long-term goals of the economy for what they see as the national interest and regulates the private sector to achieve developmental objectives. The new political economy is predicated upon the free market model in which enterprises compete with each other, with state intervention seen as dysfunctional to its dynamics.

Instead of one replacing the other, the two political economies co-exist, and the pendulum of public opinion swings back and forth between them. Although the rigidity and inflexibility of the developmental state is an issue, the free market system has been criticized for failing to provide safety nets to the weak and the marginalized and for justifying a survival-of-the-fittest mentality. Both the ruling coalition and opposition parties bear internal divisions over the two competing political economies. The issue concerns the extent to which the Japanese economy should be deregulated and the government's assets and utilities privatized in order to meet the challenge of globalization.

The LDP, now in government, is an omnibus-like and schizophrenic party. Its old guard has its conventional power base in small business and agrarian interests and therefore remains cautious about the possibility that the globally oriented market economy could damage the national regulation structure which has protected them. This position is at odds with the LDP's new guard, which has gained support in urban, white-collar, and managerial sectors invested in the development of regulation-free, market-responsive, and internationally oriented business structures. New Kōmei, the city-based ally of the LDP, also favors privatization programs.

Table 8.1   Relative characteristics of two competing political economies

Characteristic	Political economy model	
	Developmental state	Free market
Driving force	State-led planning	Market competition
Leadership sector	National bureaucracy	Private sector
Desirable size of government	Big	Small
Priorities	Defense of national interests	International expansion of business interests
Primary support bases	Rural groups; the self-employed; public-sector employees	Big business; urban professional class; cultural workers
Management practice	'Japanese-style'	Performance-based
Social inequality	Requires state-led balancing	Provides healthy incentives
De-centralization	Needs inter-regional adjustment	Encourages open contest between regions
Issues	Rigidity; inflexibility	Loss of 'publicness'

The DPJ's main power base lies in the urban middle class, so it generally favors deregulation and privatization programs that empower the private sector and weaken the influence of the national bureaucracy. However, the party receives support from *Rengō* and other labor movements worried about the erosion of their interests as a result of excessive emphasis on labor productivity and work performance.

As to the nation's international relations, the above-mentioned parties' views differ regarding the extent to which Japan should take a strategic and military role in the region, with the possibility of amending the Constitution to allow the nation to have armed forces.[5] Both the Japan Communist Party and the Social Democratic Party (SDP) are internally coherent and vocal in defending the existing Constitution as a barrier against what they see as Japan's rising militarization and in questioning the country's unequivocal alliance with the United States in strategic matters. However, the LDP comprises a wide range of politicians with differing views on international relations. Its law-makers on the right wing of the spectrum argue that the Constitution should be amended to empower Japan to be a fully fledged strategic power in the region, while those on the moderate side maintain that the constraints that the Constitution imposes on Japan's military activity have successfully enabled Japan to pursue economic objectives under the umbrella of United States

[5] For the debate on Japan's Constitution, see Hook and McCormack 2001; and Higuchi 2001.

Table 8.2   Orientations of major political parties to deregulation and the
Constitution

Constitution Deregulation	Favor the acceleration of deregulation	Have reservations about excessive deregulation
Positively disposed to the amendments of the Constitution	Democratic Party Liberal Democratic Party	Liberal Democratic Party
Inclined or eager to defend the Constitution	Democratic Party New Kōmei	Japan Communist Party, Social Democratic Party

military protection. The DPJ, which comprises both economic reformists who fled from the LDP and ex-socialists who are against the revision of the Constitution, also has two wings. The right wing of the DPJ presses for Japan to become a 'normal country', one with a constitutionally legitimated military, while its left wing stance aligns with the SDP on this issue. Table 8.2 maps the distribution of ideological orientations among the major political parties between the two competing political economies and the rival stances on the constitutional issue.

1   Business Community's Push for Deregulation

The interests of most sections of business circles conflict with the regulatory power of the bureaucracy. Concerned for the efficient operation of their business ventures, private enterprises increasingly find the intervention of the bureaucracy frustrating, as their activities become more diversified, sophisticated, and multinational. These circumstances contrast with the past, where the Japanese business world needed national coordination to make a comeback from World War II and to establish an export-oriented high-growth economy. The obstructive nature of bureaucratic regulation has become more evident in the 1990s with the prolonged recession, the appreciation of the yen, and the increased domestic demand for relatively cheap imported goods. Furthermore, the multinationalization of Japanese corporations poses a threat to the system of government intervention, inasmuch as the national bureaucracy finds it difficult to oversee offshore operations. As corporate Japan expands beyond national boundaries and embraces much more than geographical Japan, it is inevitable that powerful business groups press for deregulation.

However, while supporting the *tatemae* of deregulation, some industries are reluctant to facilitate it at the *honne* level, to protect their vested interests. Agricultural organizations which have much political clout make every attempt to defend Japan's uncompetitive agriculture. Some wholesale, retail, and other distribution outlets which have complicated *uchi* networks resist the participation of newcomers from outside. Many construction companies which have enjoyed a number of collusive arrangements have concerns about opening the market to outsiders who do not know much about the *ura* side of the industry.

Yet three dominant national centers for corporate interests are united in demanding speedy deregulation, though they differ in their internal composition. The Nihon *Keidanren* (Japanese Federation of Economic Organizations) acts as the public face of the business community and wields considerable power as the central body which collects political donations from business. The leaders of the manufacturing industries are the elite of the federation. It also focuses its activity upon industrial relations and acts as a principal body to strengthen employer solidarity against unions. The *Nisshō* (Japan Chamber of Commerce and Industry) represents more than five hundred chambers of commerce and industry in major cities across the nation and, therefore, to a considerable extent reflects the interests of small businesses. Finally, the *Keizai Dōyūkai* (Business Friendship Society) draws its membership from individual business people and aims to assess the national economy from a broad perspective without directly dealing with the specific interests of particular sectors or industries. Although these three major organizations remain separate, each performing different functions, there is overlap in their leadership. The big three have, on occasion, issued joint statements on crucial national issues. For instance, in 1960 they collectively denounced nationwide demonstrations over the ratification of the security treaty between the United States and Japan. At the time of the oil crisis in 1974, these organizations warned the business community against taking advantage of opportunistic price rises. During the 1984 budget compilation, they opposed an increase in corporation tax and proposed a radical reduction in government expenditure. In the 1990s and the early 2000s, they collectively challenged the bureaucracy with a chorus of calls for deregulation. In the 2010s, they put pressure on the government for Japan to join the Transpacific Partnership scheme, which abolishes customs tariff and liberalizes international trade.

2   Postal Privatization and the Free Market Paradigm

The leadership of the LDP, who realized that the developmental state model required extensive corrections, made a series of attempts to curtail the public sector dominated by national officialdom and government corporations. Some administrative reforms in the 1980s proved relatively effective, with the successful privatization of the Japan National Railways, the Nippon Telegraphic and Telephone Corporation, Japan Tobacco Inc., and many other public enterprises.

Shinichirō Koizumi, a maverick populist politician within the LDP, assumed the prime ministership from 2001 to 2006 on the policy platform of streamlining the debt-ridden and inefficient government companies and implementing 'administrative reform with no sanctuary'. The targets of the reform were the so-called special-status corporations (*tokushu hōjin*) – semi-governmental organizations protected by state law and funded by the national government – including the Housing Loan Bank, the Japan Highway Public Corporation, the Japan International Cooperation Agency and the Agricultural Livestock Industry Promotion. Despite the fact that in the 1980s and 1990s successive governments had attempted to amalgamate, privatize, or abolish *tokushu hōjin*, which were increasingly unprofitable, inefficient, and redundant, by 2013 their number still amounted to thirty-three, down from a peak of more than one hundred. *Tokushu hōjin*, which mushroomed in the 1960s and throughout Japan's economic boom, contributed to the consolidation of social capital and infrastructure and to the promotion of some industries right up until the end of the 1980s. With massive cumulative deficits, however, some began to cast a heavy financial burden on the national government, whose own coffers had been operating on deficit-covering government bonds. It is widely recognized that a majority of the special-status corporations have completed their socioeconomic functions and must now either be extensively reorganized or, in some cases, abolished.

It is not surprising, however, that many of the bureaucrats and politicians who have benefited from this system have actively resisted attempts to reform it. The anti-reform camp takes a strong stand on the basis that some of these corporations still play an important buffer role, protecting certain groups and regions from the more brutal forces of globalization. In particular, high-ranking bureaucrats offer stubborn resistance because, on completion of their careers in officialdom, the special-status corporations provide them with well-paid executive positions in the cozy domains of *amakudari*.

The dominance of bureaucratic executive power is best exemplified by the Fiscal Investments and Loans Program (*zaisei tōyūshi keikaku*, or FILP), which is controlled principally by the Ministry of Finance. The FILP raises funds by selling bonds to the financial market with governmental guarantee. The funds thus procured enable the ministries of the central government and the associated semi-governmental organizations to implement their respective priority projects. Through various public finance corporations, government ministries provide low-interest loans to a wide range of priority areas in housing, construction, small business, education, key industries, local development, transportation and communication, trade and economic cooperation, and so forth. At the height of the developmental state, the FILP constituted what some observers called the 'second budget', much of which did not require parliamentary approval. With the penetration of free market ideology and the call for deregulation, the FILP has been scaled down and put under a parliamentary microscope since the early 2000s. Nonetheless, it remains the symbol of the power that the national bureaucracy wields in the formation of long-term national policies and programs.

The Koizumi reform prioritized the privatization of Japan's postal system, which was closely connected with the FILP structure. After several years of pushing and shoving between major political parties, the national postal system was divided in 2007 into six private companies, with postal workers ceasing to be public servants. These new companies, which form a group called Japan Post, separately handle postal, banking, and insurance services as private enterprises, although their stocks are still owned by the government and closed to the market.

It is not the case that the free market paradigm has replaced the developmental state paradigm. They are rivals and in competition, representing different interests around the country. The anti-reformist camp claims that the reform went too far in attempting to demolish the developmental state structure and to introduce the framework of free market competition. Many attributed the expanding inequality of Japanese society to the LDP's excessive implementation of deregulation programs and other market-oriented policies, which resulted in already wealthy regular employees and urban centers gaining strength, while poor, casual workers and rural areas experienced decline. Many senior citizens felt ill-treated as pension funds shrank, while youths found themselves marginalized with the worsening employment situation. The extent to which these conditions are attributable to the domestic privatization reform programs or the international economic crisis from 2007 onwards is a moot question.

3   The Shifting Allegiances of Interest Groups

At the level of voluntary organizations, producer and professional interest groups – such as the Japan Construction Industry Association, the Japan Automobile Manufacturers Association, and the Japan Medical Association (JMA) – once the bastion of electoral backing for the LDP, have shown internal rifts, with a considerable number of members showing dissatisfaction with the LDP's shift towards free market economy. Conventionally, pressure groups with vested interests in the government-controlled system were rock solid in support of the LDP, particularly in five areas – agriculture, construction, medicine, dentistry, and land improvement – but this is no longer the case.

A case in point is the medical profession, which constitutes a potent political force connected with the LDP and other conservative organizations. The JMA has more than one hundred and sixty thousand members, most of whom are doctors working in private practices, clinics, and hospitals across the country. They see patients every day and often occupy positions of high status in their local communities. The JMA acts as a powerful lobby group to press for the interests of doctors and to campaign for LDP candidates. Many doctors hang posters of their preferred political candidates on the walls of their waiting rooms as a way of influencing their patients' votes. In proportional representation constituencies, the JMA also sends at least one LDP candidate to the House of Councilors to secure a voice in the national parliament to defend their interests and to keep remunerations for medical treatment in doctors' favor. This pattern started crumbling in the mid-2000s because of the LDP's policy to curb social welfare spending. Many doctors did not accept this direction and saw the DPJ's alternative plans as worth pursuing. Their support for the LDP was regionally diversified and checkered. In the 2010s JMA leadership has resumed firm support of the LDP,[6] although rank-and-file members are divided on the political partisanship of the organization.

Another powerful interest group is the *tochi kairyōku*, the land improvement units mainly based in rural areas. Each unit is made up of at least fifteen farmers and is legally recognized as a juridical corporate body charged with a wide range of responsibilities in the administration of a given agricultural community. These land improvement units manage irrigation facilities, establish new farming fields, and reclaim and rezone agricultural land. Collectively, the land improvement units form the National Land Improvement Political League (NLIPL), which previously provided solid support to the LDP.

The units have often served as agents for the LDP and other conservative parties, recruiting party members and collecting political donations. Many prefectural NLIPL units allocate both the number of new party members to be recruited and the amount of financial contributions to be collected to land improvement promotion associations at the county level, which in turn allot them to community-level units of land improvement. The allocation number and amount depend upon the numbers of members and administrators of each unit and the magnitude of its project budget. Although land improvement organizations are recipients of government funds, some units illegally redirect these into the political

---

[6] AM, 15 December 2013, p. 1.

funds of LDP politicians. This practice has occasionally been exposed by the media and has drawn strong public criticism. Acting as the political grassroots of rural communities, the majority of these organizations prefer the status quo and have, in effect, been an agricultural bastion against major structural reform. However, the levels of agricultural income have declined substantially under recent LDP administrations, and this has undermined the organizational solidarity of the land improvement units in favor of the DPJ, which produced an attractive compensation system for agricultural households. It remains to be seen whether the desertion of a considerable number of members of these units from the LDP will be short-lived or prolonged.

Furthermore, a network of the managers of community post offices located throughout the country who opposed plans to privatize the Japanese postal system have also distanced themselves from the LDP. The postmasters used to form the largest occupational grouping buttressing the LDP's political machine. Community post offices operate in all urban and rural locations, even on isolated islands and in other sparsely populated regions. Entrenched in community life, the national and regional networks of local postmasters have formed a grassroots arm of the Japanese state for nearly one-and-a-half centuries.[7] Past and present postmasters, their relatives, and other individuals associated with the postal services once constituted the core of the pro-LDP political organization called *Daiju* (literally 'a big tree'), which had a total membership of about two hundred thousand.

However, the postal privatization program which the LDP promoted over the past decade made these postmasters the heads of privately managed post offices and stripped them of their public servant status. Consequently, *Daiju* virtually disintegrated, and a majority of its members now belong to a newly established organization called *Yūsei Seisaku Kenkyūkai* (Postal Policy Study Association), which altered its position as a vote-generating machine for the DPJ after the DPJ proposed to partially revise the LDP-led privatization program. However, since the LDP's return to power, the postmasters again support the governing party, a stance that they deem the last defense of their interests.

These and other changes in the loyalty patterns of interest groups at the foundation of Japan's civil society expose the rivalry between the two political economies. Although the DPJ is not a party of developmental

---

[7] Their origin dates back to the period immediately after the Meiji Restoration, when local men of property and wealth cooperated with the government to establish small, community-based postal service agents throughout the country. In 1886, they became 'third-class' post offices, as distinguished from first- and second-class post offices set up by government as state organs. In 1941, the third-class post offices were reclassified as special post offices and the first and second types as ordinary post offices.

state orientation, it benefits from the conservative voluntary organizations' dissatisfaction with the free market paradigm. Although the LDP long enjoyed its affinity with the developmental state model, its bedrock has been eroded precisely because it attempted to make a swift shift to the free market discourse. The political pendulum will swing back and forth between the two political economies and will eventually find equilibrium somewhere between the two positions.

III   The Challenge of Reforming Political Culture

Despite these recent trends, the political style of the LDP, which governed the nation for so long, has left a lasting mark upon Japanese politics. In the context of the conflicting discourses, major political parties face the challenge of reforming the fundamental features of Japan's political culture.

1   Heavy Reliance on the Bureaucracy

Japanese parliamentarians rarely draw up their own bills for consideration in the Diet. Public bureaucrats draft, formulate, and finalize an overwhelming majority of bills, which the Cabinet submits to the legislative body. By and large, the bureaucracy is the virtual legislation-maker of the nation, and the Diet simply endorses or rejects the proposed laws prepared by bureaucrats. In the heyday of bureaucratic dominance, some observers even suggested that bureaucrats determined at least 80 percent of each policy proposed and politicians the rest.[8] In recent years, the LDP government established the Cabinet Office under direct control of the prime minister and strengthened the Cabinet Secretariat to enable the prime minister to have and use his own bureaucrats for policy formulation. Within ministries, political vice-ministers, political aides to ministers, and other posts were created and occupied by parliamentarians in a bid to curb the political influence of high-ranking bureaucrats.

Interest group lobbyists consider the executive branch of government the most crucial political target, with the legislative branch nearly as important, and the judicial branch almost insignificant. On the whole, business and agricultural organizations, most of which have well-established links with the policy-making processes, tend to direct their demands towards the public bureaucracy in order to maximize their chances of influencing policy formation. Even when they approach

---

[8] Itagaki 1987, p. 31.

politicians and political parties, their final target remains the decision-making process within the bureaucracy, with interest groups approaching bureaucrats rather than politicians for consultation and solicitation.[9] With frequent changes in government ministers and intensified competition between parliamentary parties, the national bureaucracy remains stable and consolidates its power over daily policy formulation.

2 Money Politics and Its Social Basis

Political transparency forms the second challenge that Japan's parliamentary culture has faced, in which a heavy emphasis on investment-driven development paved the way for 'money politics'. In return for electoral support, members of parliament are expected to bring government-supported construction projects, railways, and trunk roads into their constituencies in order to expand their *jiban* (solid blocs of voters). In this pork-barreling process, *kōenkai* (supporters' associations) for each parliamentarian play important roles as informal grassroots units in distributing the benefits their representative acquires for them.

Against this background, the LDP culture nurtured the so-called *zoku*[10] parliamentarians, who represent special interest groups and exercise much political influence over the process of governmental and bureaucratic policy formulation. They have specialist knowledge of particular sectors of the economy: agriculture, construction, commerce, telecommunications, transport, or education. In return for serving as spokespersons for particular interest groups and swaying the law-making process in their favor, these politicians secure enduring financial support bases in influential business communities. This mutual support structure has consolidated the vast foundations of the LDP's hold on government power. Many recent prime ministers have acted as *zoku* politicians to rise though the LDP ranks and to expand their spheres of influence within the party hierarchy.[11]

---

[9] Tsujinaka 2002, p. 174. According to Tsujinaka 1988, this pattern contrasts sharply with the US situation where lobby groups and pressure organizations give the highest priority to persuading legislators in Congress and the Senate.

[10] *Zoku* literally means a tribe or the same kind.

[11] The late Nobusuke Kishi (prime minister from 1957 to 1960) was widely regarded as the boss of the *zoku* group in control of commerce and industry and wielded enormous power in the key industries under the guidance of the Ministry of International Trade and Industry. Zenkō Suzuki (1980–82) was influential in the Ministry of Agriculture, Forestry and Fisheries and had strong links with agricultural cooperatives throughout the nation. Toshiki Kaifu (1989–91) was a leader of the education *zoku* group influential in the Ministry of Education. This coterie has expanded its coffers by procuring political donations from nationwide networks of the owners of private schools and kindergartens.

The Ministry of Economy, Trade and Industry sits at the hub of the political–industrial–bureaucratic complex of industrial policy formulation. Because the ministry has the power to grant and reject licenses and the authority to offer administrative guidance to the private sector, politicians attempt to influence its decision-making process for the benefit of corporate contributors to their political funds. In turn, they expect those beneficiaries to make continued and increasing donations to their political coffers. Some legislators take advantage of the aging society and put pressure on the Ministry of Health, Labour, and Welfare over the interests of nursing homes and hospitals for the aged, whose owners and managers give electoral support.[12]

Undoubtedly, such financial transactions put *zoku* politicians in precarious situations. In order to protect themselves against possible legal complications, they often have private secretaries deal with any pecuniary matters. These aides do not normally formulate policies or draft bills. Instead, they spend much time receiving and entertaining local bureaucrats, business people, and other lobbyists who visit Tokyo to entreat their parliamentary representatives for political assistance. The secretaries also frequently use their positions to find employment or arrange introductions to influential people for children and relatives of voters in their bosses' constituencies. Beneficiaries are expected to return these favors during elections.

The current electoral system prohibits individual politicians from receiving political donations personally. Each politician can establish a single fund-management organization to which enterprises, groups, and individuals can donate up to half a million yen per annum. Each political party is entitled to receive an annual grant-in-aid from public coffers. The amount which a party is granted depends on its number of elected national parliamentarians and votes received in the previous national election. Furthermore, the guilt-by-association system has been strengthened so that if a chief campaign manager, campaign treasurer, or other electoral leader is arrested and found guilty of election irregularities, the elected politician is supposed to be forced from office.

More generally, pecuniary scandals, rife at the highest levels of the Japanese political hierarchy, reflect the popular practice of gift-giving on private occasions. Gift giving is regarded as an expression of intimacy and affection. This social custom sometimes blurs the line between illegal acts and accepted informal exchanges. For many Japanese it is an established custom to bring a gift when making a visit. Formal gift giving is an institutionalized practice in summer and winter. Gifts and gift certificates are

---

[12] AM, 14 October 2013, p. 4.

sent, either directly or through department stores and shops, to acquaintances, friends, and relatives in the middle and at the end of each year as *chūgen* (mid-year gifts) and *seibo* (year-end gifts). Taking advantage of this convention, those who wish to acknowledge, or who seek, a favor from superiors or business connections send them expensive presents.

Cash gifts are normal on ceremonial occasions. At marriage receptions, well-wishers are expected to donate the yen equivalent of a few hundred dollars to the marrying couple as an expression of congratulations. The family keeps meticulous records of who gave and returns the gift in kind a few weeks later. At funerals, mourners usually make monetary offerings to the family of the deceased. A majority of employees in large corporations find it socially necessary to make sizeable cash gifts of congratulations and condolence not only to members of their own families, but also to senior and junior company colleagues. On New Year's Day, children collect monetary gifts from parents, relatives, and other adults. In temples and shrines, the names of large donors and the amounts of their gifts are listed conspicuously.

In this environment, it is accepted that powerful individuals make lavish cash contributions on such occasions as wedding ceremonies, funerals, and community festivals.[13] To maintain the continuing support of their electorate, politicians require a constant flow of cash, though funds legally received by legislators do not cover the costs of operating their offices. In reality, they rely upon corporate and other organizational donations for substantial portions of their office incomes. They manage an office or two in Tokyo and a few in their own constituencies, hire a dozen or so secretaries, and attend a number of wedding ceremonies, funerals, and New Year and year-end functions.

When conclusively tainted, some politicians resign from ministerial posts and party positions. Others quit the Diet or leave politics for a short period of time. The object of resigning is to seek and obtain sympathetic indulgence. In most areas, pragmatic judgments override ethical considerations, and the electorate usually re-elects disgraced politicians. The re-elected parliamentarians then resort to Shintoist metaphors and claim that re-election implies the completion of the purification ceremony for their past blemish. Since they have performed absolutions, they maintain that they are qualified to make a fresh start. Using this type of logic, discredited political heavyweights usually make successful comebacks as powerbrokers in national politics. To some degree, such community tolerance reflects the daily reality of electors who themselves see nothing wrong in seeking favors by giving expensive gifts to those who may aid them. The practice of those at the helm of the

---

[13] These occasions are collectively called *kankon sōsai*.

establishment corresponds with the social customs of people at the grassroots.[14]

3   Local Politics against the National Bureaucracy

Local governments in Japan have considerable autonomy in some areas, in spite of Japan's highly centralized political and bureaucratic structures. Pluralistic competition exists between the central and local governments, with the latter having two tiers, including forty-seven prefectural governments, and within each prefecture, municipal governments of cities, towns, and villages.[15] As the rivalry between various levels has intensified in recent years, prefectural governors and mayors of major cities in particular have joined forces to press for the decentralization of resources and authorities into local governments. The major issue is that the amount of local tax that each local government can collect is limited so that it must rely upon the subsidies of national ministries, which have the final decision-making power over crucial elements of its finances. Though all political parties advocate that the national bureaucracy's power over prefectures and municipalities be reduced, the realities of local governance complicate the process of decentralization.

(a)   Project Implementation

Every local government has its own regional demands and requirements and attempts to reflect them in the lobbying process. The central government does not uniformly impose its strategy upon local governments, which have the right to request and lobby for the subsidized projects they prefer. They have day-to-day know-how regarding a number of social welfare programs, which are practically their business rather than that of the state. These programs include the establishment and operation of day-care centers, homes for the aged, public housing for the poor, and other welfare institutions. Unsatisfactory implementation of these programs sometimes means the loss of electoral support for local politicians, who thus have reason to press for their successful management and expansion. In most projects of this kind, significant input by local government into the process is inevitable, making traffic two-way between the state and localities. The central government formulates the general

---

[14] See Befu 1974 on how law tangles with culture in Japan.
[15] For more on the discussion in this section, see Muramatsu 1988 and 1997; and Muramatsu, Igbal, and Kume 2002.

direction according to what it regards as the national interest, municipal governments implement the projects, and prefectural governments perform mediating functions.

(b)   Routine Lobbying

Prefectural governors, municipal mayors, local legislators, and provincial business representatives visit Tokyo from time to time to negotiate with ministry bureaucrats to win as large a share as possible of the national government's budgetary and project allocations. Members of parliament who represent the constituencies of these lobby groups play vital roles in bringing political pressure to bear on the decision-making process of ministries. National parliamentarians from rural areas exercise great influence as representatives of the agricultural community. On the eve of national budget formulation, it is routine for a variety of local lobbyists to fill the corridors of ministry buildings, where national officials hold a series of hearings with local representatives concerning their situations.

(c)   Inter-regional Competition

Ministerial sectionalism, which filters through local governments, has taken its toll but represents only one side of the coin. There is also lateral rivalry between municipalities and between prefectures to maximize their performance in local politics and administration. Local governments are conscious of their position in the national ranking and are keen to compete with those of comparable size and status to obtain subsidies, projects, and other preferential treatment. Neighboring municipalities and adjacent prefectures insist on similar deals, in view of their proximity to favored regions. Appealing to regional identities, local politicians run campaigns to raise the standard of their area, a demand that national bureaucrats cannot easily ignore, for political reasons. Local bureaucrats, too, often succeed in gaining salary levels and working conditions similar to those in comparable prefectures or municipalities. Relatively poor prefectures and municipalities actively seek large-scale projects as a means of redressing the inter-regional balance. Local initiatives have been essential to such major projects as the establishment of nuclear energy plants, extension of the bullet-train lines, provision of super-highways, development of resort centers, and so forth. Inter-regional rivalry of this kind puts pressure on national bureaucrats in their decision-making.

Table 8.3   Orientations of major power players to decentralization and deregulation

	Structural Makeup	
Orientation	Centralized	Decentralized
Bureaucratic regulation	National bureaucracy; some national business organizations	Local governments; some resident movements
Deregulation	Most national business organizations; national political parties	Local business community; local political interest groups; some resident movements

(d)   The Rise of Antiparty Swing Voters

Since the mid-1990s, large proportions of the electorate have refrained from commitment to any political party and have become nonpartisan, swing voters. Various nationwide surveys in the 2000s and the 2010s suggest that about half to one-third of eligible voters fall into this category. A series of political scandals, mergers, party splits, and changes in party platforms without principles contributed to a mass desertion of the party faithful. Cynical and skeptical, these floating voters find political expression through candidates who are unaffiliated with political parties and take a strong anti-establishment stance. Tired of political clichés and bored with interparty horse-trading, these voters regard themselves as the audience of a political playhouse and expect surprise performances from politicians. Using mass media as an effective form of communication, sensational populist politics is played out to attract the swing voters, who form a formidable force which established political parties can no longer ignore.[16]

Table 8.3 locates the major players on two axes. One dimension is that of competition between centralized and decentralized power structures. The other contrasts orientations in favor of bureaucratic regulation with those favoring deregulation. Although the three power blocs displayed in Figure 8.1 exist in the centralized sector, their activities and orientations are influenced and constrained by various local forces.

IV   'History War'

Some seven decades after the end of World War II, Japan is still embroiled in a 'history war' with neighboring countries about what the Japanese

---

[16] See Tanabe 2013, particularly Chapters 7 and 8.

military did or did not do during the war. While Germany is now accepted as a leading nation in Europe after full apologies and compensations for its fascist past, Japan still bears the brunt of criticism by Korea and China for remaining equivocal about the country's wartime activities. Three historical issues in particular have provoked bitter and highly charged controversy over the interpretation of Japan's military past.

One long-burning problem pertains to the so-called comfort women issue. Many women, mainly from Korea, which was a Japanese colony at the time, were recruited to frontline brothels to provide sexual services to Japanese soldiers. These women's accounts indicate that they were kidnapped by Japanese authorities and forced to work as 'sex slaves', an exploitation which has angered Korean public opinion, as well as human rights associations and feminist groups in Japan. In August 1993 the Cabinet secretary of the Japanese government issued a statement to the effect that the Japanese military had initiated the establishment and management of the brothels, engaged in the transfer of the women, and was involved in the brothels' operations not only indirectly but also directly. In many cases, at the request of the military, commercial dealers mainly recruited the women, often against their will. The authorities were directly privy to these activities. The women's lives in the brothels were miserable. Observing that the comfort women endured many pains and incurable psychological and physical damage, the Japanese government expressed 'sincere apologies' and made thorough self-examinations in an official statement. Yet, some Japanese politicians, historians, and right-wing ideologues dispute the government's formal position, arguing that these comfort stations were commercial brothels, with no documented evidence to show enforcement by the Japanese military in existence.

The second issue concerns the so-called Nanking Massacre, in 1937, in which a large number of Chinese soldiers, prisoners, and citizens were murdered in the largest city in southern China by the Japanese military in its war against China. On one end of the spectrum, those who were massacred are estimated at more than three hundred thousand, a claim mainly advanced by Chinese advocates. Japanese historians tend to suggest smaller numbers, although they still range from tens of thousands to more than a hundred thousand. At the other extreme, some revisionist historians in Japan maintain that the entire incident is an outright fabrication.

The third divisive issue revolves around the Yasukuni Shrine, where the war dead are enshrined, including the fourteen leaders of the Japanese military who were executed as class A war criminals at the International Military Tribunal for the Far East immediately after World War II, often referred to as the Tokyo Trial. Located in the center of Tokyo, the shrine was established in 1869 specifically for the repose of soldiers and military officers who lost their lives on battlefields, and it holds a special place in the Shinto system. The shrine is closely connected to the state and has been visited, in either official or private capacity, by prime ministers, Cabinet ministers, and parliamentarians who are committed to nationalistic principles and patriotic doctrines. Against these visits, ill feelings run high in East and Southeast Asian countries, a theater of World War II, where many find it offensive that Japanese politicians pay homage to the wartime military leaders.

At a different level of historical dispute, two sets of uninhabited islands, which the Japanese government has assumed to belong to Japan – Senkaku (Okinawa prefecture) and Takeshima (Shimane prefecture) – are contested respectively by China (as well as Taiwan) and South Korea as their territories.

On 15 August 1995, on the fiftieth anniversary of the war's end, then Prime Minister Tomiichi Murayama issued a statement which read:

During a certain period in the not too distant past, Japan, following a mistaken national policy, advanced along the road to war, only to ensnare the Japanese people in a fateful crisis, and, through its colonial rule and aggression, caused tremendous damage and suffering to the people of many countries, particularly to those of Asian nations. In the hope that no such mistake be made in the future, I regard, in a spirit of humility, these irrefutable facts of history, and express here once again, my feelings of deep remorse and state my heartfelt apology. Allow me to express my feelings of profound mourning for all victims, both at home and abroad, of that history.

While the statement has represented the official position of successive Japanese governments for two decades, a significant number of parliamentarians question whether Japan's military activity was an act of aggression. Some go so far as to maintain that Japan engaged in the war as the liberator of Asian countries under the colonial rule of Western nations. Others argue that Japan is unfairly singled out as the guilty nation despite similar past acts committed by Western nations.

In conservative politics in Japan, ideology which is labeled ultra-nationalistic and extremely right wing in most Western societies occupies a legitimate position and enjoys noticeable popular support. In particular, Tōru Hashimoto (mayor of Osaka) and Shintarō Ishihara (ex-governor of Tokyo), co-leaders of the Japan Restoration Association, have emerged as populist politicians in presenting themselves as ordinary people and attacking Japan's established institutions – the mainstream political parties, national bureaucracy, and labor unions. Their targets include foreign countries, especially the dominance of the Caucasian West and the threat of rising Asian neighbors. These leaders tend to advance a sharp dichotomy of the populace versus the elite, and the foes versus the allies, and represent themselves as heroes defending the common people in the fight against the enemies.

Supporters of these populist leaders are apt to share patriotic and authoritarian ideas, as well as neoliberal competitive principles. In terms of demographic distribution, the self-employed stand out as the support base of Japan's populism in comparison with other occupational groups.[17] Although the unemployed, non-regular workers, and other socially marginalized groups appear to be visible in nationalist and anti-foreigner street demonstrations, the populist leaders also appear to draw support from shopkeepers, small factory owners, independent businessmen, and other self-employed people who have relatively solid occupational bases.

Right-wing populist views continue to galvanize national politics into bitter and emotional debate. In May 2013, for instance, Mayor Hashimoto generated a controversy by openly claiming that the comfort women system had been necessary during the war for Japanese soldiers who were psychologically agitated amid showers of bullets and who needed to rest. He also suggested that United States soldiers stationed in Okinawa should make more use of sex-related entertainment to release their sexual energy and thereby reduce sex crimes around the military bases. Such views have considerable support,[18] although his remarks invited sharp criticism both domestically and internationally, with an overwhelming majority of Japanese voters finding them problematic and inappropriate.

V The Media Establishment

Japan's fourth estate, the world of the mainstream media, is an influential bloc which exists separately from, but closely linked with, the three centers of power.[19] It has several distinctive characteristics. Media organizations exhibit a high degree of centralization and *keiretsu* arrangements similar to those in the corporate circles of manufacturing and trading. They enjoy close links with establishment institutions through exclusive 'reporters' clubs'. Furthermore, the educational and social backgrounds of journalists in large media firms resemble those of elites in other spheres.

---

[17] Matsutani 2013, pp. 115–19. See also Higuchi 2014.

[18] A survey of the *Asahi Shimbun* shows that 75 percent of respondents regarded the Hashimoto remarks as 'problematical', with 20 percent thinking otherwise (AM, 20 May 2013, p. 1). A *Mainichi Shimbun* survey also demonstrates that 71 percent believe that they are 'inappropriate', with 21 percent considering them 'appropriate' (MM, 20 May, p. 1).

[19] Akhavan-Majid 1990; Pharr and Krauss 1996; Krauss 2000.

1   High Degree of Centralization

Japan's print media establishment is highly centralized; the concentration of major media industries in Tokyo facilitates ideological centralization, as discussed in Chapter 3. Five nationally distributed dailies, *Asahi*, *Yomiuri*, *Mainichi*, *Nikkei*, and *Sankei*, collectively claim about half the market. All have their headquarters in Tokyo, maintaining major editorial offices and printing facilities in Osaka and a few other large Japanese cities. These newspapers enjoy mammoth circulations, with the *Yomiuri*, the most widely circulated newspaper in the world, printing some ten million copies daily.

On the whole, these newspapers remain politically neutral so as to maintain their large readership and avoid antagonizing subscribers. The *Asahi* and the *Mainichi* tend to be critical of the government, and the *Yomiuri* and the *Sankei* are regarded as more pro-government, but none of them editorially supports any political party in elections.

In major urban areas, these newspapers appear in both morning and evening editions, and stories in the morning edition are continued in the evening edition. Each edition has several sub-editions distributed to different regions. The contents of each sub-edition differ substantially to cater for local interests. Each morning edition has local news pages, which staff writers at prefectural bureaus write and edit.

The book industry is also highly centralized, with some 80 percent of publishers operating in Tokyo. There is at least one bookshop in every shopping area and near to almost every railway station, with some fourteen thousand bookshops operating throughout the country as community outlets of the knowledge industry. Most editors and writers are Tokyo-based because of the high concentration of book and magazine publishers there.

Two book-sales agents based in Tokyo, *Tōhan*, and *Nippan*, together nearly monopolize distribution networks; bookshops purchase books through them, not directly from publishing houses. Thus a bookshop in Nagano, for example, cannot normally buy books directly from Nagano publishers, who must ship them first to the agents of the Tokyo-based distributors, who in turn sell them to the bookshop. Publishers who publish news and current affairs magazines are unwilling to operate outside the metropolis because they cannot afford to make such a detour in marketing their magazines.

In electronic media, the NHK networks, which are partly funded by the government, occupy a special place and are in the strongest position with regard to funding, prestige, and ratings.[20] Broadcasting since

---

[20] See Krauss 2000 for the political dimensions of NHK's news coverage.

1925, NHK has a long history and monopolized nationwide radio networks until the early 1950s, when commercial radio stations were given licenses. NHK began television broadcasting in 1953, before commercial networks entered the field. It has two nationwide radio networks, two nationwide terrestrial digital television networks, and two satellite television channels beamed across the nation. NHK may be considered partly a pay-television organization, as its budget comprises not only government subsidies but also fees that television viewers are supposed to pay to it.

2   Similarities with Other Large Corporations

The internal structure of Japan's mainstream media organizations resembles that of many other large business corporations. For commercial operations, major media organizations use *keiretsu* arrangements similar to those of large industrial and trading companies. Five key television stations in Tokyo and Osaka are directly connected with five national dailies, with their executives moving across the print and electronic spheres of their organizations, a practice analogous to the *amakudari* system discussed earlier.

In the distribution market, *keiretsu* principles prevail: of more than eighteen thousand newspaper distribution agents around the country, a majority are exclusive or semi-exclusive outlets of major dailies. The big three newspapers – *Asahi*, *Mainichi*, and *Yomiuri* – have their own chains of distribution agents across the nation and compete fiercely for subscribers. *Asahi* paperboys deliver *Asahi* and its associated newspapers only, not *Mainichi* or *Yomiuri*, and vice versa. The sales division of each major newspaper sends sales agents to households across the nation to persuade them to subscribe. Newspapers frequently give away various commodities, such as detergents, towels, watches, travel tickets, and gift vouchers, to expand their long-term market share. In this respect, Japanese newspapers epitomize the market expansion strategy of Japanese corporations. Their blatantly intrusive methods of soliciting for subscription have attracted public criticism, revealing a discrepancy between the high moral principles they advocate in their publications and the manipulative tricks they use in order to increase sales.

Journalists in major media organizations stay with the same company for their entire working lives. Although some exceptionally high-profile star journalists permit themselves to be head-hunted, moving from one organization to another, the overwhelming majority resemble the salarymen and salarywomen in other large firms, remaining loyal to their corporations for some forty years.

Multi-skilling and lateral promotion are also part of the training of print-media journalists. Reporters beginning their careers with major national dailies commence work in a local bureau. Usually, they are first assigned to a police newsbeat, covering cases of homicide, suicide, robbery, embezzlement, fire, traffic accidents, natural disasters, and other incidents in which police are involved. This initiation is aimed at developing general skills in young journalists. In this way it resembles the training of employees in other large enterprises and of officials in the public bureaucracy.

Newspaper companies and television networks rely on the same labor supply as other major corporations in recruiting prospective graduates from universities. Thus, journalists and members of the bureaucratic and business establishment in Japan have quite similar social backgrounds, with a majority of news writers being male graduates of high-ranking universities. Although they may be a countervailing force to Japan's establishment, their sociological attributes are similar to those of the Japanese power elite and differ vastly from those of the majority of the population.

3   Institutional Linkage with the Establishment

Japan's mass media tend to be docile because of the way in which information-gathering units are based in government and business establishments. Government ministries, prefectural and municipal governments, police headquarters, and business and union organizations all provide reporters of major print and electronic media with office space called *kisha kurabu* (reporters' clubs). These clubrooms are normally equipped with telephones and other communication machines, service personnel, and other facilities. Media organizations use them at nominal charge. In almost all cases, club membership is restricted to the reporters of major news organizations and is not open to journalists from minor presses or to foreign journalists. In return, government officials, politicians, and business and union leaders use these clubs as venues for prepared public announcements which the reporters write up as news stories. By constantly feeding information to reporters in this environment, representatives of the institutions which provide club facilities can obliquely control the way in which it is reported to the public. Reporters cannot risk being excluded from their club, because they would then lose access to this regular flow of information. The sentiment of mutual cooperation among all parties involved runs deep, and club members at times agree to place reporting embargoes on sensitive issues.[21] The media establishment is also involved in the policy-making process of government by sending their representatives to its advisory councils.

Japan remains a country where freedom of the press is generally ensured and established. Yet the relationship between major media organizations and political and economic institutions contains elements of congenial rivalry and cordial coordination. Such affinities derive from the media's reliance on Japanese business practice and from the information-gathering infrastructure of exclusive reporters' clubs.

VI   Five Rifts in the Elite Structure

Various elements within Japan are poised to contend with each other. To recapitulate the major points made in this chapter, one might identify five divisions in the elite structure in Japan today.

There is, first, a sharp rivalry between the nationalistic, racist, and particularistic elite on the one hand, and the more internationally minded, purely profit-oriented, and universalistic elite on the other. The symbolic embodiment of the former type is the head of the Japanese Imperial Family, *tennō* (the emperor). The latter type is exemplified by *shōsha*, the well-known Japanese trading houses which have acted as intermediaries between Japanese domestic enterprises and overseas companies in exporting and importing and thereby have contributed to the international stature of the Japanese economy. *Tennō* capitalism and *shōsha* capitalism were compatible as long as the economy was not fully incorporated into the international market. With Japan becoming a global economic superpower, however, *shōsha* capitalism has become increasingly multinational, locating both its production bases and its consumption outlets beyond Japan's national boundaries on a massive scale. For multinational organizations, domestic considerations are only part of a broad international strategy. In contrast, *tennō* capitalists find it difficult to accept encroachment on Japan's domestic priorities; they vigorously oppose the liberalization of agricultural imports and the acceptance of Asian workers in the domestic labor market. They favor moral education and strict discipline in schools, defend Japan's activities during World War II, and attack foreign criticisms of Japan.

The second rift appears between economic superpower expansionists and strategic power-seekers. The former believe that the nation must continue to give priority to the economy-first policy of postwar Japan,

---

[21] See De Lange 1997 for a detailed account of Japan's press club system.

make efforts to further strengthen its economic superpower status, and refrain from taking political and strategic leadership in the international context. According to these advocates, the Constitution should be maintained, and chauvinism and jingoism should be avoided in favor of the economic wellbeing of the nation. In contrast, strategic power-seekers take the view that Japan must explore the possibility of assuming international responsibilities in political and strategic areas in accordance with its economic position in the world. These contenders stress the importance of the Japanese Self-Defense Forces participating in United Nations peacekeeping operations, suggest the possibility of amendments to the Constitution for the nation to become a fully fledged military power, and recommend vigorous efforts to acquire a permanent seat on the United Nations Security Council.

The third division appears to be emerging between United States–oriented and Asia-oriented capitalists. In the late 2000s, China displaced the United States as the most important country for Japanese exports and overtook Japan as the second-largest economy in the world, a development that has inevitably compelled the Japanese economic establishment to calculate the relative importance of the United States and Asian economies for Japan. Japanese companies now expand their off-shore production in Asia, where cheap labor and facilities are available. Japanese business finds vast and attractive markets in the booming economies of East and Southeast Asia. In this context, economic pragmatism overpowers ideological dogma. It is not surprising that the Asia-oriented business elite finds it helpful for the Japanese political establishment to make public apologies for, and to engage in self-criticism over, Japan's wartime atrocities in Asia. This helps smooth the way for Japanese business in the region. In the long run, they argue, the conciliatory stance of some leaders towards Asian countries will pay dividends. Meanwhile, the pro-American group finds it essential for Japan to give top priority to United States–Japan transactions in every sphere of international relations, since the United States is still the most powerful and innovative country with which Japan shares the fundamental values of democracy and advanced market capitalism. The nation's general prosperity owes much to the strategic protection of the region by the military might of the United States. This pro-American group contends that Japan's long-term benefits lie in its stable relationship with the United States, which has enabled the country to establish its economic and technological status in the world.

The fourth area of competition is between rural and urban interests. For a long time, the National Federation of Agricultural Cooperative Unions has delivered votes to the LDP, which in return refused to open the agricultural market to imports. The export-oriented urban manufacturing and service sectors of the economy, however, see the possibility of such protectionism backfiring and making it difficult for them to export goods and commodities overseas on a reciprocal basis. In view of the fact that the farming population is now a small minority in comparison with the workforce in export industries, the business hierarchy of Japan has deserted rural interests in pressing for Japan to join the Transpacific Partnership scheme, which attempts to remove customs tariffs across the board among its membership countries.

The fifth contest, between those who give top priority to economic competition and those who emphasize the importance of political protection of the weak, underlies arguably the most fundamental ideological cleavage in contemporary Japan. On the whole, the economic efficiency argument seems to have the upper hand, given the obvious economic interests of the nation. Since the collapse of socialist systems around the world, economic indices have become universally regarded as the most significant measures of national status. Economy-first principles have become established more firmly than ever as the dominant ideology of Japanese society. However, Japan's very prosperity has now sensitized its public to the quality of life, ecology, and the environment, and to democratic representation and other fairness issues that the nation's elites cannot ignore. Those who press for the protection of the weak regard contemporary Japan as a society whose concern with social justice has become tenuous in favor of economism.

All these rifts seem to have emerged as a consequence of Japan acquiring economic superpower status in the international community and undergoing profound cultural changes domestically. It is also noteworthy that different groups in the dominant segment of Japanese society have different interests on each issue. At one end of the continuum, there are groups staunchly committed to the status quo. At the other end are those advocating major reforms on all fronts. In between, diverse groups form complex networks of alliance and rivalry, thereby creating an increasingly pluralistic structure of power competition.

9 Popular Culture and Everyday Life

Japanese newspapers carried an intriguing story in early July 2006.[1] Two French girls, both aged sixteen, who lived in the suburbs of Paris, were taken into police custody in Poland after making a train trip through Belgium and Germany. Their final destination was Japan. Fascinated by Japanese *manga* and pop music, they had planned to make train connections across Europe and Russia to the Korean peninsula and then travel by ship to Japan, which they fantasized about as the land of *manga* and a dreamlike lifestyle. Not knowing that visas were required to cross national borders, the girls left France with a small amount of money, a mobile phone, a portable audio-player, and *manga* books but were detained by border police when they attempted to enter Belarus. They were good school friends and were enthralled by Japanese *ninja manga* series *NARUTO*, girls' *manga* series *Peach Girl*, visual rock music, and other popular Japanese art forms. Longing to live in the fairyland of Japan's fantastic culture, the girls had left home without letting their parents know, in the belief that the adventure they embarked upon could realize their exciting dreams.

The episode itself could constitute a comical *manga* story, and one can laugh at the girls as naïve and gullible. Yet, although extreme, eccentric, and far-fetched, their ideas of Japan appear to resound in the predominating representations of the nation, which are influenced by the global explosion of Japanese pop culture and range from *manga*, animation, and *sushi* to television dramas. Although these elements do represent aspects of Japanese society, interpretations based excessively or merely on these lenses lose sight of Japan's variegation and heterogeneity and verge on a new kind of stereotyping. Since Japanese society embraces a rich variety of cultural forms that reflect its tradition, stratification, and regional stretch, this chapter examines the internal diversity of Japanese culture

---

[1] See, for example, AM, 5 July 2006, p. 6. The story was based on an article in a French newspaper, *Libération*. The factual detail and accuracy of the report are not the focus of analysis here.

as thoroughly as possible and then returns at the end to the Japanese cultural presence in the transnational context.

I   Two Dualities of Japanese Culture

Broadly, two types of duality cut across the whole landscape of Japanese culture. One pertains to a contrast between elite and popular culture, and the other concerns a disparity between traditional and imported culture.

1   Elite Versus Popular Culture

As in any society, the primary bearers of high and popular forms of Japanese culture can be differentiated along class lines. In the main, a small number of elites relish such traditional cultural styles as classic literature, flower arrangements, tea ceremonies, *noh* and *kyōgen* plays, *koto* music, *bunraku* puppet shows, and classic Japanese *buyō* dancing. They also enjoy Western classical music, opera, art exhibitions, and theatrical performances. Golf is regarded as an elite sport.

These trends tend to belong to the elite culture, not that of most Japanese. Ordinary citizens of Japan adopt much more informal, vulgar, unassuming, ostentatious, and down-to-earth cultural styles. In contrast to the organized subculture of companies and schools, Japan's city life abounds with hedonism, intemperance, and overindulgence. The Japanese also enjoy various forms of traditional grassroots culture, ranging from colorful agrarian festivals to local folk dances. Further, Japan has a range of countercultural groups even though their public visibility may be limited.

2   Traditional Versus Imported Culture

In the depths of the Japanese cultural configuration lies a profound division between traditional native culture and imported Western culture, a dichotomy that is evident in almost every sphere of cultural life in Japan today. In the world of painting, *Nihonga* (Japanese-style painting) and *yōga* (Western oil painting) form two distinct styles. In popular music, *min'yō* (locally developed folk songs) and *enka* (popular ballads)[2] represent native songs with traditional Japanese-style lyrics and melodies, as distinct from the genre of Western pop music, which ranges from rock

---

[2] *Enka* initially designated those songs that street singers sang to musical accompaniment in the late nineteenth century and the early twentieth century but now stands for the style of tunes which follow this tradition.

Table 9.1 Japanese view of 'Japanese culture' of which Japan can be proud

Culture	%
Traditional performing arts	64.7
Historical buildings and remains	56.4
Food	31.5
Dramas, dances, and public entertainment	28.8
Media art	25.3
Seikatsu[a] (everyday life)	25.3
Fine arts	24.7
Literature	18.0
Music[b]	13.5
Pop music	6.2
Other	0.2

Source: Cabinet Office 2009.
Notes: The survey allowed multiple responses.
[a] See Chapter 10, Section I.
[b] This category does not include pop music.

to folk songs. To many Japanese, *sumo*, *judo*, *karate*, and other traditional sports of Japan have different appeals from domesticated popular
sports like baseball and soccer. The duality of culture in Japan – between
traditional and imported – reflects the nation's 'late-developer' status
(discussed in Chapter 1) and culturally peripheral position in which
it has had to learn from 'early developers' that have enjoyed cultural
supremacy internationally. Studies of cultural consumption in Japan,
therefore, should bear this historical context in mind and refrain from
the unqualified application of the Western models to the country's contemporary cultural circumstances.

The term 'culture' is notoriously elusive, ambiguous, and multifaceted.
Independent of academic debate about what it means, the Japanese are
generally tradition-oriented in assessing what they regard as 'proudly
Japanese culture', according to a national survey (Table 9.1); a majority
list 'traditional performing arts' (*dentō geinō*) and 'historical buildings
and remains' as such items. They would include various forms of the
native art of public entertainment, ranging from *kabuki* to local festivals.
In comparison, food culture, media art, and pop music, which have
attracted global attention and interest, rank relatively low in the mass
evaluations of 'Japanese culture'.[3]

Quantitatively, of course, consumers of popular culture dominate
the nation's cultural panorama. Although Japan's popular culture is
multifarious, it represents the ways of life that the common people enjoy

[3] Cabinet Office 2009.

Table 9.2   Relative characteristics of three types of popular culture

Characteristic	Mass culture	Folk culture	Alternative culture
Historical origin	Recent/contemporary	Traditional	Contemporary/traditional
Mass means of communication	Essential	Minimal/absent	Minimal/absent
Considerations of marketability	Imperative	Peripheral	Minimal
Consumption orientation	High	Limited	Low
Durability of contents	Subject to consumer popularity	Relatively durable	Subject to internal group cohesion
Geographic basis	Diffusion from urban areas	Both rural and urban	Variable
Concentration pattern	Tendency towards centralization	Regionally diversified	Tendency towards decentralization
Producers	Mostly specialists	Some specialists, mostly amateurs	Mostly amateurs, some specialists
Basis of sharedness	Shared media information	Shared historical memories	Shared defiance against established order
Size of the population involved	Large	Large	Small (though many people may be attracted, they have no means to practice)
Emic category of people	*Taishū*, *shōshū*, or *bunshū*	*Jōmin*	*Seikatsusha* or *jinmin*

and share. For analytical purposes, this chapter divides popular culture into three categories: mass culture, which has spread with the expansion of the consumer market and the development of mass communication; folk culture, which is based upon conventions, mores, and customs of the indigenous tradition; and alternative culture, which a small number of ordinary citizens generate spontaneously as a counterculture challenge to the cultural status quo. Table 9.2 provides a conceptual map of these three classes of popular culture and their characteristics. The brief descriptions that follow sketch something of their diversity.

II   Mass Culture

Mass culture in contemporary Japan is a lively and potent force that affects numerous people through mass media. It relies on its marketability because it cannot survive unless it is consumed by a large number of people; it is consumer-oriented because the size of the market determines its viability. Japan's mass culture today includes:

- television and radio entertainment culture, which is the most pervasive vehicle of mass entertainment;
- the popular press, which appeases the mass appetite for gossip, scandals, and other grubby realities of life;
- fashion and trend culture, where mass-produced and mass-distributed goods are accepted and rejected;
- the entertainment culture that develops around theaters, restaurants, amusement facilities, and sex shops;
- high-tech culture, in which computers and computer-based information networks serve as the major intermediaries; and
- commercialized traditional elite culture, in which masters of flower arranging, tea ceremonies, and the like instruct in traditional cultural practices for high fees.

With these dimensions overlapping, Japan's mass culture flourishes in diverse forms and styles, all of which use channels of mass information distribution, such as television, advertisements, computers, or other forms of large-scale publicity, to generate a sense of doing things together.

This chapter surveys Japan's mass culture by first browsing the world of electronic and print media and then scanning four phenomena peculiar to contemporary Japan, several of which have achieved widespread international popularity: *manga, pachinko, karaoke,* and love hotels and other products of the love industry. Finally, it takes a brief look at the ways in which traditional elite culture is commercialized and popularized at the community level by the masters of various schools of traditional art.

1   Entertainment Media

(a)   Television and Radio

With approximately 90 percent of Japanese watching television every day, for about three hours and fifty-four minutes on average on weekdays,[4] the television industry has the most powerful homogenizing effect on the public, who share the same visual information across the country. This pattern occurs around the world. Many Japanese television programs, like television programs elsewhere, are designed to incite curiosity, envy, and anger. For instance, most major commercial stations televise morning entertainment shows filled with scandal, gossip, and other sensational stories, about which a panel of self-styled and complacent social commentators makes moralizing comments. Many afternoon programs targeting housewives have a similar format. Even newscasters openly make

---

[4] NHK 2011, p. 23.

evaluative comments between news stories, taking one side and accusing the other. With high ratings, these shows contribute greatly to the formation of homogeneous social views.

As is the case with many other societies, Japan's prime-time television is filled with nonsense and funny programs, because television stations' ratings determine their annual profits. In a bid to win the largest slice of the audience, major commercial stations' programs are full of slapstick comedies, knockabout competition games, and voyeuristic shows. Many families have developed the habit of watching television during dinner, losing the sphere of family conversation and subjecting themselves nearly exclusively to what television programs feed them.

The centralized organization of mass media in general, and television in particular, makes it easy for central image-makers to capture the nation's curiosity. This contributes to Japan's frequent nationwide crazes, including those for tea mushrooms in 1975, UFO searching in 1978, Rubik's cubes in 1980–81, and family computers in 1985–86. In the middle of the oil shock in 1973, toilet paper sold out in supermarkets around the country because of the unfounded but widely circulated rumor that Japan might face a paper shortage. In 1994, when the government imported rice because of a poor rice crop the previous year, some sections of the nation went into near hysteria and attempted to buy up domestic rice from rice dealers. In 1995, the discovery of a number of poisonous redback spiders in the Osaka area led to a nationwide search for them, with rumors of venomous spiders hiding in every community. Even in the 2000s, booms in herbal remedies come and go, so that a fad for eating certain vegetable roots is quickly replaced by one for eating special kinds of seaweed, which is in turn replaced by a fashion for decocting certain herbs. In all of these cases of fads and mass hysteria, the media, and especially television, has played a major role in stirring up feelings of insecurity and inciting a sense of national panic.

Radio listeners have declined in number with the arrival of television. Only about 13 percent of Japanese tune in to radio, yet those who do listen for more than two-and-a-half hours a day.[5] Among occupational groups, a markedly high proportion of self-employed persons listen to radio while doing their work. For carpenters, noodle-shop owners, and hairdressers, radio is an important source of information and entertainment during work. More than a dozen radio stations operate in major city areas, and each has a different group of listeners. While young fans tune in to FM music stations, some late-night radio programs are important to many older people. Unlike television, radio thus addresses segmented audiences with differing needs and requirements.

[5] NHK 2011, p. 23.

(b)   Tabloid Press and Weekly Magazines

Japan has many sensationalist, scandal-hungry, and exposé-oriented tabloid newspapers and weekly magazines whose approaches contrast sharply with those of the established and sanitized broadsheet newspapers. *Fuji* and *Nikkan Gendai* are the two leading tabloids. This category of publications also includes scandalous photographic weeklies, such as *Friday*. In addition, some fourteen sports newspapers cover mainly baseball, *sumo* wrestling, soccer, and general entertainment news, selling a total of some 3.8 million copies per day.[6] All major newspapers and established publishing houses produce these papers and magazines, cashing in on the public's desire for non-sterilized stories.

In contrast to the sanitized and balanced major newspapers and television networks, weekly magazines unashamedly publish muckraking stories, sex scandals, and revelations of trickery, often at the risk of being sued for defamation. Because mainstream media produce stories only in socially correct ways, readers who are interested in 'dirty *honne* and *ura* realities' turn to these yellow magazines. *Shūkan Bunshun, Shūkan Shinchō, Shūkan Posuto, Shūkan Gendai,* and many others compete in the weekly magazine market. The vitality of these publications suggests that a large proportion of the Japanese public identifies with popular culture at this level. Their contents differ depending on their readership. A majority of the weeklies target salarymen, running sexist, nationalist, and anti-government stories. Some weeklies regularly feature color pictures of nude women and sex-life confessions of movie stars and television personalities. Other magazines, such as *Sapio*, have followers among anti-establishment youngsters and offer behind-the-scenes stories written in sensational language. Various women's weeklies, such as *Josei Seven, Josei Jishin,* and *Shūkan Josei,* focus on stardom, royal families, and female sexuality.

These papers and magazines target the commuting public in addition to general readers, selling in large quantities at newsstands and kiosks at railway and subway stations. Because many company employees in major metropolitan areas travel long distances between home and the workplace, reading is common on commuter trains.

These publications not only reveal a deviant, hidden side of Japanese society but also reflect variations in both overt and covert desires of Japan's reading public. Editors of publications oriented to the male readership run bluntly sexist and violent cartoons. Some magazines for young

---

[6] Data compiled in 2013 by the Management Department of the Japan Newspaper Publishers and Editors Association. For a brief survey of sports journalism in Japan, see Okazaki 2001.

women highlight stories about how to look feminine and how to please and seduce men. The market for the popular press is highly differentiated and is catered for by a wide variety of magazines, including magazines for career women, established businessmen, teenage girls, leisure-oriented men, and housewives. Their diversity also demonstrates that the types of aspirations, frustrations, and grievances they publish reflect the social locations of their readers.

2   Four Japanese Phenomena

Even casual observers of Japan's mass culture cannot overlook four obvious phenomena. One, pertaining to reading taste, is that so many Japanese, including adults, are avid readers of cartoons (*manga*). Another, in the area of solitary amusements, is the obsession of many Japanese with playing *pachinko* pinball games in *pachinko* parlors. The third, in the sphere of collective entertainment, is the nationwide popularity of *karaoke* singing. The fourth is the commercialization of love and sex in ways that have given rise to several unique Japanese institutions.

(a)   Manga

Manga (literally 'funny pictures') is a generic term that covers cartoons, comic strips, and caricatures. In 2011 the sales value of *manga* books and magazines comprised some 22 percent of all published titles in Japan. The total circulation of *manga* books and magazines exceeds 968 million copies, approximately one-third of the total distribution of all publications combined,[7] a pattern that does not exist in any other industrialized society. The weekly *manga* magazine for young boys, *Shūkan Shōnen Jump*, sells some 2.9 million copies per week and is the bestselling magazine in Japan. *Shūkan Shōnen Magazine* occupies second place, selling 1.5 million copies per week.[8] More than two thousand comic books are published every year. Many of these books and magazines are story *manga* that have clear themes and narratives. Further, amateur *manga* writers publish their own magazines, often with a small coterie of enthusiasts, and sell them through private channels or at the so-called comic markets (abbreviated as *comike*), where like-minded *manga* lovers exchange information and market their products.

In the second half of the twentieth century Japan's popular culture interacted with that of the United States with great intensity.

[7] Shuppan Kagaku Kenkyūsho 2012, pp. 3–4 and 231.
[8] Shuppan Kagaku Kenkyūsho 2012, pp. 238–40.

Immediately after the defeat in World War II and the United States' occupation of Japan, the nation's cultural 'other' was almost exclusively 'American culture' in the context of the United States' dominance in many spheres of Japanese life. Osamu Tezuka, the founding father of Japan's postwar breed of *manga* and animation, attempted to absorb and compete with the techniques developed by Walt Disney. The author of *Astro Boy*, Tezuka first published its Japanese original under the title *Atomu taishi* (Ambassador Atom) in 1951, during the Allied occupation period, while emulating American animation. With main characters featuring big eyes, story lines full of high-tech devices, and a tenuous link to Japanese scenery, Tezuka's style founded the *modus operandi* of Japan's *manga* and animation writers.[9] In 2009, the *Astro Boy* film was released globally, highlighting the contemporary relevance of Tezuka's original work and the international popularity of this genre.

While *manga* are generally designed to provoke laughter in readers, a genre known as *gekiga* (dramatized pictorial stories) is a *manga* form which depicts the dark side of human existence. Like long novels, *gekiga* have complex story lines, mostly with an undertone of malice, hostility, and bitter sarcasm towards the established order. *Gekiga* initially won popularity in the 1960s among youngsters uprooted from rural areas to become blue-collar workers in factories in large cities. Uneducated and exploited, at the bottom of Japan's high-growth economy, these young workers empathized with the *gekiga* figures who resisted and challenged their powerful rulers and moral authorities, often through illegitimate and unconventional means. A series of peasant uprisings during the feudal period formed the central theme of seventeen volumes of *Ninja bugei-chō* (Ninjas' martial arts notebooks), the landmark *gekiga* that established the genre.[10] The solidarity of dissident groups also provided a theme for some *gekiga*, which had a wide readership among student rebels during campus turmoil in the late 1960s and early 1970s.

Women cartoonists have played significant roles in *manga* production. The best-known postwar Japanese cartoonist, Machiko Hasegawa, was a woman who penned the comic strips that centered on the everyday life of a housewife named *Sazae-san*, and her family members. Serialized in the morning edition of the *Asahi* newspaper for more than three decades, *Sazae-san* became a household name and popularized a housewife's perspective on Japanese society throughout the postwar period. Since the 1970s, an increasing number of talented women cartoonists have published *manga* specifically addressed to teenage girls. Attracting a wide range of readers, some of these authors have moved beyond the genre of girls' *manga* and have become the engine of contemporary *manga* culture.

---

[9] Schodt 2007.   [10] The animation version was released in 2009 as *Kamui Gaiden*.

The *manga* industry is another example of the orientation towards the mass customization of Japan's cultural capitalism, as it targets a large variety of socio-cultural groups that have different interests, identities, and curiosities – for example, *kodomo manga* for children, *shōjo manga* for girls, *shōnen manga* for boys, *sararīman manga* for office employees, family *manga* for middle-class households, *supōtsu manga* for sports fans, gourmet *manga* for epicureans, *gekiga* for social dissidents, and so on.[11]

While the socioeconomic status of individual *manga* readers conditions their preferred genre, *manga* enjoy great popularity across a wide range of age groups. Some observers attribute this to increasing social pressures of compliance brought to bear upon the school, work, and community lives of many Japanese. In a world of intense *tatemae* conformism, readers of *manga* find freedom in the peculiar and often iconoclastic fantasies, often laced with sex and bloody violence, in boys' *manga*. Other analysts see the popularity of *manga* against the background of the increasingly visually oriented lifestyles of the high-tech age, and regard the Japanese as trailblazers in this field. Section VI below will scrutinize these trends.

Both the prosperity generation and the global generation described in Chapter 3 are hooked into the cultural environment expanding from the world of *manga* into that of animation films, internet-based illustrated characters, doll-like or life-sized figures, and other assorted *manga*-related products.[12] These cultural goods are often interactively produced and packaged. Animation heroine and hero dolls, for example, are marketed after the popularity of their *anime* film counterparts is established, as is the case with Pokémons and the marketing of their figurines.

Violence and sex have been both the strength and the weakness of Japanese *manga*. On the one hand, these aspects make the story lines complex and provide intricate plots that simple children's cartoons generally do not have. Both violence and sex constitute realities of life that individuals must face. To that extent, these elements have contributed to the increasing sophistication of Japan's popular visual art products. On the other hand, commercialism and profit-motives have led to an increase in levels of graphic violence and brutality featuring rape scenes, cruel murder plots, and sadistic savagery that would offend the majority of society. In 2009, the United Nations Committee on the Elimination of Discrimination against Women urged Japan to ban 'the sale of video games or cartoons involving rape and sexual violence against women which normalize and promote sexual violence against women and girls'.[13]

[11] See Norris 2009, pp. 238–40.
[12] Japan's popular culture in general and *manga* and *anime* in particular continued to be the subject of scholarly studies in the 2000s, including Napier 2005; and Craig 2000.
[13] AM, 20 August 2009, p. 8; AM, 12 September 2009, p. 31.

Although Japan's *manga* have increased their presence internationally, their domestic consumption has declined over time (see Figure 1.1). The bestselling weekly *manga* magazine, *Shūkan Shōnen Jump*, which sold more than six million copies per week at its peak in 1995, published far less than half this number in 2007, a downturn that reflects a similar trend across the domestic *manga* magazine industry.[14] The trend is attributable to the changing consumption patterns of the younger generation who now choose to spend their money primarily on mobile phones, the internet, and other forms of digital life and only secondarily on the products of print media, which they deem unfashionable, tasteless, and tacky. The proliferation of coffee shops with *manga* libraries, shops which rent comics for a small fee, and used-book stores selling *manga* continues to satisfy the appetites of this generation, although the digitalization of their lifestyles makes it inevitable that *manga* contents will be increasingly consumed through virtual media. Japanese visual culture appears to be fast moving towards the futuristic end of the spectrum of cultural capitalism.

(b)   Pachinko

Pachinko pinball, a nationwide pastime enjoyed by more than 10 percent of the population,[15] allows players to divert their minds from their cares. In a *pachinko* saloon with hundreds of computer-operated pinball machines, filled with cigarette smoke and resounding with popular music, many people spend hours attempting to put pinballs into holes on the board. When a ball goes into a hole, the *pachinko* machine returns a large number of balls to the player, who can exchange them not only for such prizes as chocolates and cigarettes, but also for cash. Although cash prizes are prohibited, an overwhelming majority of winners cash their acquired pinballs at backstreet cashing shops. In this sense, *pachinko* is a very accessible form of gambling; the annual sales figure of the *pachinko* industry far exceeds the yearly total turnover of the more visible forms of gambling, such as horse, bicycle, speedboat, and car races. The number of *pachinko* parlors exceeds ten thousand,[16] twice as many as that of high schools in Japan.

Although there is controversy over the international birthplace of *pachinko*,[17] there is little dispute that in Japan it originated immediately

---

[14] AM, 7 September 2008, p. 33.

[15] Japan Productivity Center 2013 demonstrates that some 11.1 million enjoyed *pachinko* in 2012 throughout Japan. The annual turnover amounted to some 1.9 billion yen.

[16] An estimate made by the National Police Agency 2011. See <www.nichiyukyo.or.jp/condition/shop.php>.

[17] Pierre Baudry maintains that *pachinko* originated in the late nineteenth century in France (*Nihon Keizai Shimbun*, 13 December 1994, morning edition, p. 36).

after World War II in Nagoya, where many military aircraft manufacturing firms clustered in the region had to find a profitable way of using countless surplus ball bearings. Resourceful entrepreneurs devised a simple *pachinko* machine, which provided the masses with cheap amusement and spread across the country. The machine became more sophisticated as technological innovations were added.

Some mass culture observers attribute the popularity of *pachinko* in Japan, particularly among blue-collar workers, to its affinity with the pattern of their work, in which they compete with each other in finger dexterity on assembly lines in the same noisy surroundings.[18] These workers entertain themselves as an extension of their work environment. This is why the number of *pachinko* parlors increased most rapidly during Japan's economic growth and in the areas where the working environment became quickly mechanized. One may also argue that *pachinko* attracts so many Japanese partly because it is essentially detached from direct human interaction. Playing *pachinko* does not require players to interact face-to-face with others. To the extent that mass culture points to daily realities which the masses wish to evade, the non-interactive quality of *pachinko* games indirectly testifies to the intensity of group pressures and constraints on the working and community lives of the Japanese.

(c)   Karaoke

Karaoke became a popular form of mass entertainment relatively recently in Japan and worldwide. It is believed[19] to have originated in the 1970s in a snack bar in Kobe, where management recorded a tape for use at practice sessions for professional singers. In 1976 an electronics company commenced selling a machine called Karaoke 8, which selected an eight-track cartridge tape containing four tunes. This prototype developed into laser-disk *karaoke*, VHD *karaoke*, CD *karaoke*, and so on, as this sort of equipment became standard in entertainment establishments popular with salarymen. Many customers had a good time diverting their minds from their cares by drinking and singing with a microphone in hand. The taped accompaniment of *karaoke* gave them the fantasy of singing like professional singers on stage. As various types of family *karaoke* equipment appeared on the market, the vogue that started in amusement venues spread to some well-to-do households. More than one-third of Japanese are estimated to have participated in *karaoke* in 2012, and it is now established as the most popular pastime activity in Japan, with more

---

[18] Tada 1978, pp. 42–51.   [19] AE, 25 July 1992, p. 5.

than half of all teenagers and those in their twenties enjoying this form of diversion.[20]

Although *karaoke* singing takes place in the apparently collective environment of bars and pubs, singers face a television screen which displays lyrics and song-related pictures, while those who are waiting to sing are busily scanning the song list in order to choose a song, without listening to the person singing. The singer's co-workers usually clap loudly in appreciation, but in this ambience, meaningful conversation is impossible, and this appears to give a sense of relaxation to Japanese *karaoke* participants.[21] It is no wonder that the so-called *karaoke* boxes, where singers can behave more audaciously, have become widespread in Japan since the late 1980s. Proliferating in the streets of busy quarters, they provide small, self-contained, soundproofed rooms where anybody can sing to the tune of *karaoke* music. These *karaoke* boxes enable song lovers to give vent to their emotions and have gained popularity among housewives, young women workers, and students. It may not be wide of the mark to speculate that the mass culture of *karaoke* has established itself, like *pachinko*, as an avenue by which ordinary people can escape the stringent realities of Japanese work and community life.[22]

(d)   The Love Industry

Japan's sex industry reflects the underside of Japanese society. For instance, the love hotels that thrive in Japanese cities reflect the resourcefulness of pragmatic hotel operators. These hotels openly provide rooms to couples wishing to have sex. Some spend a few hours and pay hourly rates. Others stay overnight, generally at a reasonable rate. These hotels do not have a lobby, a restaurant, or even a coffee room. For obvious reasons, lodgers are not required to register their names and addresses. Establishments of this kind, which exceed six thousand in number across the country,[23] flourish partly because of the high frequency of premarital sex and adultery and partly because of the unfavorable housing conditions in Japanese cities.

The prostitution industry prospers despite the Prostitution Prevention Law implemented in 1965. Illicit underground groups arrange 'lovers' banks' and 'date clubs' and play cat-and-mouse with police. 'Soap land' joints, which offer private rooms, each with a bath, are virtually brothels

---

[20] Japan Productivity Center 2013, pp. 38, 42.   [21] Satō 1994, p. 114.

[22] See Mitsui and Hosokawa 2001 for the influence of *karaoke* in different parts of the world.

[23] National Police Agency 2013.

where 'massage girls' work as sex workers. Called Turkish baths in the past, these houses of ill repute, which exist in almost all cities, testify to the uninhibited flourishing of the sex industry.[24]

Although the sexual revolution has enabled and empowered young women to have active sex lives and to choose their sexual partners freely, some have been trapped in exploitative sexual situations, as observed in the growing cases of *enjo kōsai* (paid dating), a practice in which teenage girls typically offer sexual services to middle-aged men in return for monetary compensation. Online dating sites provide opportunities for strangers to meet and explore sexual encounters, a system which sometimes leads to tragic criminal cases.

On the other side of the equation, the marriage industry has played up images of romantic love and luxurious wedding receptions to manipulate the aspirations of the prosperity and global generations. As a result, marriage ceremonies and receptions for young upper middle class Japanese have become so lavish that their cost sometimes exceeds their participants' annual salaries. Hotels and ceremonial halls display advertisements for weddings in subways and trains, Japanese urban scenery indicating the sizeable market. The marriage industry turns wedding receptions into lavish performances. In a standard package, the couple appears in a gondola and in the dark, with candles, dry ice 'smoke', laser lights, and other stage effects to dramatize the occasion. Although the increasingly harsh economic conditions in recent years have forced many couples to hold plainer and more sober ceremonies, a contrast between the *omote* spectacles of the marriage industry and the *ura* realities of the sex industry remains stark and even intriguing.

Mass culture depends on its market. Once the consumers of mass culture weary of it, it must change to maintain its appeal. Thus, popular songs come and go. Fashion is by definition temporary and changing. The *pachinko* industry changes its machine format to satisfy players' appetite for change and high technology. Fluidity, variability, and transformability characterize contemporary mass culture.

3   Cross-status Cultural Consumption

Japan's pattern of cultural consumption shows that an increasing number of people relish both elite culture and popular culture at the same time. Two discernible trends cutting across class lines might be labeled

---

[24] There were more than 1,200 'soap lands' around the country in 2012 (National Police Agency 2013). Kadowaki 2002 estimates that the illegal income of the sex industry amounts to 1.2 trillion yen, more than 1 percent of the national budget.

omnivorous consumption.[25] One is a 'downward' move in which high-status individuals come to enjoy popular culture in addition to elite culture, a pattern that reflects an elite strategy to blur status lines by sharing the same conditions and appearances with subordinates. In many Japanese factories, middle managers wear the same work clothes as blue-collar workers and have lunch in the same dining room with them. Enterprise unions, prevalent in large corporations, are formed by all non-executive employees and make little distinction based on occupational classification. As an extension of the ostensibly inclusive approach of this kind, it is not uncommon for business managers to enjoy singing in *karaoke* bars with workers or drinking and eating in inexpensive taverns.

The other trend is an 'upward' process in which the masses go beyond their popular culture sphere to familiarize themselves with elite culture. The popularization of high culture has led to a sphere of activities which can be labeled as popular elite culture. Although emanating from the elite sector, it has many followers. To facilitate this process, three avenues are noticeable.

First, and most importantly, educational institutions play significant roles in popularizing elite culture through their formal curricula. Most Japanese pupils learn about high culture at school by studying Chinese classical literature (called *kanbun*), practicing calligraphy, and playing such Western musical instruments as piano, violin, and flute. Many schools have extracurricular club activities called *bukatsu*, in which students engage in artistic activities such as literary writing, drama performance, *kyudo* (Japanese archery), *igo* (a board game), and flower arrangement. Students have been trained to appreciate these cultural forms and to acquire the skills associated with them as a necessary condition of being culturally educated individuals.

In particular, many of them obtain the artistry of Western classical music, Western-style painting, and Western literature through school structures rather than through family-based processes on which the European analysis of cultural consumption tends to focus. In this sense, most Western high culture acquirers in Japan are school-based 'cultural parvenus' who rarely suffer from inferiority complexes and instead take pride in their achievements. Most Japanese are thus more or less familiar with high cultural activities, although only a small segment of the population regularly practices them after school life.

The second avenue comprises social education, a sphere of cultural learning mainly for adults who have completed formal education and desire to study high culture. Most notably, 'culture centers' of various

---

[25] See Kataoka 2000, although she focuses primarily on the 'downward' process discussed below.

kinds now operate in urban areas, mostly under the management of mass media organizations, and attract millions of avid learners. The courses offered cover a wide range of subjects – traditional Japanese poetry writing, *shigin* (recitation of Chinese poems), calligraphy, English conversation, *bonsai* gardening, and professional photography, to name only a few. Students are predominantly female, with women in the age group of the fifties and above comprising more than half of all students. Their appetite for artistic learning exceeds that of men, and beats a significant path towards cultural attainment.

The third avenue involves home-based private lessons. Most notably in the sphere of traditional elite culture, this path has been institutionalized by the *iemoto* system, in which *iemoto*, the head family of a school of an established art form, oversees nationwide hierarchical networks of followers with various levels of teachers as middle managers. In the case of tea ceremonies, two major schools exist, each having its *iemoto*. In flower arranging, several schools compete with each other with similar *iemoto* structures. Under the authorization of *iemoto*, most teachers in these disciplines run teaching sessions at their homes and receive tuition fees from students. When students finish a course, they can acquire certificates from the *iemoto* to certify that they have the required skills, but they must pay considerable sums to the *iemoto* through their teacher, who retains some of the money. After arriving at a certain level, students can become qualified teachers. This licensing system ensures the *iemoto* households receive not only social prestige but also material gains, with some of them managing vocational schools and junior colleges of their own. They prosper from the successful proliferation of the notion that middle-class women must have some knowledge of tea ceremonies and flower arranging before marriage. On the whole, the home-based mode of cultural capital reproduction appears to be more closely associated with Japan's traditional high culture.

Less structured civic cultural groups also operate in communities. Lovers of Japanese, Western, and Chinese painting and woodblock printing attend private tutorial sessions conducted by experts for a fee, with some devotees forming clubs with regional and national networks. At many Buddhist temples, priests teach brush calligraphy to children. Private *juku* lessons, where students learn academic subjects at the homes of instructors, also follow the tradition of home-based cultural teaching.

Against the backdrop of these intersecting paths of cross-status cultural consumption, numerous literary coterie magazines exist around the nation, and they are edited, distributed, and read by avid composers of poems and novels. Many contributors to these magazines are amateur writers from various walks of life who find satisfaction in creative writing. Chinese chess, *igo*, which a small circle of elites enjoyed in the past, is so popular that some communities have parlors where enthusiasts play against each other. With an established national association, nearly two thousand amateur learners of *kanshi* (classic Chinese poems) around the country enjoy composing poetry in accordance with the rules of rhyming and writing established in China in the eighth century, an amazing number considering their complexity.

The popularized elite culture does not really reach the bottom of the social scale and remains the pastime of the relatively well off, if not the very rich. Yet contemporary Japanese society has solid layers of local intelligentsia and grassroots artists who are popular practitioners of high culture.

4   Compartmentalization and Solitary Culture

In the age of computers, the internet, and mobile phones, solitary mass culture has proliferated among Japanese youths, whose lifestyles are increasingly compartmentalized with the expansion of the virtual world. Nintendo computer games and Sony Walkman initially set the pace, enabling mass culture consumers to play antisocially with cultural products in a closed sphere and to disengage from face-to-face social interaction. Emails, text messages, blogs, iPads, and other cyberspace operations have accelerated the pattern of social isolation and provided fertile ground for misanthropic youths, called *otaku*. In extreme cases, they are obsessed with animation, *manga*, computer games, and other unsocial hobbies, shunning direct human interactions, locking themselves in their rooms, and sharing their interests online with other youngsters under similar conditions. Whether creative or pathological, the lifestyle of this type of youth, which appears to be highly discernible in Japan, the birthplace of many *otaku* goods, has heralded a new form of subculture internationally. Some three in ten men aged between their twenties and forties deem themselves part of *otaku* culture.[26] Section VI of this chapter discusses this phenomenon in some detail.

The spread of *otaku* culture is caused in part by the casualization of the labor force in a globalized economy. While the number of regular employees whose job security is guaranteed has shrunk, the number of casual employees who work on a short-term, hourly basis has grown at the same time to promote economic rationalism and efficiency, as discussed in Chapter 4. With precarious work conditions, low wages, and irregular working hours, casual employees stand in diametric

---

[26] See the survey conducted by the *Asahi Shimbun* and reported in AM, 3 January 2006, p. 9.

opposition to workaholic permanent staff in their work ethic and aspirations. As their everyday life does not follow a corporate, systematic, and organized routine, casual workers find meaning and satisfaction in becoming addicted to cheaply and readily available entertainment in their isolated world.

These tendencies prompt a considerable number of youths to withdraw from school and society and to stay at home in seclusion. *Hikikomori* (social withdrawal) has become a national phenomenon,[27] and it constitutes a brooding ground for *otaku* culture. To this extent, *otaku* culture has sprung from the competitive education that generates a sharp divide between conformist students and alienated non-conformists.

Some male *otaku* youths hold the erotic orientation known as *moe*, a strong fetish obsession for the characters of computer games and animation stories.[28] These characters are generally young, good-looking, and 'cute' girls with big eyes, images born of a virtual world. Life-sized figures, large dolls, and other so-called character goods fill the floors of computer shops in Akihabara, a quarter in Tokyo lined with electronic stores known as the epicenter of *otaku* culture.[29] This is a virtual sphere far removed, for instance, from the sensual and fleshly world of *geisha* culture.

III Folk Culture

Folk culture is the type of popular culture that has been conventionalized in the everyday life of the populace. It includes local festivals, seasonal holidays, and traditional playful art. Having taken root over decades or centuries, the content of folk culture differs from place to place and relies on the historical memories of people in a region. Folk culture requires neither mass products nor mass media, and, while it does not have to be mass consumed, it normally involves a large number of people in a locality or region, or even throughout Japan.

1   Local Festivals as Occasions of *Hare*

Japan's ethnographers and ethnologists have long regarded three Japanese emic concepts – *hare*, *ke*, and *kegare* – as fundamental categories for understanding Japanese folk culture. *Hare* represents situations where formal, ceremonial, and festive sentiments prevail. On these occasions (*hare no hi*), people dress in their best clothes (*haregi*) and eat gala meals

[27] See Zielenziger 2006.   [28] Kijima 2012.
[29] This is why *otaku* culture is also called *Akiba-kei*, with *Akiba* standing for Akihabara in abbreviated form and *kei* meaning type or clique.

(*hare no shokuji*). In contrast, *ke* stands for routine life in which people do things habitually, conventionally, and predictably. As they consume energy in *ke*-based daily lives, they arrive at a condition of *kegare*, in which their vitality withers. Some analysts argue that *hare* occasions are organized to animate, invigorate, and restore vivacity.[30] Others suggest that the characteristics of a given folk society are determined by whether it regards opposite types as being *hare* and *ke* or *hare* and *kegare*.[31] Japanese folk-culture researchers also debate the extent to which these concepts correspond to the conventional sociological distinction between the sacred and the profane.

Local festivals which represent important *hare* affairs are closely linked with the tradition of community Shintoism, Japan's indigenous religion, understanding of which requires knowledge of the ways in which religion is practiced in Japan. To begin with, sociologists estimating the distribution of individual religious affiliation in Japan encounter difficulties because the total membership of all religious groups, sects, and denominations appears to exceed the population of Japan. This apparent anomaly derives from the fact that many Japanese belong to two or more religious groupings without feeling inconsistent. A number of Japanese families have both a household Shinto shrine and a Buddhist altar. Most Japanese find it quite acceptable to visit Shinto shrines on festive days, have a marriage ceremony in a Christian church, and worship the souls of their ancestors at a Buddhist temple. In this sense, the Japanese religious system is non-exclusivist, eclectic, and syncretic.

Shintoism has no scriptures; it developed a mythology that the Japanese nation was created by the goddess of the sun, when she emerged from a rock hut and performed a strip dance in front of it. The Japanese term *kami*, which corresponds to 'god' in English, originally meant 'that which excels in its act, be it good or bad'. Belief in *kami*, therefore, does not imply faith in a single god. Instead, the most native of Japan's religions is based on worship of *mana*, the supernatural or mystical power that resides not only in human beings but also in animals, plants, rivers, and other natural things. Most Shintoist shrines deify human figures who excelled in some way. Thus, for example, Tenjin shrines in many parts of the country enshrine Michizane Sugawara, a ninth century politician and scholar, as the god of scholarship. The Izumo Shrine in Shimane prefecture is well known as a shrine dedicated to a mythological character, Ōkuninushi no Mikoto, a figure believed to have excelled in medical and magical matters and worshipped as a god who presides over marriage. The Meiji Shrine in the heart of Tokyo enshrines Emperor Meiji, the first

---

[30] Sakurai 1982.   [31] Namihira 1979.

emperor of modern Japan. Inari shrines across Japan venerate foxes and their alleged supernatural power.

Shintoism also includes elements of animism, the veneration of spirits which are believed to dwell in people and in non-human beings such as trees and rocks. The animistic tendency in Japanese thinking manifests itself on ceremonial occasions. At the commencement of construction work, even some mega-scale multinational corporations will organize a purification ceremony to appease the 'god of earth'. Although animism is often accompanied by superstition, some ecologists and environmentalists in Japan observe that the tradition of animism must be seriously studied and selectively revitalized as a system of values for the protection of nature, to counter the scientific industrialism that has brought about the worldwide environmental crisis.

Traditionally, those who live near a Shinto shrine are called *ujiko*, children under the protection of the community deity, and contribute to the organization and proceedings of their community festivals. As the most momentous *hare* occasions, these celebrations provide *ujiko* with the opportunity to energize themselves by happily abandoning daily routines. They shoulder portable shrines together, dance in the street collectively, and enjoy a sense of liberation and rapture. In agrarian Japan, community festivals have been connected with the timing of harvest.

In the everyday life of most Japanese, Buddhism has lost visible significance except at most funerals, in which Buddhist priests play a major role. Although some Buddhist temples are tourist attractions and many care for family graves and tombs, they have only limited relevance in the area of popularized elite culture, such as tea ceremonies, flower arrangements, and calligraphy. Still, the Buddhist heritage is evident in the short period in August during which ancestors' souls are supposed to return to their native locality. In this mid-summer interval known as *bon*, many city dwellers take holidays to visit their home villages and towns where their relatives still reside. This is also the season when many communities organize various kinds of *bon* dances, communal dances which local residents perform in streets, playgrounds, and other public areas to the accompaniment of traditional folk songs. Like other Japanese folk dances, *bon* dancing involves no physical contact; participants dance in a circle or advance in rows. Each locality has its own style, perhaps the most famous being the Awa dance, in Tokushima prefecture, where people dance through one street after another. Even in some housing complexes in Tokyo, children and adults dance to the relatively recent tune of the Tokyo Song. On the last day of the *bon* festival, some communities organize a colorful event at which drawings are made on paper lanterns, which are floated on a river to carry away the spirits of the dead.

Many Japanese families celebrate certain festival days that reflect the rhythm of changing seasons. On New Year's Day, arguably the most significant national holiday, most households enjoy eating *zōni* (rice cakes boiled with vegetables), herring roe, dried young anchovies, and other festive delicacies. During the New Year season, people fly kites on which they have painted unique pictures. On the day before the beginning of spring, in February, some families scatter parched beans to drive evil spirits out of their houses. March 3, when peach blossoms are at their best, is the day of the Girls' Festival, when girls and their parents display dolls on a tiered stand. In April, in various parts of the country, large parks are full of people who come to view the cherry blossoms, some drinking, eating, and singing on a mat spread on the ground under cherry trees in full bloom. Many Japanese write their wishes on strips of paper that they hang on a bamboo tree on 7 July, the day of the Festival of the Weaver, when two lover stars, Altair and the Weaver, on opposite sides of the Milky Way, are believed to meet by crossing it. On the spring and fall equinoxes, people follow the custom of visiting their family tomb, cleaning and washing it, and dedicating flowers to it. They fold their hands in front of the grave to pray that the departed souls of their ancestors will protect them from misfortune and lead them to prosperity. Most Japanese engage in such activity at least once a year,[32] visits to the family grave ranking highest among the religious and quasi-religious activities of the Japanese.

2   Regional Variation of Folk Culture

Folk culture exhibits much regional diversity. As discussed in Chapter 3, different areas have different folk songs, folk dances, and folk crafts. The plurality of folk culture across Japan can be seen in Okinawa, the southernmost prefecture, and in Hokkaidō, the northernmost major island.

In Okinawa, neither Shintoism nor Buddhism has been influential. Across the Ryūkyū islands, each village has an *utaki* shrine, where the souls of village ancestors are worshipped and gods descend from heaven. The prevailing belief is that the gods who bring happiness to people visit on festive occasions from utopias that exist beyond the ocean. Many annual festivals on these islands are related to the sea. Ryūkyū dance, which is performed on festive occasions, is well known for the wave-like movement of the dancers' fingers, similar to that found in dances in Southeast Asia. The Okinawan system of musical scales differs from those in other parts of Japan, resembling those of Indonesia, Malaysia,

---

[32] Nishi 2009, p. 70.

and the Philippines. Since Okinawa was occupied by the United States until 1972, the American influence remains more pervasive than in other parts of Japan.

Folk culture in some areas of Japan is on the verge of extinction because of the penetration of more dominant cultural forms. Ainu folk culture is a conspicuous example. Before the invasion of the Japanese pushed them from the northern parts of Honshū island into a small corner of Hokkaidō, Ainu communities had a different language, a distinct tradition of festivals, and a separate belief system. Traditional Ainu clothes are furs or dresses made of linens with special embroidery. Ainu used to engage in hunting and fishing and have special techniques of carving, tattooing, and extrasensory perception. Ainu hold highly animistic beliefs, deeming every physical object to contain a kind of spiritual being which puts it in motion. According to Ainu folk belief, good and bad supernatural beings exist and positively or negatively influence the object in which they have landed. Hence, the everyday life of the Ainu community includes a variety of religious ceremonies and practices which are presumed to propitiate these invisible divine forces. In the house, various gods are supposed to reside underneath a fire-place, at the rear, and near the entrance. *Ianu*, pieces of shaved wood, are put in appropriate places to serve as intermediaries with gods. The bear festival, regarded by Ainu as the most important ceremony for praying for a successful hunting season, was celebrated until recently. Some Ainu communities are making attempts to preserve their folk *yukar* – lyric poems which will otherwise sink into oblivion.

These cultural practices are all parts of Japan's folk culture, although some are less visible or are dying out. It would be erroneous to assume that all grassroots cultural traditions have been cast in the same mold. Commercially organized events have, to a large extent, supplanted folk festivals in recent years. At the community level, local shopping areas stage parades, fairs, and galas with the explicit aim of improving business turnover. City and prefectural governments hold one exhibition after another and are often involved in musical, sporting, and other planned events. In collaboration with the mass media, large corporations sponsor such festival-like events as ladies' marathons, music concerts, and trade fairs. On the whole, these manufactured events acquire the characteristics of mass culture and fail to inherit those of folk culture.

3   Marginal Art

In classifying art forms, Shunsuke Tsurumi, an analyst of popular culture, distinguishes between three analytical categories – pure, mass, and

Table 9.3 Types of marginal art

Type of action	Concrete examples
Moving one's body	Gesture in everyday life; rhythm in work; the New Year's parade of fire brigades; play; courting; applause; *Bon* festival dance; walking on stilts; bouncing a ball; *sumo* wrestling; *shishimai* (ritual dance with a lion's mask)
Constructing, making, living, using, and watching	Housing; the appearance of houses lining the street; miniature garden; *bonsai*; straps of a *geta* thong; paper flowers that open when placed in a glass of water; knot making; building blocks; cocoon balls; tombs
Singing, talking, and listening	Calls used to enliven physical labor; speaking in a singsong tone; tongue twisters; song variations; humming a tune; nicknaming; *dodoitsu* (Japanese limerick); two-person *manzai* comic acts; mimicry
Painting and drawing	Graffiti; votive wooden tablets; battledores; picture painting on kites; New Year cards; picture drawing on paper lanterns floated on a river
Writing and reading	Letters; gossip; calligraphy; conventional *haiku* poem writing; decorations on the day of the Festival of the Weaver
Performing	Festivals; funerals; *miai* meetings; family albums; family videos; *karuta* (Japanese playing cards); *sugoroku* (a Japanese variety of parcheesi); *fukubiki* lotteries; visits to a family tomb; political demonstrations

Source: Adapted from Tsurumi 1967, p. 70.

marginal art types – and argues that the third type deserves serious examination.[33] In what he calls pure art, producers are professional artists and those who appreciate it are specialists with some degree of expert knowledge. Its concrete forms include *noh*, symphonies, and professional paintings. Mass art, whose modes include television shows, popular songs, posters, and detective stories, is often regarded as pseudo-art or vulgar art, inasmuch as its production is based on collaboration between professional artists and media organizations, and its recipients are non-specialist masses. In contrast, marginal art is seen as a domain at the intersection between everyday life and artistic expression. As Table 9.3 shows, its forms range from graffiti to gestures in daily interaction, New Year's cards, song variations, building blocks, and room decorations. Even the ways in which people interact in communal baths (*sentō*) and hot springs would be a kind of marginal art; people of different backgrounds meet naked, engage in unpretentious conversation, and thereby generate an artistic form of communication in the space of a mini-democracy. Marginal art is based on amateur activities to the extent that both its producers and consumers are laypersons without specialist or professional

[33] Tsurumi 1967, Chapter 1. See also Sugimoto 2008.

expertise. Although such art forms have existed since ancient times, the development of mass media and democratic economic and political systems have paved the way for the dichotomy between pure and mass art and have removed marginal art from the sphere of legitimately recognized art. Once one accepts the realm of marginal art thus conceptualized, one can see many popular activities today as reflections of Japan's folk culture, as in Table 9.2.

IV   Alternative Culture

Alternative culture is composed of indirect, devious, and not necessarily overtly political forms of mass dissent against the institutionalized order. Some are reformist or even radical, while others are simply troublesome and threatening. All are located at the margin of Japanese society and challenge the patterns of the routine lives of ordinary citizens in various ways.

Japanese history abounds with so many activities of this type that only a few illustrations would suffice. Many Buddhist religious sects which today enjoy established status initially started as alternative culture with a charismatic leader who had enthusiastic followers ready to defy the social order of the day. This is true, for example, of Shinran, the priest who established the *Jōdo Shinshū* sect in the thirteenth century as a kind of protestant movement in defiance of established Buddhist sects. He attracted peasants and the urban populace as firm believers. The same applies to Saint Nichiren, who started the *Nichiren* sect in the thirteenth century, vigorously attacked other Buddhist groups, and was condemned by the government to exile on Sado island. Many newer religions in modern Japan, including *Sōka Gakkai*, *Ōmotokyō*, and *Konkōkyō*, resisted the military government's attempts to unite the public into supporting Japan's war activities during World War II. In the area of literature, Bashō, the seventeenth-century poet who elevated *haiku* (a mode of Japanese poem with seventeen syllables) to a respected literary field, challenged the existing circles of *haiku* poets with serious alternative artistic styles, traveled extensively around the nation in solitude, and won the admiration of devoted followers who were dissatisfied with the literary status quo. At a more popular level, urban residents in feudal Japan enjoyed writing poems called *senryū*, which are similar to *haiku* in style but more sarcastic and wittier in substance, mocking the ways of the world and the rulers of the day. Even today, most newspapers have *senryū* sections to which avid amateurs contribute satirical observations on world affairs in the form of short poems.

Contemporary Japan is full of alternative culture. The following sections delineate only a few aspects of it.

1 'Mini-communication' Media and Online Papers

Despite the immense power of mass media, small-scale publications flourish in grassroots Japan. Community newsletters, consumer group pamphlets, voluntary association magazines, ecological newspapers, and many other types of 'mini-communication' publications thrive throughout the country. Called *mini-komi*, these publications proliferated especially from the mid-1960s to the mid-1970s in the context of the collapse of social movements opposing the United States–Japan Security Treaty and the rise of those against the Vietnam War and university authorities. This was a time when politically committed citizens consciously developed a counterculture with networks of small groups in deliberate opposition to the mass media's depictions of the world. The waves of small communication media subsided with the good performance of the Japanese economy and the decline in open political confrontations. Nonetheless, *mini-komi* media play significant roles in environmental movements, notably those against nuclear electricity plants. Groups concerned about the safety of food are active in the publication of newsletters, pamphlets, and mini-magazines. Other alternative groups, in their *mini-komi*, question the Japanese quality of life, which does not seem to reflect the nation's apparent material wealth. In addition, free newspapers and community journals, which are more informational than countercultural, are thriving with the increasing ease of editing techniques, publication methods, and online technology.

In this context, a few online 'citizens' newspapers' are in operation, including *NikkanBerita*, *Wikinews*, and *NPJ* (News for the People of Japan), which are all independent of the established media. Ordinary citizens and freelance writers contribute to these newspapers as correspondents. Although journalists working for the established press tend to be suspicious of the quality control of the articles that appear in online newspapers, some of these sites attract several hundred thousand hits per day and provide reports and commentary that are alternative to the mainstream media. Although they struggle financially, the potential of online newspapers cannot be underestimated as a possible, economically viable engine of civil society in Japan.

Using feeble radio transmissions that do not require legal authorization, mini-FM stations have proliferated since the 1980s. These small, community-based 'free radio' stations try to mirror the needs and views of small groups of listeners not catered for by the major radio stations. Since 1992, more substantial community FM radio stations have commenced operation throughout the country. Staffed by small groups of employees and volunteer workers, these stations reflect the voices of marginalized groups much more than large commercial radio stations and operate in the hope that they might become significant grassroots media.

The development of high technology by the Japanese and the international corporate world has provided these small groups with efficient modes of communication. With the advent of online networking, alternative group activists are able to exchange and disseminate information about their movements. With the expansion of online communication systems (including Facebook and Twitter), an increasing number of youngsters participate in discussions on various issues. This type of 'high-tech conversation' provides a new mode of social intercourse which enables people to have democratic access to electronically controlled but open conversations with strangers, often cutting across spatial boundaries. As discussed in Chapter 10, a series of anti-nuclear demonstrations after the explosions at the nuclear plants in Fukushima in 2011 were spontaneously and efficiently organized by means of online information dissemination. Relying on similar communication networks, volunteer workers emerged at the same time from various parts of the nation to help rescue the tsunami victims.

2   Countercultural Events and Performances

Alternative theaters figure in the countercultural scenery in urban Japan. They challenge the formalist styles of drama performed in established theaters and seek to offer independent, intentionally scandalous, and 'non-routinized' entertainment in show tents, small playhouses, and underground halls. These theaters reject the convention of following prepared scripts and defy the formal division between the actors (as players on stage) and the audience (as spectators). They involve both in interactive situations, use non-verbal symbols including human bodies and physical objects on stage to the maximum extent, and invite spontaneity in a bid to 'demolish' time and space. The flesh, dreams, emotions, and 'alien substances' play major symbolic roles in these theaters, where primitive sentiments are to be revitalized against the background of the modern, technological, and mechanical environment. These small theaters have been gradually absorbed into the mainstream since their heyday in the 1960s and 1970s, but still function as dissonant voices against the increasing influence of mass media.

At a more spontaneous level, new waves of pop art, street performance, and stylish fashion come and go in urban centers, where lavish shops and postmodern buildings abound. In Tokyo, for instance, railway terminals such as Shinjuku and Shibuya and entertainment districts such as Harajuku and Roppongi provide a milieu where trendy youth culture bubbles and talk-of-the-town social cliques flourish. A case in point is the so-called bamboo shoot tribe,[34] teenagers who regularly appeared in the 1980s in unconventional clothes in Tokyo's Harajuku-Yoyogi area on Sundays when the streets were closed to vehicular traffic. These youngsters danced in the streets, wearing a variety of richly colored and eye-catching clothes, including Japanese happi coats, Chinese dresses, and Hawaiian muumuus. They worked as ordinary company employees during the week but at the weekend liberated themselves in this manner from daily routine. In the early 2000s, a relatively small number of adolescent girls employed unconventional makeup called *ganguro* for its shock value.[35] Painting their faces black, while brightening the areas surrounding their eyes and mouth with white, they used this striking makeup as a means of self-expression and self-actualization.

Likewise, costume plays, often referred to as 'cosplays' or *kosupure*, have established themselves as part of urban youth culture. Wearing mainly the costumes of *manga* and animation characters in a playful fashion, enthusiastic youths show off their dresses and makeup in indoor and outdoor gatherings in an attempt to break the monotonous routines of participants' everyday lives. Cosplay events have spread internationally with the global popularity of Japanese popular culture, enabling its young overseas audience to enjoy momentary escape and fun by having imaginary identities in a festive atmosphere.

3   New Religions

New religions come and go, capturing marginalized individuals and giving them some fantasies of salvation. In the immediate postwar decades, when Japan was in both material and spiritual turmoil, established religions were challenged by new religious groups, including *Sōka Gakkai*, a Buddhist sect with a political grouping called New Komei within both national and local politics, and *Seichō no Ie*, a right-wing religious organization with a nationalist ideology and an anti-abortion commitment.

[34] The term is attributable to the fact that the youngsters wore clothes that they bought at the boutique known as Takenoko, meaning 'bamboo shoots'.

[35] Klippensteen 2000.

They lost their initial populist fervor and became institutionalized over time. In their place, small but rapidly expanding fresh religious groups came to the fore after the nation gained stability and affluence in the 1970s. Although relatively small in membership, they make their presence felt by energetic campaigns and by forming subcultures which differentiate them from the prevailing patterns of life in contemporary Japan. These new religious subcultures display a few distinct characteristics.[36]

First, many of the new religions engage in occultism and mysticism and use magic and necromancy in contradiction to the rationalist approach of modern religion. *Shinreikyō* (God-Soul Sect), *Mahikari Kyōdan* (True Light Sect), and *Kiriyama Mikkyō* (Kiriyama Esotericism) fall into this category. They all set forth a doctrine of various types and worlds of souls in an invisible space and elaborate on the ways in which both good and bad souls govern the happiness, health, and life of each individual. These sects also claim to have secret exorcist rituals to remove deleterious souls from possessed people. Adherents seem to be interested primarily in participating in the acts of incantation and enchantment.

Second, the tenets of most new religions are based on spectacular images of the cosmos, where groups of souls are thought to form constellations. The teaching is that the apocalyptic dramas that unfold in such a vast universe, with souls, angels, and demons as main actors, influence the everyday life of individuals in this world. Some of these new religions are also oriented towards eschatological fundamentalism, which teaches that the end of the earth is drawing close. Stirring fear and anxiety and smacking of science fiction, these grandiose visions appear to captivate those who feel profoundly alienated in the automated, predictable, and regulated environment of the modern world. Some of the religions make maximum use of mass media. The founder of *Kofuku no Kagaku* (Science of Happiness), for example, published a few hundred books with a total of several million copies sold. These organizations also hold spectacular mass religious performance sessions in baseball stadiums and large halls.

Finally, believers in these religions take much interest in developing what they regard as supernatural capacities, such as extrasensory perception and psychokinesis. Followers engage in ascetic practices in an attempt to acquire these abilities. Leaders of *Aum Shinrikyō*, the group which in 1995 released deadly nerve gas in the Tokyo subway system, became the focus of nationwide criticism for having given followers chemical drinks and injections of dangerous doses of drugs throughout their spiritual training sessions, allegedly to induce a high level of enlightenment. On the pretext of enabling followers to elevate their spiritual

---

[36] Shimazono 2004; Nishiyama 1979.

capacities, the group confined adherents to its precincts, arrested deserters by force, and compelled new participants to offer all their personal assets and belongings to the sect. In these ways, followers were forced to give total loyalty to the guru in return for the supposed acquisition of supernatural skills.

The absence of firm political ideology after the end of the Cold War provides a breeding ground for new religious groups. Growing frustrations, particularly among the youth, with regimented school life and stern company life pave the way for commitment to irrational alternatives.

4   Socially Deviant Groups

Deviant groups are countercultural in their defiance of authorities. 'Bikies', or motorcycle freaks, for instance, form countercultural youth gangs.[37] Clad in singular costumes, they ride their motorcycles in groups, generate much noise pollution (often at night), and cause a public uproar from time to time. Many of them live at the fringe of society, having dropped out of school and taken menial jobs. They despise and resent the stability of middle-class culture and find satisfaction in disturbing it. These groups are reproduced from one generation to another, yielding an intergenerational cycle of non-conformity.[38]

At a more serious level, *Yakuza*, Japan's mafia groups, construct a particular pattern of antisocial culture, engaging in all sorts of illegal activities from blackmail, extortion, and fraud to murder. Their groups have a strict hierarchical order, demand total devotion from members, and, in some cases, require each new member to have his little finger cut off at an initiation ceremony, although the practice is believed to be gradually disappearing. Many members come from the bottom of society and have a unique sense of bonding, unity, and comradeship among themselves. Their marginal background sometimes makes them side with the powerless and the poor despite their generally parasitic existence in society. These outlaw groups developed the moral code of *ninkyō*, a kind of chivalrous spirit with which each member is supposed 'to assist the weak and resist the powerful', 'to help others with total disregard for his own life', and 'not to be ruled by avarice despite being a ruffian'. These formulae do not represent the realities of the toughs, but constitute expected standards for their behavior in some areas and under some circumstances. These elements of their subculture have been portrayed with some sympathy in novels and films which have attained wide circulation.

[37] See, for example, Kersten 1993.   [38] See Yoder 2004.

5 Sexually Alternative Lifestyles

Japan has an appreciable number of individuals who see themselves as either lesbian, gay, bisexual, or transgender (LGBT). An internet consumer trend survey of some seventy thousand respondents carried out in 2012 by the Research Institute of Dentsū, the largest advertising company in Japan, indicates that 5.2 percent, approximately one in twenty people, identify as LGBT, with a majority choosing not to come out.[39] These are not small numbers. If they are accurate, the LGBT population should be more than, or at least comparable to, the population of Tottori prefecture, on the Sea of Japan side of central Japan.

The Japanese legal system does not recognize same-sex marriage. The nation's Constitution states in Article 24 that marriage 'shall be based only on the mutual consent of both sexes', a principle on which Japan's civil law is predicated. This legal requirement poses not only philosophical but also material issues to same-sex couples. For example, they are not entitled to the spouse tax deductions that married couples can claim. Some same-sex couples devise defensive and instrumental strategies. A case in point is an adoption strategy in which partner A legally adopts partner B as his or her child, which enables them to have the same surname. With the same-sex couple registered in this way in *koseki*, the process of property inheritance generally encounters very few impediments – after a partner's death, the survivor can easily qualify as the legatee.

Japanese lesbians and gays gradually and openly formed homosexual groupings in the 1990s. Some run gay magazines, several of which sell tens of thousands of copies. Their market is diversified, with *Badi* and *Barazoku* for young gays, *SAMSON* for the elderly, and *G-men* for those interested in muscular types. These magazines have produced gay *manga* writers. Although lesbian magazines are less prolific, an internet magazine, *Tokyo Wrestling*, provides forums to debate lesbian concerns and establish networks for homosexual women. Some groups organize local meetings and discuss their own issues and agendas, often in open defiance of the general community. It is public knowledge that there are gay bars and saunas where gay men have casual sex. Although operating less conspicuously, some lesbian couples came out in the early 1990s[40] and they are increasingly confident of their sexual preferences. Both steady monogamous homosexual relationships and casual sexual contacts

---

[39] AM, 28 June 2013, pp. 12 and 18; MM, 18 June 2013.

[40] See, for example, the special edition of the magazine *Bessatsu Takarajima*, no. 64, published in 1991 by JICC Shuppan under the title of *Onna-tachi o aisuru onna-tachi no monogatari* (The stories of women who love women). It reported the stories of 234 lesbian women.

between homosexuals form significant alternative cultures in Japan today, although they remain relatively undetectable in public in comparison with their counterparts in Western societies – a situation attributable to the harsher ideological reality that homosexuality still remains rigidly taboo in Japan. Formal marriages between same-sex partners can never be legalized unless the *koseki* system discussed in Chapter 6 is amended.

A small number of empirical studies of homosexual subculture in Japan[41] have shown that both gay men and lesbian women expect household chores to be equally divided between partners, while heterosexual men and women tend to be less egalitarian in this respect. Homosexual people are more open to experimenting with relationships and role patterns. They also appear to value *omoiyari*, the Japanese sense of empathy, very highly in friendships and relationships, more than those who criticize gays and lesbians as immoral. Troubled by the duality of female and male, some advocates of alternative culture in this area maintain that the public should accept, or at least tolerate, transvestitism (cross-dressing) and trans-sexuality (sex change by operation) as legitimate lifestyles and redefine femininity and masculinity more liberally.[42]

The moral norm of 'proper marriage' as the only acceptable lifestyle lingers, making it difficult even for de facto heterosexual relationships and remaining unmarried to be recognized as alternatives. Yet an increasing number of women and men choose to live as singles and prove to be happy and confident. A number of books have popularized the notion of 'liberated single culture' in a positive light.[43] The younger generations are increasingly apt to choose *jijitsu-kon* (de facto relationships) as their way of life. These lifestyles are deeply discordant with Japan's narrow and marriage-based definition of sexuality, thereby shaking the dominant ideology of fixed gender roles.

6   Communes and the Natural Economy

Alternative culture finds radical expression in communes based on the natural economy and the abolition of private ownership. Cases in point include *Atarashii Mura* (New Villages) in Saitama and Miyazaki prefectures, *Shinkyō Buraku* in Nara, and *Ittō-kai* in Kyoto. *Yamagishi-kai*, founded by Miyozō Yamagishi in the 1950s, is arguably the best known and largest in Japan. Originating with a small group of mainly farmers

---

[41] See, for example, Ito and Yanase 2001; Lunsing 1995 and 2001; McLelland 2000; and Summerhawk, McMahill, and McDonald 1999.
[42] See Lunsing 2001, Chapter 7.   [43] Ueno 2009; Ebisaka 1986.

in Mie prefecture, it is now a nationwide network of small-scale communes espousing a philosophy of symbiosis with nature and total pacifism. Renouncing private property and income, commune dwellers make a lifetime commitment to the movement, adopt simple lifestyles, and remain entirely non-religious. While many of its communes manage poultry farms and engage in agricultural production, the organization's headquarters publishes newsletters, runs schools, and organizes special courses at which outsiders lodge together for a week to engage in self-introspection in interactive group discussion. *Yamagishi-kai* has attracted ex-student political activists, environmentalists, and other disenchanted reformist types.

In a broader context, networks of ecologists are formed across the country to provide organically produced agricultural goods to the public, using the symbols of cooperation and coexistence with nature. In rural communities, they challenge mechanized mass-production of produce contaminated by agricultural chemicals, and turn their attention to the traditional wisdom of environmentally sound methods. In distribution processes, the 'life-club cooperatives' based in urban communities collectively purchase organic foods directly from growers. A few take the form of 'worker collectives' in which participating members promote the establishment of distribution networks based on principles of direct democracy and flexible organization.[44] They look for ways of recycling and exchanging unwanted goods, establishing children's nurseries, and developing a kind of counter-economy among themselves.

V   The Plurality of Popular Culture

This chapter has surveyed three types of popular culture which derive from different social formations. Mass culture is constantly produced as a process of modern society in which the populace is atomized and susceptible to mass-produced merchandise and information propagated by mass media. The Japanese analytical category for this type of mass is *taishū*, although it is increasingly segmented into small units, such as *bunshū* and *shōshū* – masses which have particular requirements for certain goods, services, and information, as discussed in Chapter 4.

Folk culture has been nurtured in the soil of what Japanese ethnographers call *jōmin*, those ordinary persons who may not engage in the production of pure or mass art but who express themselves in various forms of marginal art. Folk culture has its origin mostly in the non-literary world, having little to do with written forms of communication.

---

[44] Amano, M. 2011; Maclachlan 2003.

Table 9.4   Four types of culture

Population size of appreciators	Economic resources of producers	
	Plentiful	Limited
Small	Elite	Alternative
Large	Mass	Folk

Alternative culture mirrors the dissatisfaction, grievances, and disenchantment of some sections of the community but remains small and marginal. Located at the fringe of Japanese society, alternative culture groups present images and world-views that are discordant with, or go beyond, the frameworks of both mass and folk culture. As such, they are invariably exposed to the danger of being extinguished or assimilated into mass or folk culture.

Each person embodies all three cultural elements, although their relative importance may differ between individuals. A committed commune activist may enjoy reading *manga* magazines and singing traditional folk songs. An avid Shinto believer may participate in countercultural *minikomi* publications and spend a few hours playing *pachinko* every week. Looking at the entire cultural scene at a macro level, one might be able to classify elite and popular culture in terms of the magnitude of the economic resources that producers of culture require and possess, and the proportion of the population that appreciates it. As Table 9.4 indicates, elite culture is appreciated by comparatively few but is amply supported economically, while alternative culture tends to be both small and in economic terms relatively deprived. The four types are respectively majority and minority cultures, depending upon the criteria used.

Over the past two decades or so, Japanese culture has become a focus of global attention. It is now selectively stereotyped, packaged, and exported around the world, but this representation does not necessarily reflect its rich and diverse varieties. The next section makes a brief survey of its international iterations and attempts to contextualize the fascination and the preoccupation that it has generated.

VI   Cool Japan: Potential or Mirage?

1   Cool Japan as Commercial Market

'Japanesy' cultural products are increasingly visible around the world. They range from Japanese *anime*, *manga*, computer games, *karaoke*, *sushi*, and fashion to martial arts and include knowledge commodities such as

Sudoku games, Kumon education, and the Suzuki method of teaching music. Pokémon, Ninja, and Hello Kitty are international icons. These cultural goods are as important to trade as 'industrial' commodities like cars and electronic appliances. In the context of the rise of cultural capitalism, as discussed in Chapters 1 and 4, McGray[45] created a sensation with the thesis that although Japan may no longer be an industrial superpower in terms of gross national product, it has developed into a powerhouse in terms of what he calls Gross National Cool, an index that measures the overall level of 'cool' pop culture products.

In the educational sphere, many students who study Japanese language at universities and high schools are motivated by the desire to read and understand Japanese *manga* in Japanese. Departments of Japanese around the world promote the Cool Japan vision to attract, maintain, and expand student engagement with Japanese studies.

The Japanese cultural industry, government, and mass media have been eager to promote representations of Cool Japan domestically and internationally. They are encouraged and even flattered by the view that the expansion of Cool Japan has catapulted Japan into a position as a leading soft power. The Shinzō Abe government established the post of Minister in Charge of Cool Japan Strategy in 2013; the Cool Japan Promotion Council operates within the Prime Minister's Office; and the Ministry of Economy, Trade, and Industry runs the Cool Japan Promotion Office – measures reminiscent of the now defunct Cool Britannia program championed by Tony Blair's government in the United Kingdom in the 1990s.

Cool Japan is big business. Next to the United States, Japan has the second-largest domestic contents market[46] which many analysts classify into five fields: package software, including visual, music, and game software, as well as newspapers and books; broadcasting; entertainment facilities, such as movie theaters, *karaoke* boxes, and game centers; internet-based visual and music contents, as well as advertisements; and mobile phones, including music, games, and literary information.[47] As Table 9.5 demonstrates, the size of the contents market in Japan is estimated to be over 11.77 trillion yen per annum for the past several years – an amount well over 10 percent of the national government budget – and represents a highly significant sphere of the nation's cultural capitalism, as discussed in Chapter 4. It should be noted, however, that the size of the domestic contents market is contracting rather than expanding, after peaking in the mid-2000s. Notwithstanding the consistent rise of mobile phone

---

[45] McGray 2002.

[46] HumanMedia 2012, p. 4, defines the domestic contents market as the 'market of information that is distributed and paid in exchange for its sale and advertisement via media'.

[47] HumanMedia 2012, p. 4.

Table 9.5   Size of media and contents market in
Japan (2005–11)

Year	Market size (trillion yen)
2005–06	12.96
2006–07	12.75
2007–08	12.74
2008–09	12.11
2009–10	11.83
2010–11	11.77

Source: Adapted from HumanMedia 2012.

Table 9.6   Size of media and contents markets of major countries (2010–11)

Country	Market size (trillion yen)	Country	Market size (trillion yen)
United States	25.74	Italy	2.50
Germany	5.85	Brazil	2.27
China	5.61	South Korea	1.86
United Kingdom	4.63	Spain	1.47
France	3.84	India	1.47

Source: HumanMedia 2012, pp. 20–1.

businesses, the overall decline is unmistakable, notably in the world of entertainment establishments such as *karaoke* booths and game centers. Meanwhile, the contents market abroad amounts, at the very least, to five times that of Japan's domestic market, as Table 9.6 shows, and presents a huge opportunity and challenge to the quaternary sector of the Japanese economy.

2   Cool Japan in the Image Market Abroad

Cool Japan is now a symbol around which a variety of interests compete and to which multiple interpretations are attached. Table 9.7 provides a conceptual map of the three phases of the popular images of Japan abroad, in conjunction with the predominant models of Japanese studies, as well as the changing mega-structural conditions that influenced these images and models. The current images of Cool Japan constitute the third wave, which has surged in the wake of the preceding two.

Immediately after the end of World War II, Japan was seen as culturally obscure and mysterious. The role of Japan specialists was to unravel its inscrutable and enigmatic peculiarities by focusing on traditional aspects of the country, such as *bushido, judo, noh, kabuki,* and flower

Table 9.7 Changing models of Japanese studies

Comparative criteria	Phase one	Phase two	Phase three
Peak period	1950s–1960s	1970s–1980s	1990s–2000s
Popular images abroad			
Main descriptive themes	Mysterious Japan	Groupist Japan	Cool Japan
Concrete symbols	*Bushido, judo, kabuki, noh*, tea ceremony, *geisha*	Lifetime employment, enterprise unions, quality control, *kanban*, bureaucracy	*Manga, anime, sushi, karaoke*, J-pop, fashion, cuisine
Main attributes	Inscrutable, enigmatic, highly exotic	Serious, patient, industrious, persevering, consensual	Playful, hilarious, unpredictable, sexy, fun-loving
Major image consumers	Avid Japanophiles	Businessmen, government officials	Non-elite, young, urban
Japanese studies paradigms			
Neustupný (1980)	Japanology paradigm	Area studies paradigm	Contemporary paradigm
Steinhoff (2007)	Language and area studies paradigm	Economic competition paradigm	Cultural studies paradigm
Chiavacci (2008)	Class struggle model	General middle-class society model	Social division model
General orientations			
Domestic culture	Monocultural	Monocultural	Multicultural
Key attributes		Uniquely group oriented, classless, highly integrated	Class differentiated, demographically diverse, competitive
Cultural relativism	Inter-ethnic relativity	Inter-ethnic relativity	Inter-ethnic and inter-class relativity
Contour of Japan's nationhood	Given	Taken for granted	Blurred, problematized
Definition of the 'Japanese'	Exclusive	Exclusive	Increasingly inclusive
Japanese studies in the 'world system of knowledge'	Based on Eurocentric criteria	*Nihonjinron* as cultural relativism	Part of flows of non-European ideas
English translations of Japanese scholarly work	Very few	Few	Still limited
Japan as a case in explicitly comparative studies	Few	Some	Increasing
Underlying mega-structural conditions	*Agrarian society*; US occupation and recovery from WWII	*Industrial capitalism* (dominated by manufacturing); trade surplus, 'bubble economy', vertical integration	*Cultural capitalism* (dominated by the quaternary sector); globalization, cross-border migration, aging, deflation, civil society

arrangements. Except for Japanophiles, who were attracted by Japan's exoticism, there was little interest in Japan internationally. The nation was predominantly agrarian, with a majority of the workforce in the primary sector of the economy.

With the ostensibly sudden rise of the Japanese economy in the 1970s and its global expansion in the 1980s, the international community began to pay attention to aspects deemed to be unique to Japanese culture, especially the various corporate practices that were applicable to the elite sector of Japanese company structures. Practices like lifetime employment, seniority-based wage structure, and enterprise unionism were thought to be the driving forces of Japanese economic ascendancy. It was widely believed that the Japanese orientation to groupism – as distinct from Western individualism – accounted for the phenomena that were allegedly peculiar to Japan. This was a time when the world watched the rise of Japan's industrial capitalism, particularly its manufacturing sector, with admiration, fear, and envy, and when Toyota, Nissan, Sony, and Panasonic became global household names.

The third wave of Japanese popular images emerged after the stagnation of the country's economy in the 1990s. Success stories were things of the past. This, however, was followed by the international popularization of Japan's pop culture – mostly *manga*, *anime*, *sushi*, and *karaoke* (which are sometimes referred to by the acronym MASK, which Pulvers coined[48]). Within Japan, expectations are high that an exportable Japanese culture might help lift not only the nation's prestige symbolically but its business and political interests materially.

Fun-loving, funny, entertaining, hilarious, sexy, and playful aspects of life are, on the whole, manifest in third-wave Japanese cultural products. Here, postmodern descriptors are increasingly championed in place of modern descriptors. A fresh emphasis is now placed on new orientations – fluidity rather than predictability, amorphousness rather than rationality, conviviality rather than seriousness, and ecology-consciousness rather than developmentalism – paving the way for what may be called postmodern exoticism. This is in sharp contrast with earlier portrayals of the Japanese as serious, persevering, workaholic, loyal, patient, and stoic, although the new images coexist with the old ones.

The three-phase image transformations correspond to other observations. In summarizing Japanese studies in the United States for the past several decades, Steinhoff identifies three paradigms: language and area studies (1950s–70s), the economic competition paradigm (1980s–90s), and the cultural studies paradigm (1990s–present).[49] Covering a longer

---

[48] Pulvers 2006.   [49] Steinhoff 2007 and 2013.

time span, Richter also presents a three-stage model of Japanese studies in which the latest stage began in the 1990s, with a focus on a Cool Japan built on the postmodern information service society.[50] More than three decades ago, Australian-based Neustupný distinguished three analogous paradigms in the study of Japan: the Japanology paradigm, the area studies paradigm, and the contemporary paradigm.[51] As discussed at the beginning of Chapter 2, Chiavacci presents three phases of class analysis in postwar Japan, from the class struggle model through the general middle-class society model to the social division model, each phase more or less corresponding to the above periodization.[52]

All in all, one might venture to say that these trichotomous phases observed by scholars in Japanese studies, cultural studies, and class analysis point to the interaction between popular images and scholarly models. The underlying mega-structural trends – the decline of agrarian society to the rise of cultural capitalism – have also exercised fundamental influences. In this complex context, the debate over the so-called Cool Japan phenomena came into play.

3   *Otaku* as Bearers of Cool Culture: Their Demography

The analysis is complicated by ambiguity about how the Cool Japan phenomena should be defined. Some concentrate on *manga* and *anime*, while others focus on music and fashion. Still others are primarily interested in food. Apart from the genre under observation, some analysts pinpoint the bearers of these cultural products, while others direct their undivided attention to symbols and representations. The field is thus equivocal, elusive, and often unquantifiable.

Demographically, a category of young Japanese who are deeply absorbed in some aspects of popular culture, the *otaku*,[53] are regarded as significant players in the consumption and creation of 'cool' culture. Market researchers were quick to investigate *otaku* as highly visible trend-setters and innovators for consumers of cultural commodities, although *otaku* themselves may represent only a small fraction of consumers. The Nomura Research Institute, for example, which has conducted an extensive demographic study of *otaku*, defined the group as those individuals

---

[50] Richter 2010, pp. 173–5.   [51] Neustupný 1980.   [52] Chiavacci 2008.

[53] The Japanese term *otaku* literally means 'your house' and also 'you' in formal speech. As this group has global attention, it entered the vocabulary of English so that the *Oxford English Dictionary* (2004), for example, explains its origin, saying that it was initially used by some pop culture fans as 'an affectedly formal way of addressing others with similar interests'.

who *either* psychologically get hooked on particular goods *or* purchase them without self-constraint and examined their value orientations and consumer behavior. The size of *otaku* is estimated to exceed 40 percent of the population of Japan, although the proportion of those who show *both* characteristics – psychological dependence and compulsive buying – is as small as 3.6 percent.[54] Overall, they are eager to collect the commodities with which they are obsessed and to share their interests with others, to have their own judgment criteria for the goods, to belong to the same collection group, to show off their collections, and to create original goods. These five types of desire – collecting, sharing, belonging, showing, and creating – are the defining characteristics of *otaku* people. The specific commodities of their interests and obsessions are wide-ranging and include comics, *anime*, computer games, computers, audio-visual machines, plastic models, cars, information technology gadgets, travel, fashion, cameras, airplane- or railway-related goods, postage stamps, stationery, and so forth. The *otaku* group overlaps with such groups as nerds, geeks, and freaks in other countries but covers a much wider variety.

(a) K-shape Model: Stratification of Otaku

Although the phrase 'Cool Japan' has a ring of grace and elegance, it is double-edged when it comes to its demographic base. The bearers of the so-called cool culture are stratified into two groups:[55] the affluent and the marginalized. The *otaku* phenomenon was initially prevalent in the late twentieth century among youth brought up in a privileged environment in Tokyo, who had both intellectual and financial resources to form subcultural groups committed to cool culture. Then, the pattern manifested itself at the higher echelon of Japan's class structure; one can now observe the rise of a new upper middle class that works in the globally connected contents industries involving information technology, media, art, design, and management and finds satisfaction in engaging in flexible, mobile, and creative work. Members of this class are highly competitive and champion the neoliberal ideology of the survival of the fittest. Successful and upwardly mobile in their work, they enjoy expensive, pleasurable, and urban lifestyles. The residents of Roppongi Hills, an extravagant high-rise building in the heart of Tokyo, exemplify this class. Although extremely few in number, they are visible in the media and present themselves as role models of 'cool' aspirants.

---

[54] Nomura Research Institute 2005, p. 17.   [55] Richter 2010, pp. 181–3.

At the other end of the spectrum exists a mass of *otaku* individuals who have not 'made it' in the neoliberal competitive environment, with some struggling to maintain their livelihoods. These *otaku* find refuge, escape, or even silent defiance in such 'cool' activities as online social networking, collecting cool products, reading *manga*, and idolizing idols. The extreme model of 'cool'-seeking *otaku* at this level are *freeter* (discussed in Chapter 4) who spend much of their time in internet cafés reading comics and sending and receiving messages on social media with strangers and regard their mobile phones as their most important possessions.

This dichotomy can best be summarized as a 'cool' K-shape model, with the top and bottom ends forming the key players and the middle sector taking very little part. On the whole, salarymen in bureaucratic organizations, rural residents, senior citizens, and housewives, for instance, do not figure conspicuously in the cool culture environment. Clearly, in the debate over Cool Japan, it is important to keep an eye on the class foundations of its participants.

(b) Five Types of Otaku

From a slightly different perspective, the above-mentioned Nomura Research Institute study pays attention to the broader demographic characteristics of *otaku* (numerically dominated by the second group above) and identifies five clusters, as shown in Table 9.8, which reveals their internal diversity. Although their numbers are small, they deserve analysis, given that the notion of *otaku* originated in Japan and that many overseas fans of Japan's popular culture see this group as a point of reference.

The first group mainly comprises married, middle-aged men who spend time assembling and fixing mechanical gadgetry in addition to enjoying *anime* and travel, although their expenses are limited due to their budgets. Fathers who quietly and stealthily immerse themselves in their favorite hobbies are the representative image of this type.

The second type are predominantly single men in their twenties and thirties who have strong opinions about what they take an interest in – popular entertainers, mechanical assemblage, cars, and cameras – and are able to spend a good amount of time and money pursuing their hobbies.

The third group is made up of relatively young men and women in their twenties and thirties who are sensitive to new developments in a variety of areas. They are alert to fresh information and enact the latest trends. Making use of the internet, they spend much time, but not much money, in pursuit of their interests and obsessions. This group is characterized by a high level of commitment to a multiplicity of spheres.

Table 9.8 Five types of *otaku* fandom

Type Attributes	Married, closet *otaku*	Independent, going-my-way *otaku*	Information-sensitive multi-field *otaku*	Social, activist *otaku*	Creative *otaku*
Age	Middle-aged	20s–30s	20s–30s	30s–40s	20s–30s
Gender	Male	Male	Male/female	Male	Female
Time spent	Limited	Plenty	Plenty	Plenty	Plenty
Purchase of goods	Limited	Plenty	Limited	Limited	Plenty
Orientations	Not vocal, subject to family constraint	Opinionated, manic in collecting information	Keen to get new information quickly, fond of community sites and online auctions	Active in involving others, eager to promote fixed ideas	Very strong desire for creative activities
Main areas of interest	*Anime*, assemblage of computer and audio-visual equipment, travel	Idols, assemblage of mechanical gadgets, cars, cameras	As many areas as possible, no particular concentration	Online games, idols, travel, fashion	Mainly *manga*, plus idols, games, and *anime*
Approx. % of *otaku*	25	23	22	18	12

Source: Adapted from Nomura Research Institute 2005, pp. 19–23.

The fourth cluster primarily consists of men in their thirties and forties who tend to hold their own particular views about the goods of their passion but make efforts to involve others in their pursuits. They spend time, but not money, on their hobbies and typically continue to follow ideas fixed since their teenage days.

The final, fifth group is composed predominantly of young females who actively participate in a variety of creative projects – for example, the production of coterie magazines of *manga* and novels. Internet-obsessed, they spend a great deal of time in communicating with each other. The emblematic model of this type is the job-hopping part-time woman obsessed with *manga* and *anime* characters since her younger days. These five varieties of *otaku* form the backdrop against which the Cool Japan phenomena are analyzed.

4   Promise or Illusion?

The vision of Cool Japan has kindled some controversy in at least three areas: whether it contributes to the understanding of Japanese society, whether it opens the way for Japan to be a soft power, and whether it represents postmodern counterculture or postmodern *Nihonjinron*.

(a)   Japan Literacy?

The first point concerns the relationship between the Cool Japan project and Japan literacy, where two rival observations prevail. On the one hand, it is widely argued that the spread of Cool Japan products is welcome because they provide good points of entry into a better understanding of Japanese society in the long run. Many students who take Japanese courses at universities and high schools are motivated to learn the language in order to read and understand Japanese *manga* in Japanese. Conversations carried out in *manga* balloons are usually highly colloquial and informal, and foreign learners can study the language naturally while enjoying pictorial story lines. Many creative teaching methods that exploit Japan's pop culture have been developed.

The Japanese behavior patterns and lifestyles that appear in some *anime* allow the audience a glimpse into how some Japanese behave and live. Some *manga* stories – such as *Sazae-san* and *Doraemon* – provide insights into aspects of Japanese family life. So do many Japanese dramas televised in Asia and beyond.

On the other hand, some observers are skeptical about the impact of Cool Japan items in terms of a sophisticated understanding of Japanese society. They maintain that it is questionable, or at least inconclusive, whether the current trend enhances the level of Japan literacy per se. Some simple comparisons are useful. *Spiderman* or *Snow White* arguably contribute little to a thorough comprehension of North American society. Similarly, there is no reason to believe that *Akira*, *Sailor Moon*, or *Dragon Ball* provide their readers with a better grasp of Japanese society. Needless to say, to the extent that eating spaghetti provides almost no insight into Italian society, relishing *sushi* has little to do with the enhancement of knowledge of Japanese society. The extent to which Cool Japan projects would help raise the level of their consumers' Japan literacy depends on their contents.

Furthermore, the themes of Cool Japan involve an apparent paradox: the more we study Cool Japan products in reality, the more likely we will find our initial fantasies mundane. The cool objects are cool not because they are simply beautiful and appealing but because they are somehow incomprehensible, enigmatic, or unfathomable. The elements of inscrutability, unintelligibility, and mysteriousness must be present in cool entities, be they Ninja, Hello Kitty, or *wasabi*. The 'cool' element emerges when outsiders become interested and seek to adopt elements of something they perceive as illusive and esoteric.

Sober and rational investigations into these objects, however, tend to diminish their cool luster and they cease to be cool objects with which one wishes to be fanatically involved. One cannot be unreservedly excited about Ainu artistic goods after studying the associated production and distribution structure of exploitation. We might find the big-eyed *kawaii* girl dolls cool, so long as we ignore the fact that they have little to do with real Japanese girls. In this sense, it might well be the case that coolness is built upon ignorance as a mirage and disappears when illuminated by the light of level-headed understanding. If so, the skeptics argue, MASK do in fact mask the realities of Japanese society, a deflection that might produce misleading and distorted images.

(b) Soft Power?

The second area of divided views is about whether the spread of Cool Japan is conducive to Japan acquiring 'soft power' in the international context. In pointing to the new form of power in world politics, Joseph Nye, who coined the phrase 'soft power', argues that the sources of power are increasingly cultural, psychological, and ideological rather than coercive and militaristic. Such soft power is the intangible capacity of a country to influence preferences of other countries and to achieve its

Table 9.9   Overseas contents market and earnings for Japan (2011)

Content	Overseas market (billion yen)	Income for Japan (billion yen)	% of overseas market
Movies	18.4	4.6	25
TV programs		6.3	?
Anime	266.9	16.0	6
Music			?
Manga	120.0	12.0	10
Characters	650.0	31.5	5
Game software	418.5	298.0	70
Game hardware	1,088.0	761.6	70

Source: Adapted from HumanMedia 2012, p. 329.
Notes:
1. Figures are shown in billion yen. Cells are left blank where figures are unavailable. All the numbers are based on estimates for 2011, except TV programs (2010), *manga* (recent trend), and characters (2009).
2. All figures are based on estimates for copyright earnings, except game software and hardware, which are predicated upon estimations for shipment values.

political and economic goals by 'soft' means which co-opt people instead of coercing them.[56]

McGray develops his argument about Cool Japan with this thesis in mind. His notion of Gross National Cool is not simply an index of the number of popular cultural goods; it is also an indicator of the degree to which the goods should translate into wealth accumulation in business transactions and diplomatic advantages in international politics. It is sobering, however, that Cool Japan products do not earn substantial export money. Gone are the days when Japan was accused of accumulating an excessive trade surplus.[57] The Japanese contents market has been shrinking rather than expanding over the past few years. The 2011 data indicate that while the size of Japan's domestic market is approximately 40 percent of, and second to, that of the United States, South Korea is ahead of Japan in the area of computer games. In internet advertising, China has overtaken Japan. As Table 9.9 shows, while the size of the *manga* market overseas is estimated to be approximately 120 billion yen, Japan earns about 12 billion yen, merely 10 percent, mainly as copyright earnings. The animation income is a similar story, with only 5 percent (16 billion yen) of the overseas market (266.9 billion yen) coming back to Japan. The exception is the computer game industry; its market size abroad and export returns stand out above the rest. At the individual level, some studies[58] have shown that consumers of Cool Japan products overseas do not necessarily buy other Japanese goods because of their

[56] Nye 2005.   [57] See HumanMedia 2012.   [58] Filip 2013.

exposure to Cool Japan goods, a pattern that suggests that cultural vogue does not necessarily and uniformly convert to massive economic gains.

The same applies to political and diplomatic international relations, which, on the whole, are not closely connected with grassroots culture. A Korean girl, for example, who enjoys Japanese *manga* would feel no contradiction in accusing the Japanese of wartime wrongdoings in classroom discussions to the extent that she dissociates one issue from another, a process that Befu calls 'value compartmentalization'.[59] The popularity of Japanese pop culture commodities in China and Korea has not helped to solve either historical animosity or current territorial disputes between those countries and Japan.

Moreover, demographically, the main consumers of Cool Japan differ from those of previous periods. When the representations of Japanese management prevailed, the main audience was the overseas business and government elite. In contrast, contemporary overseas fans of *manga* and *anime* are mainly non-elite, existing outside mainstream society. In the United States, the largest market in this field, *manga* and *anime* consumers are made up of two demographic groups. One comprises 'adult niche' manias of people now in their twenties and thirties who grew up with *Akira* and *Ramma 1/2* in the 1980s. The other group consists of teenagers and those in their twenties who were brought up with *Pokémon* and other games in the late 1990s and early 2000s, many of whom enjoy internet *anime* and *manga* available for hire from public libraries as inexpensive modes of entertainment. These goods command wide popularity among relatively low-income families.[60] Young girls in Taiwan, Thailand, and other Asian countries who are avid followers of Japanese fashion, food, and books have little to do with the national decision-making processes of those nations; overall, there appears to be little evidence to support the core of the Cool Japan thesis that the global spread of Japan's cultural products will increase the nation's influence as a soft power as defined by Nye.

(c)   Postmodern Nihonjinron?

The third issue pertains to the extent to which the Cool Japan discourse reflects advanced postmodern values and lifestyles or represents a new type of stereotype formation that promotes Japanese cultural essentialism.

It is true that the fresh focus on Japan's popular culture gave rise to a perspective which liberated Japan observers from the hackneyed images of Japan based on national traditional conventions or its corporate

[59] Befu 2003, p. 17.   [60] HumanMedia 2012, p. 233.

culture. Cool enthusiasts focus on the contemporary Japanese lifestyle that received little attention in the past and extol its emancipatory potential. Costume players – participants in so-called cosplay – who dress up as characters of *manga*, *anime*, or computer games, embark on this ostensibly childlike pursuit in defiance of the established values and norms of the world of adults. Elite university students and career-track employees enjoy reading *manga* and immerse themselves in the space of fictional immaturity and imagined juvenility, thereby freeing themselves from the stifling routines of their everyday lives. Cooking exotic meals can be a self-transcending experience for those who are fed up with fast food, mundane cookery, and ordinary recipes. These cool undertakings often give rise to small communities and networks in which the participants exchange information and ideas in shared defiance of conventional structures and values. To that extent, the Cool Japan discourse, in support of such activities, is either explicitly or implicitly countercultural, thereby challenging the old images of Japan as a highly bureaucratized society composed of obedient individuals.

Furthermore, the Cool Japan discourse highlights a postmodern paradigm:[61] the virtual world in which fictions and realities are entangled and inseparable, where fictions are real and realities are fictitious. The favored entertainers, idols, and *anime* characters, whom the fans have never met but watch on television every day, become their virtual family members. Fictitious heroes and heroines of *manga* penetrate into viewers' lives so much that they form part of their real environment. They might want to take part in a cosplay and dress up as characters in the imaginary world because to them it is real. Fans might also find it natural and enjoyable to indulge in collecting cool character dolls and even to feel *moe* (emotional and erotic attachments) towards them as sexual objects, as they are better looking, better shaped, and better dressed than real people. As people spend more time interacting with the virtual world than with their family and friends, the virtual world forms a universe that can appear more alive than it really is. In this process, objects of adoration are anthropomorphized. *Bishōjo* (beautiful girl character figures), for instance, which have no material existence, become more real than actual humans to their devotees.[62] Thus, the indivisibility of the fictitious and the real enables the person to relish a form of sensitivity that is not subject to the context in which they find themselves. This postmodern transcendentalism appears to account for the *otaku* phenomena, as well as the *hikikomori* (social withdrawal) phenomena (discussed earlier in this chapter and in Chapter 5), and helps to focus on those groups that rarely

[61] Azuma 2009.   [62] Kijima 2012.

drew attention in Japan and abroad in the past. Against this backdrop, some analysts have proposed *otaku* studies,[63] while others have argued for the potential of what they call Cool Japanology.[64]

At the same time, while countercultural and postmodern in many respects, the Cool Japan discourse not only contains very limited orientations to structural social reform but often comes close to cultural essentialism. The very fact that Cool Japan is approved by Japanese government and business indicates that Cool Japan culture is not a threat to the nation's socio-political system at all and is conceivably countercultural in form only. It arguably expands political and economic interests while allowing the masses to engage in acceptable diversions. In tune with Prime Minister Shinzō Abe's 2006 slogan *Utsukushii kuni Nippon* (Japan as a beautiful nation), one may even suggest that the Cool Japan campaign tacitly fosters cultural nationalism.

Underneath the Cool Japan model lies the assumption that Japanese culture encapsulates exceptionally unique characteristics that no other culture has. Here, to focus primarily on *manga* and *anime*, a new depiction of Japanese culture has emerged: pictocentrism.[65] Japanese are deemed visually oriented in contrast with the 'logocentric' and 'phonocentric' Westerners. Some have argued that Japan has had a long history of visually oriented culture. As discussed in Chapter 1, the first Japanese *manga* is said to be the *chōjū giga* scrolls produced around the twelfth century, in which a variety of birds and animals are comically illustrated. *Ezōshi*, picture books sold and read in the Edo period, are often cited as the precursor of Japan's *manga* culture today. Others suggested that *kanji* characters, originally imported from China, are ideographic rather than phonetic, each representing an image of something, and have nurtured the visually oriented culture of Japan.

Based on an Orientalist polarity of the East and the West, these observations and arguments tend to single out a limited sector of Japanese society and expand it disproportionately to build an image of national culture at large. As the above-mentioned third wave of overseas representations of Japan, it is new in the sense that an emphasis is placed on playfulness, flexibility, urbanity, and mobility – features that are regarded as postmodern. While departing from the conventional form of exoticism, this development embraces what might be regarded as postmodern Orientalism.[66] It is merely a slight leap from here to argue, as many of the Cool Japan advocates have, that 'pictocentric' Japan is postmodern and

[63] Okada 2000.   [64] Azuma 2010.
[65] See Inouye 1996; Napier 2005; Berndt 2007, pp. 137–40.   [66] Sanders 2008.

thus ahead of the 'logocentric' and 'phonocentric' West, which is stuck with logical, coherent and rational modernity. In this sense, then, the Cool Japan discourse can be positioned as a new stereotype formation, possibly called postmodern *Nihonjinron*.

It might be time for both enthusiasts and skeptics to look at the Cool Japan phenomena with a cool head.

10   Civil Society and Friendly Authoritarianism

Two ostensibly contradictory forces operate in Japanese society, as is the case in other industrialized societies. On the one hand, it is subject to many centrifugal forces that tend to diversify its structural arrangements, lifestyles, and value orientations. On the other hand, a range of centripetal forces drive Japanese society towards homogeneity and uniformity. This chapter recapitulates these two forces from a slightly different angle. The first section of the chapter examines the vibrancy of Japan's civil society as the centrifugal drive. The second part investigates the Great East Japan Earthquake in 2011 and its aftermath as a concrete test case of the interplay between civil society and the establishment. Finally, the third part attempts to locate a variety of forms of control in an analytical framework and to summarize their features as the centripetal force of Japanese society.

I   Civil Society

The liveliness of grassroots culture in Japan, detailed throughout this book, reflects the vitality of its civil society, the sphere of voluntary collective activities carried out with a significant degree of autonomy from the power of the state and the forces of the market. The characteristics of Japan's civil society have been a subject of intense debate in recent years, pointing to the possibility that new forms of voluntary association might be emerging.[1]

This section on civil society first deals with three conspicuous developments in recent years – the proliferation of volunteer activities, the spread of non-profit and non-governmental organizations, and the rise of resident movements – and then examines a variety of voluntary associations and interest groups before investigating the significance of the emic notion analogous to citizenship in the analysis of the Japanese context.

[1] Tsujinaka 2002, pp. 30–4.

1   Volunteer Activities

The English term volunteer came into wide circulation for the first time in Japanese vocabulary immediately after the Great Hanshin-Awaji Earthquake hit the heavily populated city of Kobe and its adjacent areas, killing more than sixty-four hundred persons and rendering more than three hundred homeless, in January 1995. Volunteers surged into the ruined areas to render assistance, and their numbers impressed the public, a spectacle which led some commentators to declare that this was the beginning of volunteer activities in Japan, although similar practices occurred during previous disaster situations. In 2009, when many non-regular workers lost their jobs and accommodation, a volunteer group established a tent village for them in the middle of Tokyo and demanded government assistance for those who had suddenly become homeless. Empirical evidence suggests that more than a quarter of the Japanese participate in volunteer activities, occasionally or frequently.[2]

Although the scope for civil participation in volunteer activities has expanded, some analysts maintain that volunteers are prone not so much to press for progressive reforms as to retain a rather conservative status quo. This trend arguably has some bearing upon the class backgrounds of participants in volunteer activities: there is a correlation between household income and volunteer activity participation rate[3] – well-off families tend to engage in volunteer activities more frequently than low-income families. Accordingly, these activities are often carried out without affecting the class interests of the relatively rich or with a view to promoting them. Charity activities, for example, make philanthropists feel good without challenging their comfortable lifestyles.

Other observers argue that volunteer activities are not monopolized by the upper socioeconomic groups. Some research has demonstrated a bipolar pattern, with those in the higher class bracket and those at the bottom of the scale being apt to be volunteers, while those in the middle range are least inclined.[4] These studies suggest that upper-class groups tend to participate for ideological and compassionate reasons while lower-class groups do so based on the convention of mutual assistance.

Volunteer activities have proliferated partly because of the demographic changes at the top end of the age pyramid. On the demand side,

---

[2] Ministry of Internal Affairs and Communications 2006 shows that 26.2 percent of the population participate in volunteer activities. The SSM 2005 data show a similar pattern. See Nihei 2008, p. 197.

[3] Toyoshima 2000; Nihei 2008. Regarding the elderly, see Yoshikawa 2010.

[4] This tendency is described as a K-pattern; with the class dimension on the vertical axis and the participation ratio on the horizontal axis, the empirical distribution curve shows a K shape. See Suzuki 1987; Inazuki 1994; Economic Planning Agency 1999.

the aging of the population has necessitated medical and welfare care of the elderly. On the supply side, the increasing number of retirees in good health has provided a sizeable pool of senior citizens ready to work in a humanitarian fashion. Many of those who arrived at the retirement age at the beginning of the twenty-first century were in their youth at the time when anti-establishmentarian student revolts spread across the country. Now being 'time-rich', they want to make non-monetary contributions to the society at large after spending many years of their occupational life under profit-first economic rationalism, often in conflict with their core philosophies.

2   NPOs and NGOs

If volunteer groups are generally unstructured and non-institutionalized as business organizations, non-profit organizations (NPOs) that have emerged with the enactment of the law governing them in 1998 have legal personality and corporate status, although their *raison d'être* is not profit-making but public socioeconomic support. Nearly fifty thousand NPO establishments were in operation in 2014.[5] These organizations constitute the everyday landscape of Japanese society today.

NPO activities cover a wide range of areas, the most popular of which include medical care, public health, social welfare, community planning, social education, environmental protection, child-care, and academic, cultural, and sporting activities. There are also many organizations that specialize in international cooperation, human rights, gender equality, and peace issues. While these social and cultural activities are predominant, there are also a good number of organizations that have more economic foci, such as business vitalization, occupational skill formation, employment assistance, and consumer protection.

The development of information technology has enabled small groups with limited capital and infrastructure to start NPOs with cost-effective ways to gather information from a wide range of sources and dispatch information to large audiences. Without temporal and geographic barriers, those who wish to establish NPOs can implement projects with relative ease and without huge initial funds, such as distant education, virtual visits to the aged, and internet-based disaster crisis management.

---

[5] The Cabinet Office collates statistical data and reports them on its homepage. The broader definition of NPOs includes all organizations that provide services to households, not to corporate enterprises, business establishments, or industrial associations. In this definition, it does not matter whether or not the NPOs have acquired corporate status.

These developments are in tune with the growth of cultural capitalism, discussed in Chapter 4.

The non-governmental organizations that are referred to as NGOs also operate as non-profit groups, while their areas of activity are global, with a focus on development, human rights, ecology, and disarmament. Some three hundred Japanese NGOs are active, and tens of thousands of Japanese men and women work mainly in developing countries in conjunction with the United Nations as well as international institutions. Although non-governmental, Japan's NGOs often carry out their work in cooperation with the Official Development Assistance programs of the Japanese government. NGO activities overseas are indicative of the extension of Japan's civil society beyond its national borders.

3   Rise of Resident Movements

Japan has had a variety of citizens' movements concerned with national and international issues. Peace movements that exemplify such orientations have achieved widespread support around the country. The Group of Article 9, for example, which was initially formed in 2004 to defend the peace clause of the Constitution, now has a network of civil movements with several thousand chapters throughout the nation.

Meanwhile, more locally based resident movements that address community issues prove sturdy buffers against state power. Nationwide social movements based on clear ideological causes have waned since the 1970s, but conflicts between state development programs and tenacious local community groups have become common throughout the country.[6]

Japan's spectacular economic growth produced a wide range of environmental victims and triggered two types of local protest. At one end of the spectrum, community residents stood up against development projects which they regarded as detrimental to their vested interests. The construction of high-rise condominium buildings in densely populated urban centers provoked objections from neighboring residents who lost the 'right to enjoy sunshine'. The extension of highways and roads was opposed by residents who might suffer from noise and air pollution. By and large, these protestors enjoyed a reasonably comfortable standard of living and feared the possibility of losing what they had already gained. They were not necessarily politically radical; many in fact were conservatives who wished to maintain the status quo. Most resident movements of this type have been clustered in urban areas.

---

[6] See, for example, Broadbent 1998; Hasegawa 2004.

At the other end of the scale were a smaller number of rural resident movements which often adopted more extreme forms of dissent and focused on the basic human rights of local inhabitants. Some movements arose in situations where residents of a particular area became ill or died as a direct consequence of water and air pollution. In Minamata, Kyūshū, for example, a series of anti-pollution protests, lasting for half a century, developed a distinctive dissident culture: many members of the fishing community there were crippled after eating fish poisoned by a large quantity of mercury which a chemical company in the area knowingly discharged into the sea in the 1950s and 1960s. The victims were supported by political activists from city areas, who joined forces with them in demanding both apologies and material compensation from the company and the state, whose negligence contributed to the spread of the problem.[7] Another case in point is the long-lasting protest movement against the construction of the New Tokyo International Airport in the rural town of Narita. Farmers in the area mounted a series of violent confrontations in the 1970s and 1980s, together with student radicals and supporters from Tokyo and other urban centers, protesting against the state expropriation of farmers' land.[8]

In these and similar cases, the fusion between local protestors and outside radicals generated a particular type of alternative culture; a kind of 'magnetic field' of cultural creativity was generated when permanent local residents who constituted the 'subjectivity of the movement' formed a tie with volunteer support groups which drifted into the local community from outside.[9] This kind of alternative culture is characterized by a strong sense of defiance against the state which destroyed the peaceful lives of local residents, using police to protect the expansionary programs of the business or the state. This type of dissident culture has a sharp moral tone, denouncing development programs as vicious and claiming that it is essential for their promoters to engage in sincere self-criticism and apologize.

Some other rural development programs orchestrated by technocrats in government ministries in the name of national interests have also triggered fierce, long-running protests. Cases include such large-scale national projects as the construction of bullet-train networks and nuclear plants across the country. Protest movements of this type also often involve the participation of articulate city radicals alongside local residents.

Although different in styles, both types of resident movements have taught those in power in the center a lesson; bureaucrats, politicians, and

---

[7] See Huddle and Reich 1987.
[8] See Apter and Sawa 1984.   [9] Irokawa 1989, pp. 80–1.

business leaders have become aware that they can not simply impose their development projects but must first consult with the communities potentially affected. The influence of these movements has not only been felt in connection with pollution issues but has been significant in a range of urban problems, including city planning, environmental protection, and the preservation of cultural assets. Thus, policy-makers now have to calculate both the benefits and social costs of programs, making resident movements a kind of local counterweight against the central establishment.

4   Three-dimensional Typology

Apart from these fresh developments in civil society, there are, of course, many others. Labor unions, as discussed in Chapter 4, have defended the rights and working conditions of organized workers for decades. Neighborhood associations (*chōnaikai* and *jichikai*) provide a sphere of action in geographically defined communities, although their activities are often closely linked with local governments, as discussed later in this chapter. Parent–teacher associations are vehicles of interaction between schools and parents and represent the engine of civic life in education. The associations of commerce and industry (*shōkōkai*) in cities and agricultural cooperatives (*nōkyō*) in rural areas form area-based interest groups that have channels of influence over state decision-making processes. Local cooperatives (*chiiki seikyō*), which initially emerged immediately after World War II to defend consumers' interests against raw market forces, have a long history of keeping the state at arm's length, although they have become increasingly accommodative and commercialized. These cooperatives operate in various localities throughout the nation to cater for a wide range of consumer needs, from shopping, nursing care, and ecology to hairdressing. Cooperative movements are also widespread in workplaces, universities, and medical institutions.

These voluntary associations, in which citizens participate of their own volition, form the crux of civil society as intermediary organizations sitting between socio-political institutions at the top and scattered, non-participatory individuals at the bottom. The spread of these spontaneous action groups is the best empirical index of the extent of civil society.

One can examine them in terms of three dimensions. The first pertains to the organization's relationship to, and its autonomy from, the state. The key question is whether it tends to show confrontational or indifferent tendencies vis-à-vis the state. Citizens' movements are generally organized in opposition to state policies, while hobby groups are mostly

Table 10.1   Types of voluntary organizations

Confrontational vis-à-vis the state	Institutionalized as business organization	Necessarily bound to small geographical community	Organizations
−	−	−	Volunteer groups, hobby groups, sports clubs
−	−	+	Neighborhood associations (*chōnaikai*, *jichikai*)
−	+	+	Agricultural cooperatives (*nōkyō*), local business associations (*shōkōkai*), political supporters' associations (*kōenkai*)
−	+	−	NPO, religious organizations, cultural foundations
+	+	−	Labor unions
+	−	−	Peace movements
+	−	+	Residents' movements (*jūmin undō*)
+	+	+	Life-club cooperatives (*seikatsu kurabu seikyō*), some local cooperatives (*chiiki seikyō*)

non-political. The second dimension concerns the extent to which the organization in question has an institutionalized business structure – that is, whether it is consolidated as an organization that has an annual budget and paid full-time employees. Local cooperatives have such structure, whereas most volunteer groups do not. Third, the geographical bases of voluntary organizations deserve consideration. The question is whether they require specific small geographical communities as a necessary condition for their existence.[10] Residents' movements are, by definition, founded on local community bases, while NPOs do not necessarily require them. Neighborhood associations, which are fully discussed later in this chapter, as groups both voluntary and linked to the state, are necessarily geographically based. We can then analyze how each voluntary organization operates in three-dimensional space, as shown in Table 10.1. Displaying eight analytically distinguishable types, the table attempts to offer a glimpse of the multifaceted complexity and diversity of Japan's civil society.

[10] A cluster analysis of SSM 2005 data shows that voluntary associations are divided into two clusters, geographically based and de-localized groups. See Nihei 2008, p. 201.

5   Interest Groups

With a principal focus on empirically observable organizations and quantitatively testable propositions, the Japan Interest Group Study (JIGS), led by Yutaka Tsujinaka, has produced by far the most comprehensive portrayal of what it calls civil society organizations in Japan in comparison with that of three other countries – the United States, Germany, and South Korea. Conducted in 1997 in Tokyo and Ibaraki Prefecture, the study concentrates on civil associations and unions – active non-governmental organizations with a significant degree of durability, orientation to the public interest, and concern with policy-making. This study centers its attention narrowly on politically engaged and organizationally structured interest groups and does not cover more amorphous but action-oriented civil groups – such as resident movements, unorganized volunteer groups, and unregistered civil action networks. Yet, the findings of the project are groundbreaking.

In international comparison, Japan's civil organization structure appears to be characterized by the abundance and strength of economic interest groups, particularly producer groups, closely associated with the national bureaucracy. They include, for instance, the Japan Agricultural Cooperatives, the Federation of Electric Power Companies, and the Japan Road Constructors Association. These groups attempt to influence the national political process by making representations primarily to national ministry officials and secondarily to parliamentarians, mainly those of the ruling party. This pattern reflects the power that national ministries have over economic interest groups in exercising administrative guidance, granting permits and licenses, framing legal regulations, and providing subsidies (as discussed in Chapter 8). Among various ministries, the Ministry of International Trade and Industry and the Ministry of Agriculture, Forestry and Fisheries are the frequent targets of economic interest groups. The cozy relationship between officialdom and many economic civil groups manifests itself in the personnel traffic between the two, with bureaucrats occupying the top positions of interest groups after retirement and civil organization leaders sitting on governmental advisory councils and consultative committees by ministerial invitation.

The ideology of each group plays a role in determining which state apparatus it approaches to petition and lobby. Not surprisingly, business interest groups hardly try to make representations to the Japan Communist Party. Conversely, labor unions, environmentalist organizations, and left-leaning political groups differ from the mainstream producer interest groups in accessing opposition parties and mass media rather than ministries and the ruling political party. Interest groups based in rural areas are highly active and robust in providing a powerful electioneering basis for political campaigning and vote gathering for conservative party candidates. Interest groups combine various tactics to influence state policies. Some lobby *inside* the system in direct contact with major political parties and national ministries. Others mobilize their members from *outside* by organizing letter-writing campaigns, petitions, public rallies, street demonstrations, sit-ins, and other forms of direct action. They also rely on mass media to exercise external pressure on national and local governments, holding press conferences and running advertisements in newspapers and on television.

Distinct from domestically oriented interest groups, globally oriented organizations – NGOs in particular – have proliferated since the 1980s, and a majority of them are based in localities outside Tokyo, a pattern that suggests the groups that 'think globally and act locally' are on the rise.[11] On the whole, they are small in size and tend to distance themselves from the national government while networking between themselves and making extensive use of mass media for the propagation of their perspectives. While domestically minded groups are prone to pursue their particularistic instrumental interests, international groups are inclined to press for universalistic civil objectives. The contemporary acceleration of internet, mobile phone, and other communications technology has made it possible for these small, internationally oriented organizations to act both efficiently and cost-effectively.

Japan's civil organizations appear to have been formed in three different phases.[12] In the first phase, between 1945 and 1957, immediately after the end of World War II, a majority of interest groups currently in operation were established. These are mainly producer organizations that reflect the economic and occupational configuration of Japanese society, including a variety of industrial and professional associations. The second phase, which lasted from 1957 to 1996, recorded the rise of the so-called policy beneficiary groups, whose activities are dependent on the policies of the state. Many educational and social welfare organizations fall into this category. The third wave, which surged after 1996, included the emergence of new types of civil organizations that press for fresh values ranging from environmental protection, gender equality, and aged care to international assistance.

The JIGS project also shows that the four advanced economies under investigation – Japan, the United States, Germany, and South Korea – have similar interest group structures and appears to give some credence to the convergence thesis, discussed in Chapter 1. In all these countries, three levels of engagement are apparent, with almost all interest

[11] Adachi 2002, pp. 195–7.   [12] Tsujinaka and Choe 2002, pp. 284–5.

groups showing concern with governmental policies and programs, (2) some 30 to 70 percent pursuing lobbying activities, and (3) approximately 10 to 20 percent involving themselves in overt political activities, such as conducting election campaigns for particular candidates and attempting to influence the budget appropriation process at the national and local government levels.

The JIGS identifies three axes of differentiation in portraying the overall configuration of civil organizations in contemporary Japan. The first of these concerns the extent to which groups are actively involved in the state political process or relatively autonomous and independent of it; the second relates to the degree to which they are associated with the state bureaucracy or political parties; and the third focuses on whether they are more oriented to the domestic distribution of material goods or to the global sharing of information and civic values. As Table 10.2 shows, the combination of these three dimensions produces eight types of interest groups that operate in Japanese society today.[13]

It is important to reiterate that interest groups with clear organizational structures and political directions are not the only ingredients of civil society. Spontaneous political demonstrations, civic rallies, charity campaigns, public debate forums, and even lively discussions at coffee shops and pubs constitute significant components. Japanese society abounds with these unstructured yet activist group activities. To comprehend the complexity of civil society in this context, one should be sensitized to some vernacular notions particular to Japan.

6   *Seikatsusha* as an Emic Concept of Citizens

The Japanese word for citizen, *shimin*, has wide circulation in contemporary Japan but is tinged with foreign nuances and intellectual overtones as an imported concept. A more vernacular notion, *seikatsusha*, has perhaps a ring of familiarity and reality for many Japanese as an emic concept that overlaps with the idea of citizen. The term *seikatsu* means livelihood, everyday life, or a wide range of life activities, including clothing, food, housing, folk customs, language, recreation, and entertainment, not to mention work and consumption.[14] *Seikatsusha* are the agents of

---

[13] The focus of Table 10.2 differs from that of Table 10.1. Table 10.2 investigates *interest groups* in particular, whereas Table 10.1 examines *voluntary organizations* in general. The former is a smaller category than the latter.

[14] Recognizing the popular acceptance of the concept, the Miyazawa cabinet launched a five-year plan in 1992 to make Japan a *seikatsu taikoku* (lifestyle superpower). Though the plan went nowhere, it reflected the widespread idea that, though Japan may be an economic superpower, there is much room for the improvement of its citizens' quality of life.

Table 10.2 Typology of interest groups

Relationship with the state	Actively engaged with the state		Relatively independent of the state	
Target values	Bureaucracy-oriented	Parliament-oriented	Bureaucracy-oriented	Parliament-oriented
Domestic, materialistic	Agricultural, economic, administrative organizations (Established 1955–74)	Labor organizations, welfare corporations, special semi-government corporations (1955–74)	None	Welfare organizations
Global, informational	Incorporated associations	Political organizations	Foundations, educational groups, professional associations (before 1944)	Organizations with no corporate status, citizens' groups (1975–)

Source: Adapted from of Tsujinaka 2002, p. 335, Figure 15.1.

Note: The year ranges in brackets are the periods in which the types of organizations in question were established in large numbers.

seikatsu who construct a variety of autonomous areas of civic life culture and attempt to improve their standard of living and quality of life in competition with the forces of government regulation and capitalist consumerism.

The notion of *seikatsusha* has been debated since the first half of the twentieth century.[15] Kiyoshi Miki, an uncompromising liberal philosopher in wartime Japan, attempted to explore the life culture (*seikatsu bunka*) of common people as an analytical category as distinct from national and class culture. Based on the lives of ordinary people, life culture comprises the styles of speech, cooking, customs, social interactions, pastime amusements, and other everyday activities. *Seikatsusha* are the active and skillful artists who struggle to carve out new lives built on their daily life conditions.

The styles of participant observation of *seikatsusha* have established themselves as a genre of studies. Itaru Nii, a dissident journalist during and after World War II, wandered the streets of Tokyo, witnessing and recording the lives of people buried in obscurity, and counterposed *seikatsusha* as people who lead autonomous lives vis-à-vis those who belong to officialdom, large corporations, and banks, and whose lives are subjected to allegiance to their organizations. Discontented with literature-based research, Kunio Yanagita, the founding father of Japanese ethnology and folklore studies, also traveled around Japan to observe the unrecorded histories, oral traditions, legends, practices, and customs of ordinary people, whom he called *jōmin* (literally, everyday life people), a category that comes very close to *seikatsusha*.

Immediately after World War II, Wajirō Kon was the first social scientist to propose *seikatsu-gaku* (life studies, lifeology) as a field that studies the lives of common people, their clothing, eating, and housing realities, as well as their entertainment, leisure, and education activities, not necessarily as the direct products of economic conditions. He later founded the Japan Association of *Seikatsu* Studies (*Seikatsu Gakkai*), which has received wide recognition.

Throughout postwar years, a journal entitled the 'Science of Thought' (*Shisō no kagaku*) served as a forum for debate over *seikatsusha* and published a number of studies featuring the examination of popular novels, popular songs, personal advice columns in newspapers, graffiti, *manga*, workplace accounts, and personal diaries.[16] The group that engaged in these studies attempted to listen to the voices of the 'voiceless individuals' whose philosophy was embedded in their mundane, everyday lives

---

[15] For a full English discussion of the *seikatsusha* concept, see Amano, M. 2011. For a succinct and excellent discussion on the idea, see Seifert 2007.

[16] The intellectual leader of these studies was Shunsuke Tsurumi, whose idea of marginal art was discussed in Chapter 8. See also Sugimoto 2008.

and enlightened by their own 'worm's eye views'. Their ways of thinking, developed in the school of hard knocks are not necessarily politically correct but often egoistic, devious, and crafty. This is an intellectual current in pursuit of a vision of civil society without glorification of the masses.

In the 1960s, *Beheiren*, the first large-scale citizens' movement in Japan, which called for peace in Vietnam, defined *seikatsusha* as the key actors of political action and used the term together with such phrases as *shimin, futsū no hito* (ordinary people), and *tada no hito* (run-of-the-mill people) in distinction from the conventional agents of anti-government movements, such as workers and students. Consciously formulating *seikatsusha* as weak, fragile, and inarticulate individuals, Japan's citizens' movements developed a style rooted in the daily lives and realities of the common folk that is not affiliated with such established political organizations as labor unions, student associations, and religious bodies.

The *seikatsu kurabu seikyō* (life-club cooperatives) that also commenced their activity in the 1960s have developed as a civic consumer movement in pursuit of alternative ways of life. Organized primarily by concerned housewives, these cooperatives initially challenged the systems of highly developed commercialism and took initiatives to develop their own food distribution networks. Over time, the participants in the movement involved themselves not only in food safety problems but also in other ecological issues over synthetic detergents, waste recycling, and nuclear power generation.[17] This group emphasizes the fact that its members are not simply passive consumers but active participants in the equity investment, utilization, and operation of their cooperatives. These orientations articulated the notion of *seikatsusha* as participatory civil actors and as an antonym for submissive consumers.[18]

Formulated, elaborated, and debated within Japan for more than half a century, *seikatsu* and *seikatsusha* have remained Japanese emic concepts that have not yet been examined comparatively. It has been suggested that the notion of *seikatsu* substantially overlaps with some major ideas of Western sociology when it is used in combination with other words: for instance, *Lebensführung* (Weber), lifeworld, or *Lebenswelt* (Husserl, Schütz, and Habermas) and life-chances (Dahrendorf).[19] Through interaction with these notions, *seikatsu* and *seikatsusha* would perhaps be sharpened and thus shed more light on the characteristics of civil society in Japan and beyond.

[17] See Gelb and Estevez-Abe 1998.
[18] This perspective formed a basis of worker collectives, discussed in Chapter 9.
[19] Seifert 2007, p. 4151.

II   The Case of Fukushima: Collusive Center and Civil Defiance

On 11 March 2011 the northeastern region of Japan experienced a massive earthquake, followed by a series of extremely destructive tsunamis. Nearly sixteen thousand people were killed and more than twenty-five hundred were reported missing. Many people lost their families, friends, and homes and had to live in temporary shelters for a long period of time. The crushing calamity gave rise to subsequent explosions at nuclear power plants situated on the coast of Fukushima, some 230 kilometers north of Tokyo, causing further unprecedented disaster around Fukushima prefecture and beyond. Hazardous nuclear substances spread through the nearby area, forcing residents to evacuate to safer communities, while also raising serious health concerns among citizens of adjacent prefectures – including the highly populated Tokyo metropolitan region. A considerable quantity of recycled water which was supposed to be sealed within the nuclear plant's system kept leaking into the soil and underground water and eventually leached into the sea – awakening alarm among the fishing industry and consumers of marine products. With nowhere to go, contaminated debris accumulated in the areas affected by the earthquake, tsunamis, and nuclear explosions, but few prefectures or municipalities were willing to accept responsibility. No one knows exactly how many years or decades it will take to clean up the radioactive soil and water on the plains, hills, and mountains and in the ocean. This is undoubtedly the greatest nuclear plant disaster that Japan has suffered in the nation's memory.

The responses of Japanese society to this unprecedented calamity dramatically exhibited both the centripetal and the centrifugal forces at work as the rival undercurrents of Japanese society. This section focuses both on the way in which the national center has made deliberate attempts to conceal and underestimate the repercussions of the disaster and on the extent to which concerned citizens have tried to mount anti-nuclear campaigns and demonstrations – a specific case of tug-of-war between the establishment and civil society, whose outcome will seriously affect the future configuration of Japanese society.

1   TEPCO and the 'Nuclear Village'

The Fukushima tragedy was manmade at every step. Although the earthquake itself was unavoidable, much of the resulting human tragedy could have been prevented if Japanese decision-makers had taken a different path before, during, and after 11 March 2011. In particular, the Fukushima nuclear explosion and its ensuing disaster revealed collusion at the top level of the country, involving the nuclear power industry, the national bureaucracy, and the political circles (the three-way alliance discussed at the beginning of Chapter 8). Most mainstream mass media, as well as nuclear science academia, were also enmeshed in the complicated web of mutual collaboration and complicity. The network of nuclear power promoters, often referred to as the 'nuclear village', formed the complex that generated and disseminated the so-called 'myth of safe nuclear energy' and benefited from it.

(a)   Structural Complicity

A deep-seated structure of complicity has been built around the Tokyo Electric Power Corporation (TEPCO) which ran the Fukushima nuclear plants and therefore must assume the primary responsibility for the calamity. The Nuclear and Industrial Safety Agency, the key government body which is supposed to oversee the safety of nuclear power plants from an independent and neutral perspective, is part of the Ministry of Economy, Trade and Industry, which promotes nuclear electricity generation as the mainstay of its national energy program. Furthermore, for decades some high-ranking officials of these government entities have secured executive positions with TEPCO after retiring from their official posts, a practice known as *amakudari* (landing from heaven) that enables the bureaucracy and the big corporations under its supervision to develop collusive arrangements.

Nuclear experts also enjoy similar cozy interdependence with the government and power companies, which provide them with large research funds. On the whole, these academics are pro-nuclear scientists who tend to argue that radiation risks are limited. Nuclear scientists who have voiced concerns about the dangers of nuclear power plants have not shared in the benefits of such grants and, in some cases, have been prevented from obtaining higher positions in universities. A well-known case in point was a small group of middle-aged, and now retired, concerned nuclear specialists based at Kyoto University, who were forced to remain at the level of research assistant throughout their academic careers.

TEPCO is the most powerful of the nine regionally based power companies that monopolize both the production and the delivery of electricity across the nation. These power companies have been able to maintain exclusive rights despite the step-by-step privatization of most monopoly sectors, including postal services, national railways, airways, and telephones. These electricity companies, notably TEPCO, embody the old-style management model lauded internationally in the 1980s as the engine of the so-called 'Japanese miracle', for its internal cohesion, employee loyalty, and behind-closed-doors decision-making practices.

TEPCO has a checkered history when it comes to transparency. A decade ago, it was revealed that the company had concocted data on the levels of radioactivity in its plant, a record which only adds to the current community suspicion that the full extent of the ongoing risks and dangers is being downplayed to protect the future of Japan's nuclear industry and shield corporate and ministerial interests. TEPCO's possible concealment of information regarding the details of the nuclear situation is already subject to severe ongoing criticism from specialists in the field. In old-style Japanese corporate culture, the flow of information is often delayed due to the multiple and complex layers of communication channels and consensus formation processes. In the context of the current crisis, crucial data were withheld by prolonged internal consultations at various levels.

TEPCO operates within the conventional 'convoy system' in which government ministries protect companies that are in trouble while supervising and overseeing the private sector in the name of national interest. In peaceful situations, the system cultivates close links between large corporations and governmental agencies in a collusive fashion. Closed to 'outsiders', the structure failed to incorporate the assessments of the many international experts who arrived in Japan to examine the situation. Meanwhile, Japan's major banks, which lie within this circle, have been quick to support TEPCO while being slow to offer aid to individual citizens.

Major companies in Japan in this mold are situated at the top of the corporate pyramid, above their own associated enterprises, subsidiaries, and subcontracting companies. This hierarchy is known as a dual structure (as discussed in Chapter 4), where a small number of large businesses prevail over a large number of smaller ones. Many workers who continue to battle *kamikaze*-style on the dangerous frontline in and around the nuclear plant to control the disaster are not TEPCO employees but workers from the lower-level companies under its command.

Japan's conventional corporate culture reflects the community values in which perseverance, patience, and self-control are emphasized. When applied to the 'convoy system', however, such moral principles give priority to the collective and organizational interests of government ministries and leading corporations. Closely knit and tightly structured, the ministry–industry complex is based on employees' quiet loyalty and devotion and is consistent with the values of individual self-restraint and endurance. Virtually no voices of concern or dissent have been openly articulated from within this structure.

2   Manipulation of Hardship on the Periphery

The disasters drew public attention to regional inequality and the disparity between urban and rural areas. The destruction of small car-parts production factories, which are concentrated in the Tōhoku region, paralyzed the car industry in Japan, as well as overseas, an indication of the dependency of multinational car companies on their subsidiaries and subcontractors in the hinterland.

The Tohoku district has long been regarded as the nation's backwater which has supported the prosperity of the metropolis of Tokyo. Located away from the national center and faced with the danger of nuclear radiation, Fukushima and other regions housing nuclear plants in Tohoku have supplied nuclear-generated electricity to the glittering megacities in and around the capital, where one-third of electricity was nuclear-dependent. The shortage of power ensuing from the shutdown of the Fukushima plants suddenly limited electricity usage in the major cities and forced residents to realize that their comfortable lifestyles owe much to the supply of energy generated in distant locations that bear the attendant risks.

Yet, it is telling that those who live outside the nuclear-contamination zones are either covertly reluctant or openly opposed to various programs to move radioactive debris to their communities, a kind of regional egoism in which the center remains unwilling to share the plight of the periphery. In retrospect, the Japanese-language book *Build Nuclear Power Plants in Tokyo*, published under this provocative and sarcastic title more than two decades ago by an anti-nuclear journalist,[20] hits the mark.

Most cities, towns, and villages where nuclear plants are situated allowed their construction and operation in exchange for substantial grants and subsidies from the central government and power companies. With no profitable industries and limited employment opportunities, these localities were attracted to the 'financial carrots' dangled in front of them and succumbed to the whims of the national ministries and powerful corporations. The Fukushima incident exposed the center–periphery relationship to the public eye while making weak municipalities aware of the broader costs a nuclear accident entails. They appear to be increasingly unwilling to accept short-term economic incentives in return for extensive and long-term dangers to their populace.

[20] Hirose 1986.

3   Division in the Business and Civil Communities

The Japanese are still divided over the continuation of nuclear power supply. The business community is not uniform. At one end of the spectrum, *Keidanren* (Japanese Federation of Economic Organizations), the most influential employer organization, takes a pro-nuclear stance and actively explores the possibility of exporting Japanese nuclear power plant packages to Vietnam, Turkey, Jordan, South Korea, and Russia. Meanwhile, the knowledge industry tends to favor the expansion of sustainable energy and calls for environmentally friendly developments. Masayoshi Son, chief executive officer of Softbank, a leading mobile phone company, presses for the establishment of nationwide networks of solar panels in cooperation with local municipalities across Japan. Hiroshi Miyatani, the head of Rakuten, a leading online shopping mall, resigned from *Keidanren* in June 2011 in protest against its pro-nuclear stance. Studio Ghibli, the most well known Japanese *anime* production company, which has produced such internationally acclaimed films as *Spirited Away*, *My Neighbor Totoro*, and *Nausicaa of the Valley of the Wind*, attracted much public attention in 2011 by placing a huge banner on the office building of the company which said 'we want to make films without using electricity produced by nuclear power'. These enterprises constitute the driving force of Japan's new economy and take a non-nuclear line, which is not only ethically and morally more seemly but also economically compatible with their business opportunities and interests – a reflection of the wider division between industrial and cultural capitalism, which is now becoming evident in the Japanese economy in general (as discussed in Chapter 4).

At the community level, the proportion of nuclear skeptics has significantly increased since the Fukushima disaster. The image of a technologically sophisticated nation is now accompanied by the depiction that it is both highly vulnerable and unresponsive to natural disasters and the realization that the advance of science has hazardous side effects. The risks and dangers were highlighted for the emerging skeptics who had benefitted from cheap, reliable power and had long and unquestioningly believed in the 'myth of safe nuclear energy'. Yet, many of them would prefer to pursue a less nuclear-dependent society slowly, without drastically altering their present lifestyles of convenience, efficiency, and comfort. These gradualists are willing to refrain from overusing air-conditioners and to turn off electricity at home as frequently as possible, and thereby reduce the overall level of power consumption, but are unwilling to accept substantial hikes in electricity bills, which non-nuclear alternatives might bring about. The DPJ, which was in government at the time of the Fukushima incident, takes this line of thinking and has adopted *datsu genpatsu* (de-nuclearization) by the 2030s as its official policy.[21]

4 Test of Civil Society

At the other end of the spectrum, the earthquake and the ensuing Fukushima situation showed the strength of Japan's civil society. Two major groups emerged: anti-nuclear demonstrators who demanded the immediate and permanent shutdown of all nuclear plants around the country, and volunteer workers who came from various areas of the nation to help disaster victims recover from the devastating conditions.

(a) Anti-nuclear Demonstrations

Diametrically opposed to the pro-nuclear groups and distant from moderate nuclear skeptics, many civic groups demanded the immediate and permanent shutdown of all nuclear plants and pressed for alternative and sustainable energy supplies (including hydro-electric, geothermal, and wind power). The most visible dissent from Japan's nuclear programs emerged as anti-nuclear demonstrations that spread through the main streets, parks, and train stations of Tokyo and other cities (including areas near the prime minister's official residence). These public protests continued with remarkable tenacity, with the number of participants fluctuating between a few hundred and two hundred thousand. Predominantly in their thirties or below, many of these protestors took part in mass political action for the first time, with mobile phones, emails, Twitter, Facebook, and other forms of social media playing the key role in the process of mobilization.[22] These young and fresh activists reflect an emerging sector of civil society, which is spontaneous, internet-savvy, and environmentally conscious. Their communication mode differs from that of the seasoned political left, who tend to use posters, leaflets, handouts, newsletters, and other conventional means to disseminate information and marshal support. Quick, instantaneous, and interactive, the younger generation's style has the power of sudden and explosive mobilization, although it is transient, momentary, and ephemeral at times.

Participants in street demonstrations have traditionally been students, housewives, and pensioners who can easily afford to spend time participating in demonstrations. However, the anti-nuclear protests attracted

---

[21] The DPJ is in a dilemma because it is supported by the national umbrella organization of labor unions, *Rengō*, which includes the powerful electricity unions, whose stance does not differ from that of the power companies.

[22] Hirabayashi 2013.

workers in the prime of their working lives, including casual employees, kindergarten teachers, executives of foreign-owned companies, artists and singers, tradesmen, and so on. This reflects the diversification of the workforce and reveals an increased participation rate of people working flexible hours, who now have free time to take part in protest action.[23] Anti-nuclear demonstrators appear to have come voluntarily from a cross-section of the population – except the conventional Japanese corporate world, in which dedicated salarymen work prohibitively long hours. In the second half of 2012, a combination of factors (obsolete equipment, legally required inspections, and the community's fear of nuclear dangers) compelled every nuclear plant to come to a standstill – a situation in which anti-nuclear activists' demands were partially brought into reality.

(b)   Volunteer Work

At a different level, the strength of civil society manifested itself with an aggregate total of 1.3 million volunteers working at the disaster sites, mainly in Iwate, Miyagi, and Fukushima prefectures, to provide assistance for three-and-a-half years after the disaster.[24] To alleviate the dire circumstances, they endeavored to help professionals and government workers in clearing up debris, sorting and distributing donated goods, running evacuation sites and emergency shelters, caring for the elderly and children, cleaning, and even reconstructing some damaged houses. The speed with which civil NPOs mounted quick and effective action contrasted sharply with the slow and ineffective responses of government bureaucracies which were lauded as the efficacious engine of the 'Japanese miracle' during the nation's high-growth period.

The web of *chōnaikai*, the primary disaster damage prevention organizations on which disaster victims were supposed to rely, functioned only in a limited way. These associations had justified their existence as community networks for mutual assistance in disaster situations and frequently engaged in emergency drills. In place of the conventional and old-style community networks, the new civil groups showed their presence. The volunteer system that assisted disaster victims was better established in 2011 than in 1995 when the Great Hanshin-Awaji Earthquake hit central Japan. It was almost taken for granted that volunteers would arrive at the Fukushima disaster sites, as they had acquired considerable experience since 1995. Immediately after the catastrophe, an extensive support network initiated by various NPOs, charity groups, student organizations, and other private associations sprang up – a sign

---

[23] Oguma 2013, p. 15.   [24] Zen Nihon Shakai Fukushi Kyōgikai 2013.

that the volunteer movement had been well prepared for calamities of this scale.

It is notable that some social practices prevalent in Japanese society served as a mechanism of moderation and cooperation and ultimately made the volunteers' work easier. Immediately after the earthquake, the victims displayed an impressive level of restraint, orderliness, and self-discipline without the looting, theft, and other crimes often associated with disasters of this scale in other countries. At the distribution centers for rescue goods, for instance, victims queued up peacefully, showing perseverance, patience, and self-control, values often emphasized in everyday life in Japan. It is common practice for most Japanese to stand in well-organized queues at schools, shops, and stations, and this pervasive habit also manifested itself in the sudden and unexpected disaster situation around Fukushima. At many evacuation centers, small groups (called *han*) were formed in aid of mutual assistance and efficient communication, a structure to which most Japanese are fully accustomed. These values are routinely inculcated in the hearts and bodies of many Japanese (often as a means of control), and they provided temporary stability and endurance in this crisis situation – an indication that every deep-rooted convention entails multiple consequences.

The case of Fukushima has presented a crucial test of Japan's civil society, which now seems to show an appreciable and increasing level of maturity, soberness, and sophistication. Although the past twenty years might have been the 'lost decades' economically, they appear to have been the 'civilizing decades' in social and cultural terms.

III   Friendly Authoritarianism

Japanese society has various forms of regimentation that are designed to standardize the thought patterns and attitudes of the Japanese and make them toe the line in everyday life. Although these pressures exist in any society, in Japan they constitute a general pattern which one might call friendly authoritarianism, which exerts a powerful centripetal force.[25] It is authoritarian to the extent that it encourages each member of society to internalize and share the value system which regards control and regimentation as natural and to accept the instructions and orders of people in superordinate positions without questioning. As a system of micro-management, friendly authoritarianism:

---

[25] Davidson 2013 uses the concept for his study of a Japanese suburb.

- uses small groups as the basis of mutual surveillance and deterrence of deviant behavior (a kind of lateral control within a small group compels each member to compete with the others to comply with the expected norms and standards);
- institutes an extensive range of mechanisms in which power is made highly visible and tangible;
- legitimizes various codes in such a way that superordinates can use ambiguities to their advantage (arrangements couched in vague terms allow power holders to reinterpret them as the occasion requires); and
- inculcates various forms of moralistic ideology into the psyche of every individual, with a particular stress on minute and trivial details (spontaneous expressions and free actions of individuals are generally discouraged).

Japan's authoritarianism does not normally exhibit its coercive face, generally dangling soft incentives of various kinds.[26] It is 'friendly' to the extent that it:

- resorts, wherever possible, to positive inducements rather than negative sanctions – 'carrots' rather than 'sticks' – to encourage competition to conform;
- portrays individuals and groups in power positions as congenial, cordial, and benevolent, and uses socialization channels for subordinates to pay voluntary respect to them;
- propagates the ideology of equality and the notion of a unique national homogeneity, ensuring that images of class cleavage are as blurred as possible; and
- relies upon joyful, amusing, and pleasant entertainments such as songs, visual arts, and festivals to make sure that authority infiltrates without obvious pains.

When ineffective, these friendly elements are abandoned, and recourse is given to more coercive controls. Although Japan's formal institutions are no doubt organized in accordance with democratic principles, there lingers a suspicion that the Japanese system is arranged to downplay the human rights that are regarded as the cornerstone of democracy.[27]

---

[26] Soft control in Japanese society has been discussed by such writers as Broadbent 1998; Pharr 1989; and Garon 1997.

[27] Some who accuse the Japanese system of being undemocratic have been criticized for applying the Western yardstick of democracy to a different cultural context. Yet, unlike

1   Mutual Surveillance within Small Groups

The first element of Japanese friendly authoritarianism relies on the capacity of small groups to evoke from members maximum compliance with the dominant norms of society. These groups are often pitted against each other to achieve intra-group mutual surveillance by dint of inter-group competition. The most prevalent form of this method is *han*, a small unit composed of five to ten individuals. All children in Japan learn the *han* system in primary school, where each class is subdivided into *han* units.[28] They are expected to compete with each other in conforming to such school norms as high academic achievement and good behavior. On classroom walls, teachers and pupils often display the outcomes of daily, weekly, or monthly competition among *han* groups, ranging, for example, from mathematics test results, the number of pupils who failed to complete homework assignments, and scores for tidiness, to the number of pupils who forgot to clip their nails. As each *han* is praised or blamed as a collective unit, there is constant intra-group pressure on members to comply with the expected standard.

The total quality control (TQC) movement, to which Japanese economic success is often attributed, perhaps best epitomizes the Japanese technology of human control through mutual surveillance. The initial version of quality control in the United States was statistical quality control, where a random sample of commodities was checked thoroughly so as to decrease the number of defective goods shipped out of the firm. After the importation of this method from the United States, Japanese management expanded its application to the workers themselves.

The basic unit of the TQC movement in Japanese firms is a group of ten to fifteen members in the same section or division. Each group is expected to present as many proposals as possible to improve both the quality of products and the efficiency of work arrangements, in order to maximize productivity and marketing efficiency. Since the number of proposals per group is the crucial index of competition, each group member is under constant pressure to think of ways to improve his or her company. In this process, employees often unconsciously conceptualize their work setting not from the worker's but from the manager's point of view. Although the primary function of this movement is quality improvement and does not involve physical coercion, it tends to produce employees highly devoted to the company. In some firms, the TQC movement is called JK (*jishu kanri*) activity (literally, voluntary control). The phrase epitomizes latent

the leaders of some other Asian nations, most Japanese elites appear to accept democracy as a desirable goal even though they may neither articulate nor practice it.

[28] Lewis 1988, particularly pp. 168–70.

aspects of the activity, drawing attention to the extent to which employees are controlled under the guise of voluntary commitment.

The ideology that the members of a collective unit are jointly responsible for its performance places restraints on each member. When one or a few members of a unit indulge in culpable behavior, all members bear the blame collectively. When one pupil plays a mischievous trick or disobeys the rules, teachers sometimes punish the entire class by making all pupils stay late, organizing a soul-searching session, or, as in one controversial case, ordering all boys in the class to cut their hair short.[29] If a member of a promising high-school baseball team engages in delinquent behavior, the principle of shared responsibility can force the entire team to withdraw from a national tournament. The whole group assumes collective responsibility (*rentai sekinin*) for the wrongdoings of each member.

Every community has a *han* network. In the lowest reaches of government, Japanese communities have neighborhood associations composed of several to a few dozen households. These associations are variously called *chōnaikai* or *chōkai* (town-block associations). They are called *jichikai* (self-government associations) or simply *han* in some areas, and *burakukai* or *kukai* (hamlet associations) in rural localities. There are nearly three hundred thousand associations of this kind,[30] based in almost all municipalities around the country. Once formed, they normally involve an overwhelming majority of households in a community. Only a small fraction of Japanese, mostly resident in metropolitan areas, are not members of such a group.

Neighborhood associations are characterized by several features.[31] First, they engage in a wide range of activities and function as all-purpose organizations. At a social level, their members organize and take part in community gatherings, fetes, outings, and festival dances. Once in a while they are called upon to clean gutters, engage in activities for the prevention of crime and fire, and collect donations for community causes. Many associations manage and maintain a community hall. Almost all of them serve as distribution networks for circulars, fliers, and information leaflets from their municipal government.

Second, the unit of association membership is the household, not the individual. This means that associations tend to be male-dominated, because the head of the family, who is usually male, attends association

---

[29] This case, which took place in a boys' high school in Fukuoka prefecture, in Kyūshū, in March 1995, generated much controversy. See AE, 3 March 1995, p. 15.

[30] Ministry of Internal Affairs and Communications 2003. Some 39 percent of these associations identify themselves as *jichikai*, and 22 percent as *chōnaikai*. For the most recent analysis of these community organizations, see Tsujinaka, Pekkanen, and Yamamoto 2009.

[31] Kurasawa and Akimoto 1990; Nakata 2007.

meetings and participates in association activities as the household representative. The directory of an association's membership normally lists the names of family heads only.

Third, it is semi-compulsory for a household to join a neighborhood association. When a family moves into a locality, its neighborhood association often automatically enlists the family as a member and requests its subscription. Association membership is not voluntary, as the family is given little choice. Furthermore, because only one neighborhood association exists per area, residents do not have alternative options.

Chōnaikai associations function as the grassroots *han* units, which transmit governmental and semi-governmental programs at community level in a variety of ways. One of them is the practice of vertical quota allotment typical of nationwide fund-raising campaigns. In a community chest drive, for example, the semi-governmental National Community Chest Organization first sets the national target of the total amount of funds to be raised and allocates an amount to each prefecture on the basis of its population. Each prefectural government then divides its allocated figure among all municipal governments in proportion to their populations, and each municipal government issues quota figures to all *chōnaikai* on the same basis. The leaders of each association then normally send the exact amount to the municipal government. The donations thus raised flow to the national level after prefectural governments have collected them through municipal governments. Because of this system, community chest drives in Japan rarely fail to achieve their targets.

As community-based *han* units, neighborhood associations cooperate in many ways with various branches of local government and semi-governmental agencies. A section of a *chōnaikai* often collaborates with police in crime prevention programs in its area. *Chōnaikai* frequently act as the basic units in fire drills and other disaster prevention exercises organized by the local fire defense headquarters. Members of *chōnaikai* also come into close cooperative contact with government-backed associations concerned with local hygiene, social welfare, and compliance with tax laws.

A survey[32] suggests that an overwhelming majority of Japanese support the existence of *chōnaikai*, although there is much regional variation in the grounds for support. Residents in regional cities place the significance of neighborhood associations in their capacity to organize such social functions as local galas, entertainment gatherings, and *bon* festival dances. Those who live in Tokyo, however, regard crime prevention and sanitation as the prime functions of *chōnaikai*. To the extent that there is community support for grassroots state apparatus,

---

[32] For more details, see Tsujinaka, Pekkanen, and Yamamoto 2009; and Iwasaki, Ajisaka, Ueda, Takagi, Hirohara, and Yoshioka 1989.

the mechanism of mutual surveillance within each *han* group continues to operate, blurring the line between voluntary dedication and state
manipulation.

The prototype of *han* ideology is discernible in Tokugawa Japan, in the
feudal regime's implementation of a nationwide network of five-family
neighborhood units, known as the *go-nin gumi* system. This served as a
quasi-espionage organization. Families in a neighborhood were required
to watch each other for any signs of deviant activities. During World
War II, a similar system was devised under the name *tonari gumi* (neighborhood watch) to promote conformity and solidarity at the community
level in support of war activities. Even today, although this type of community network no longer serves as machinery for military propaganda,
it is a significant channel through which the power of the state permeates
into every part of Japanese society in the form of community voluntary
cooperation.

The *han* system is effective in ensuring attitudinal and behavioral conformity among its members precisely because it is not predicated upon
the imposition of authority from above. Instead of vertical control, the
system counts on a kind of horizontal control, where the policing of
people of the same status in a small unit – classmates, work colleagues,
or neighborhood acquaintances – makes it difficult for them to diverge
from the standard expected;[33] while higher status persons are connected
to each *han*, those who control a person are not necessarily above but
beside them.

2   Visible and Tangible Power

The second aspect of the Japanese style of friendly authoritarianism is
the way in which power and authority are made visible and tangible in
everyday life rather than being abstract and conceptual; attempts are
made to ensure that the dominant moral order is reproduced at the level
of face-to-face 'existential' situations.

This tendency is most conspicuous in the area of law enforcement.
The Japanese police system penetrates into every corner of society. More
than half a million households, or about one in fifty, are organized as
'households for crime prevention' and are closely associated with police
stations. About 40 percent of Japanese police officers are stationed in
small community-based police boxes known as *kōban*, or in substations
called *chūzaisho*.

---

[33] See Ashkenazi 1991 for a different interpretation of traditional small group organizations
and their functions in Japan.

Although this system has received international attention as a way of reducing crime rates, it imposes close surveillance on the private lives of individuals. Each *kōban* or *chūzaisho* police officer routinely visits households and business establishments within his or her jurisdiction to obtain information about them and to inquire whether any 'suspicious figures' hang around the neighborhood. Although performed in the name of the maintenance of public safety, this practice, known as *junkai renraku* (patrol liaison), often verges upon invasion of individual privacy.

As an essential part of this exercise, police provide a liaison card to each household, requesting details such as its telephone number, the date of residents' settlement at that present address, the identification of the household head, each member's name, date of birth, occupation, place of work or school, and the address and telephone number of a contact person in an emergency. For enterprises such as firms and shops, the card covers such items as the type of business, the person in charge, the number of employees, the hours which it is open for business, the days it is regularly closed, and whether the business owns a dog. Officially, the system is intended to make it easy for police officers in the community to show the way to visitors, make contact in emergencies, and facilitate other public services. Community residents are not legally required to fill out these cards and return them to police.

In reality, however, nearly all households do so. Many genuinely believe that the system prevents neighborhood crime and improves police services. Others accept it because they fear that declining to fill out the card might incur police suspicion that they are rebels or criminals, and police might bring them under close surveillance. Only a tiny minority of civil libertarians are willing to risk the likelihood of police suspicion. The practice serves to test the level of community cooperation with police activities. The performance of police officers who are assigned to *kōban*, *chūzaisho*, and other small, community-linked police stations is evaluated in terms of the extent to which they have secured 'voluntary cooperation' from the community under their jurisdiction. Such appraisal includes the number of households about which they have succeeded in acquiring information through *junkai renraku*.[34] Although the system is based on the voluntary cooperation of the public, most households are willing to expose themselves to police data-gathering machinery. Effective community control thus occurs even though its implementation takes the form of supposed individual voluntarism.

In the area of education, teachers actively present themselves as moral authorities in their school district. At primary-school level, home-room teachers routinely visit the home of every child under their charge to meet his or her parents at least once a year. The teachers are expected to discuss

[34] AM, 3 June 1989, p. 30; AM, 19 November 2004, p. 14.

the child's scholastic and social development and exchange views with the parents. Although this practice allegedly facilitates good communication between schools and homes, it is virtually compulsory, in the sense that parents do not have the option of welcoming or declining these visits. Teachers frequently perform policing functions, making parents serve as quasi-agents to control children at home in line with the school's ethos. It is not unusual for teachers, together with police and parents, to patrol amusement arcades and shopping areas to make sure pupils are not straying from the fold after school.

In community life, the Japanese encounter a steady flow of verbal and visual instructions from authorities about expected behavior. Japanese train conductors constantly announce what passengers should and should not do, saying, for instance, 'Do not stand near the door', 'Hold on to a strap', 'Make room for other people', and 'Let us offer seats to senior citizens'. Railway stations broadcast such announcements as 'Please stand behind the white line as a train is approaching the station', 'Stand in two rows in an orderly manner until the train arrives', and 'Would you kindly not jostle one another when you step into the train'. Streets and public places are studded with signs bearing such instructions as 'Keep out' and 'No admittance'.

These techniques softly control the populace by ensuring that the dominant moral order is reproduced in face-to-face situations. The power of the state does not remain an abstract concept but is brought into daily experience in a moralistic fashion.

3   Manipulation of Ambiguity

The third ingredient of Japan's friendly authoritarianism relies on an ideology which encourages ambiguity in a variety of circumstances. This enables those in positions of authority to interpret various situations at their discretion.

In the sphere of law, police enjoy extensive discretionary power. A case in point concerns the supplementary jail system, in which lockup cells at police stations are used as substitutes for prison. Police are supposed to send an arrested suspect to a house of detention under the jurisdiction of the Ministry of Justice within forty-eight hours of arrest. However, in reality, a majority of suspects are kept in police detention under the Jail Law, enacted in 1908 and still enforced. In an exception clause, this law allows police to use their lockup cells as an alternative to an official detention house. While the Ministry of Justice wishes to retain this practice, the Japan Federation of Bar Associations and human rights groups oppose it as an arrangement which allows investigators to question suspects for inordinately long periods, resulting in numerous false charges based on groundless confessions wrung out of suspects under duress. A dubious exception clause of a law enacted over a century ago has thus been used as a basis for modern, general police practice simply because it suits law enforcement authorities.

The interpretation of the Constitution, particularly Article 9, has also been a locus of ambiguity. The article states:

Aspiring sincerely to an international peace based on justice and order, the Japanese people forever renounce war as a sovereign right of the nation and the threat or use of force as means of settling international disputes.

In order to accomplish the aim of the preceding paragraph, land, sea, and air forces, as well as other war potential, will never be maintained. The right of belligerency of the state will not be recognized.

When the Constitution was promulgated, in 1946, the spirit of the article was that Japan would never again possess armed forces of any kind. With the Cold War escalating in East Asia, the Police Reserve Forces were established in 1950 without parliamentary approval, claiming that they were not military troops. Soon they changed their name, first to the Public Security Forces and then to the Guard Forces after the ratification of the peace treaty. In 1954 they became the Self-Defense Forces and have since developed into armed forces of some quarter of a million troops equipped with sophisticated weaponry. While the Self-Defense Forces are organized to defend the country against acts of aggression from outside, some members have served as part of United Nations peacekeeping operations abroad and as disaster relief units domestically.

These step-by-step shifts in the interpretation of the same text reflect what Japanese call *nashikuzushi*, the pragmatic strategy that many Japanese power-holders at various levels use to adapt gradually to changing circumstances. The term *nashikuzushi* originally meant payments by installment, but in this context it implies that players achieve their final goal by making a series of small changes in the meaning of key terms in a document. The technique does not call for alteration of the text itself. The point is not so much the validity of the changing interpretations as the almost imperceptible way in which they have been brought about, little by little.

In all these circumstances, equivocation rather than articulation is promoted, allowing those in dominant positions to manipulate what is meant, what is right, and what should be done. In many companies, as suggested in Chapter 4, fresh employees are not given formal contracts or job specifications, and their supervisors can use their discretion in defining the tasks which subordinate employees should perform, a practice which partly accounts for the long working hours in Japan. As discussed in Chapter 8, the practice of administrative guidance (*gyōsei shidō*) enables public bureaucrats to maneuver the private sector without clear statutory basis, because the representatives of companies are aware that the bureaucrats have the power to apply implicit sanctions against those who do not follow their instructions. The school textbook authorization system, described in Chapter 5, gives the Ministry of Education censors broad scope for subjective revisions of submitted manuscripts, enabling them to exercise unspecified control over textbook writers. In effect, ambiguity offers advantages to power-holders, as they can use it to enforce their will on subordinates at their discretion, in the absence of clearly documented rules and regulations.

4   Moralizing and 'Mind Correctness'

The fourth element of Japan's friendly authoritarianism is the extent to which various moralizing techniques are used to appeal deeply to the psyche of individuals. An example is the way in which Japanese authorities require offenders against laws and rules to express total contrition for their wrongdoing. For even minor offenses, such as traffic violations and unintended trespassing, the authorities regard it as insufficient for an offender to lose a license or pay a fine; they also demand that the offender write or sign a letter of apology (*shimatsusho*). It is usually a form letter containing such sentences as 'I am very sorry for breaching a public regulation' and 'I endeavor never to repeat the same error'. The letter is normally addressed to the holder of a public office, such as the head of district police or the mayor of the municipality where the offense occurred. This practice has no statutory basis but is enforced with the reasoning that offenders need to cleanse their spirits completely to conform to social norms in the future. This thinking gives priority to 'mind correctness' of citizens. Various means are supposed to achieve such attitudinal conformity.

(a)   Physical Correctness

The first of these focuses on 'physical correctness'. Japanese schools make it a rule for pupils to clean their classrooms each day after school. At every Japanese school, pupils do keep-fit exercises to the well-known tunes of a radio program broadcast at a set time every day through a national public radio network. At school, each Japanese child is taught how to bow correctly, how to stand correctly, how to sit correctly, how to walk correctly, and so on. At work, many companies train employees how to greet customers, how to address superiors, and how to exchange name cards in an appropriate fashion. With this type of repeated training, many Japanese acquire a disposition to attend to details. In controlled situations, they tend to give heed to such matters as how to wrap gifts, how to present meals, and how to blow their nose.

(b) Emotive Moralizing

The second focus is the notion that people should learn conformity through emotive means. In this respect, collective singing plays an important role in generating a sense of group solidarity. All schools, including primary schools, have their own school song which has many moralistic lines, and pupils sing it on such occasions as morning assemblies, athletic meets, and entrance and graduation ceremonies. Many companies also have their own enterprise song which exalts the virtues of hard work and job commitment. Employees are expected to sing it daily at a morning gathering and on ceremonial occasions. Cities and other municipalities have a song that, in most cases, glorifies the natural beauty and historical tradition of their locality. Given that singing is generally fun blended with sentimental emotion, the Japanese method of enhancing solidarity combines such gaiety with the inculcation of values that praise organizational dedication. This technique strikes a responsive chord in participants and so tends not to give them the impression that they are being psychologically steered in a certain direction. Conscious of the power of collective singing for mass mobilization, Japan's leaders observed during World War II that popular 'songs are military commodities'.[35]

Against the background of the widespread practice of collective singing, it comes as no surprise that *karaoke* singing has become common in Japan's entertainment quarters. As a combination of merriment and tension management, this popular culture, which has become an epidemic since the late 1970s, reflects the extent to which emotive conformity and collective singing interact in Japanese society.

(c) A Community of Sanctions

The socially constructed images of a community that exercises sanctions against acts of deviance are a third means of generating psychological compliance. For this purpose, emic notions are often invoked as those which penetrate into the soul of the Japanese, an example being the concept of *seken*, an imagined community that has the normative power of approving or disapproving of and sanctioning individual behavior. *Seken* extends beyond primary groups, such as immediate kin, workmates, and

---

[35] The comment of Navy Captain Ikuo Hirade of the Cabinet Information Bureau in 1941. See Hirade 1942.

Table 10.3   Four Japanese emic conceptions of social
relations

| Group size | Kinship relationship (either real or symbolic) | |
	Absent	Present
Large	*Seken*	*Harakara*[a] (fraternity)
Small	*Nakama*	*Miuchi*[b] (relatives or
	(mates, fellows)	comrades)

Source: Adapted from Yoneyama 1990, p. 98.
Notes:
[a] This concept is often used to describe 'we, the Japanese'
(*ware ware Nihonjin*) as the largest imagined kinship unit.
[b] This notion refers to a small, fictitious kinship unit in
which *oyabun* (patriarchal godfather figure) and *kobun* (his
devoted followers) form family-like relationships.

neighbors, but does not encompass the entire society of Japan, and still
less overseas societies. As an intermediate network, *seken* makes its presence felt in the minds of many Japanese as the largest unit of social
interaction not implying blood relations[36] (see Table 10.3). In reference
to *seken*'s censuring functions, it is often said that if one deviates from
social norms, *seken* will not accept one. If one does something shameful,
one will not be able to face *seken*. One should not expect *seken* to be
lenient and permissive. When an organization is found to be involved
in an unacceptable practice, its leaders often make public apologies for
disturbing *seken*. When one refers to *seken* accepting or renouncing a
certain choice or behavior, one envisages *seken* not only as the standard
gauge or rule but as those individuals who compel it. As an imagined but
realistic entity, *seken* presents itself as a web of people who provide the
moral yardsticks that favor the status quo and traditional practices.

(d)   Ideology of Egalitarian Competition

Finally, the Japanese establishment has promoted an ideology of equality of opportunity and generally discourages ascriptive inequality based
on family origin. Although the framework has not covered women and
minority groups, it has nevertheless championed the meritocratic doctrine that every Japanese has an equal chance of achieving high status
through persistent effort. In the world of secular symbols, this notion
is translated into the phrase *risshin shusse*, the 'careerism' in which one
can get ahead in life and rise in the world through arduous endeavor and
perseverance. Even if born in a deprived peasant family, a bright boy who

[36] See Yoneyama 1971 and 1990, pp. 98–9.

Table 10.4   Four Japanese strategies for moral indoctrination

	Negative moral sanctions	Positive moral inducements
Behavioral	(A) Physical correctness	(C) Collective singing
Ideational	(B) *Seken*	(D) Equality of opportunity

studies hard is legitimately expected to get into a top university and eventually attain a high-ranking position in an important company. Prewar textbooks abound with legends of self-made men of this sort. Popular writings argue that one's success in life depends solely on the extent to which one mobilizes the spirit of *ganbari* (determination), which everyone possesses intrinsically and equally. Invoking the principle of fairness to all, most public and private universities in Japan accept or reject students exclusively on the basis of their scores at entrance examinations, without considering their other attributes. In this limited sense, Japan is an egalitarian, achievement-oriented society. In reality, those who have risen to the higher echelons of society from lower family backgrounds comprise only a small portion of the total population. Therefore, Japan is, on a mass basis, a pseudo-egalitarian society. Nevertheless, the illusion, and occasional reality, that everybody is given equal opportunities to succeed is sufficiently prevalent to drive many Japanese in a quest for educational, occupational, and material achievements.

This fantasy obscures the fact that opportunities are unevenly distributed across different social groups and strata. More importantly, it enables status-holders to defend themselves as rightful winners of contests which have supposedly given everybody equal chances. It also makes it difficult for status-losers to hold grievances against successful achievers, because of the dominant myth that losers have been given an equitable opportunity but simply could not make it. Losers take the blame on themselves and accept the supremacy and authority of those who have succeeded in climbing the ladder. Thus, the ideology of equality of opportunity leads to individualized and fragmented self-accusations by those who have failed and blinds them to the structural inequalities they are subject to. In this sense, the Japanese experience appears to demonstrate that the ideology of equality of opportunity justifies the reality of the inequality of outcomes more plausibly than does the doctrine which rationalizes inequality of opportunities.[37]

These four aspects of moral indoctrination in Japan can be summarized schematically. Table 10.4 combines the two dimensions of inculcation. One dimension is whether the method in question emphasizes negative sanctions or positive inducements. For example, while *seken* imposes

[37] Kumazawa 1993, pp. 105–20, shows how this process operates in workplaces.

Table 10.5 Orientations of various types of friendly authoritarianism in Japan

Sphere of control	Type of control			
	Mutual surveillance within small groups	Visible and tangible power	Manipulative ambiguity	Moralizing and mind correctness
Law	Family registration; resident card system	*Kōban* (police box)	Constitution; supplementary jail system	*Shimatsusho* (apology letters)
Community	Neighborhood associations	Police household checks	Extensive gift-giving practices	Sanction of *seken*
Business	TQC movement	Long working hours; service overtime	Unaccounted expenses; *dangō*	Company songs; company mottoes
Education	*Han* groups in classrooms	Corporal punishment; *katei hōmon* (teachers making calls at pupils' homes)	School textbook authorization system	Classroom cleaning; militaristic ethic

negative constraints singing songs relies on the positive sense of releasing one's feelings. The other dimension concerns whether mind correctness is achieved behaviorally or ideationally. For instance, while training through physical learning requires behavioral rectification (Cell A), the ideology of equality of opportunity is propagated in the ideational sphere (Cell D). The other combinations are self-explanatory. The Japanese system compounds these elements to ensure behavioral and ideational compliance through both negative and positive pressures.

Both institutional and ideological systems manipulate the everyday life of the Japanese, from a variety of angles in a wide range of spheres, so as to maintain the moral order of Japanese society. Table 10.5 shows some examples of the control mechanisms discussed in this book.

A finely blended combination of these control pressures in Japanese daily life has yielded the friendly authoritarianism which counteracts the diversified and stratified realities of society. This constraining force operates unevenly in different sectors of society. A tug-of-war between centripetal and centrifugal forces remains an ongoing process which produces dissimilar outcomes at different times.

The characteristics of Japanese society cannot be fully determined without defining its population base. It would be one-sided to define Japaneseness in a unitary way on the basis of observations of the elite sector or the consumers of pop culture only, without thoroughly analyzing the characteristics of a wide range of subcultural groups. The recognition of internal variation in Japan has implications for recognizing possible international similarities with counterparts in other societies, and for subcultural group communications and interactions across national boundaries. Comparative studies based on such awareness would underscore the ways in which forces of friendly authoritarianism produce conformity and order in Japan. As diversity counteracts uniformity and subcultural groupings countervail control and regimentation, Japan literacy requires an in-depth understanding of the ways in which a shifting balance is struck in Japan between economic efficiency and political equity, between social stability and cultural reform, and between collective integration and individual dignity.

References

Newspaper Abbreviations

AM   *Asahi Shimbun*, morning edition.
AE   *Asahi Shimbun*, evening edition.
MM   *Mainichi Shimbun*, morning edition.
ME   *Mainichi Shimbun*, evening edition.

Abbreviations of the Social Stratification and Mobility Study

SSM 85 *Gendai Nihon no kaisō kōzō* (Social stratification in contemporary Japan) 1990. Final reports on the 1985 Social Stratification and Mobility Study, 4 volumes. Tokyo: Tokyo Daigaku Shuppankai.

SSM 95a *Nihon no kaisō shisutemu* (Social stratification system in Japan) 2000. Final reports on the 1995 Social Stratification and Mobility Study, 6 volumes. Tokyo: Tokyo Daigaku Shuppankai.

SSM 95b *Gendai Nihon no shakai kaisō ni kansuru zenkoku chōsa kenkyū' seika hōkokusho* (Reports on the results of the 1995 national survey on social stratification in contemporary Japan) 1998. Reports on the 1995 Social Stratification and Mobility Study, 21 volumes. Tokyo: 1995 SSM Survey Research Committee.

SSM 05a *Gendai Nihon no kaisō shakai* (Stratified society in contemporary Japan) 2011. Final reports on the 2005 Social Stratification and Mobility Study, 3 volumes. Tokyo: Tokyo Daigaku Shuppankai.

SSM 05b *Gendai Nihon kaisō shisutemu no kōzō to hendō ni kansuru sōgō-teki kenkyū' seiika hōkokusho* (Reports on the results of the 2005 comprehensive survey on the structure and transformation of the contemporary Japanese stratification system) 2008. Reports on the 2005 Social Stratification and Mobility Study, 17 volumes. Sendai: 2005 SSM Survey Research Committee.

Surveys of Governmental and Semi-governmental Organizations

Cabinet Office (Naikakufu) 2009, *Bunka ni kansuru yoron chōsa* (Public opinion survey on culture).

Cabinet Office, Economic and Social Research Institute (Naikakufu, Keizai Shakai Kenkyūsho) 2006, *Kokumin keizai keisan nenpō* (Annual report of the system of national accounts).

Cabinet Office, Gender Equality Bureau (Naikakufu, Danjo Kyōdō Sankakukyoku) 2002, *Danjo kyōdō sankaku ni kansuru kokusai hikaku chōsa* (International comparative survey of gender equality).

Cabinet Office, Gender Equality Bureau (Naikakufu, Danjo Kyōdō Sankakukyoku) 2011, *Danjo-kan ni okeru bōryoku ni kansuru chōsa* (Survey on violence between men and women).

Cabinet Office, Gender Equality Bureau (Naikakufu, Danjo Kyōdō Sankakukyoku) 2013a, *Heisei 25-nendo ban danjo kyōdō sankaku hakusho* (2013 white paper on gender equality).

Cabinet Office, Ministerial Secretariat, Public Relations Section (Naikakufu, Daijin Kanbō, Kōhōshitsu) 2007, *Danjo kyōdō sankaku shakai ni kansuru yoron chōsa* (Public opinion survey on gender equal society).

Cabinet Office, Ministerial Secretariat, Public Relations Section (Naikakufu, Daijin Kanbō, Kōhōshitsu) 2012a, *Danjo kyōdō sankaku shakai ni kansuru yoron chōsa* (Public opinion survey on gender equal society).

Cabinet Office, Ministerial Secretariat, Public Relations Section (Naikakufu, Daijin Kanbō, Kōhōshitsu) 2012b, *Kazoku no hōsei ni kansuru yoron chōsa* (Public opinion survey on family legislation).

Cabinet Office, Ministerial Secretariat, Public Relations Section (Naikakufu, Daijin Kanbō, Kōhōshitsu) 2012c, *Kokumin seikatsu ni kansuru yoron chōsa* (Public opinion survey on people's livelihood).

Cabinet Office, Ministerial Secretariat, Public Relations Section (Naiakufu, Daijin Kanbō, Kōhōshitsu) 2013b, *Kazoku no hōsei ni kansuru yoron chōsa* (Public opinion survey on laws governing families).

Economic Planning Agency 1999, *Kokumin seikatsu senkōdo chōsa* (National survey of life preferences).

Hokkaidō Prefectural Government 2006, *Utari seikatsu jittai chōsa* (Life conditions of the Utari). Sapporo: Hokkaidō-chō.

Institute of Labor Administration (Rōmu Gyōsei Kenkyūsho) 2003, 'Jinji kanri tenkin ni kansuru toriatsukai no jittai (Realities of personnel management and job relocations)', *Rōsei jihō* (Labor administration news), issue 3571, pp. 2–33.

Institute of Statistical Mathematics (Tōkei Sūri Kenkyūsho) 2009, 'Kokuminsei no kenkyū: 2008-nen dai 12-kai zenkoku chōsa' (Studies of national character: the 12th national survey, conducted in 2008). *Tōkei chōsa kenkyū report.*

International Monetary Fund 2013, *World Economic Outlook Database.*

Japan Family Planning Association (Nihon Kazoku Keikaku Kyōkai) 2012, *Dai 6-kai danjo no seikatsu to ishiki ni kansuru chōsa* (The fourth survey on the life and consciousness of men and women).

Japan Institute of Labor (Nihon Rōdō Kyōkai) 2001, *'Dai 4-kai kaigai haken kinmusha no shokugyō to seikatsu ni kansuru chōsa'* (Fourth survey on the occupations and the lifestyles of employees posted to overseas offices).

Japan Institute of Labor Policy and Training (Nihon Rōdō Kenkyū Kikō) 2000, *Kinrō seikatsu ni kansuru chōsa 1999* (A survey of work life in 1999). Nihon Rōdō Kenkyūsho.

Japan Productivitiy Center (Nihon Seisansei Honbu) 2013, *Rejā hakusho* (White paper on leisure). Nihon Seisansei Honbu.

Japan Student Services Organization (Nihon Gakusei Shien Kikō) 2014, *Heisei 22-nendo gakusei seikatsuhi chōsa* (2010 survey of students' life).

Management and Coordination Agency 2000, *Kisei kanwa hakusho* (White paper on deregulation). Ōkurashō Insatsukyoku.

Management and Coordination Agency, Bureau of Statistics (Sōrifu, Tōkei-kyoku) 1996, *Shakai seikatsu tōkei shihyō* (Statistical indices of social life), 1996 edition. Nihon Tōkei Kyōkai.

Management and Coordination Agency, Office for Gender Equality (Sōrifu, Danjo Kyōdō Sankaku-shitsu) 2000, *Danjo-kan ni okeru bōryoku ni kansuru chōsa* (A survey on violence between men and women). Ōkurashō Insatsukyoku.

Ministry of Education and Science (Monbu Kagakushō) 2007a, *Gakkō kihon chōsa* (School basic survey).

Ministry of Education and Science (Monbu Kagakushō) 2007b, *Heisei 19-nendo monbu kagaku hakusho* (White paper on education and science 2007).

Ministry of Education and Science (Monbu Kagakushō) 2009a, *Dēta kara miru Nihon no kyōiku 2008* (Japan's education at a glance 2008). Nikkei Insatsu.

Ministry of Education and Science (Monbu Kagakushō) 2009b, *Gakkō kihon chōsa* (School basic survey).

Ministry of Education and Science (Monbu Kagakushō) 2010, *Gakkō kihon chōsa* (School basic survey).

Ministry of Education and Science (Monbu Kagakushō) 2011a, *Gakkō kihon chōsa* (School basic survey).

Ministry of Education and Science (Monbu Kagakushō) 2011b, *Heisei 23-nendo gakusei nōfukin chōsa* (2011 survey of students' payments).

Ministry of Education and Science (Monbu Kagakushō) 2013a, *Gakkō kihon chōsa* (School basic survey).

Ministry of Education and Science (Monbu Kagakushō) 2013b, *Taibatsu chōsa: Dai 2-ji hōkoku* (Corporal punishment survey: second report).

Ministry of Education and Science (Monbu Kagakushō) 2013c, *Heisei 13-nendo jidōseito no mondai kōi-tō seito shidōjō no shomondai ni kansuru chōsa ni tsuite* (On the 2013 survey of various issues on student guidance, involving cases of students' and pupils' problematic behavior).

Ministry of Education and Science (Monbu Kagakushō) 2013d, *Heisei 25-nendo zenkoku gakuryoku gakushū jōkyō chōsa* (2013 national survey of scholastic ability and study situations).

Ministry of Foreign Affairs (Gaimushō) 2013, *Kaigai zairyū hōjinsū tōkei* (Annual report of statistics of Japanese nationals overseas).

Ministry of Health, Labour and Welfare (Kōsei Rōdōshō) 2006a, *Heisei 18-nenban rōdō keizai no bunseki* (Analysis of labor economics, 2006).

Ministry of Health, Labour and Welfare (Kōsei Rōdōshō) 2006b, *Kon'in ni kansuru tōkei* (Marriage statistics).

Ministry of Health, Labour and Welfare (Kōsei Rōdōshō) 2007, *Chingin kōzō kihon chōsa* (Basic survey on wage structure).

Ministry of Health, Labour and Welfare (Kōsei Rōdōshō) 2008, *Heisei 20-nendo kōsubetsu koyō kanri seido no jisshi shidō jōkyō* (Implementation and guidance of employment management systems for career-based paths in 2008).

Ministry of Health, Labour and Welfare (Kōsei Rōdōshō) 2010, *Kokumin seikatsu kiso chōsa* (Basic survey of the life conditions of the Japanese).

Ministry of Health, Labour and Welfare (Kōsei Rōdōshō) 2011, *Koyō kintō kihon chōsa* (Basic survey on equal employment).

Ministry of Health, Labour and Welfare (Kōsei Rōdōshō) 2012a, *Rōdō kumiai kiso chōsa* (Basic survey on labor unions).

Ministry of Health, Labour and Welfare (Kōsei Rōdōshō) 2012b, *Jinkō dōtai chōsa* (Vital statistics).

Ministry of Health, Labour and Welfare (Kōsei Rōdōshō) 2012c, *Chingin kōzō kihon tōkei chōsa* (Basic statistical survey on wage structure).

Ministry of Health, Labour and Welfare (Kōsei Rōdōshō) 2012d, *Heisei 23-nendo kōsei nenkin hoken kokumin nenkin jigyō no gaiyō* (An overview of the Welfare Pension Insurance scheme and the National Pension scheme in 2011).

Ministry of Health, Labour and Welfare (Kōsei Rōdōshō) 2013a, *Koyō kintō kihon chōsa* (Basic survey on equal employment).

Ministry of Health, Labour and Welfare (Kōsei Rōdōshō) 2013b, *Eisei gyōsei hōkoku-rei* (Annual statistical report on hygiene administration).

Ministry of Health, Labour and Welfare (Kōsei Rōdōshō) 2013c, *Shūrō jōken sōgō chōsa* (Comprehensive survey of working conditions).

Ministry of Health, Labour and Welfare (Kōsei Rōdōshō) 2013d, *Heisei 24-nendo ni okeru nō, shinzō shikkan oyobi seishin shōgai ni kakawaru rōsai hoshō jōkyō* (A survey of worker compensation payouts for brain, heart and mental disorders in 2012).

Ministry of Health, Labour and Welfare (Kōsei Rōdōshō) 2013e, *Rōdō kumiai kiso chōsa* (Basic survey on labor unions).

Ministry of Health, Labour and Welfare (Kōsei Rōdōshō) 2013f, *Jinkō dōtai chōsa* (Vital statistics).

Ministry of Internal Affairs and Communications (Sōmushō) 2003, *Chien ni yoru dantai no ninka jimu no jōkyō tō ni kansuru chōsa* (A survey on official authorization work on locally based social groups).

Ministry of Internal Affairs and Communications (Sōmushō) 2006, *Shakai seikatsu kihon chōsa* (Social life basic survey).

Ministry of Internal Affairs and Communications (Sōmushō) 2008, *Rōdōryoku chōsa* (Labor force survey).

Ministry of Internal Affairs and Communications (Sōmushō) 2009a, *Zenkoku shōhi jittai chōsa* (National survey of family income and expenditure).

Ministry of Internal Affairs and Communications (Sōmushō) 2009b, *Keizai sensasu kiso chōsa hōkoku* (Economic census basic survey report).

Ministry of Internal Affairs and Communications (Sōmushō) 2011, *Shakai seikatsu kihon chōsa* (Social life basic survey).

Ministry of Internal Affairs and Communications (Sōmushō) 2012, *Keizai sensas* (Economy census).

Ministry of Internal Affairs and Communications (Sōmushō) 2013a, *Shūgyō kōzō kihon chōsa* (Basic survey of employment structure).

Ministry of Internal Affairs and Communications (Sōmushō) 2013b, *Rōdōryoku chōsa* (Labor force survey).

Ministry of Internal Affairs and Communications (Sōmushō) 2013c, *Tōkei de miru to-dō-fu-ken no sugata* (Statistical profiles of prefectures).

Ministry of Internal Affairs and Communications (Sōmushō) 2013d, *Jinkō suikei nenpō* (Annual report on current population estimates).

Ministry of Internal Affairs and Communications 2013e, *Chihō kōkyō dantai no gikai no giin oyobi chō no shozoku tōhabetsu jin-in shirabe tō, Heisei 24-nen 12-gatsu 31-nichi genzai* (Survey of party affiliations of members and heads of prefectural and municipal assemblies as of 31 December 2012).

Ministry of Justice (Hōmushō) 2013a, *Zairyū gaikokujin tōkei* (Statistics on resident foreigners).

Ministry of Justice (Hōmushō) 2013b, *Heisei 24-nen ni okeru nanmin ninteishasū tō nit suite* (Report on the number of refugees officially accepted in 2012).

Ministry of Justice (Hōmushō) 2013c, *Kika kyoka shinseisha suu tō no suii* (Trends in the numbers of applicants and accepted cases for naturalization), <www.moj.go.jp/TOUKEI/t_minj03.html>.

National Institute of Population and Social Security Research (Kokuritsu Shakai-hoshō Jinkō Mondai Kenkyūsho) 2001, '*Shokugyō-betsu danshi shūgyōsha no 20-saiji heikin jumyō: 1970–90*' (Life expectancy table of male workers at the age of twenty in different occupations: 1970–90).

National Institute of Population and Social Security Research (Kokuritsu Shakai-hoshō Jinkō Mondai Kenkyūsho) 2011a, '*Dai 14-kai shusshō dōkō kihon chōsa*' (The fourteenth national basic trend survey on marriage and birth).

National Institute of Population and Social Security Research (Kokuritsu Shakai-hoshō Jinkō Mondai Kenkyūsho) 2011b, '*Kekkon to shussan ni kansuru zenkoku chōsa*' (A national survey on marriage and birth).

National Personnel Agency (Jinji-in) 2012, *Ippan shoku no kokka kōmuin ninyō jōkyō chōsa* (A survey of the employment situation of the general public service personnel in the national bureaucracy).

National Police Agency (Keisatsu-chō) 2013, *Heisei 24-nendochū ni okeru fūzoku kankei jihan no torishimari jōkyō tō ni tsuite* (On the control of the crimes in the sex industry in 2012).

National Tax Agency (Kokuzeichō) 2011, *Heisei 23-nen minkan kyūyo jittai tōkei chōsa* (2011 fact-finding survey of salary levels in the private sector).

Nippon Junior High School Physical Culture Association 2012, *Kamaikō chōsa shūkei* (Tabulation of member school surveys) <www18.ocn.ne.jp/~njpa/kamei.html#h24join>.

Organization for Economic Cooperation and Development 2011a, *Divided We Stand: Why Inequality Keeps Rising*. Paris: OECD.

Organization for Economic Cooperation and Development 2011b, *Society at a Glance 2011*. Paris: OECD.

Organization for Economic Cooperation and Development 2013, *OECD Skills Outlook 2013: First Results from the Survey of Adult Skills*. Paris: OECD.

Prime Minister's Office (Sōrifu) 1993, *Dōwa chiku jittai haaku tō chōsa* (A survey of the actual conditions of *buraku* communities).

Tokyo Metropolitan Government, Bureau of Industry and Labor (Tokyo-to Sangyō Rōdō-kyoku) 2006, *Kigyō ni okeru josei koyō kanri to sekushuaru harasumento no torikumi tō ni kansuru chōsa* (A survey on female employment administration in enterprises and their attempts to grapple with sexual harassment).

United Nations, Department of Economics and Social Affairs, Population Division 2008, *World Fertility Prospects: The 2008 Revision*.

Books, Journal Articles

Abegglen, James C. 1958, *The Japanese Factory: Aspects of Its Social Organization.* Bombay: Asia Publishing House. AERA, Asahi Shimbun.

Akhavan-Majid, Roya 1990, 'The press as an elite power group in Japan', *Journalism Quarterly*, vol. 67, no. 4 (Winter), pp. 1006–14.

Amano, Ikuo 2011, *The Origins of Japanese Credentialism.* Melbourne: Trans Pacific Press.

Amano, Masako 2011, *In Pursuit of the Seikatsusha: A Genealogy of the Autonomous Citizen in Japan.* Melbourne: Trans Pacific Press.

Amanuma, Kaoru 1987, *'Ganbari' no kōzō: Nihonjin no kōdō genri* (Structure of 'endurance': principle of Japanese behaviour). Tokyo: Yoshikawa Kōbundō.

Ambaras, David R. 2006, *Bad Youth: Juvenile Delinquency and the Politics of Everyday Life in Modern Japan.* Berkeley: University of California Press.

Amino, Yoshihiko 1990, *Nihonron no shiza* (Perspectives on theories of Japan). Tokyo: Shōgakukan.

Amino, Yoshihiko 1992, 'Deconstructing Japan', *East Asian History*, vol. 3, pp. 121–42.

Amino, Yoshihiko 1994, *Nihon shakai saikō* (Reconsidering Japanese society). Tokyo: Shōgakukan.

Amino, Yoshihiko 2000, *'Nihon' to wa nani ka* (What is 'Japan'?). Tokyo: Kōdansha.

Anderson, Benedict 1983, *Imagined Communities: Reflections on the Origins and Spread of Nationalism.* London: Verso.

Aoki, Hideo 2006, *Japan's Underclass: Day Laborers and the Homeless.* Melbourne: Trans Pacific Press.

Aoki, Hideo 2009, 'Buraku culture', in Yoshio Sugimoto (ed.), *The Cambridge Companion to Modern Japanese Culture.* Melbourne: Cambridge University Press, pp. 182–98.

Apter, David and Sawa, Nagayo 1984, *Against the State: Politics and Social Protest in Japan.* Cambridge, Massachusetts: Harvard University Press.

Arai, Kazuhiro 2000, *Bunka no keizaigaku: Nihon shisutemu wa warukunai* (The economics of culture: Japan's system is not so bad), Tokyo: Bugei Shunjū.

Arnason, Johann P. 2002, *The Peripheral Centre: Essays on Japanese History and Civilization.* Melbourne: Trans Pacific Press.

Asada, Akira 1983, *Kōzō to chikara* (Structure and power). Tokyo: Keisō Shobō.

Asahi Shimbun 'Lost Generation' Shuzai-han 2007, *Lost generation: samayou 2-sen mannin* (The lost generation: straying twenty million). Tokyo: Asahi Shimbunsha.

Asakawa, Akihiro 2003, *Zainichi gaikokujin to kika seido* (Foreigners resident in Japan and the naturalization system). Tokyo: Shinkansha.

Ashkenazi, Michael 1991, 'Traditional small group organization and cultural modelling in modern Japan', *Human Organization*, vol. 50, no. 4 (Winter), pp. 385–92.

Azuma, Hiroki 2009, *Otaku: Japan's Database Animals.* Minneapolis: University of Minnesota Press.

Azuma, Hiroki (ed.) 2010, *Nihonteki sōzōryoku no mirai: Kūru Japanorojii no kanōsei* (Future of Japanese imagination: potential of Cool Japanology). Tokyo: NHK Books.

Beardsley, Richard K., Hall, John W., and Ward, Robert E. 1959, *Village Japan*. Chicago: University of Chicago Press.

Befu, Harumi 1974, 'Bribery in Japan: How law tangles with culture', in Elinor Lenz and Rita Riley (eds), *The Self and the System*. Los Angeles: UCLA Western Humanities Center, pp. 87–93.

Befu, Harumi 1980, 'A critique of the group model of Japanese society', *Social Analysis*, nos. 5/6 (December), pp. 29–43.

Befu, Harumi 1989, 'The emic–etic distinction and its significance for Japanese studies', in Yoshio Sugimoto and Ross Mouer (eds), *Constructs for Understanding Japan*. London: Kegan Paul International, pp. 323–43.

Befu, Harumi 1990a, *Ideorogī to shite no Nihon bunka-ron* (Theories on Japanese culture as ideology), revised version. Tokyo: Shisō no Kagakusha.

Befu, Harumi 1990b, 'Conflict and non-Weberian bureaucracy in Japan', in S. N. Eisenstadt and Eyal Ben-Ari (eds), *Japanese Models of Conflict Resolution*. London: Kegan Paul International, pp. 162–91.

Befu, Harumi 2001, *Hegemony of Homogeneity: An Anthropological Analysis of Nihonjinron*. Melbourne: Trans Pacific Press.

Befu, Harumi 2003, 'Globalization theory from the bottom up: Japan's contribution', *Japanese Studies*, vol. 23, no. 1, pp. 3–22.

Bellah, Robert 1957, *Tokugawa Religion: The Values of Pre-industrial Japan*. New York: Free Press.

Benedict, Ruth 1946, *The Chrysanthemum and the Sword: Patterns of Japanese Culture*. Boston: Houghton Mifflin.

Berger, Peter L. and Hsiao, Hsin-Huang Michael (eds) 1988, *In Search of an East Asian Development Model*. New Brunswick: Transaction Books.

Berndt, Jacqueline 2007, *Manga no kuni Nippon* (Japan as a *manga* country). Tokyo: Kadensha.

Borthwick, Mark 1992, *Pacific Century: The Emergence of Modern Pacific Asia*. Boulder: Westview Press.

Bourdieu, Pierre 1986, *Distinction: A Social Critique of the Judgement of Taste*, Richard Nice (trans.). London: Routledge.

Brinton, Mary C. 1992, *Women and the Economic Miracle: Gender and Work in Postwar Japan*. Berkeley: University of California Press.

Broadbent, Jeffrey 1998, *Environmental Politics in Japan: Networks of Power and Protest*. New York: Cambridge University Press.

Bungei Shunjū Henshūbu 2001, 'Shin kaikyū shakai Nippon (Japan as new class society)', in Chūō Kō ron Henshūbu, *Ronsō chūryū hōkai* (Debate on the collapse of the middle class), Chūō Kōronsha, pp. 44–74. Originally published in *Bungei shunjū*, May 2000.

Buraku Kaihō Jinken Kenkyūsho (ed.) 2001, *Buraku mondai to jinken jiten* (Encyclopedia of *buraku* and human rights issues). Osaka: Kaihō Shuppansha.

Buraku Kaihō Jinken Kenkyūsho (ed.) 2013, *Buraku kaihō jinken nenkan 2013* (Yearbook on human rights 2013). Osaka: Kaihō Shuppansha.

Burenstam Linder, Staffan 1986, *The Pacific Century: Economic and Political Consequences of Asia-Pacific Dynamism*. Stanford: Stanford University Press.

Cave, Peter 2007, *Primary School in Japan: Self, Individuality and Learning in Elementary Education*. London: Routledge.

Chapman, David 2008, *Zainichi Korean Identity and Ethnicity*. London: Routledge.

Chiavacci, David 2008, 'From class struggle to general middle-class society to divided society: Models of inequality in postwar Japan', *Social Science Japan Journal*, vol. 11, no. 1, pp. 5–27.

Chūō Kōron Henshūbu and Nakai, Kōichi (eds) 2003, *Ronsō: Gakuryoku hōkai* (Debate on the disruption of academic ability). Tokyo: Chūō Kōronsha.

Clammer, John 2001, *Japan and Its Others: Globalization, Difference and the Critique of Modernity*. Melbourne: Trans Pacific Press.

Craig, Timothy J. (ed.) 2000, *Japan Pop! Inside the World of Japanese Popular Culture*. Armonk, NY: M. E. Sharpe.

Dale, Peter 1986, *The Myth of Japanese Uniqueness*. London: Routledge.

Davidson, Ronald A. 2013, '"Friendly authoritarianism" and the bedtaun: Public space in a Japanese suburb', *Journal of Cultural Geography*, vol. 30, no. 2, pp. 187–214.

Davis, John H. 2000, 'Blurring the boundaries of the *buraku(min)*', in J. S. Eades, Tom Gill and Harumi Befu (eds), *Globalization and Social Change in Contemporary Japan*. Melbourne: Trans Pacific Press, pp. 110–22.

De Lange, Willem 1997, *A History of Japanese Journalism: Japan's Press Club as the Last Obstacle to a Mature Press*. Richmond, Surrey: Curzon Press.

Denoon, Donald, Hudson, Mark, McCormack, Gavan, and Morris-Suzuki, Tessa (eds) 1996, *Multicultural Japan: Palaeolithic to Postmodern*. Melbourne: Cambridge University Press.

Dentsū (ed.) 2008, *Nihon no kōkokuhi* (Japan's advertising expenditure). Tokyo: Dentsū.

Dentsū Sōken and Nihon Research Center (ed.) 2008, *Sekai shuyōkoku kachikan dēta buhhu* (Data book on values of major countries in the world). Tokyo: Dōbunkan.

De Roy, Swadesh R. 1979, 'A one-class society?', *Japan Quarterly*, vol. 26, no. 1, pp. 204–11.

Deutschmann, Christoph 1987, 'The Japanese type of organisation as a challenge to the sociological theory of modernisation', *Thesis Eleven*, no. 17, pp. 40–58.

Deutschmann, Christoph 1991, 'Working-bee syndrome in Japan: An analysis of working-time practice', in Karl Hinrichs, William Roche, and Carmen Sirianni (eds), *Working Time in Transition: The Political Economy of Working Hours in Industrial Nations*. Philadelphia: Temple University Press, pp. 189–202.

De Vos, George and Wagatsuma, Hiroshi 1966, *Japan's Invisible Race: Caste in Culture and Personality*. Berkeley: University of California Press.

De Vos, George and Wetherall, William O. (updated by Kaye Stearman) 1983, *Japan's Minorities: Burakumin, Koreans, Ainu and Okinawans*. London: Minority Rights Group.

Doi, Takeo 1973, *The Anatomy of Dependence*. Tokyo: Kodansha International.

Dore, R. P. (ed.) 1967, *Social Change in Modern Japan*. Princeton: Princeton University Press.

Dore, R. P. 1973, *British Factory – Japanese Factory*. Berkeley: University of California Press.

Dore, R. P. (ed.) 1987, *Taking Japan Seriously: A Confucian Perspective on Leading Economic Issues*. London: Athlone.

Eades, J. S., Goodman, Roger, and Hada, Yumiko (eds) 2005, *The 'Big Bang' in Japanese Higher Education*. Melbourne: Trans Pacific Press.

Ebisaka, Takeshi 1986, *Shinguru raifu: Onna to otoko no kaihō-gaku* (Single life: liberation strategy for women and men). Tokyo: Chūō Kōronsha.

Edwards, Walter Drew 1989, *Modern Japan Through Its Weddings: Gender, Person and Society in Ritual Portrayal*. Stanford: Stanford University Press.

Eisenstadt, S. N. 1996, *Japanese Civilization: A Comparative View*. Chicago: University of Chicago Press.

Famighetti, Robert (ed.) 1994, *The World Almanac and Book of Facts 1995*. Mahwah, New Jersey: Funk & Wagnalls.

Filip, Ruxandra 2013, 'The future of Cool Japan: A case study of the Japanese video game industry'. Unpublished MBA thesis submitted to the Graduate School of Business Administration, Meiji University, Tokyo.

Fujita, Wakao 1984, *Sayonara, taishū* (A farewell to masses). Kyoto: PHP Kenkyūsho.

Fujiwara, Masahiko 2005, *Kokka no hinkaku* (The grace of the Japanese nation). Tokyo: Shinchōsha.

Fujiwara, Shō, Itō, Takashi, and Tanioka, Ken 2012, *Senzai kurasutaa bunseki o mochiita keiryō shakaigaku-teki apurōchi* (A quantitative sociological approach using latent cluster analysis), *Nenpō ningen kagaku* (Human science annual report), issue 33, pp. 43–68.

Fukuoka, Yasunori 2000, *Lives of Young Koreans in Japan*. Melbourne: Trans Pacific Press.

Fukutake, Tadashi 1949, *Nihon nōson no shakai-teki seikaku* (Social characteristics of Japanese agricultural villages). Tokyo: Tokyo Daigaku Shuppankai.

Fukuzawa, Rebecca Erwin and LeTendre, Gerald K. 2001, *Intense Years: How Japanese Adolescents Balance School, Family and Friends*. New York: Routledge Falmer.

Funabashi, Yōichi 2000, *Aete eigo kōyō-ron* (Venturing to argue in favor of making English an official language in Japan). Tokyo: Bungei Shunjū.

Garon, Sheldon 1997, *Molding Japanese Minds: The State in Everyday Life*. Princeton: Princeton University Press.

Gelb, M. and Estevez-Abe, M. 1998, 'Political women in Japan: A case study of the *Seikatsusha* network movement', *Social Science Japan Journal*, vol. 1, pp. 263–79.

Gill, Tom 2000, 'Yoseba and ninpudashi: Changing patterns of employment in the fringes of the Japanese econonomy', in J. S. Eades, Tom Gill, and Harumi Befu (eds), *Globalization and Social Change in Contemporary Japan*. Melbourne: Trans Pacific Press, pp. 123–42.

Granovetter, Mark 1984, 'Small is bountiful: Labor markets and establishment size', *American Sociological Review*, vol. 49, pp. 323–34.

Gravett, Paul 2004, *Manga: Sixty Years of Japanese Comics*. New York: Collins Design.

Hakuhōdō Seikatsu Sōgō Kenkyūsho 1985, *'Bunshū' no tanjō* (The emergence of segmented masses). Tokyo: Nihon Keizai Shimbunsha.

Hakuhōdō Seikatsu Sōgō Kenkyūsho 1989, *Kyūjū-nen-dai kazoku* (Families in the 1990s). Tokyo: Hakuhōdō.

Haley, John Owen 1978, 'The myth of the reluctant litigant', *Journal of Japanese Studies*, vol. 4, no. 2 (Summer), pp. 359–90.

Hamaguchi, Eshun 1985, 'A contextual model of the Japanese: Toward a methodological innovation in Japanese studies', *Journal of Japanese Studies*, vol. 11, no. 2 (Summer), pp. 289–321.

Hamaguchi, Eshun 1988, '*Nihon-rashisa*' *no sai-hakken* (Rediscovering 'Japanese-like' qualities). Tokyo: Kōdasha.

Hamashima, Akira 1991, *Gendai shakai to kaikyū* (Contemporary society and class). Tokyo: Tokyo Daigaku Shuppankai.

Hara, Junsuke 2000, 'Kindai sangyō shakai Nippon no kaisō shisutemu (Social stratification system in Japan as a modern and industrialized society)', SSM 95a, I, pp. 3–43.

Hara, Junsuke and Seiyama, Kazuo 2006, *Inequality amid Affluence: Social Stratification in Japan*. Melbourne: Trans Pacific Press.

Hasegawa, Koichi 2004, *Constructing Civil Society in Japan: Voices of Environmental Movements*. Melbourne: Trans Pacific Press.

Hashimoto, Kenji 2003, *Class Structure in Contemporary Japan*. Melbourne: Trans Pacific Press.

Hashimoto, Kenji 2011, 'Rōdōsha kaikyū wa dokokara kite doko e ikunoka (Where do the working class come from and where do they go?)', in Hiroshi Ishida, Hiroyuki Kondō, and Keiko Nakano (eds), *Kaisō to idō no kōzō* (Structure of social stratification and mobility), SSM 05a, vol. 2, pp. 53–69.

Hayashi, Yūsuke 2008, 'Gendai Nihon shakai no tagenteki kaisō shisutemu (The multidimensional stratification system in contemporary Japan)', SSM 05b, vol. 15, pp. 153–69.

Herbert, Wolfgang 1996, *Foreign Workers and Law Enforcement in Japan*. London: Kegan Paul International.

Hidaka, Rokuro 1984, *The Price of Affluence: Dilemma of Contemporary Japan*. Tokyo: Kodansha International.

Higuchi, Naoto 2014, *Nihon-gata-haigai-shugi* (Japanese-style exclusionism). Nagoya: Nagoya Daigaku Shuppankai.

Higuchi, Yōichi (ed.) 2001, *Five Decades of Constitutionalism in Japanese Society*. Tokyo: University of Tokyo Press.

Hirabayashi, Yūko 2013, 'Nani ga "demo no aru shakai" wo tsukuru no ka (What produces a "society with public demonstrations"?)', in Shigeyoshi Tanaka, Harutoshi Funabashi, and Toshiyuki Masamura (eds), *Higashi Nihon Daishinsai to shakaigaku* (The Great East Japan Earthquake and sociology). Kyoto: Minerva Shobō, pp. 163–95.

Hirade, Hideo 1942, 'Daitōa sensō to ongaku (The Great Asia War and music), *Ongaku no tomo* (Friends of music), May, pp. 14–24.

Hirose, Takashi 1986, *Tokyo ni genpatsu o* (Build nuclear power plants in Tokyo). Tokyo: Shūeisha.

Hofstede, Geert 1984, *Culture's Consequences: International Differences in Work-related Values*. Beverly Hills: Sage Publications.

Hook, Glenn D. and McCormack, Gavan 2001, *Japan's Contested Constitution: Documents and Analysis*. London: Routledge.

Horioka, Charles Yuji 1995, *Household Saving in Japan: The Importance of Saving for Specific Motives*. Amsterdam: Elsevier Science.

Huddle, Norie and Reich, Michael 1987, *Island of Dreams: Environmental Crisis in Japan*. Cambridge, Massachusetts: Schenkman Books.

HumanMedia 2012, *Nihon to sekai no media x kontentsu shijō data base* (Media and contents markets in Japan and the world), vol. 6. Tokyo: HumanMedia.

Huntington, Samuel P. 1993, 'The clash of civilizations', *Foreign Affairs*, vol. 72, no. 3, pp. 22–49.

Huntington, Samuel P. 2011, *The Clash of Civilizations and the Remaking of World Order*. New York: Simon and Shuster.

Ihara, Ryoji 2007, *Toyota's Assembly Line: A View from the Factory Floor*. Melbourne: Trans Pacific Press.

Imada, Takatoshi 1987, *Modan no datsu-kōchiku* (Deconstructing the modern). Tokyo: Chūō Kōronsha.

Imada, Takatoshi 2000, 'Posto moden jidai no shakai kaisō (Social strata in postmodern age)', in Takatoshi Imada (ed.), *Shakai kaisō no mosto modan* (The postmodern in social stratification), SSM 95a, vol. 6, pp. 3–53.

Imazu, Kōjirō 1991, 'Kyōiku: Tōkō kyohi o chūshin ni (Japanese education with a special focus on school-refusal cases)', in Tsutomu Shiohara, Nobuko Iijima, Michiharu Matsumoto, and Mutsuto Ara (eds), *Gendai Nihon no seikatsu hendō* (Lifestyle changes in contemporary Japan). Kyoto: Sekai Shisōsha, pp. 71–89.

Inazuki, Tadashi 1994, 'Borantia kōzōka no yōin bunseki (A factor analysis of the structuration of volunteers)', *Kikan shakai hoshō kenkyū* (Social security studies: a quarterly), vol. 29, no. 4, pp. 334–47.

Inoguchi, Takashi 2006, *Japanese Politics: An Introduction*. Melbourne: Trans Pacific Press.

Inoguchi, Takashi, Tanaka, Akihiko, Sonoda, Shigeto, and Dadabaev, Timur (eds) 2006, *Human Beliefs and Values in Striding Asia*. Tokyo: Akashi Shoten.

Inoue, Teruko and Ehara, Yumiko (eds) 2005, *Josei no dēta bukku* (Data book on women), 3rd edition. Tokyo: Yūhikaku.

Inouye, Charles S. 1996, 'Pictocentrism: China as a source of Japanese modernity', in Sumie Jones (ed.), *Imaging/Reading Eros*. Bloomington: East Asian Studies Center, Indiana University Press, pp. 148–52.

Inui, Akio 1990, *Nihon no kyōiku to kigyō shakai* (Education and corporate society in Japan). Tokyo: Ōtsuki Shoten.

Irokawa, Daikichi 1989, 'Popular movements in modern Japanese society', in Gavan McCormack and Yoshio Sugimoto (eds), *The Japanese Trajectory: Modernization and Beyond*. Cambridge: Cambridge University Press, pp. 69–89.

Ishida, Hiroshi 1993, *Social Mobility in Contemporary Japan*. London: Macmillan.

Ishida, Hiroshi 2000, 'Sangyō shakai no naka no Nihon (Japan in comparison with other industrial societies)', SSM 95a, vol. I, pp. 219–48.

Ishida, Hiroshi 2010, 'Does class matter in Japan? Demographics of class structure and class mobility from a comparative perspective', in Hiroshi Ishida and David H. Slater (eds), *Social Class in Contemporary Japan: Structures, Sorting and Strategies*. London: Routledge, pp. 33–56.

Ishida, Hiroshi, Goldthorpe, John H., and Erikson, Robert 1991, 'Intergenerational class mobility in postwar Japan', *American Journal of Sociology*, vol. 96, no. 4 (January), pp. 954–92.

Ishida, Hiroshi and Slater, David H. (eds) 2010, *Social Class in Contemporary Japan: Structures, Sorting and Strategies*. London: Routledge.

Ishida, Takeshi 1983, *Japanese Political Culture*. New Brunswick: Transaction Books.

Ishikawa, Akira 1985, 'Shōwa 55-nen shokugyō-betsu danshi shūgyōsha no seimeihyō (1980 life expectancy table of male workers in different occupations), *Jinkō Kenkyū* (Population studies), vol. 173.

Itagaki, Hidenori 1987, *'Zoku' giin no kenkyū* (A study of *zoku* politicians). Tokyo: Keizaikai.

Ito, Satoru and Yanase, Ryuta 2001, *Coming Out in Japan*. Melbourne: Trans Pacific Press.

Itō, Shuntarō 1985, *Hikaku bunmei* (Comparative studies of civilizations). Tokyo: Tokyo Daigaku Shuppankai.

Iwabuchi, Koichi 2002, *Recentering Globalization: Popular Culture and Japanese Transnationalism*. Durham: Duke University Press.

Iwabuchi, Kōichi 2007, *Bunka no taiwa-ryoku* (Cultural dialogue power). Tokyo: Nihon Keizai Shimbun Shuppansha.

Iwama, Akiko 2011, 'Jendaa to shakai sanka (Gender and social participation)', SSM 05a, vol. 3, pp. 325–40.

Iwasaki, Nobuhiko, Ajisaka, M., Ueda, N., Takagi, M., Hirohara, S., and Yoshioka, N. (eds) 1989, *Chōnaikai no kenkyū* (Studies of neighborhood associations). Tokyo: Ochanomizu Shobō.

Iwata, Masami and Nishizawa, Akihiko (eds) 2008, *Poverty and Social Welfare in Japan*. Melbourne: Trans Pacific Press.

Iwata, Ryūshi 1981, *Gakureki shugi no hatten kōzō* (Development structure of educational credentialism). Tokyo: Nihon Hyōronsha.

Izumi, Seiichi and Gamō, Masao 1952, 'Nihon shakai no chiiki-sei (Regional characteristics of Japanese society)', in Hiroshi Satō and Misao Watanabe (eds), *Nihon chiri shin-taikei* (New series in Japanese geography), vol. 2. Tokyo: Kawade Shobō.

Japan Newspaper Publishers and Editors Association (Nihon Shimbun Kyōkai) 2012, *Shinbun tsūshinsha jūgyōin-sū to kisha-sū no suii* (Changes in the number of employees and that of reporters in newspaper and news services). Available at <www.pressnet.or.jp/>.

Japanese Trade Union Confederation (Rengō) 2006, *Rengō 2006 seikatsu ankēto* (*Rengō* 2006 life conditions survey).

Japanese Trade Union Confederation (Rengō) 2010, *Kōsei shoshiki, chihō rengōkai ni okeru josei no rōdō kumiai katsudō e no sankaku ni kansuru chōsa* (Survey of gender equality in labor union activities at the levels of national industrial unions and prefectural unions).

Johnson, Chalmers 1982, *MITI and the Japanese Miracle*. Stanford: Stanford University Press.

Johnson, Chalmers 1990, 'The Japanese economy: A different kind of capitalism', in S.N. Eisenstadt and Eyal Ben-Ari (eds), *Japanese Models of Conflict Resolution*. London: Kegan Paul International, pp. 39–59.

Kadowaki, Takashi 2002, *Nihon no chika keizai* (Japan's underground economy). Tokyo: Kōdansha.

Kamata, Satoshi 1984, *Kyōiku kōjō no kodomatchi* (Children in education factories). Tokyo: Iwanami Shoten.

Kariya, Takehiko 2001, *Kaisōka Nippon to kyōiku kiki* (Stratified Japan and the educational crisis). Tokyo: Yūshindō Kōbunsha.

Kariya, Takehiko 2008, *Gakuryoku to kaisō* (Academic achievements and social strata). Tokyo: Asahi Shimbun Shuppan.

Kashima, Yoshihisa, Yamaguchi, Susumu, Kim, Uichol, Choi, San-Chin, Gelfand, Michele, and Yuki, Masaki 1996, 'Culture, gender, and self: A perspective from individualism-collectivism research', *Journal of Personality and Social Psychology*, vol. 69, no. 5, pp. 925–37.

Kataoka, Emi 1987, 'Shitsuke to shakai kaisō no kanren ni kansuru bunseki (An analysis of the relationship between family socialization and social class)', *Osaka Daigaku Ningen Kagakubu kiyō*, vol. 13, pp. 23–51.

Kataoka, Emi 1992, 'Shakai kaisō to bunkateki saiseisan (Social and cultural reproduction processes in Japan)', *Riron to hōhō*, vol. 7, no. 1, pp. 33–55.

Kataoka, Emi (ed.) 1998, *Bunka to shakai kaisō* (Social stratification and cultural reproduction), SSM 95b, vol. 18.

Kataoka, Emi 2000, 'Bunka-teki kanyōsei to shōchō-teki kaikyō (Cultural tolerance and symbolic boundaries)', in Takatoshi Imada (ed.), *Kaisō shakai no posuto modan* (Postmodernity in stratified society), SSM 95a, vol. 5, pp. 181–220.

Katō, Tetsurō 1992, *Shakai to kokka* (Society and the state). Tokyo: Iwanami Shoten.

Kawamura, Nozomu 1980, 'The historical background of arguments emphasizing the uniqueness of Japanese society', *Social Analysis*, nos. 5/6, pp. 44–62.

Kawanishi, Hirosuke 1992, *Enterprise Unionism in Japan*. London: Kegan Paul International.

Kenessey, Zoltan 1987, 'The primary, secondary, tertiary and quaternary sectors of the economy', *Review of Income and Wealth*, vol. 33, issue 4, pp. 359–85.

Kerr, Clark, Dunlop, T. John, Harbian, Frederick, and Myers, Charles A. 1960, *Industrialism and Industrial Man: Problems of Labor and Management in Economic Growth*. Cambridge: Cambridge University Press.

Kersten, Joachim 1993, 'Street youth, bosozoku and yakuza: Subculture formation and societal reactions in Japan', *Crime and Delinquency*, vol. 39, no. 3, pp. 277–95.

Kijima, Yoshimasa 2012, 'Why make e-*moe*-tional attachments to fictional characters? The cultural sociology of the post-modern', in Katsuya Minamida and Izumi Tsuji (eds), *Pop Culture and the Everyday in Japan*. Melbourne: Trans Pacific Press, pp. 149–70.

Kim, Myeongsu and Inazuki, Tadashi 2000, 'Zainichi kankokujin no shakai idō (Social mobility of resident Koreans in Japan)', in Kenji Kōsaka (ed.), *Kaisō shakai kara atarashii shimin shakai e* (From stratified society to new civil society), SSM 95a, pp. 181–99.

Kimoto, Kimiko 2006, *Gender and Japanese Management*. Melbourne: Trans Pacific Press.

Kimura, Sakae and Baba, Ken'ichi 1988, *Boshi yuchaku* (Mother–child adhesion). Tokyo: Yūhikaku.

Kitayama, Shinobu 1998, *Jiko to kanjō* (The self and emotion). Tokyo: Kyōritsu Shuppan.

Kitayama, Shinobu, Markus, H. R., Matsumoto, H., and Norsakkunkit, V. 1997, 'Individual and collective processes in the construction of the self', *Journal of Personality and Social Psychology*, vol. 72, pp. 1245–67.

Klippensteen, Kate 2000, *Ganguro Girls: The Japanese 'Black Face'* (photographs by Everett Kennedy Brown). Köln: Könemann.

Kohn, Melvin L. 1977, *Class and Conformity: A Study in Values*, 2nd edition. Chicago: University of Chicago Press.

Kohn, Melvin and Schooler, Carmi 1983, *Work and Personality: An Inquiry into the Impact of Social Stratification*. Norwood, New Jersey: Ablex Publishing.

Koike, Kazuo 1988, *Understanding Industrial Relations in Modern Japan*, trans. Mary Saso. London: Macmillan.

Koike, Kazuo and Watanabe, Ikuo 1979, *Gakureki shakai no kyozō* (School-based career society: fact and fantasy). Tokyo: Tōyō Keizai Shimpōsha.

Koiso, Kaoru 2009, 'Nihonjin eigo shiyōsha no tokuchō to eigo nōryoku (The characteristics of English users among the Japanese and their English proficiency)', *JGSS Research Series*, no. 6 (March), pp. 123–37.

Kokuritsu Josei Kyōiku Kaikan (National Education Center for Women) 2012, *Danjo kyōdō sankaku tōkei dēta bukku 2012* (Statistical data book on gender equality 2012). Tokyo: Gyōsei.

Komai, Hiroshi 2001, *Foreign Migrants in Contemporary Japan*. Melbourne: Trans Pacific Press.

Kondō, Katsunori (ed.) 2007, *Kenshō kenkō kakusa shakai* (Examining Japan as health-based disparity society). Tokyo: Igaku Shoin.

Kosaka, Kenji (ed.) 1994, *Social Stratification in Contemporary Japan*. London: Kegan Paul International.

Kosaka, Kenji and Ogino, Masahiro (eds) 2008, *A Quest for Alternative Sociology*. Melbourne: Trans Pacific Press.

Kosugi, Reiko 2008, *Escape from Work: Freelancing Youth and the Challenge to Corporate Japan*. Melbourne: Trans Pacific Press.

Krauss, Ellis S. 2000, *Broadcasting Politics in Japan: NHK and Television News*. Ithaca: Cornell University Press.

Krauss, Ellis S. and Pekkanen, Robert 2010, *The Rise and Fall of Japan's LDP: Political Organizations as Historical Institutions*. Ithaca: Cornell University Press.

Kumazawa, Makoto 1993, *Shinpen Nihon no rōdōshazō* (Profiles of Japanese workers: revised edition). Tokyo: Chikuma Shobō.

Kurasawa, Susumu and Akimoto, Ritsuo (eds) 1990, *Chōnaikai to chiiki shūdan* (Neighborhood associations and local groups). Kyoto: Mineruva Shobō.

Kusayanagi, Daizō 1990, *'Nihon-rashisa' no shin-dankai* (New stage of 'Japanese-like' qualities). Tokyo: Rikurūto Shuppan.

Kuwayama, Takami 2004, *Native Anthropology: The Japanese Challenge to Western Academic Hegemony*. Melbourne: Trans Pacific Press.

Kyūtoku, Shigemori 1997, *Fugenbyō* (Father-pathogenic disease). Tokyo: Daiwa Shuppan.

Lee, O-Young 1984, *Smaller Is Better: Japan's Mastery of the Miniature*, trans. Robert N. Huey. Tokyo: Kodansha International.

Lehmeyer, Jan 2006, 'Population statistics' at <www.populstat.info>.

Lewis, Christine C. 1988, 'Japanese first-grade classrooms: Implications for US theory and research', *Comparative Education Review*, vol. 32, no. 2, pp. 159–72.

Lie, John 2001, *Multiethnic Japan*. Cambridge: Harvard University Press.

Lunsing, Wim 1995, 'Japanese gay magazines and marriage advertisements', *Journal of Gay and Lesbian Social Services*, vol. 3, no. 3, pp. 71–87.

Lunsing, Wim 2001, *Beyond Common Sense: Sexuality and Gender in Contemporary Japan*. London: Kegan Paul International.

McGray, Douglas 2002, 'Japan's gross national cool', *Foreign Policy*, vol. 44, no. 11, May–June, pp. 44–55.

Maclachlan, Patricia 2003, 'The struggle for an independent consumer society: Consumer activism and the state's response in postwar Japan', in Frank J. Schwartz and Susan J. Pharr (eds), *The State of Civil Society in Japan*. New York: Cambridge University Press, pp. 214–32.

McLelland, Mark J. 2000, *Male Homosexuality in Modern Japan: Cultural Myths and Social Realities*. Richmond, Surrey: Curzon Press.

McVeigh, Brian J. 2000, *Wearing Ideology: State, Schooling and Self-presentation in Japan*. Oxford: Berg.

Mahathir Bin Mohamad 1999, *A New Deal for Asia*. Subang Jaya: Pelanduk Publications.

Mahathir Bin Mohamad and Ishihara, Shintarō 1996, *The Voice of Asia: Two Leaders Discuss the Coming Century*. Tokyo: Kodansha International.

Markus, H. R. and Kitayama, Shinobu 1991, 'Culture and the self: Implications for cognition, emotion, and motivation', *Psychological Review*, vol. 98, pp. 225–53.

Maruyama, Masao 1963, *Thought and Behavior in Modern Japanese Politics*. Oxford: Oxford University Press.

Maruyama, Masao, Katō, Shūichi, and Kinoshita, Junji 1991, *Nihon bunka no kakureta katachi* (Hidden shape of Japanese culture). Tokyo: Iwanami Shoten.

Matsumoto, Koji 1991, *The Rise of the Japanese Corporate System*. London: Kegan Paul International.

Matsutani, Mitsuru 2013, 'Populism', in Shunsuke Tanabe (ed.), *Japanese Perceptions of Foreigners*. Melbourne: Trans Pacific Press, pp. 107–20.

Minamida, Katsuya and Tsuji, Izumi (eds) 2012, *Pop Culture and the Everyday in Japan*. Melbourne: Trans Pacific Press.

Min, Kwan Sik 1994, *Zainichi Kankokujin no genjō to mirai* (The present and future conditions of Korean residents in Japan). Tokyo: Byakuteisha.

Mitsui, Toru and Hosokawa, Shuhei (eds) 2001, *Karaoke around the World*. London: Routledge.

Mitsuyoshi, Toshiyuki 1991, 'Kazoku (1): Shūren to kakusan (The family, section 1: convergence and divergence)', in Sōkichi Endō, Toshiyuki Mitsuyoshi, and Minoru Nakata (eds), *Gendai Nihon no kōzō hendō* (Structural transformation in contemporary Japan). Kyoto: Sekai Shisōsha, pp. 123–42.

Miwa, Satoshi and Ishida, Hiroshi 2008, 'Sengo Nihon no kaisō kōzō to shakai idō ni kansuru kiso bunseki (A basic analysis of class structure and social mobility in postwar Japan)', SSM 05b, vol. 1, pp. 73–93.

Morioka, Kōji 2009, *Hinkonka suru howaito karā* (The impoverished white-collar). Tokyo: Chikuma Shobō.

Morris-Suzuki, Tessa 1998, *Re-inventing Japan: Time, Space, Nation*. New York: M. E. Sharpe.

Mouer, Ross and Kawanishi, Hirosuke 2005, *A Sociology of Work in Japan*. Cambridge: Cambridge University Press.

Mouer, Ross and Sugimoto, Yoshio 1986, *Images of Japanese Society*. London: Kegan Paul International.

Mouer, Ross and Sugimoto, Yoshio (eds) 1987, *Kojin kanjin Nihonjin* (Individuals, interpersonal relations and society in Japan). Tokyo: Gakuyō Shobō.

Mouer, Ross and Sugimoto, Yoshio 1995, '*Nihonjinron* at the end of the twentieth century: A multicultural perspective', in Yoshio Sugimoto and Johann P. Arnason (eds), *Japanese Encounters with Postmodernity*. London: Kegan Paul International, pp. 237–69.

Murakami, Yasusuke 1984a, *Shin chūkan taishū no jidai* (The age of new middle masses). Tokyo: Chūō Kōronsha.

Murakami, Yasusuke 1984b, '*Ie* society as a pattern of civilization', *Journal of Japanese Studies*, vol. 10, no. 2, pp. 281–367.

Murakami, Yasusuke, Kumon, Shunpei, and Satō, Seizaburō 1979, *Bunmei to shite no ie shakai* (*Ie* society as civilization). Tokyo: Chūō Kōronsha.

Muramatsu, Michio 1988, *Chihō jichi* (Local autonomy). Tokyo: Tokyo Daigaku Shuppankai.

Muramatsu, Michio 1994, *Nihon no gyōsei* (Japanese public bureaucracy). Tokyo: Chūō Kōronsha.

Muramatsu, Michio 1997, *Local Power in the Japanese State*. Berkeley: University of California Press.

Muramatsu, Michio, Igbal, Farrukh, and Kume, Ikuo (eds) 2002, *Local Government Development in Postwar Japan*. Oxford: Oxford University Press.

Muramatsu, Michio, Itō, Mitsutoshi, and Tsujinaka, Yutaka 1986, *Sengo Nihon no atsuryoku dantai* (Pressure groups in postwar Japan). Tokyo: Tōyō Keizai Shimpōsha.

Nagashima, Hironobu 1977, 'Nihon-teki shakai kankei (The Japanese mode of social relations)', in Yoshio Masuda (ed.), *Nihonjin no shakai* (The society of the Japanese), vol. 6 of *Kōza hikaku bunka* (Series on comparative culture). Tokyo: Kenkyūsha Shuppan, pp. 185–213.

Nagayama, Sadanori 1998, 'Bunka geijutsu to gender statistics (Cultural art and gender statistics)', *Bunka keizaigaku* (Economics of culture), vol. 1, no. 2, pp. 1–6.

Naitō, Asao 2009, *Ijime no kōzō* (Structure of bullying). Tokyo: Kōdansha.

Nakamura, Hideichirō 1990, *Shin chū ken kigyō-ron* (A new theory on middle-sized enterprises). Tokyo: Tōyō Keizai Shimpōsha.

Nakamura, Hideichirō 1992, *Nijū-isseiki gata chūshō kigyō* (Medium- and small-sized businesses of the twenty-first-century type). Tokyo: Iwanami Shoten.

Nakane, Chie 1967, *Tate shakai no ningen kankei* (Interpersonal relationships in a vertically structured society). Tokyo: Kōdansha.

Nakane, Chie 1970, *Japanese Society*. London: Weidenfeld & Nicolson.

Nakane, Chie 1978, *Tate shakai no rikigaku* (Dynamics of a vertically structured society). Tokyo: Kōdansha.

Nakanishi, Yūko 2000, 'Gakkō ranku to shakai idō (School ranks and social mobility)', in Hiroyuki Kondō (ed.), *Sengo Nihon no kyōiku shakai* (Educational society in postwar Japan), SSM 95a, vol. 3, pp. 37–56.

Nakano, Shōichirō and Imazu, Kōjirō (eds) 1993, *Esunishitī no shakaigaku: Nihon shakai no minzoku-teki kōsei* (Sociology of ethnicity: the ethnic composition of Japanese society). Kyoto: Seikai Shisōsha.

Nakano, Yumiko 1974, 'Kaisō to gengo (Class and language)', *Kyōiku shakaigaku kenkyū*, no. 29, pp. 146–60.

Nakata, Minoru 2007, *Chihō bunken jidai no chōnaikai jichikai* (Local associations in the age of decentralization). Tokyo: Jichitai Kenkyūsha.

Nakayama, Ikuo 1942, 'Dai tōa sensō to ongaku (The Great Asia War and music)', '*Ongaku no tomo* (Friends of music)', May, vol. 2, no. 5, pp. 14–24.

Nakazawa, Wataru 2007, 'Zainichi gaikokujin no taka to gaikokujin ni taisuru henken to no kankei (Correlations between the number of foreign residents and the extent of prejudice towards them)', *Soshioroji* (Sociology), vol. 52, pp. 75–91.

Namihira, Emiko 1979, 'Hare to ke to kegare (*Hare, ke* and *kegare*)', *Nippon no minzoku shūkyō* (Japan's folk religion), vol. 1. Tokyo: Kōbundō.

Napier, Susan J. 2005, *Anime from Akira to Howl's Moving Castle: Experiencing Contemporary Japanese Animation*, undated edition. New York: Palgrave Macmillan.

Neustupný, J. V. 1980, 'On paradigms in the study of Japan', *Social Analysis*, no. 5/6 (December), pp. 20–8.

NHK Hōsō Bunka Kenkyūsho (ed.) 2006, *Nihonjin no seikatsu jikan, 2005* (Patterns of time usage of the Japanese). Tokyo: NHK Shuppan.

NHK Hōsō Bunka Kenkyūsho (ed.) 2011, *Nihonjin no seikatsu jikan, 2010* (Patterns of time usage of the Japanese). Tokyo: NHK Shuppan.

NHK Special 'Working Poor' Shuzai-han 2007, *Working Poor: Nippon o mushibamu yamai* (The working poor: the disease that gnaws away at Japan). Tokyo: Poplasha.

NHK Yoron Chōsabu 1992, *Zusetsu Nihonjin no seikatsu jikan 1990* (Patterns of time usage of the Japanese, 1990). Tokyo: Nippon Hōsō Kyōkai.

Nihei, Norihiro 2005, 'Boranitia katsudō to neo-riberarizumu no kyōshin mondai o saikō suru (Re-examining the problems of resonance between volunteer activities and neo-liberalism)', *Shakigaku hyōron* (Japanese sociological review), vol. 56, no. 2, pp. 485–99.

Nihei, Norihiro 2008, '"Sanka-gata shimin shakai" no kaisōteki, seijiteki fuchi (Stratificational and political constellations of "participatory civil society")', SSM 05b, vol. 7, pp. 189–210.

Nihon Bengoshi Rengōkai (Japan Federation of Bar Associations) 2012, *Bengoshi hakusho* (White paper on lawyers).

Nihon Seikyōiku Kyōkai (Japanese Association for Sex Education) 2013, '*Wakamono no sei*' hakusho (White paper on 'youth sex'). Tokyo: Shōgakukan.

Nihon Shoseki Shuppan Kyōkai (Japan Book Publishers Association) 2011, *Jisedai shoshi jōhō o kyōtsūka ni muketa kankyō seibi* (Preparations for the proper environment for the standardization of data on next-generation books), report submitted to the Ministry of Internal Affairs and Communications).

Nijūisseiki Shokugyō Zaidan 2000, *Sōgōshoku josei no jittai chōsa* (A survey on female career-track employees). Tokyo: Nijūisseiki Shokugyō Zaidan.

Nikkei Digital Media 2011, *Nikkei Who's Who*. Tokyo: Nihon Keizai Shimbunsha.

Nippon no Shachō Kenkyū-kai 1994, *Nippon no shachō-tachi* (Company presidents in Japan). Tokyo: Daiyamondosha.

Nishi, Kumiko 2009, '"Shūkyō-teki na mono" ni hikareru Nihonjin (The Japanese are attracted to "the religious")', *Hōsō kenkyū to chōsa* (Broadcasting studies and surveys), May, pp. 66–81.

Nishiyama, Shigeru 1979, 'Shin shūkyō no genkyō (The present situation of new religions)', *Rekishi kōron*, vol. 5, no. 7 (July), pp. 33–7.

Nitoda, Rokusaburō 1987, *Tatemae to honne: Nihonjin no ura to omote* (*Tatemae* and *honne*: *ura* and *omote* of the Japanese). Tokyo: Mikasa Shobō.

Noguchi, Michihiko 2000, *Buraku mondai no paradaimu tenkan* (A paradigm shift in *buraku* issues). Tokyo: Akashi Shoten.

Nomura Research Institute (Nomura Sōgō Kenkyūsho) 2005, *Otaku shijō no kenkyū* (A study of *otaku* marketing). Tokyo: Tōyō Keizai Shimpōsha.

Norris, Craig 2009, '*Manga, anime* and visual art culture', in Yoshio Sugimoto (ed.), *The Cambridge Companion to Modern Japanese Culture*. Melbourne: Cambridge University Press, pp. 236–60.

Nye, Joseph S. 2005, *Soft Power: The Means to Succeed in World Politics*. New York: Public Affairs.

Odaka, Kunio 1961, 'Nihon no chūkan kaikyū: Sono ichizuke ni kansuru hōhōron-teki oboegaki (Japan's middle classes: methodological notes on their conceptualization)', *Nihon rōdō kyōkai zasshi*, no. 22, pp. 4–27.

Oguma, Eiji 2002, *A Genealogy of 'Japanese' Self-images*. Melbourne: Trans Pacific Press.

Oguma, Eiji (ed.) 2013, *Genpatsu o tomeru hitobito* (The people who stop nuclear power). Tokyo: Bungei Shunjū.

Oguma, Eiji 2014, *The Boundaries of the 'Japanese'*, Melbourne: Trans Pacific Press.

Ohmae, Kenichi 1990, *The Borderless World: Power and Strategy in the Interlinked World*. Cambridge, Massachusetts: Ballinger Publishing Company.

Ohmae, Kenichi 1995, *The End of the Nation State: The Rise of Regional Economies*. New York: Free Press.

Ōishi, Shunichi 2005, *Eigo teikoku shugi ni kōsuru rinen* (Principles against English-language imperialism), Tokyo: Akashi Shoten.

Okada, Toshio 2000, *Otaku-gaku nyūmon* (An introduction to *otaku* studies), Tokyo: Shinchōsha.

Okano, Kaori 1993, *School to Work Transition in Japan*. Clevedon: Multilingual Matters.

Okano, Kaori 2009a, 'School culture', in Yoshio Sugimoto (ed.), *The Cambridge Companion to Modern Japanese Culture*. Melbourne: Cambridge University Press.

Okano, Kaori 2009b, 'Education reforms in Japan: Neo-liberal, neo-conservative, and "progressive education" directions', in Dave Hill (ed.), *The Rich World and the Impoverishment of Education*. London: Routledge, pp. 238–58.

Okano, Kaori and Tsuchiya, Motonori 1999, *Education in Contemporary Japan: Inequality and Diversity*. Melbourne: Cambridge University Press.

Okazaki, Mitsuyoshi 2001, 'Sports journalism: Potentials and dilemmas', *Japanese Book News*, no. 35 (Fall), pp. 1–2.

Okumura, Hiroshi 1991, *Hōjin shihonshugi* (Corporate capitalism), revised edition. Tokyo: Asahi Shimbunsha.

Osaka University of Commerce, JGSS Research Center 2003, Japanese General Social Surveys (JGSS).

Ōsono, Tomokazu 1991, *Hitome de wakaru kigyō keiretsu to gyōkai chizu* (Enterprise groupings and the industry map at a glance). Tokyo: Nippon Jitsugyō Shuppansha.

Ōtake, Fumio and Horioka, Charles Yuji 1994, 'Chochiku dōki (Motives for savings)', in Tsuneo Ishikawa (ed.), *Nihon no shotoku to tomi no bunpai*

(Distribution of income and wealth in Japan). Tokyo: Tokyo Daigaku Shuppankai, pp. 211–44.

Ōtsuki, Shigemi 2008, 'Gaikokuji ni taisuru ishiki taipu (Types of orientation to foreigners)', SSM 05b, vol. 7, pp. 107–20.

Ōtsuki, Shigemi 2013, 'Coexistent society in Japan', in Shunsuke Tanabe (ed.), *Japanese Perceptions of Foreigners*. Melbourne: Trans Pacific Press, pp. 42–55.

Ōtsu, Tōru 1985, 'Ritsuryō kokka to kinai: Kodai kokka no shihai kōzō (The Kinki district in ancient Japan and its structure of domination)', *Nihon shoki kenkyū*, vol. 13. Tokyo: Hanawa Shoten.

Ozawa, Masako 1989, *Shin kaisō shōhi no jidai* (New age of stratified consumption). Tokyo: Asahi Shimbunsha.

Parsons, Talcott 1951, *The Social System*. New York: Free Press.

Pempel, T. J. 1998, *Regime Shift: Comparative Dynamics of the Japanese Political Economy*. Ithaca: Cornell University Press.

Pharr, Susan J. 1989, *Losing Face: Status Politics in Japan*. Berkeley: University of California Press.

Pharr, Susan and Krauss, Ellis S. (eds) 1996, *Media and Politics in Japan*. Honolulu: University of Hawaii Press.

Piller, Ingrid and Choi, Jinhyun 2013, 'Neoliberalism as language policy', *Language in Society*, vol. 42, no. 1, pp. 23–44.

Piller, Ingrid, Takhashi, Kimie, and Watanabe, Yukinori 2010, 'The dark side of TESOL: The hidden costs of the consumption of English', *Cross-cultural Studies*, vol. 20 (August), pp. 183–202.

Poisson, Barbara Aoki 2002, *The Ainu of Japan*. Minneapolis: Lerner Publications.

Pulvers, Roger 2006, 'Who out there cares about "Cool Japan"', *The Japan Times*, 9 April.

Ramseyer, J. Mark 1988, 'Reluctant litigant revisited: Rationality and disputes in Japan', *Journal of Japanese Studies*, vol. 14, no. 1 (Winter), pp. 111–23.

Reischauer, Edwin O. 1977, *The Japanese*. Cambridge: Belknap Press of Harvard University Press.

Rengō Sōken (Research Institute of the Japanese Trade Union Confederation) 2012, *Kinrōsha tankan* (Short-term survey of workers' conditions). Tokyo: Rengō.

Richter, Steffi 2010, 'Yōroppa ni okeru "kūru Japanorojii" no kizashi (Signs of "Cool Japanology" in Europe)', in Hiroki Azuma (ed.), *Nihon-teki sōzō ryoku no minrai: Kūru Japanorojii no kanōsei* (The future of Japanese imagination: the potential of Cool Japanology). Tokyo: NHK Books, pp. 169–85.

Russell, John 1991a, 'Race and reflexivity: The black other in contemporary Japanese mass culture', *Cultural Anthropology*, vol. 6, no. 1 (February), pp. 3–25.

Russell, John 1991b, 'Narratives of denial: Racial chauvinism and the black other in Japan', *Japan Quarterly*, vol. 38, no. 4 (October–December), pp. 416–28.

Sagami Gomu Kōgyō 2013, *Nippon no sekkusu* (Japanese sexual behavior), <www.nipponnosex.com>.

Saitō, Takashi 2001, *Koe ni dashite yomitai Nihongo* (The Japanese language that we want to read in a powerful voice). Tokyo: Sōshisha.

Sakaiya, Taichi 1980, *Dankai no sedai* (The baby-boomer generation). Tokyo: Bungei Shunjū.

Sakaiya, Taichi 1991, *Nihon to wa nanika* (What is Japan?). Tokyo: Kōdansha.
Sakaiya, Taichi 1993, *What is Japan?* Tokyo: Kodansha International.
Sakakibara, Fujiko 1992, *Josei to koseki* (Women and the family registration system). Tokyo: Akashi Shoten.
Sakamoto, Kōji 2011, *Nihon de ichiban shiawase na kenmin* (In which prefecture do the happiest people reside?). Kyoto: PHP Kenkyūsho.
Sakurai, Tokutarō 1982, *Nippon no minzoku shūkyō-ron* (On Japan's folk religion). Tokyo: Shunjūsha.
Sakurai, Tokutarō et al. 1984, *Kyōdō tōgi: hare, ke, kegare* (A collective discussion on *hare, ke* and *kegare*). Tokyo: Seidosha.
Sanders, Leonard Patrick 2008, *Postmodern Orientalism: William Gibson, Cyberpunk and Japan*, Unpublished PhD thesis in English, Massey University, New Zealand.
Sataka, Shin 1992a, *Nippon ni igi ari* (Dissenting from Japan). Tokyo: Kōdansha.
Sataka, Shin 1992b, 'Hanran shite iru seishin shugi kenshū (A flood of spiritualist training sessions for company executives)', AM, 23 May, p. 8.
Sataka, Shin 1993a, *'Kaisha kokka' o utsu* (Denouncing Japan as a 'corporation country'). Kyoto: Kamogawa Shuppan.
Sataka, Shin 1993b, *Kigyō genron* (An introduction to Japanese business practices). Tokyo: Shakai Shisōsha.
Satō, Bunmei 1991, *Koseki ga miharu kurashi* (Everyday life controlled by the family registration system). Tokyo: Gendai Shokan.
Satō, Machiko 1994, *Gōrei no nai gakkō* (Schools without words of command). Tokyo: Chikuma Shobō.
Sato, Machiko 2001, *Farewell to Nippon: Japanese Lifestyle Migrants in Australia*. Melbourne: Trans Pacific Press.
Sato, Nancy 2003, *Inside Japanese Classrooms: The Heart of Education*. New York: Garland.
Satō, Toshiki 2000, *Fubyōdō shakai Nippon* (Japan: not an egalitarian society). Tokyo: Chūō Kōronsha.
Satō, Toshiki 2011, 'An explosion of inequality consciousness: Changes in postwar society and "equalization" strategy', in Sawako Shirahase (ed.), *Demographic Change and Inequality in Japan*. Melbourne: Trans Pacific Press, pp. 16–45.
Schodt, Frederik 2007, *The Astro Boy Essays: Osamu Tezuka, Mighty Atom, and the Manga/Anime Revolution*. Berkeley: Stone Bridge Press.
Schoolland, Ken 1990, *Shogun's Ghost: The Dark Side of Japanese Education*. New York: Bergin & Garvey.
Schwartz, Frank J. and Pharr Susan J. (eds) 2003, *The State of Civil Society in Japan*. New York: Cambridge University Press.
Seifert, Wolfgang 2007, '*Seikatsu/seikatsusha*', in George Ritzer (ed.), *The Blackwell Encyclopedia of Sociology*, vol. viii, pp. 4150–3.
Seisaku Jihōsha 1999, *Seikan yōran* (Handbook on politics and ministerial bureaucracy). Tokyo: Seisaku Jihōsha.
Seiyama, Kazno 1994, 'Intergenerational occupational mobility', in Kenji Kosaka (ed.), *Social Stratification in Contemporary Japan*. London: Kegan Paul International.
Shibata, Kōzō 1983, *Hō no tatemae to honne* (*Tatemae* and *honne* in law). Tokyo: Yūhikaku.

Shimazono, Susumu 2004, *From Salvation to Spirituality: Popular Religious Movements in Modern Japan*. Melbourne: Trans Pacific Press.

Shimono, Keiko 1991, *Shisan kakusa no keizai bunseki* (An economic analysis of asset disparity). Tokyo: Nagoya Daigaku Shuppankai.

Shimono, Keiko and Ishikawa, Miho, 2002, 'Estimating the size of bequests in Japan: 1986–1994', *International Economic Journal*, vol. 16, no. 3, pp. 1–21.

Shindō, Muneyuki 1992, *Gyōsei shidō* (Administrative guidance). Tokyo: Iwanami Shoten.

Shirahase, Sawako 2008, 'Shōshika shakai ni okeru kaisō ketsugō to shiteno kekkon (Marriage as class bondage in a society with a declining birthrate)', SSM 05b, vol. 2, pp. 63–81.

Shirahase, Sawako (ed.) 2011, *Demographic Change and Inequality in Japan*. Melbourne: Trans Pacific Press.

Shirahase, Sawako 2012, 'Marriage as an association of social classes in a low fertility rate society', in Hiroshi Ishida and David H. Slater (eds), *Social Class in Contemporary Japan*. London: Routledge, pp. 57–83.

Shufu to Seikatsusha 1992, *Todōfuken-betsu kankonsōsai daijiten* (Dictionary of prefectural variations in the ceremonies of coming of age, marriage, funeral, and ancestral worship). Tokyo: Shufu to Seikatsusha.

Shuppan Kagaku Kenkyūsho 2012, *Shuppan shihyō nenpō 2012* (Annual report on publication indicators 2012). Tokyo: Zenkoku Shuppan Kyōkai Shuppan Kagaku Kenkyūsho (Research Institute for Publications of the Japan Publication Association).

Sofue, Takao 1971, *Kenmin-sei* (Prefectural character). Tokyo: Chūō Kōronsha.

Steinhoff, Patricia 2007, *Japanese Studies in the United States and Canada: Continuity and Opportunity*. Honolulu: University of Hawaii Press for The Japan Foundation.

Steinhoff, Patricia 2013, 'Japanese studies are alive and well in the United States'. Paper presented at the conference 'Engaging with Japanse studies' held at the Nissan Institute of Japanese Studies, Oxford University, 14–15 March.

Stevenson, David Lee and Baker, David P. 1992, 'Shadow education and allocation in formal schooling: Transition to university', *American Journal of Sociology*, vol. 97, no. 6 (May), pp. 1639–57.

Stevenson, Harold W. and Stigler, James W. 1992, *The Learning Gap: Why Our Schools Are Failing and What We Can Learn from Japanese and Chinese Education*. New York: Summit Books.

Stickland, Leonie R. 2008, *Gender Gymnastics: Performing and Consuming Takarazuka Revue in Japan*. Melbourne: Trans Pacific Press.

Sugimoto, Yoshio 1993, *Nihonjin o yameru hōhō* (How to cease to be Japanese), 2nd edition. Tokyo: Honnoki.

Sugimoto, Yoshio 1999, 'Making sense of Nihonjinron', *Thesis Eleven*, no. 57 (May), pp. 81–96.

Sugimoto, Yoshio 2006, 'Nation and nationalism in contemporary Japan', in Gerard Delanty and Krishan Kumar (eds), *The Sage Handbook of Nations and Nationalism*. London: Sage Publications, pp. 473–87.

Sugimoto, Yoshio 2008, 'Tsurumi Shunsuke: Voice of the voiceless', in Gloria Davies, J. V. D'Cruz, and Nathan Hollier (eds), *People in Courage: Political Actors and Ideas in Contemporary Asia*. North Melbourne: Australian Scholarly Press, pp. 30–42.

Sugimoto, Yoshio (ed.) 2009, *The Cambridge Companion to Modern Japanese Culture*. Melbourne: Cambridge University Press.

Sugimoto, Yoshio 2010, 'Kyōsei: Japan's cosmopolitanism', in Gerard Delanty (ed.), *Routledge Handbook of Cosmopolitan Studies*. London: Routledge, pp. 452–62.

Sugimoto, Yoshio and Mouer, Ross 1980, *Japanese Society: Reappraisals and New Directions*. A special issue of *Social Analysis*, nos. 5/6 (December). Adelaide: University of Adelaide.

Sugimoto, Yoshio and Mouer, Ross (eds) 1989, *Constructs for Understanding Japan*. London: Kegan Paul International.

Sugimoto, Yoshio and Mouer, Ross 1995, *Nihonjinron no hōteishiki* (The Japanology equations). Tokyo: Chikuma Shobō.

Summerhawk, Barbara, McMahill, Cheiron, and McDonald, Daren (eds) 1999, *Queer Japan: Personal Stories of Japanese Lesbians, Gays, Transsexuals, and Bisexuals*. Norwich, Vermont: New Victoria Publishers.

Suzuki, Atsuko (ed.) 2008, *Gender and Career in Japan*. Melbourne: Trans Pacific Press.

Suzuki, Hiroshi 1987, 'Borantia-teki kōi ni okeru "K" patān ni tsuite (The "K" pattern of volunteer activities)', *Tetsugaku nenpō*, issue 46, pp. 13–32.

Tachibanaki, Toshiaki 1998, *Nihon no keizai kakusa* (Economic disparity in Japan). Tokyo: Iwanami Shoten.

Tachibanaki, Toshiaki 2005, *Confronting Income Inequality in Japan: A Comparative Analysis of Causes, Consequences, and Reform*. Cambridge: MIT Press.

Tachibanaki, Toshiaki 2010, *The New Paradox for Japanese Women: Greater Choice, Greater Inequality*. Tokyo: I-House Press.

Tachibanaki, Toshiaki and Yagi, Tadashi 1994, 'Shotoku bunpai no genjō to saikin no suii (The present situation and the recent trend of income distribution)', in Tsuneo Ishikawa (ed.), *Nippon no shotoku to tomi no bunpai* (The distribution of income and wealth in Japan). Tokyo: Tokyo Daigaku Shuppankai, pp. 23–58.

Tada, Michitarō 1978, *Asobi to Nihonjin* (Play and the Japanese). Tokyo: Chikuma Shobō.

Takahara, Kimiko 1991, 'Female speech patterns in Japanese', *International Journal of the Sociology of Language*, no. 92, pp. 61–85.

Takano, Yōtarō 2008, *Shūdan shugi to iu sakkaku: Nihonjinron no omoichigai to sono yurai* (Illusion of groupism: the misapprehension of *Nihonjinron* and its origin). Tokyo: Shinyōsha.

Takano, Yōtarō and Ōsaka, Eiko 1999, 'An unsupported common view: Comparing Japan and the US on individualism/collectivism', *Asian Journal of Social Psychology*, vol. 2, issue 3 (December), pp. 311–41.

Takarajima Henshūbu 2007, 'Shirarezaru Nippon no tokken kaikyū (Japan's unacknowledged class of privilege)', *Bessatsu Takarajima* (Special edition, Takarajima), issue 1479.

Takatori, Masao 1975, *Nihon-teki shikō no genkei* (The original pattern of Japanese-style thinking). Tokyo: Kōdansha.

Takeuchi, Kiyoshi 1993, 'Sei to bunka no shakaigaku (Sociology of student culture)', in Takahiro Kihara et al. (eds), *Gakkō bunka no shakaigaku* (Sociology of school culture). Tokyo: Fukumura Shuppan, pp. 107–22.

Takeuchi, Yō 1981, *Kyōsō no shakaigaku* (Sociology of competition). Kyoto: Sekai Shisōsha.

Takeuchi, Yō 1991, 'Myth and reality in the Japanese educational selection system', *Comparative Education*, vol. 27, no. 1 (March), pp. 101–12.

Takezawa, Yasuko (ed.) 2011, *Racial Representations in Asia*. Kyoto: Kyoto University Press.

Tanabe, Shunsuke 2001, 'Gaikokujin e no haitasei to sesshoku keiken (Exclusion of foreigners and contact experience with them)', *Shakaigaku ronkō* (Sociological studies), vol. 22, pp. 1–15.

Tanabe, Shunsuke 2012, 'What does it mean to be a "Japanese"?', in Katsuya Minamida and Izumi Tsuji (eds), *Pop Culture and the Everyday in Japan*. Melbourne: Trans Pacific Press, pp. 260–81.

Tanabe, Shunsuke (ed.) 2013, *Japanese Perceptions of Foreigners*. Melbourne: Trans Pacific Press.

Tanaka, Shigeyoshi, Funabashi, Harutoshi, and Masamura, Toshiyuki (eds), *Higashi Nihon Daishinsai to shakaigaku* (The Great East Japan Earthquake and sociology). Kyoto: Minerva Shobō.

Tanigawa, Gan 1961, 'Nippon no nijūkōzō' (Japan's dual structure), *Gendai no hakken* (Discovering contemporary Japan), vol. 13. Tokyo: Shunjūsha.

Tanioka, Ichirō, Nida, Michio, and Iwai, Noriko (eds) 2008, *Nihonjin no ishiki to kōdō* (Consciousness and behavior of the Japanese). Tokyo: Tokyo Daigaku Shuppankai.

Tanno, Kiyoto 2013, *Migrant Workers in Contemporary Japan*. Melbourne: Trans Pacific Press.

Tokyo Daigaku Kōhō Iinkai (University of Tokyo Public Relations Committee) 2012, *Gakunai kōhō* (University of Tokyo newsletter), no. 1432, 14 December.

Tominaga, Ken'ichi 1982, 'Problems of viewpoint in interpreting Japanese society: Japan and the West', Ostasiatisches Seminar, Freie Universität Berlin, Occasional Papers, no. 38.

Tominaga, Ken'ichi 1988, *Nihon sangyō shakai no tenki* (Turning points of Japanese industrial society). Tokyo: Tokyo Daigaku Shuppankai.

Tose, Nobuyuki, Okabe, Tsuneharu, and Nishimura, Kazuo (eds) 1999, *Bunsū ga dekinai daigakusei* (University students cannot solve fractional equations). Tokyo: Tōyō Keizai Shimpōsha.

Tose, Nobuyuki, Okabe, Tsuneharu, and Nishimura, Kazuo (eds) 2000, *Shōsū ga dekinai daigakusei* (University students cannot handle decimals). Tokyo: Tōyō Keizai Shimpōsha.

Tōyō Keizai Shimpōsha 2006, *Yakuin shikihō jōjō kaishaban* (Trend survey of directors of major companies). Tokyo: Tōyō Keizai Shimpōsha.

Toyoshima, Shinichirō 2000, 'shakai-teki katsudō (social activities), SSM 95a, vol. 6, pp. 143–59.

Tsuda, Yukio 2003, *Eigo shihai to wa nani ka* (What is English domination?). Tokyo: Akashi Shoten.

Tsujinaka, Yutaka 1988, *Rieki shūdan* (Interest groups). Tokyo: Tokyo Daigaku Shuppankai.

Tsujinaka, Yutaka (ed.) 2002, *Gendai Nihon no shimin shakai, riekidantai* (Civil society and interest organizations in contemporary Japan). Tokyo: Bokutakusha.

Tsujinaka, Yutaka and Choe, Jae Young 2002, 'Rekishiteki keisei (Historical development)', in Yutaka Tsujinaka (ed.), *Gendai Nihon no shimin shakai, riekidantai* (Civil society and interest organizations in contemporary Japan). Tokyo: Bokutakusha, pp. 255–86.

Tsujinaka, Yutaka, Pekkanen, Robert, and Yamamoto, Hidehiro 2009, *Nippon no jichikai chōnaikai* (Neighborhood associations in Japan). Tokyo: Bokutakusha.

Tsurumi, Shunsuke 1967, *Genkai geijutsu-ron* (On marginal art). Tokyo: Chikuma Shobō.

Tsurumi, Shunsuke 1986, *An Intellectual History of Wartime Japan, 1931–1945*. London: Kegan Paul International.

Twu, Jaw-yann 1990, *Tōyō shihon-shugi* (Oriental capitalism). Tokyo: Kōdansha.

Ueno, Chizuko 1988, 'The Japanese women's movement: The counter-values to industrialism', in Gavan McCormack and Yoshio Sugimoto (eds), *The Japanese Trajectory: Modernization and Beyond*. Cambridge: Cambridge University Press, pp. 167–85.

Ueno, Chizuko 1990, *Kafuchōsei to shihonsei* (Patriarchy and capitalism). Tokyo: Iwanami Shoten.

Ueno, Chizuko 1991, 'Josei no henbō to kazoku (Women's transformation and the family system)', in Sōichi Endō, Toshiyuki Mitsuyoshi and Minoru Nakata (eds), *Gendai Nihon no kōzō hendō* (Structural transformation in contemporary Japan). Kyoto: Sekai Shisōsha, pp. 141–65.

Ueno, Chizuko 2004, *Nationalism and Gender*. Melbourne: Trans Pacific Press.

Ueno, Chizuko 2007, *Ohitori-sama no rōgo* (Living a single life in one's old age). Tokyo: Hōken.

Ueno, Chizuko 2009, *The Modern Family in Japan: Its Rise and Fall*. Melbourne: Trans Pacific Press.

Umehara, Takeshi (ed.) 1990, *Nihon to wa nannanoka* (What is Japan?). Tokyo: Nihon Hōsō Shuppan Kyōkai.

Umesao, Tadao 1986, *Nihon to wa nanika* (What is Japan?). Tokyo: Nihon Hōsō Shuppan Kyōkai.

Umesao, Tadao 1987, *Nihon santo-ron* (On three Japanese cities: Tokyo, Osaka, and Kyoto). Tokyo: Kadokawa Shoten.

Umesao, Tadao 2002, *An Ecological View of History: Japanese Civilization in the World Context*. Melbourne: Trans Pacific Press.

Vogel, Ezra F. 1979, *Japan as Number One: Lessons for America*. Cambridge: Harvard University Press.

Vogel, Steven Kent 2006, *Japan Remodeled: How Government and Industry Are Reforming Japanese Capitalism*. Ithaca: Cornell University Press.

Watanabe, Hiroyuki 2009, *Japan's Whaling: The Politics of Culture in Historical Perspective*. Melbourne: Trans Pacific Press.

Watanabe, Masao 1997, 'Class differences and educational opportunities in Japan,' *Hitotsubashi Journal of Social Studies*, vol. 29, no. 2 (December), pp. 49–71.

Watanabe, Osamu 1990, *'Yutakana shakai' Nippon no kōzō* (The structure of 'affluent Japanese society'). Tokyo: Rōdō Junpōsha.

Watanabe, Shōichi 1989, *Nihonshi kara mita, Nihonjin, Kodai-hen, 'Nihon-rashisa' no gensen* (The Japanese in Japanese history: ancient period. The origin of 'Japanese-like' qualities). Tokyo: Shōdensha.

Weiner, Michael (ed.) 2009, *Japan's Minorities: The Illusion of Homogeneity*. 2nd edition. London: Routledge.

White, Merry 1987a, *The Japanese Educational Challenge: A Commitment to Children*. New York: Free Press.

White, Merry 1987b, 'The virtue of Japanese mothers: Cultural definitions of women's lives', *Daedalus*, vol. 116, no. 3 (Summer), pp. 149–63.

White, Michael and Trevor, Malcolm 1984, *Under Japanese Management: The Experience of British Workers*. London: Heinemann Educational.

Wolferen, Karel Van 1990, *The Enigma of Japanese Power*. New York: Vintage Books.

World Economic Forum 2013, *The Global Gender Gap Report 2013*. Geneva: World Economic Forum.

Yamada, Masahiro 1999, *Parasaito shinguru no jidai* (The age of parasite singles). Tokyo: Chikuma Shobō.

Yamada, Masahiro 2001, 'Excess affluence lies behind young unemployment', *Nihon rōdō kenkyū zasshi*, no. 484 (April), pp. 34–5.

Yamamoto, Shichihei 1989, *Nihonjin to wa nanika* (What are the Japanese?). Kyoto: PHP Kenkyūsho.

Yasuda, Kōichi 2012, *Netto to aikoku: Zaitoku-kai no 'yami' o oikakete* (The internet and patriotism: investigating the 'darkness' of the Civil Association that does not allow the privileges of *Zainichi Koreans*). Tokyo: Kōdansha.

Yoder, Robert Stuart 2004, *Youth Deviance in Japan: Class Reproduction of Non-Conformity*. Melbourne: Trans Pacific Press.

Yoneyama, Shoko 1999, *Japanese High School: Silence and Resistance*. London: Routledge.

Yoneyama, Toshinao 1971, 'Nihon-teki shakai kankei ni okeru "kihon-teki gainen gun" ("Basic conceptual clusters" in Japanese social relations)', *Kikan jinruigaku*, vol. 2, no. 3, pp. 56–76.

Yoneyama, Toshinao 1976, *Nihonjin no nakama ishiki* (The Japanese sense of mateship). Tokyo: Kōdansha.

Yoneyama, Toshinao 1990, *Ima, naze bunka o tounoka* (Why do we examine culture, now?). Tokyo: Nihon Hōsō Shuppan Kyōkai.

Yoshikawa, Gōshu 2010, 'Membership in community organizations', in Katsunori Kondo (ed.) *Health Inequalities in Japan: An Empirical Study of Older People*. Melbourne: Trans Pacific Press, pp. 151–70.

Yoshino, Kōsaku 1992, *Cultural Nationalism in Contemporary Japan: A Sociological Enquiry*. London: Routledge.

Yoshino, Kōsaku 1997, *Bunka nashonarizumu no shakaigaku* (Sociology of cultural nationalism). Nagoya: Nagoya Daigaku Shuppankai.

Yoshitani, Izumi 1992, *Nippon no chūshō kigyō* (Medium-sized and small-scale enterprises in Japan). Tokyo: Shin-Nippon Shuppansha.

Yuzawa, Yasuhiko 1987, *Zusetsu gendai Nihon no kazoku mondai* (Illustrated accounts of family problems in contemporary Japan). Tokyo: Nihon Hōsō Shuppan Kyōkai.

Yuzawa, Yasuhiko 1995, *Zusetsu kazoku mondai no genzai* (Illustrated accounts of family problems today). Tokyo: Nihon Hōsō Shuppan Kyōkai.

Zen Nihon Shakai Fukushi Kyōgikai (National Council of Social Welfare) 2013, *Zen Shakyō hisaichi shien saigai borantia jōhō* (NCSW's information about volunteers for disaster areas), <www.saigaivc.com>.

Zielenziger, Michael 2006, *Shutting out the Sun: How Japan Created Its Own Lost Generation*. New York: Vintage Books.

Index